Latinx Histories

Lori A. Flores and
Michael Innis-Jiménez,
editors

Series Advisory Board
Llana Barber
Adrian Burgos Jr.
Geraldo Cadava
Julio Capó Jr.
Miroslava Chávez-García
Kaysha Corinealdi
María Cristina García
Ramón Gutiérrez
Paul Ortiz

This series features innovative historical works that push
boundaries in the study of race, ethnicity, sexuality,
gender, migration, and nationalism within and around
Latinx communities, premised on the view that Latinx
histories are essential to understanding the full sweep
of history in the United States, the Americas, and the
world.

A complete list of books published in Latinx Histories is
available at https://uncpress.org/series/latinx-histories/.

AWAITING THEIR FEAST

Latinx Food Workers and Activism

from World War II to COVID-19

Lori A. Flores

The University of North Carolina Press

Chapel Hill

© 2025 The University of North Carolina Press
All rights reserved

Designed by April Leidig
Set in Garamond by Copperline Book Services

Manufactured in the United States of America

Cover art designed by Vivian Lopez Rowe.

Complete Cataloging-in-Publication Data for this
title is available from the Library of Congress at
https://lccn.loc.gov/2024046657.

978-1-4696-7985-3 (cloth: alk. paper)
978-1-4696-7986-0 (pbk.: alk. paper)
978-1-4696-7987-7 (epub)
978-1-4696-7988-4 (pdf)

CONTENTS

vii List of Illustrations

ix Acknowledgments

xiii Note on Terminology

INTRODUCTION

1 A National Craving and Contradiction

PART I

We Need to Be Fed:
Latinx Guestworker and Farmworker
Food Activism, 1940–1980

CHAPTER ONE

15 Appetites Gained and Lost:
Mexican and Puerto Rican Guestworkers and Food

CHAPTER TWO

45 The United Farm Workers' Northeastern Food Boycotts
and Discourses of Hunger

PART II

How Latinx Newcomers Transformed
Foodscapes, 1980–2011

CHAPTER THREE

77 Changing Mexican Foodscapes and
Food Entrepreneurs in New York City

CHAPTER FOUR

105 Not Everybody's Vacationland:
The Lives of Latinx Food Workers in Maine

PART III

Food Labor Flows and Futures, 1990–2024

CHAPTER FIVE

131   Latinx Seafood Workers on the New England Coast

CHAPTER SIX

153   Empty Cups:
      Latinx Dairy and Wine Workers in
      Vermont and New York State

CHAPTER SEVEN

181   COVID-19 and the Food Labor Chain

CONCLUSION

197   Food Is Pleasurable *and* Political

203   Notes

245   Index

ILLUSTRATIONS

FIGURES

35   1.1. Puerto Rican officials visit farmworkers in their mess hall, ca. 1956

54   2.1. UFW volunteer picketing at the New England Produce Market

63   2.2. UFW volunteers picketing in front of an A&P store

85   3.1. Zarela Martínez meeting Ronald Reagan, 1983

87   3.2. Press photo of Zarela Martínez

121   4.1. Vasquez's Mexican restaurant, Milbridge, Maine, 2018

123   4.2. Wyman's blueberry workers' camp, Deblois, Maine, 2018

159   6.1. Vermont dairy farm, 2019

168   6.2. *Paquetero* service van, Brooklyn, New York, 2021

189   7.1. Street vendor permit protest, New York City Hall, 2023

194   7.2. Community fridge, Brooklyn, New York, 2023

GRAPH

58   2.1 The UFWOC boycott's effect on California grapes, 1968–1969

MAPS

100   3.1 Mexican enclaves in New York City's boroughs

135   5.1 Downeast Maine region

TABLES

17   1.1. Contracted guestworkers in the United States, 1947–1964

24   1.2. Sample weekly bracero commissary menu, ca. 1945

33   1.3. Puerto Rican farmworkers placed on US mainland farms, 1955–1961

ACKNOWLEDGMENTS

Writing my second book has taken place in different, and at times more difficult, circumstances than my first, but what has stayed the same is my immense gratitude to those who lent their time, energy, or resources to me along the way.

I want to thank the many fellowships and institutions that allowed me to conduct the research, travel, and periods of concentrated writing that this manuscript required. My home institution of Stony Brook University (SUNY) provided research funds and grants for archival trips and allowed me to spend a year as a fellow at the Russell Sage Foundation, where I used a beautiful Upper East Side office for many late nights of furious typing. My fellow fellows—who included Gary Fine, Mae Ngai, and Kim Phillips-Fein—were inquisitive and encouraging, and RSF staff members Alejandro "Galo" Falchettore and Katie Winograd helped me immensely with mapmaking and newspaper research. A monthlong writing residency at the Rockefeller Foundation's Bellagio Center in Italy was something out of a dream, and yielded me wonderful friends in Hiba Bou Akar, Kate Desmond and Tom Rice, and Niko Sullivan. Closer to home, an autumn writer's residency on Glynwood Farm in Cold Spring gave me further inspiration to write about upstate New York. The Walter P. Reuther Library at Wayne State University in Detroit supported my feverish forays into United Farm Workers records with a Sam Fishman Travel Grant. I am so grateful to Abraham Schechter at Portland Public Library, the staff of Centro (the Center for Puerto Rican Studies) at CUNY, and the National Archives in College Park for their enthusiastic assistance. A final weeklong writing residency at the Whiteley Center on San Juan Island was cold, magical, and clarifying.

As a historian of modern America, I not only feel a responsibility to interview living subjects for my work, but these conversations always remind me why I love what I do. I give my deepest thanks to Jorge Acero, Edward Bonuso, Rafael Flores, Mike Guare, Deirdre Heekin, Donald Hoenig, David Keck, Zarela Martínez, Mary Mendoza, Hannah Miller, Christina O'Campo, Juana Rodríguez Vásquez, Blanca Santiago, Todd Trzaskos, Ian Yaffe, and my stepfather Richard Rocha, who were all generous with their time, observations, and memories and allowed me to integrate their words into my own historical interpretations. I am also grateful for the other oral historians who recorded interviews with food workers in previous eras that I have used throughout the book.

I am so grateful to the many colleague-friends who encouraged this work, and much of their scholarship is cited within my chapters. Adam Arenson invited me to present at the Writing History Workshop at Columbia, Jim Scott kindly hosted me at the Agrarian Studies Colloquium at Yale, and Megan Elias, Alison Lefkovitz, Vanessa May, and Lara Vapnek gave me a great community of readers in the US Women's and Gender History Workshop at the New York Historical Society. Colleagues who invited me to speak at their institutions also reenergized me. Alejandra Bronfman brought me to beautiful Vancouver, Felipe Hinojosa and Sonia Hernández invited me back to my home state of Texas, Mireya Loza put me in dialogue with NYU's food studies crowd, Jennifer Rogers Brown facilitated connections with the organization Rural Migrant Ministry, Brenda Elsey and Benita Sampedro brought me to Hofstra, and Lana Dee Povitz and Heather Roller offered final opportunities to connect with their students at Colgate and Middlebury. Years ago I started a Second Book Writing Group in the History Department at Stony Brook, and am grateful to Jennifer Anderson, Eric Beverley, Alix Cooper, and April Masten for their engagement with a very early version of chapter 3. I also thank Hasia Diner and Heather Lee for feedback on that same chapter. For years, I have enjoyed the support and friendship of Paul Gootenberg, Sara Lipton, Shobana Shankar, and Eric Zolov at Stony Brook. I also thank my former doctoral students Fernando Amador II and Ximena López Carrillo—now both professors—for their help with newspaper research for chapter 3 and their hard work on our accompanying "Mexican Restaurants of NYC" digital history project. To Al Camarillo, Karl Jacoby, Natalia Molina, Jeffrey Pilcher, and Steve Pitti—I admire you all, and thank you for always being kind and in my corner.

From the time I began working on this book, I wanted its home to be UNC Press. I am honored to be published in the Latinx Histories Series, which I now help to coedit with the indefatigable Michael Innis-Jiménez, who has supported my work since I was in graduate school. In those early years, I met Debbie Gershenowitz in passing at a conference, and she made me feel glittering and special in the span of two minutes. Little did I know I would get to work with her years later as my editor. I thank all the other people at UNC Press who labored on this book including Valerie Burton, Alexis Dumain, Vivian López Rowe, Alex Martin, Peter Perez, Lindsay Starr, and the anonymous readers who pushed me to make this manuscript sharper and better.

Whether it was by letting me crash for the night during a research trip or taking me out for distraction, friends have filled my cup so generously. Carmen Greenlee, Elizabeth Newman, Susan Tananbaum, Allen Wells, and Ian Yaffe gave me comfortable guest beds, boat rides, lighthouse walks, travel tips, research leads, and their own cars during my research trips in Maine. Laura D. Gutiér-rez bestowed generous and thorough pointers about navigating bracero records in the Archivo General de la Nación in Mexico City. Daniel Pérez offered his warm and laidback hospitality in Coyoacán, and did a fantastic job indexing this book. The wonderful Mary E. Mendoza hosted me multiple times in Vermont and organized a dairy farm tour, accompanied me on interviews, and indulged my need for apple cider donuts. Jeannette Estruth gifted me a much-needed sum-mer writing retreat in her lovely Hudson home. Meredith Garagiola, Haninah Levine, and Steve Velásquez always fed me well and lifted my spirits in Wash-ington, DC. In other cities, Mohamad Ballan and Rosabel Ansari, Andrew Ro-bichaud and Liz Beers, Jared Farmer and Magda Maczynska, Joel and Naomi Rosenthal, David Stanley and Jenna Ushkowitz, and Ruth and Katie Yemane took great care of me.

To Caitlin Dean, Sylvia Delgadillo, Simon Doubleday, Alina Gorokhova, Lani Harwood, Kelsey Haskins, Kris Klein, Beth and Casey Lew-Williams, Jamie Martin, Dodie McDow, Declan McGinley, Carol and Scott McKibben, Maria Montoya and Roderick Hills, Casandra Rosenberg, Roxanne Rosenberg, Rachel St. John, and Simon Tschinkel—thank you for caring about me during the hard things, and helping me celebrate the good things. To Ala Alryyes, with whom I could be most myself, I treasure the many laughs, conversations, café writing sessions, and travel adventures we shared. You also took my ramblings about this book's content and designed a structure for it that made so much sense.

To Mona Chopra and Isabel Sánchez Sachs, thank you for listening, keeping me well, and helping me to learn more about myself.

Finally, my constant loves—my doves—are my mother Mary Ann and sister Gina. They have cheered my life on in ways that teach me how to be more tender-hearted and optimistic about what's ahead. This book is for them.

NOTE ON TERMINOLOGY

In this book I use *Latinx* as a gender-neutral term to refer to individuals and communities of Latin American descent (whether migrant or citizen) living and working in the United States. I acknowledge that Latinx is a recent term (recognized by the Oxford and Webster dictionaries in 2015 and 2018, respectively) and that older, working-class, or nonacademic communities do not tend to use it. However, there are some reasons to defend its usage. Contrary to assumptions that the "x" is an English-language imposition, the "x" can be interpreted as an indigenizing, radical move (similar to Chicano/Chicana being rewritten as Xicano/Xicana). Additionally, "Latinx" is used by younger generations—including the students I hope my book will reach—because they desire a term that does not conform to the masculine/feminine binary of Latino and Latina. "Latiné" is another option, but it has origins in Europe and is not as widely used a term as Latinx in the current moment, though this may change. As a historian, I realize that solely using "Latinx" to speak about people of past eras would be anachronistic; thus, I will use Latinx as an umbrella term at certain points, and use nationality or subjects' preferred identifying terms at other moments.

AWAITING THEIR FEAST

A National Craving and Contradiction

In the modern world, hunger is not just about the
relation between a person and food, but about
the relations between people.
—Stephen Minister, "Food, Hunger, and Property"

O n an autumnal day in September 2000, Mexican migrant workers Víctor Estrada, Omar González, and Christo Gutiérrez entered Poncho's
Cantina in the small town of Auburn, Maine. The restaurant's name
and menu items seemed familiar and inviting. At this time, 98 percent of Auburn's residents identified as white, but in recent years the town had
absorbed about 1,000 Mexican and Central American immigrants working in
the local apple, broccoli, blueberry, and egg industries. After sitting down, the
three men began conversing in Spanish within earshot of the restaurant's owner,
Patricia Varnum. As they remembered, Varnum slammed her hand down on
the bar and exclaimed, "If you're going to be here, you have to speak in English
because this is my place! If you don't like it, leave." The men, who were all capable
of speaking English, promptly left and shared their experience with family members in Texas, who then relayed it to the Mexican consulate in Boston. The three
men were advised to file a complaint with Maine's Human Rights Commission.
When interviewed later by the media, Varnum insisted she had not forbidden
the men from speaking Spanish with each other but had told them, "I don't
speak Spanish. . . . You have to speak English to me to get served." One of the
men slyly replied to her in English, "Can we speak Spanish to you if we speak real
slow?" which likely irritated her further.[1]

    This nonsensical, even darkly comical, moment of customers being scolded
for speaking Spanish in a Mexican restaurant illustrates a deep contradiction in
the United States. It is a nation that desires and embraces *foodways* that have migrated from Latin America, but has a much more fraught relationship with *people*
of Latin American origin or descent. Disturbingly similar incidents to the one

in Auburn have continued to occur in food spaces, and spiked during Donald Trump's presidency. In May 2018 at a restaurant in midtown Manhattan, a white lawyer yelled at employees and customers for speaking Spanish with each other, and was captured on video ranting, "My guess is they're not documented. So my next call is to ICE [Immigration and Customs Enforcement] to have each one of them kicked out of my country. . . . I pay for their welfare. I pay for their ability to be here. The least they can do . . . is speak English." A few months later in Colorado, a white woman persistently harassed two women for speaking Spanish in a grocery store. In the spring of 2019, a woman threatened to call ICE on a food truck operating in a Dallas neighborhood, assuming its owner Claudia López was undocumented. When interviewed by the media about her kneejerk racism, the woman said she was simply frustrated by eyesores that hindered the sale of her home. "I like tacos! Just not in my neighborhood!" she exclaimed. In July 2019 in Eustis, Florida, two white customers told Burger King manager Ricardo Castillo to "go back to Mexico" when they heard him speaking Spanish with an employee. Castillo retorted that he was of Puerto Rican descent and demanded they leave his restaurant.[2] Though hearing Spanish is the frequent trigger for these outbursts, it is noteworthy that debates and violence over whether Latinx people belong in the United States often take place in realms of food provision or service. As geographer Rachel Slocum has pointed out, "Race is produced and racism reinforced through foodspace."[3]

When Latinos for Trump founder Marco Gutierrez warned Americans on national television that Latinx culture would become so "dominant" that we would have "a taco truck on every corner," his words went viral. A few years later, we are living in that reality—a 2024 report from the Pew Research Center shows that 99 percent of Americans live near a Mexican restaurant or food establishment. For decades, a burrito or taco was seen as a poor field-worker's lunch, and Mexican American students' homemade food was ridiculed in school cafeterias. "There was a lot of shame eating a taco back then. . . . So I had to hide my food," remembered Robert "Bobby" Vasquez, the owner of the restaurant Tamale House in Austin. "Now everybody's eating tacos. It's not just Mexicans anymore."[4]

If Latin American food seems more beloved—and increasingly appropriated and capitalized upon—with each passing year, why do we still see incredible xenophobia, racial tension, and violence against Latinx people in food spaces? One might hope that experiencing another community's foodways would inspire greater appreciation, curiosity, empathy, and respect for that group. But as Lucy M. Long writes of "culinary tourism," it can constitute "a colonialist enterprise in which individuals . . . exploit other cultures for their own pleasure, entertainment, or edification. . . . Eating does not necessarily lead to understanding or respect." Scholar Mark Padoongpatt adds that food adventurism constitutes a "superficial way of engaging racial and ethnic difference and an arms-length approach to inclusion."[5] Eating multiculturally can signify an openness to "Others," but dining experiences often allow one to consume on a surface level without delving deep into the complex histories of migration that have made certain ingredients or dishes available in the first place. Often the very same people who crave and consume Latin American food express distance or disgust toward Latinx people (migrant and citizen) and treat them as invisible labor or hyper-visible cultural and legal threats. Trump's infamous social media post of enjoying a taco bowl on Cinco de Mayo, captioned "I love Hispanics!" crisscrossed with damaging generalizations about Mexicans such as "They're bringing drugs. They're bringing crime. They're rapists." Due to historical US-Mexico border policing and tensions, Mexican-origin people have received the brunt of xenophobia and vilification, but as more Central American, South American, and Haitian migrants present themselves at the border out of hope and desperation, hostility has enveloped more people from Latin America and the Caribbean, inevitably affecting their coethnics who already live in the United States.

Unlike waves of European migration, Latin American migration to the United States has continued into the twenty-first century because of economic inequality and political turbulence, in which the United States has often played a part. Despite Latin American people being framed as a continuing immigration "crisis," the cuisine remains desirable. As historian Vicki Ruiz observed about politically conservative Orange County, California, customers can eat happily at a Mexican restaurant while complaining about "illegal aliens" during the same meal.[6] Opinions about immigrants being job stealers, economic drains on the nation, criminals, or polluters of "American" culture literally hover over tables as people pass fajitas, tostadas, guacamole, and margaritas. The late restaurateur and food critic Anthony Bourdain called attention to this hypocrisy ten years ago, referencing Mexican food and food workers in particular: "We consume nachos, tacos, burritos, tortas, enchiladas, tamales and anything resembling Mexican in enormous quantities. . . . Despite our ridiculously hypocritical attitudes towards immigration, we demand that Mexicans cook a large percentage of the food we eat, [and] grow the ingredients we need to make that food. . . . As any chef will tell you, our entire service economy—the restaurant business as we know it—in most American cities, would collapse overnight without Mexican workers."[7]

One must fully digest the reality that many of those who make desirable food experiences happen, and who power the US food industry—from farmworkers to meatpacking workers to restaurant employees and street vendors—are of

Latin American descent or origin. Yet whether they are US citizens, temporary guestworkers, or undocumented migrants, Latinx food workers experience high levels of discrimination, invisibility, criminalization, and exploitation in their daily lives. A memorable example of this dissonance occurred in June 2018, when protesters confronted Trump's Department of Homeland Security (DHS) Secretary Kirstjen Nielsen as she dined at a sleek Mexican restaurant near the White House. At the time, the DHS was separating children from their parents at the border. "Get activists here," one diner texted his friend. Members of the Metro DC Democratic Socialists of America assembled and marched inside to where Nielsen was sitting, flanked by Secret Service. Shouting "Shame!" and "If kids don't eat in peace, you don't eat in peace!" the group streamed the encounter on Facebook. "Homeland Security Secretary Kirstjen Nielsen is in a Mexican restaurant of all places! The fucking gall!" one activist shouted on the livestream. Customer Brent Epperson recalled, "More than half the restaurant . . . started clapping," and protester Amanda Werner said "a lot of the [Latino] waiters and busboys were kind of smiling at us and seemed to be enjoying the fact that we were calling this woman out." After about ten minutes, Nielsen left and so did the demonstrators, where they were high-fived and thanked by a few customers who followed them outside.[8] This protest disrupted the usual DC practice of leaving politicians alone while eating, and Nielsen learned she could not get away with enjoying Mexican food while endorsing the trauma of Mexican and Central American families at the southern border.

While some might ask, "Why must we bring politics into food? Can't we just enjoy this pleasurable thing, without analyzing it?" the answer is we cannot, precisely because the US food system is built on the mistreatment and invisibility of multiple groups of people. If one considers all the links in the food chain—from crop harvesting to processing to transportation to provision to service and delivery—millions of workers are required to get our food to us every day. More than 20 million people work in the US food system, and of that number, people of color and immigrants hold most of the low-wage jobs.[9] American history has consisted of feasting for some and scarcity for others, and since the era of plantation slavery the occupation of food labor has stayed physically dangerous, economically precarious, and starved of basic protections. US consumers only enjoy the food prices they do because most food workers are in the precariat and earning poverty-level wages. In October 2016 in Buffalo, New York, for example, ICE agents raided Mexican market and taco counter La Divina in search of owner Sergio Mucino, who had been harboring undocumented workers in various homes and employing them at four restaurants. Two dozen people were seized during the raids. Local conservative radio talk show host Tom Bauerle recalled receiving numerous comments from listeners praising the ICE sweep but who "[were] disappointed because apparently these places made awesome tacos" for $2.50 apiece.[10]

Awaiting Their Feast argues that beginning in the 1940s, the United States gained in tandem an appetite for Latinx *food* and Latinx food *labor*, and then devalued both from then on. This dual appetite was fed first by the poverty and itinerancy of US citizen farmworkers (who included a large Latinx contingent) abandoned by the New Deal, and then major wartime guestworker programs negotiated between the US government and Mexico and the Caribbean. During these programs, the US agricultural, railroad, and food processing industries all grew accustomed to continuously "ordering" and importing contracted foreign labor. Employers also benefited from a parallel stream of undocumented labor that emerged alongside this legal recruitment. With desperate US citizens, guestworkers, and undocumented workers competing for food labor jobs, the wages of all were depressed. People were left metaphorically hungry for better conditions and, in many cases, literally hungry because of a lack of access to affordable and adequate food for themselves.

The food industry, of course, is not the only industry functioning this way in modern America. Many economic sectors have purposefully accelerated the process of ethnic succession—replacing one wave of workers with a new one—to try to disorganize and preclude workers' political organization. In meat and poultry processing, for example, employers have hired undocumented Central American laborers as a more vulnerable workforce and disruptive presence to Black and Mexican workers' occupational knowledge and politicization. Similarly, guestworkers who lack a formal right to unionize have been intentionally recruited alongside (and instead of) US citizen workers to displace them over time. If today's food workers are overwhelmingly Latinx, guestworker, and undocumented, they are more vulnerable to exploitation and deportation at work, and also become targets of xenophobia and hostility in public space.

Moving the reader through time from World War II to COVID-19, *Awaiting Their Feast* analyzes several case studies to historicize how Latinx food workers have been rendered invisible as racialized or migrant subjects but also rendered invisible *structurally* in the food system by being tucked away in spaces like fields, warehouses, or the backs of restaurants. Food labor realms are often intentionally designed to be less visible or completely invisible to consumers, even if one is trying to be an informed and ethical eater. In restaurants there is often a gradation as one moves from the front to the back of the house—lighter to darker skinned, citizen to undocumented, English speaking to non-English speaking. In grocery stores, undocumented workers labor in stockrooms or freezers, and in the seafood industry immigrant processors are found inside of plants rather than on docks. These layered invisibilities contrast starkly with how hyper-visible Latinx foodways tend to be in commercial and popular culture. Meanwhile, Latin American food itself has undergone its own devaluation in the United States since World War II—it is often considered "authentic" only if it is cheap. By no coincidence, this belief has strengthened as more Latin American migrants have become visible as a food labor precariat in the United States. Framing this workforce as grateful for any dollars they make in *el norte* compared to their home countries, more Americans assume the price of the food and the price of the people should be inherently low.

Though it tells a national story, this book zooms in on the US Northeast in particular. For a region that has long claimed inhabitants from Latin America and the Caribbean, the Northeast is still very understudied in Latinx history. This is partly because New England and the Northeast are still imagined to be "white" places, even though they have claimed a Latinx demographic for centuries. During the 1600s Dominicans, Brazilians, and Spaniards began arriving in New York with the Dutch and other Europeans. Soon after, ships traveling between Connecticut and Puerto Rico were trading grain and lumber for molasses, rum, and enslaved people. Then, during the 1800s, Spaniards, Cubans, and Puerto Ricans living in the Caribbean began self-exiling and migrating to the East Coast amid rebellions against Spanish imperial control. By 1890 Boston claimed a Cuba-Borinquen Club and a chapter of the Partido Revolucionario Cubano. In the aftermath of the Spanish American War of 1898, US imperialistic restructuring of Puerto Rico and Cuba led to further instability, creating unemployment and overcrowding in cities and provoking migration off the islands and up north. Cubans settled in places such as Portland, Maine; and Providence, Rhode Island. Similarly spurred north by the Mexican Revolution, Mexican migrants came to the Northeast by train or ship and settled in Providence, Boston, and New York City by the 1920s. Trickles of other Latin American migrants—including Chileans, Colombians, Ecuadorians, Peruvians, and Venezuelans—arrived in the Northeast over subsequent decades, along with US-born Latinx people migrating internally throughout the nation.[11]

Another pressing reason we should attend to the Northeast is because it is part of the "other" border zone that is the US-Canadian borderlands. This other borderland is arguably just as significant as the US-Mexico border in histories of Latinx labor, race relations, and community formation. In fact, many Latinx stories have begun, and stayed, in the North.[12] Using the angle of food labor to cut across an increasingly diverse and complex Latinx demographic, this book draws together often-siloed histories of Mexican, Caribeño, and South and Central

American communities. As can be expected in any work that discusses multiple groups of people, there is much that does not appear in this book. I hope, however, that it will inspire further meditations on the Latinx Northeast.

Awaiting Their Feast also bridges the fields of Latinx, labor, immigration, and food studies. In their work, food historians and journalists have offered cultural analysis of American eaters' desires and critiqued the US food export economies that have negatively impacted health outcomes in Latin America, where diabetes and obesity have risen from processed foods and sugar. Meanwhile, commodity studies have analyzed the production and flow of items such as tamales, tortillas, and tacos from Latin America to the United States, as well as the relations between the various actors and institutions involved in their distribution. Labor scholars have exposed the problematic nature of both the US and global food systems—most workers in them are not paid a living wage, and have physically and emotionally suffered as they serve and nourish others. Finally, studies in anthropology, political science, law, and sociology have discussed how pervasive the idea of a social, cultural, and political "Latino threat" continues to be in the United States.[13] This book dialogues with all these literatures while staying rooted in historical narratives and methods. It relies on a mixed archive to do so. Latinx communities have often been denied access to and inclusion in more traditional textual records, particularly as creators or "main characters" of documents. Instead, they are part of the archivally "underdocumented."[14] In addition to mining manuscript and government collections, I rely on sources including newspaper articles, court cases, restaurant reviews, and historical menus. Additionally, interviews that others and I have conducted comprise an essential source base. As personal memories are complex and mutable, these oral histories are cross-referenced with corroborating information as much as possible.

Awaiting Their Feast is divided into three parts that draw new waves of Latinx food workers into the story and show how certain labor struggles have been tidal and repeating while others have resulted in noticeable change. Each chapter revolves around one or two nucleus case studies, telescoping out at moments to provide national context. Part I, "We Need to Be Fed," focuses on farmworkers—the first workers in the food chain—and details important moments of their food activism between the 1940s and 1980s. Chapter 1 discusses two World War II guestworker initiatives, the Bracero Program with Mexico and the Migration Division Farm Labor Program with Puerto Rico, and their impacts upon the "Garden State" of New Jersey, northern New York, and Pennsylvania. All three places had absorbed diverse agricultural workforces over time, which included US southern Blacks, Italian and Polish immigrants, Bahamians, and Jamaicans. After Mexican and Puerto Rican guestworkers displaced these workers in fields and vegetable processing plants, they became quite vulnerable themselves in terms of their own racial marginalization, deportability, and "foreignness." Despite these precarities, both Mexican and Puerto Rican guestworkers agitated for better living and working conditions. While these guestworker programs have been studied by scholars, this chapter tells a new story about these programs and food. Even though guestworkers had been recruited to produce food for the Allies during World War II, and then for the general American populace after the war, they received highly inadequate provisions themselves while working. Thus one of their consistent demands, across regions and decades, was better-tasting and culturally familiar meals. Guestworkers wrote letters to Mexican consulates and Puerto Rican bureaucrats, filed complaints against companies and supervisors, walked off the job, and proposed specific changes to their labor camp cooks, kitchens, and meal routines. Contrary to the assumption that food issues were trivial compared to other labor rights violations, workers placed their food protests squarely alongside their grievances about wage theft, a lack of medical care, and hazardous working conditions. During the war years, Mexican braceros framed their food grievances as a gastro-diplomatic and Good Neighbor Policy issue. Beyond wartime, both Mexican and Puerto Rican workers used a politics of disgust to assert their right to culturally and calorically nourishing food. Ironically, while these Latin American guestworkers were asking for these things, Mexican and Tex-Mex food was becoming more available to US consumers in restaurants and grocery stores by midcentury.

Chapter 2 moves into the civil rights protest period of the 1960s and 1970s to explore how Latinx farmworkers urged consumers to think about their shopping and eating choices as part of a moral economy. The most famous Latinx-led food boycotts in US history were the ones led by the United Farm Workers union (UFW), headed by Cesar Chavez, Dolores Huerta, and Larry Itliong. Representing mostly Mexican American farmworkers in California, the UFW conducted nationwide consumer boycott campaigns against grapes, lettuce, and wine. To keep the pressure on employers, the union needed to attract diverse allies, cultivate a wide reach, and stay financially afloat. The union deployed organizers to every region of the country, and the Northeast—which claimed major fruit and vegetable markets and distribution hubs—proved crucial for keeping the union's message in front of consumers. Again, this chapter places a new twist upon California or Southwest-centric histories of the UFW by focusing on its activity in the Northeast. It also examines how Chavez and other union leaders used fasting as a technique to gain food shoppers' sympathy. Capitalizing on global and national attention to the issue of hunger, the UFW emphasized that malnourishment and starvation could be found at home among farmworkers as much as in the developing world. The shock and irony of the nation's food workers going hungry was enough to garner support and fundraising dollars from northeastern contingents ranging from wealthy elite liberals to the Black and Puerto Rican working class to suburban housewives. Ultimately, however, though the UFW made slight attempts to become involved in northeastern farmworker movements, it never achieved truly transregional organizing. Additionally, Cesar Chavez's characterization of undocumented workers as strikebreakers limited the union's expansion of its membership, as did an overall xenophobic climate in the 1980s that balked at Central American refugeeism and "amnesty" legislation such as the Immigration Reform and Control Act (IRCA).

While activists were shaping discourses about food labor and hunger, there was also very real change taking place in US culinary culture due to Latinx presence in and migration to the Northeast. Part II, "How Latinx Newcomers Transformed Foodscapes," describes how Latinx labor shaped food in the urban and rural Northeast between the 1980s and the 2010s. Chapter 3 traces the dual histories of how high-end and more modest Mexican food entrepreneurs transformed New York City. Following the Tex-Mex craze of the early 1980s, regional Mexican cuisine captured diners' attention via creatives like the pioneering Latina chef Zarela Martínez, whose eponymous restaurant in Manhattan operated for almost twenty-five years. Martínez was part of a class of shrewd immigrant food entrepreneurs who helped to create (and cash in on) New Yorkers' fascination with Mexican food. When the 1994 North American Free Trade Agreement (NAFTA) began destabilizing rural economies in Mexico, an influx of migrants came to the Big Apple and entered many sectors of the food industry. From bakeries and bodegas to taquerías and tortilla factories, these newcomers' enterprises offered New Yorkers a much wider range of Mexican food options. Complications arose, however, as the American public saw more hole-in-the-wall Mexican restaurants and street food on display and came to believe that "authentic" Latin American food should be fast and cheap. This monetary devaluation—which by no coincidence occurred as Latin American immigrants became more associated with food service in the United States—made it more difficult for *everyone* along the Latinx food-providing chain, including Martínez, to demand a certain level of money and respect. This chapter, in telling the story of a relatively privileged restaurateur alongside humbler food workers, argues for placing interclass and intersecting histories of Latinx success and struggle on the same plate.

The 1980s and 1990s were an important period when both Latin American migrants and US-born Latinx people moved to non-metropolitan places and began making lives for themselves. Chapter 4 moves to the far Northeast and explores how Latinx food labor migration and settlement occurred in the nation's demographically whitest state: Maine. Not only did Mexican Americans from the Southwest and Southeast begin coming to Maine to piece together seasonal harvest jobs, but the US government reincarnated the Bracero Program in the late 1980s through the H-2 visa program, which brought new Jamaican, Haitian, and Mexican labor to the United States.[15] In the Northeast, H-2 workers began displacing older waves of Native American, Canadian, southern Black, and Puerto Rican labor. This chapter explores the overlapping migrations and relationships between the US Latinx, Latin American, and Caribbean workers who contributed to Maine's egg, blueberry, vegetable, and seafood industries. It intentionally includes Haitians as Latinx workers in Maine, acknowledging their overlapping identities as Black, Caribeño, and migrant. As neighbors with the Dominican Republic, which goes unquestioned as part of Latin American and Latinx history, Haitians have experienced violent intimacies with Dominican political administrations that have unabashedly showcased their anti-Blackness. Lorgia García Peña and others have urged us to pay attention to and translate Blackness in Latinx history, particularly when intertwined histories of colonialism, violence, multiracialism—and, in the case of this book, food labor migration—are at play.[16] This chapter also pushes back against the problematic label of "unskilled" that is often affixed to seasonal labor. Instead, I argue that these communities in Maine are some of the most agile and resourceful workers in the nation. They rotate through several industries in a single calendar year and must constantly flex their physical and emotional muscles to adapt to different labor, environmental, legal, and social environments. If not for these workers, many food-related economies in demographically "graying" states like Maine would not have thrived in the ways they did during the late twentieth century. It was also during the 1990s and early 2000s that some Latinx Mainers—much like Zarela Martínez did in an earlier era—became food entrepreneurs and restaurant owners who transformed a landscape devoid of varied Mexican cuisine into a burgeoning one.

Part III, "Food Labor Flows and Futures," examines the period between the 1990s and the 2020s to show how diverse Latinx people have boosted (or even saved) certain food-related and touristic economies of the Northeast. Chapter 5 tackles seafood, tracing how Latin American immigrants became sea cucumber and lobster processors in Downeast Maine and fish processors in New Bedford, Massachusetts. In each place, Latinx workers entered the seafood industry at a time when a Euro-American workforce was waning. Despite filling this crucial labor niche, Latinx seafood workers have received mixed responses from locals. Residents in the town of Milbridge, Maine bristled when Latinx newcomers tried to live there year-round, and even tried to block them from affordable housing options. In New Bedford, many community members have accepted a Latin American (and often undocumented) immigrant workforce out of economic pragmatism, but the town is not free from its own structural inequalities and xenophobia.

Chapter 6 turns to drinks, and the Latinx laborers who are propping up the bucolic, artisanal image of the dairy and wine industries of Vermont and New York State. Dairy products like milk, butter, cheese, and ice cream, along with wine and cider, are consumed by locals and tourists alike as seasonal charms of New England and the Northeast. Both dairy farmers and vineyard owners began hiring Latin American migrant labor in the late twentieth century to stabilize their paltry workforces. Vermont and New York State present unique cases of spatial unfreedoms because of their proximity to the US-Canada border and thus to heightened surveillance in our contemporary era of criminalized immigration (*crimmigration*). Fearing apprehension by the Border Patrol or ICE, undocumented dairy workers in Vermont and upstate New York feel confined to their employer-provided housing and unable to move freely in public space. For this reason, finding opportunities to control their own grocery shopping and food procurement through cultural brokers or *paqueteros* became supremely important to them to recover some limited autonomy. As Ashanté M. Reese has used the phrase "Black food geographies" to describe the myriad ways Black communities have obtained and made the food they wanted, Latinx communities have done the same.[17] Meanwhile, in the North Fork wine region of Long Island, workers navigate their own zones of policing and are struggling to enforce recent state legislation that allows them to bargain collectively. Like their counterparts in Vermont, Latinx Long Islanders have persisted in creating culinary havens and nourishing themselves in a climate of isolation and inequality.

Before 2020, Latinx food and drink laborers had proved essential to multiple food industries' profitability and longevity. This was only magnified during the first year of the COVID-19 pandemic, when Americans feared the links in the national food chain would break. Largely based on journalism from the COVID years, this book's final chapter zooms out to the national level and traces the severe impacts of the pandemic upon US food workers, who were treated as essential yet disposable. Farmworkers, processing and transportation workers, grocery store and restaurant employees, street vendors, and delivery workers were all interconnected via their vulnerability. Politicians and employers pushed to keep farms and factories operating, banking on mere slaps on the wrist for noncompliance regarding personal protective equipment, sick leave, and distanced worker transportation and housing. A horrific number of employees in the agricultural and meat-processing sectors became infected with COVID or died from it. Meanwhile, shuttered restaurants wrestled with asking anxious employees to return to work, especially when some customers ignored health etiquette and violated staff's personal boundaries. Outside, street food vendors—whom many people depended on for quick, open-air, and affordable meals during the pandemic—encountered heightened regulations, ticketing, and criminalization. Zigzagging through the streets, *deliveristas* (food delivery workers) on bikes risked contracting the virus through exchanges with restaurants and customers, became victims of assault and robbery, and struggled to understand wage and tipping systems on delivery apps. Compounding all these precarities was the fact that many food workers experienced noticeable food insecurity during the pandemic. In response, mutual aid efforts such as food boxes and community fridges sprung up, as did new public protests from workers who did not want to be "essential but invisible" any longer.

This book reveals the multiple and profound ways that Latinx communities have sustained and shaped the US food industry, at the same time that they have expanded and electrified so much of what we think is culinarily desirable and exciting. Without their labor, all the links in our national food chain would likely suffer or fail. *Awaiting Their Feast* lifts out some key moments in which these food workers contested their invisibility and made moves to make themselves seen, heard, and better compensated. In addition to more familiar routes of collective protest such as union strikes, rallies, or marches, they have engaged in gastropolitical demonstrations by stopping food production for others; asking for better food for themselves while working; using or seeking out food to challenge power relations; or becoming food entrepreneurs themselves when other workscapes did not serve them. While this book excavates histories of struggle and hardship, it also emphasizes food workers' agency, fuller lives and desires, and alternative visions regarding more just worlds of food.

The hunger spoken of here is twofold. The first is physiological, related to a shortfall of calories and nutrition. The second is emotional—a longing for other dignities. Without the privileges they deserved, Latinx food workers have found ways throughout history to talk about and fight for food that meant something to them. This book exposes uncomfortable truths about how the modern US food system has stayed in operation, and how Latinx foodways have been fetishized and appropriated. Yet it also highlights the powerful moments when people—who were designed and told to stay out of view—articulated their hungers in impressive and disruptive ways.

PART I

We Need to Be Fed

Latinx Guestworker and Farmworker
Food Activism, 1940–1980

CHAPTER ONE

Appetites Gained and Lost

Mexican and Puerto Rican
Guestworkers and Food

After a long day of building railroads in Philadelphia in the summer heat, two dozen exhausted Mexican guestworkers (braceros) returned to their labor camp for dinner. They were among the thousands of Mexican men recruited during World War II to fill labor shortages in the US agricultural and railroad industries. The war would end the next month with Japan's surrender, but as far as everybody knew at the time, railroad work needed to continue in haste to facilitate the transportation of crops, foodstuffs, rubber, and other cargo across the country. The famished crew examined their mess hall dinner—it was egg sandwiches, and little else. Resigned, they ate. They had become accustomed to being disappointed by their meals.

Shortly after, the entire group suffered debilitating food poisoning. One worker was in such severe pain that the others decided to call an ambulance. Since their supervisor did not sleep at the camp and there was not a telephone on the premises, a worker had to stagger out into the street and flag down a passing police car. After this incident, which made the men miss valuable hours of work and pay the next day, the bracero crew requested a meeting with the Mexican consulate and officials of the Railroad Retirement Company. The men initially extended an invitation for the authorities to eat lunch with them at the camp, but when nobody accepted, the braceros brought samples of their rancid food to them. Claiming the cold cuts in their sandwiches were often "wormy," they told the officials that their food would be much safer, and more satisfying, if they could cook for themselves instead of paying for commissary meals. After hearing the complaints, the Mexican consular official added that the railroad company should compensate the workers for the time they were incapacitated.[1]

This was one of many incidents regarding food that occurred during the nation's participation in three overlapping guestworker initiatives that began in the World War II years. The US and Mexican governments negotiated the

Bracero Program; Puerto Rico established the Farm Placement Program (FPP) with the mainland; and the British West Indies Temporary Alien Labor Program (BWITALP) imported laborers from Jamaica, St. Lucia, St. Vincent, Barbados, and Dominica. All three programs were framed by the US government as emergency measures to fill labor shortages amid the military draft, but they lasted far longer in reality. The BWITALP imported more than 20,000 workers a year from 1943 to 1947. The Bracero Program lasted for more than twenty years (1942–64) and distributed between 4.6 and 5.2 million labor contracts to Mexican men dispersed across almost every US state. Finally, the FPP (1943–93) sent several thousand Puerto Rican workers to the Midwest, Eastern Seaboard, and Northeast. These hybrid citizen-guestworkers harvested and canned fruits and vegetables in New Jersey, picked cranberries on Cape Cod and apples in the Hudson Valley, and were essential to the Pennsylvania mushroom and Connecticut River Valley tobacco industries.[2]

The World War II era was not the first time the United States had experimented with guestworkers or absorbed laborers from Latin American and Caribbean countries (see table 1.1). Between 1911 and 1921, Jamaicans worked widely across the Americas, including on the Panama Canal and in a variety of food industries. Thirty thousand Jamaicans came to the United States to pick fruit, and 10,000 cut sugar cane in Cuba every year.[3] As for Puerto Rico, it was no coincidence that the Jones Act of 1917 granted Puerto Ricans US citizenship in a time of war. In addition to drafting them for the military, the US Department of Labor (USDOL) began recruiting their labor for war-related industries, guaranteeing them wages of three dollars for eight-hour workdays and overtime pay on weekends. By July 1918 more than 18,000 Puerto Ricans were participating in this program, mostly working in the US South. At first, the program seemed a welcome escape from economic hardships on the island. A few months in, however, workers had filed multiple complaints about substandard wages, food, housing, and medical care on the mainland. When ninety-three Puerto Rican workers died in Arkansas between October 1918 and February 1919, investigations were launched and the USDOL sponsored workers' return. Despite this controversy, the federal government contracted Puerto Rican workers again in the 1920s to work in Arizona agriculture. Outside these programs, other Puerto Ricans made their personal decisions to migrate. In 1920, 11,811 Puerto Ricans were recorded on the mainland, and this number rose to 52,774 by 1930 and 69,967 by 1940.[4]

Meanwhile, Mexican and Mexican American migration was changing US demographics. During the late 1800s and early 1900s, southwestern Tejanos followed *enganchadores* (labor recruiters) to strawberry, sugar beet, and other

TABLE 1.1. Contracted guestworkers in the United States, 1947–1964.

Year	Mexicans	Puerto Ricans	British West Indians	Bahamians	Canadians	Others*	Total
1947	19,632	1,241	1,017	2,705	7,421	—	32,016
1948	35,345	4,906	2,421	1,250	5,900	—	49,822
1949	107,000	4,598	1,715	1,050	3,000	—	117,363
1950	67,500	7,602	4,425	1,800	2,800	—	84,127
1951	192,000	11,747	6,540	2,500	2,600	—	215,387
1952	197,100	12,277	4,410	3,500	5,200	—	222,487
1953	201,380	14,930	4,802	2,939	6,200	—	230,251
1954	309,033	10,637	2,159	2,545	7,000	—	331,374
1955	398,850	10,876	3,651	2,965	6,700	—	423,042
1956	445,197	14,969	4,369	3,194	6,700	390	474,819
1957	436,049	13,214	5,707	2,464	7,300	685	465,419
1958	432,857	13,067	5,204	2,237	6,900	315	460,580
1959	437,643	10,012	6,622	2,150	8,600	405	465,432
1960	315,846	12,986	8,150	1,670	8,200	863	347,715
1961	291,420	13,765	8,875	1,440	8,600	40	324,140
1962	194,978	13,526	11,729	1,199	8,700	404	230,536
1963	186,865	13,116	11,856	1,074	8,500	923	222,334
1964	177,736	14,628	14,361**	—	7,900	25	214,650

*Includes Japanese and Filipino workers.

**Number includes Bahamians.

Source: Data from Ismael García-Colón, *Colonial Migrants at the Heart of Empire: Puerto Rican Workers on U.S. Farms* (Oakland: University of California Press, 2020), 170.

agricultural work in the Midwest. Others answered the call of steel and auto factories in Chicago and Detroit. In the Northeast, Mexican-origin people appeared in noticeable numbers at the beginning of the twentieth century (the Census recorded 300 Mexicans in New York City in 1900), and records of them can be found in 1920s ship manifests, newspaper reports, and money orders. Mexican anthropologist Manuel Gamio, for example, found almost 500 money orders sent from New York to points in Mexico in the summer of 1926.[5] This excerpt from the 1929 folk song "Corrido Pensilvanio" speaks to those who left cotton picking in Texas for work in Pennsylvania steel:

Adiós estado de Texas	Goodbye state of Texas
con toda tu plantación,	With all your plantations,
Ya me voy pa' Pensilvania	I am going to Pennsylvania
por no piscar algodón.	To pick cotton no more.
Adiós, Fort Worth y Dallas,	Goodbye, Fort Worth and Dallas,
pueblos de mucha importancia,	Cities of great importance
Ya me voy pa' Pensilvania	I am going to Pennsylvania
por no andar en la vagancia.	To wander aimlessly no longer.[6]

Across the border, the turbulence of the Mexican Revolution created another northward diaspora of Mexicans throughout the 1910s and 1920s. In the interest of hiring cheap foreign labor, agricultural employers lobbied the federal government to exclude Mexicans from the immigrant head taxes and literacy tests applied to others at the time. It soon became obvious that employers preferred Mexican nationals to Puerto Rican laborers because of the former's deportability. "We cannot handle them like Mexicans. A Porto Rican . . . cannot be deported as can a Mexican," said a Los Angeles Chamber of Commerce leader in 1927.[7]

Even though Latin American and Caribbean labor was nothing new to the US mainland on the eve of World War II, the 1940s were the decade during which the United States began developing an insatiable appetite for contracted labor from this part of the world. The workers, however, quickly discovered how lacking their wages, food, and housing conditions were. As historians Cindy Hahamovitch and Maria L. Quintana have both argued, guestworkers exist in a liminal realm between slavery and freedom, a "no man's land between nations."[8] Because of a lack of federal oversight and inspectors on the ground, employers could and did skimp on workers' necessities.

Meanwhile, to US citizens already struggling to find steady work in agriculture, guestworker programs were threatening and frustrating. The Great Depression had ravaged the nation, and the New Deal had intentionally excluded farmworkers and domestic workers from important protective legislation. The National Labor Relations Act (also known as the Wagner Act), which permitted workers to join collective bargaining units, and the Fair Labor Standards Act—which established a forty-four-hour workweek, a national minimum wage, overtime pay, and prohibited child labor—only applied to industrial workers. In response, strike flurries occurred in fields and canneries during the 1930s and early 1940s. The Cannery and Agricultural Workers' Industrial Union spearheaded successful multiracial strikes in California. In New Jersey, 2,000 cannery workers at the Campbell Soup Company (including Barbadian and Puerto Rican workers) went on strike in 1934. In 1941, workers at New Jersey's Seabrook Farm won higher wages, seniority rights, and paid vacation. But victories like these were rare. A combination of redbaiting, deportations of union leaders, and collusions between grower associations and police forces meant that strikers often faced physical violence, firing, and blacklisting. American agribusiness preferred to keep importing nonunionized guestworkers rather than answer citizen farmworkers' calls for better treatment.

Building on existing studies of these guestworker programs, this chapter asks new questions and tells a new story about these programs and food. Considering so many of these guestworkers were recruited to work in food production and distribution for the United States, what kind of food did they receive themselves? What types of nourishment, and deprivation, did they experience during their time as laboring allies and "guests"? Food from a home country becomes incredibly important to a migrant's life and identity once they are in a new place. *Nostalgia*, rooted in the Greek *nostos* (to return home) and *algia* (a painful condition), refers to a desire to journey back or call the past into the present.[9] Guestworkers, separated from their kin networks and assigned to unfamiliar locations in the United States, understandably wanted culinary reminders of home. This chapter examines how guestworkers protested for their right to nutritionally and culturally nourishing food during the World War II years and after. Because the British West Indies programs were small and short-lived, this chapter focuses on the longer-lasting Mexican and Puerto Rican programs but offers information about the West Indies counterpart when relevant.

Though some might assume that issues of food did not reach the same level of urgency as guestworkers' other grievances, they rivaled and at times even superseded complaints about wage theft, a lack of medical care, and substandard housing. Workers' protests against food deprivation can be found in Puerto Rican and Mexican government records dating from the 1920s until the early 1990s.[10] As noncitizens, Mexican braceros sought help from their consulates, while Puerto Rican workers felt emboldened to approach both mainland and island authorities. The chapter discusses the Bracero Program first, focusing on the World War II–era crews of Mexican railroad workers who were deprived of nourishment despite being expected to facilitate flows of food throughout the nation. During wartime, braceros framed their need for better food as a diplomatic issue, invoking the language of the Good Neighbor Policy. The chapter then moves to Puerto Rican vegetable processing workers of the 1950s to 1970s, who conducted similar protests around food and mistreatment and sometimes quit their contracts altogether to seek new lives in northeastern cities.

Asking for higher-quality and culturally desirable food was important to these guestworkers, not only because they were being charged for their food daily but because they yearned for meals that could quiet their homesickness. Mexicans and Puerto Ricans constantly imagined and executed other ways of eating and procuring food they desired. If they resided in smaller labor camps, workers pooled money to buy ingredients and cook meals in their own kitchens. In larger camps with mess halls, workers threw their cold sandwiches, soggy rice, unsalted beans, and inedible proteins on the floor and conducted work stoppages. Both groups, in different time periods, used a politics of disgust to assert that they deserved better, and were not mere tools of labor without taste or opinions. If disgust was a sentiment reserved for those in power—for those who felt entitled to denigrate or judge others' foodways, habits, or hygiene—Latin American guestworkers flipped the script on US employers, who did not expect them to complain.

Though this chapter addresses guestworkers' food protests in the Northeast, these complaints transcended region. One historian of the Pacific Northwest wrote that bad food was "the source of more discontent and work stoppages than any other single aspect of [bracero] camp life." Labor activist Ernesto Galarza wrote of Michigan, "The protests concerning food sometimes reach the stage of mild violence," and similarly observed that "food complaints became so insistent that violence was narrowly averted" in California. In that latter state, workers even convinced some employers to contract with Latino and Filipino food suppliers who could bring spices, ingredients, and tortilla presses to them. Meanwhile, a California commissary company hired several hundred Chinese Mexican cooks who had experience working in Mexican restaurants.[11]

Ironically, it was during the mid-twentieth century that Latin American (and specifically Mexican) food started becoming more available to US consumers in grocery stores and restaurants across the nation. As they shopped for Mexican or Tex-Mex food items and engaged in culinary adventurism, Americans likely had no idea there were guestworkers confined to labor camps who were begging for these same things. This chapter ends around 1970, when the British West

Indies and Bracero Programs had already ended and Puerto Rico's Farm Placement Program was on the decline. Across all three groups, a significant number of workers decided not to return home. As they blended in with 1950s and 1960s waves of Latin American migrants from South America and the Caribbean, these ex-guestworkers began establishing stronger footholds—and foodways— in both rural and urban northeastern communities.

We Need to Be Fed:
Mexican Braceros' Wartime Food Protests

Over its lifetime, the Bracero Program sent an annual average of 200,000 Mexican men to the United States, giving them labor contracts of about six to nine months (though some workers found ways to extend them). Women and children were not permitted to migrate under the program, primarily because US employers did not want to encourage Mexican families' reproduction and permanent settlement. In April 1943, President Franklin D. Roosevelt moved control of the Bracero Program from the Farm Security Administration to the newly established Office of Labor and the War Food Administration.

Archival records show how desperate Mexican citizens were to become braceros; the papers of President Manuel Ávila Camacho include hundreds of petitions for bracero contracts. Writing individually and collectively, men (and even some women) pleaded with the president and his staff to let them migrate, including any information they felt could bolster their case. Many writers emphasized that they had voted for Ávila Camacho, or were registered members of his political party. A man named Mariano García wrote that he worked in a train that Ávila Camacho once took from Nayarit to Sinaloa.[12] Other men declared they needed to become braceros because of natural disasters. When a volcano erupted in Paricutín, Michoacán, in February 1943, ash fell for weeks and destroyed farmers' crops.[13] When flooding struck the state of Coahuila, the Unión Civil de Obreros sin Trabajo (Unemployed Workers' Union) demanded work in the United States and threatened to go on hunger strike in Mexico City. A hurricane in the state of Nayarit brought even more letters.[14] Some women even asked to be considered. Ángela Velarde de Madrigal requested spots for her and her husband, as his salary alone was not enough to sustain them and their four children. Another woman, Elvira Moreno, requested information about how to apply for a job in fruit packing companies in California.[15]

The men ultimately selected for the agricultural and railroad Bracero Programs in the war years were welcomed with a Good Neighbor discourse that characterized Mexican men as allied soldiers producing and transporting "food for victory."[16] The first trainloads of braceros were sent to southwestern states like California and Texas, but over time more crews were sent to the Midwest, Deep South, Pacific Northwest, and Northeast to harvest crops or work on railroad infrastructure. The New York Central Railroad was a major northeastern employer, as was the New Haven Railroad, which employed hundreds of men for track and engine house duties and housed them in towns including North Haven, Connecticut; Providence and East Greenwich, Rhode Island; and East Hartford and Springfield, Massachusetts. Railroad braceros earned about fifty cents an hour. In the agricultural sphere, farms in northeastern communities like North Kingstown, Rhode Island; and Portsmouth, New Hampshire, employed agricultural guestworkers from both Mexico and Puerto Rico.[17] Residents of towns that received braceros tried to acknowledge and welcome the newcomers. When a group of fifty braceros arrived in the small town of Beaver Dams, New York, in the depths of winter, townspeople and railroad officials gave them coats and warm clothes. It was a good thing they did; the men's housing was a row of unheated train crew cars. In this town and others, residents organized English classes, leisure activities, and social events for braceros, often under the auspices of YMCA chapters.[18]

Though they were promised decent mess hall food or their own kitchens during their contract term, braceros had to pay daily fees for food if it was provided by their employer or a commissary company. The deducted cost from their paychecks ranged from 75 cents to $1.50 a day in the early 1940s (the equivalent of $16 to $33 a day in 2024). Portions were often so small that workers had to supplement their meals by buying canned beans, fruit, sardines, and cheese from the commissary or outside their camp. Braceros were surprised by these unexpected costs, and it did not help when some governmental representatives mocked braceros' food complaints. A US State Department official remarked, "Mexico's Juan Trabajador . . . likes his corn-meal tortillas, his beans, and his chili, and no amount of ham 'sanweech' will quite satisfy." Ernesto Galarza, a scholar, labor activist, and representative for the Pan-American Union, visited a group of braceros and observed one bracero's tragicomic campaign of "planting" his sandwich lunch every day in the fields "to see 'if it would grow tortillas.'"[19]

In addition to cold sandwiches and fruit at midday, braceros complained about small portions and repetitive or stale ingredients. A typical workweek menu exhibited this repetition, with the most variety on Friday:

1. Potatoes, meat, beans, hard rolls, milk.
2. Potatoes, meat, vegetable stew, tortillas, bread, milk, pie.

3. Potatoes, meat, beans prepared in three different ways, bread, milk, coffee.
4. Potatoes, meat, green beans, tortillas, bread, milk, coffee.
5. Potatoes and gravy, tongue, carrots and peas, stewed tomatoes, chili beans, bread, tortillas, green salad, lemonade, sweet rolls and stewed apricots.[20]

Likewise, a menu from California's Threlkeld Commissary Company revealed the same overfeeding of simple, cheap, fast-burning carbohydrates (see table 1.2). Boiled potatoes were served at all three meals a day for six days out of the week; white bread and oleo (margarine) were served seven days a week at every meal except one; and oatmeal was served for four days. Protein in the form of eggs was provided every day, various beans were a staple, and different meats (beef, pork, chicken, lamb) were alternated with offal like heart, kidneys, and pigs' feet. Fish was offered only once during the week, and desserts consisted of stewed fruits, cake, punch, Jell-O, or pudding. In response to bracero complaints about a lack of Mexican-style food, Threlkeld worked with the State Department to hire several hundred Chinese Mexican cooks from Mexico. Chorizo, menudo, and "Spanish" or "Mexicana" style vegetables were integrated into menus, and lunch was redesigned to be the bigger meal because braceros needed more fuel for their afternoons of work. Threlkeld even tried to get the State Department to increase their red food ration points from 72 (five pounds of meat per man per month) to 150 instead. "I think you will agree that . . . [a] lack of appetizing food would do much to undermine a friendly and co-operative attitude on the part of these Nationals towards the United States," a Threlkeld official wrote. The War Food Administration denied the request, stating that the commissary's menu appeared sufficient.[21]

Alimentary unhappiness reigned at most bracero camps, and food protests manifested in many ways. Some men tried to modify the food they were given into what they wanted it to be. In one large camp, a group of braceros asked for pancakes at dinner. The confused camp cooks made stacks of flapjacks and watched as the men used them as tortilla substitutes, stuffing their dinner of spare ribs, beans, tomatoes, and lettuce into them and topping it all with hot sauce. Caribbean workers also complained about a lack of culturally familiar food, and labor camps in the Northeast scrambled to find Jamaican-born cooks when protests erupted in mess halls. Some company bosses even instructed local restaurants to override their usual discrimination policies if their workers arrived and wanted to eat. When Bahamian workers of New Jersey's Seabrook Farms entered a restaurant and were refused service for being Black, the men "jumped over the counter and started breaking up the dishes, [and] tearing up the place."

TABLE 1.2. Sample weekly bracero commissary menu from the Threlkeld Company, ca. 1945.

Day of week	Breakfast	Lunch	Dinner
Monday	Corn flakes with milk, soft boiled eggs, hot biscuits, boiled potato, jelly, oleo, bread, coffee	Spanish meatloaf, string beans with onions and tomatoes Spanish style, boiled potatoes, stewed apples, bread, oleo, coffee	Braised honeycomb tripe (menudo) with garbanzo beans Spanish style, new green cabbage with tomatoes and onions, salsa salad, sheet cake, grape punch, bread, oleo
Tuesday	Oatmeal with milk, chariza [sic] sausage mixed with scrambled eggs, hot biscuits, boiled potato, jelly, oleo, bread, coffee	Sliced beef heart with thick Creole sauce (celery, onions, hot chili peppers, tomatoes), pink beans, boiled potato, one orange, bread, milk (fresh), oleo	Braised pig's feet Spanish style with salad, stewed corn Spanish style, boiled potato, bread, oleo, chocolate pudding, coffee, milk
Wednesday	Oatmeal with milk, soft boiled eggs, fried kidney beans, hot biscuits, boiled potato, jelly, oleo, bread, coffee	Stewed beef kidneys with onions, tomatoes, and green peas Spanish style, red kidney beans, boiled potato, stewed prunes, bread, oleo, orange punch	Beef stew with carrots, onions, and tomatoes, green peas Mexicana style, Spanish rice, boiled potato, salsa salad, stewed dried peaches, iced tea, bread, oleo
Thursday	Chariza [sic] sausage mixed with scrambled eggs, hot cakes with maple syrup, boiled potato, jelly, oleo, bread, coffee	Barbecued pork spare ribs with Hot Mexicana sauce, new green cabbage with tomatoes and onions, slice of sheet cake, orange punch, milk, bread, oleo	Braised short ribs of beef Spanish style, stewed summer squash Spanish style, boiled potato, salsa salad, bread, oleo, fruit jello, milk
Friday	Oatmeal with milk, soft boiled eggs, fried kidney beans, hot biscuits, boiled potato, jelly, oleo, bread, coffee	Roast leg of mutton, Mexicana sauce, boiled potato, stewed summer squash, fried kidney beans with chopped onions and cracklings, one orange, iced tea, bread, oleo	Baked salmon with Creole sauce, stewed tomatoes Spanish style, boiled potato, salsa salad (consists of Mexican chili, peppers, tomatoes, shredded lettuce, onion, and vinegar), sherbert, coffee, bread, oleo

TABLE 1.2 (*continued*)

Day of week	Breakfast	Lunch	Dinner
Saturday	Corn flakes with milk, soft boiled eggs, hot cakes with maple syrup, fried kidney beans, jelly, butter, bread, coffee	Stewed beef kidneys, Mex. style, string beans with tomatoes and onions, boiled potato, salsa salad, bread, oleo	Honeycomb tripe with garbanzo beans, stewed chipeña squash Spanish style, stewed corn, boiled potato in jacket, stewed apples, milk
Sunday	Oatmeal with milk, charizo [*sic*] sausage mixed with scrambled eggs, boiled potato, jelly, oleo, bread, coffee	Braised chicken with Spanish sauce, stewed summer squash with tomatoes Spanish style, boiled potato, coffee, bread, oleo, fruit jello	Barbecued fresh pork shoulder with Mexicana sauce, salsa salad, pink beans, boiled potato, coffee, bread, chocolate cupcake, oleo

Source: RG 59: Department of State, Mexico file, folder 811.504, box 4852, National Archives and Research Administration, College Park, Maryland.

The restaurant staff called company owner John Seabrook, who replied, "Feed them. You better feed them."[22]

Mexican braceros also fought for the right to eat away from camp and opt out of their mandatory daily fees for food. They became incensed when employers deducted these fees from their paychecks anyway, regardless of whether they ate or skipped a meal. Some companies defended this deduction practice, claiming they were only trying to shield braceros from the racist restaurant service of the outside world.[23] Enough braceros filed complaints about these deductions that in May 1944, the New York Mexican consulate released a letter authorizing braceros to eat offsite whenever they chose, as long as they gave camp cooks twenty-four hours' notice. Later that summer, however, New York bracero Reynaldo Elizalda García complained he had not eaten in his camp cafeteria for over a month but still received reduced pay. In September 1945, fifty braceros working for the Baltimore and Ohio Railroad in Philadelphia signed a petition to the Railroad Retirement Board and Mexican consulate demanding an end to this wage theft. During the summer of 1946, a group of braceros in Maine went on strike for the right to eat outside of camp, all threatening to return to Mexico if this freedom was not granted.[24]

The volume of letters sent to the Mexican government and consulate spurred some authorities to travel to the United States and see bracero conditions for themselves. One official who accompanied a group of northeastern railroad braceros along their route observed them living in "carro-casas" (train-car homes) and reported back to the Mexican government that the braceros were not permitted to eat in their own train's dining cars. At breakfast the men had to file into the dining car to fill paper plates with scrambled eggs, sausage, potatoes, and bread, and then return to their dwelling cars. By the time they sat down to eat, their coffees had sloshed out of their paper cup and their food was cold. Ernesto Galarza wrote vividly of poorly ventilated dwelling cars, heated by coal stoves that blanketed braceros' belongings in soot.[25] Andrés Iduarte, a labor inspector who reported to the Mexican secretary of labor and social welfare, made multiple visits to the Northeast. On a trip to New York in late January and early February 1945, Iduarte was lavished with attention (or closely surveilled) by labor contracting and camp officials. He visited braceros on the Erie Railroad in East Buffalo and reported that the camp's kitchen ingredient inventory did not seem varied or interesting. At another camp in the area, Iduarte sat down to talk with a group of braceros after dinner. The men complained their company charged them $1.20 a day for three meals, and $1.50 on days they did not work. In addition to demanding more heating in their carro-casas, the group requested that their coworker Antonio Ortiz be named cook, since he had cooked for groups of 700 in California. "The issue of cooking is fundamental for the satisfaction and best work of the braceros," Iduarte wrote in his report, and recommended the camp take its workers' suggestions seriously. He traveled on to Camp Stewart near Niagara Falls, where workers complained about wage theft, a verbally abusive Italian American foreman, and an alcoholic cook who left them without food. These braceros also asked for a Mexican man to serve as their camp chef.[26] Though they knew their meals would not exactly match the Mexican food they remembered from home, they hoped for cooking techniques and substitutions of proteins and grains (more beef and beans instead of processed ham, and corn tortillas instead of white bread) that would close the long distance they felt between Mexico and the Northeast.

Unwittingly, braceros across the nation were complaining in unison about their food. In Ypsilanti, Michigan, braceros working on the New York Central Railroad complained of an overreliance on "starchy foods like potatoes and macaroni" and animal parts like joints, oxtail, and pigs' feet. Meanwhile, Galarza wrote that these workers' milk tasted "like a concentrated emulsion of powdered chalk and chlorinated kerosene." To supplement their unsatisfactory meals, braceros felt forced to buy cans of sardines, jars of green peppers, and bottled milk from grocery stores, which only further depleted their meager wages. During his visit to this camp, Galarza encouraged the thirty-six-man crew to write to the

War Manpower Commission. They did so, represented by one bracero named Ernesto Vieyra Avendaño. One month later, after no reply, the men wrote a second letter to the WMC and sent copies to Galarza and the Mexican consul in Detroit. It read in Spanish,

> Our dissatisfaction is not only with the manner that this food is prepared but its poor quality and scarcity. Sometimes the meat is decomposing and rotten and has a bad odor.... It has been two or three months that we have not had any sugar in the camp; it's only reserved for the bosses.... There have been times when we have refused to eat the food at lunch and we have ... return[ed] to supper where we have been served exactly the same food that we left behind at the lunch hour.

Whenever the crew complained, the letter continued, the boss threatened to call the police or cancel their contracts and send them back to Mexico. In fact, one of their coworkers who had argued strongly had been fired and nobody had heard from him since. The letter demanded to know that worker's whereabouts and asked for WMC employees to come to the camp because "nuestra situación empeora cada día [our situation worsens every day]." A particularly powerful statement, surely felt by braceros elsewhere, read, "Con un trabajo tan duro como el nuestro necesitamos alimentarnos de lo contrario no podemos trabajar con buena voluntad" (With a job as hard as this we need to feed ourselves [be fed]. Otherwise, we cannot work with goodwill).[27] Braceros were asking for the Good Neighbor Policy to be made real, in a culinary sense. Across the country, they were becoming so frustrated that they marched to consulates and government agencies carrying their food. In one case, a crew of men sent their stale food by air mail. By intertwining their complaints about food with other issues like discriminatory treatment and low wages, braceros communicated that all were of equal importance. Anthropologist James C. Scott has termed these acts "everyday forms of resistance" or "weapons of the weak." One must not only look for big demonstrations such as strikes or riots, he points out, but recognize how "vital territory is being won and lost here too" in people's daily and smaller struggles over work pace, leisure, and food.[28]

Railroad companies and government officials wrote to each other about workers' food protests, worrying they would have ruinous effects on the industry. Santa Fe Railroad representative G. H. Minchin wrote to John D. Coates, chief of the WMC's Foreign Labor Section, explaining that the "inability [to] secure meat is causing much unrest, and indications are may lose several hundred [workers]." Coates then wrote to Leon Bosch, associate director of the Food Rationing Division of the Office of Price Administration. "Unless ... [braceros'] food grievance can be eliminated the number who desert and return to Mexico may seriously cripple railroad operations," he wrote.[29] Government and consular officials also received letters from concerned US citizens who used Good Neighbor Policy rhetoric. A young student named Thomas C. Murray Jr. wrote to John Willard Carrigan, chief of the Division of Mexican Affairs in the Department of State, expressing concern about braceros' treatment in his New Jersey hometown. Mentioning that he had attended summer school in Mexico the previous year, Murray affirmed, "The hospitality shown me by the Mexicans is unsurpassed. Truly, Mexico is doing its part in the Good Neighbor Policy." To his dismay, when eighty Mexicans came to Metuchen, New Jersey, to work for the Pennsylvania Railroad, locals exhibited a mixed response. While some (including Murray himself) started giving braceros free English lessons weekly at the local YMCA, it was not long before several Metuchen residents began to complain "that they didn't want the Mexicans using the swimming pool, gymnasium, and pool tables of the 'Y.'" The branch then denied braceros use of the facility except to take the English class. Murray also reported that "some of the bus drivers in that vicinity refuse passage to the Mexicans and tell them to take the next bus." He concluded, "The citizens of Metuchen are denying the Mexicans of recreational facilities and, in general, are tearing down the Good Neighbor Policy." Whether by luck or his pointed rhetoric, Murray's letter received attention from Carrigan right away, who reached out to rectify conditions on the ground in New Jersey. Ultimately, the Metuchen YMCA directors voted to give braceros an additional night of access each week for social activities.[30]

Elsewhere in the Northeast, braceros were experiencing racial rejection and gendered segregation. In rural Plainsboro, New Jersey, the YMCA designed a summer recreation program "to help find a solution to the Mexican problem." It consisted of English classes, some sports (softball, soccer, badminton, croquet, volleyball), and opportunities to play musical instruments. Over 100 braceros attended at first out of curiosity or loneliness, but after some months only a few remained because no locals mixed with them in these leisure activities. Trenton began a similar program, but like Plainsboro, it made activities same-sex only after local girls' interactions with braceros stoked residents' fear of sexual mixing.[31] In Maine, these fears manifested in the immediate arrest of a forty-nine-year-old railroad bracero named José Salas Vásquez, who was accused of statutory rape of a seven-year-old girl in May 1945. As Salas Vásquez worked at an intersection, the daughter of his labor contractor walked by him. Reminded of his own seven-year-old daughter back in Mexico, Salas Vásquez picked her up and kissed her before giving her a dime. The girl's father called police and claimed Salas Vásquez "was about to take [his daughter] into the woods" to commit an "assault of a high and aggravated nature." Andrés Iduarte—the same Mexican authority who inspected bracero camp and food conditions—went to the Portland jail to visit Salas Vásquez, who was being held on $3,000 bond. The child, who in Iduarte's opinion had given "vague" testimony, was not given a medical exam. "Everyone I've talked to about the case has either clearly or timidly said the matter is unjust, produced by lack of knowledge about Mexican character, racial or national prejudice and because in this area there has been two grave sexual crimes recently," Iduarte wrote in his report. In Salas Vásquez's eyes, he simply showed affection to a child who reminded him of his own four children in Mexico, whom he desperately missed. Though Portland lawyer Maurice Davis took Salas Vásquez as his client and was ready to defend him, the girl's father decided not to appear and testify at the grand jury hearing. The jury refused to indict, and Salas Vásquez was released back to work.[32]

Anything but naive, braceros knew they were being portrayed as social and sexual threats by locals in their surrounding communities. During the summer of 1945, the Alianza de Braceros Nacionales de México en los Estados Unidos de Norteamérica (National Alliance of Mexican Braceros in the United States) reminded US and Mexican government officials that they needed their moral support. In a letter to President Ávila Camacho, they wrote that inspectors and consulates had not intervened enough on their behalf. Braceros suffered from "una soledad torturante, depresión moral" (a torturous solitude and low morale) and had no one protecting them from employer greed. Moreover, they lacked medical care, social lives, and meaningful interaction with locals. The Alianza asked the government to prove "que la Patria no es vocablo hueco" (that the Homeland is not an empty concept) and that it was "una entidad viviente y sensible que se alargan hasta donde está el más ultimo, el más anónimo y más modesto de los mexicanos, para auxiliarlo, para levantarlo y para consolarlo en sus graves quebrantos" (a living and sensitive entity that helps the very last anonymous, humble Mexican citizen and aids, lifts, and comforts him in his gravest breakdowns).[33] If the United States needed to treat braceros like good neighbors, they argued, Mexico also needed to treat them as loved sons and citizens who would not be forgotten as soon as they left the homeland.

In the last months of the wartime railroad bracero program, Mexican workers in the Northeast spoke out against medical neglect and workplace repression, in addition to food. On a basic level, their shoddy housing provided little protection from the cold weather, and illnesses such as flu and pneumonia spread rapidly. Braceros were getting injured and even killed at work because safety signage was not bilingual, and any resulting medical costs were foisted upon them instead of their companies. At a railway camp in Plainsboro, bracero José Flores-López was struck in the right eye by a chipped piece of ballast. The next morning he notified his foreman, who sent him to a medical examiner in Trenton, where he was diagnosed with a corneal abrasion. Though he was initially charged for all medical expenses, Flores persisted in filing a workers' compensation claim and received money for his injury and lost days of work. Things turned out differently, however, for his coworker Antonio Feliciano Ramírez, who also suffered a corneal abrasion and a lower back injury. As a Zapotec man with no knowledge of English or Spanish, Ramírez encountered much more hostility from the company investigator, who declared him to be "slightly demented or greatly faking" in a written report. Ultimately, Ramírez did not receive any compensation and was painted as a difficult worker by the company. "His persistent refusal to return to the track, because of his physical condition, resulted in the cancellation of his contract and his return to Mexico," the company's report concluded. Many other braceros were taken aback by their medical bills when they were injured on the job. An investigation of over 175 bracero railroad camps in New York, New Jersey, and Connecticut revealed that many workers had unknowingly signed away their workmen's compensation rights in their contracts.[34] Camp translators, even if they were Mexican themselves, often did not explain agreements fully to Spanish-speaking braceros. The situation was even more confounding if one was an Indigenous bracero who spoke another language that was not Spanish.

By the end of World War II, it was clear that US employers had developed a growing appetite for cheaper, nonunionized Mexican labor. In 1945, 13,000 bracero camps existed across the nation, housing anywhere from 20 to 200 men apiece.[35] Though the railroad component of the Bracero Program ended in 1945, US agribusiness lobbied Congress to renew the agricultural component. All signs pointed to the continued exploitation of foreign-born farmworkers, especially since citizen farmworkers were not faring any better. In 1947, President Harry S. Truman's Federal Interagency Committee on Migrant Labor produced a report remarking on "almost unbelievable" child labor in the fields. Average wages for farmworkers in the late 1940s were $5 per day and $514 per year, and by 1950 a quarter of US agricultural workers (1 million people) were peripatetic. This itinerancy limited individuals' and families' eligibility for residential rights related to school admission, public aid, and voting. Truman appointed a Commission on Migratory Labor to conduct twelve hearings around the nation in 1950, but—despite all its revelations and recommendations for the improvement of US farmworker conditions—Congress voted to extend the Bracero Program via Public Law 78.[36] To avoid continued scrutiny and critique of the program's many problems, the federal government withdrew from its role of facilitator. All recruitment, contract negotiations, transportation and housing arrangements, and worker grievances would be handled by growers' associations and the Mexican government.

With the US federal government abdicating all responsibility, attention to braceros' food issues vanished altogether. One could see this neglect in an April 1946 letter from Veracruz man José Olivera, the father of a dead bracero, who wrote to the US president that he believed food poisoning had killed his son.[37] In an echo of the food poisoning episode described at the beginning of this chapter, poor provisions continued to be part and parcel of the neglect that Mexican braceros, and the Puerto Rican guestworkers who followed them, would experience well into the 1960s.

Boricua Braceros: Puerto Ricans' Food Protests

While the US government began importing braceros from Mexico, it also entered into agreements with Caribbean countries for guest labor. In 1942, 5,000 Bahamian men and women between the ages of twenty and forty arrived by plane to perform farm work in the United States. Though these workers were initially allowed to bring their families, women were quickly banned when immigration authorities discovered a few of them had initiated their own abortions when employers threatened them with deportation for getting pregnant. Bahamian men were rapidly substituted with Jamaican and Barbadian men.[38] The WMC began importing Puerto Rican laborers in 1942 but soon realized this contingent would present a unique challenge because of their freedom as citizens to leave their worksites if dissatisfied. Indeed, 60 percent of the Puerto Ricans hired to work on the Baltimore and Ohio Railroads in Maryland, the Campbell Soup Company in New Jersey, and copper mines in Utah had deserted these jobs six months into the guestworker initiative. The US government decided to turn over all recruitment responsibilities to employers, who then decided to use labor contractors as middlemen.[39]

Puerto Rican authorities and technocrats were motivated to keep their guestworker program going, precisely because it offered an economic safety valve and remittance flow to the island. To that end, the Puerto Rican government created a Bureau of Employment and Migration (BEM) within the US Department of Labor. Nestled within the BEM, the Farm Placement Program (FPP) recruited people through radio and newspaper advertisements and selected workers based on health certificates, a farmer's recommendation, and a good conduct certificate from the police. In the first large-scale airborne migration of guestworkers to the

United States, FPP men were sent to New Jersey, Pennsylvania, Connecticut, Massachusetts, Indiana, New York, Minnesota, Washington, Delaware, Michigan, and Wisconsin. During its first year, the BEM placed 5,796 Puerto Ricans in jobs in island and mainland agriculture. As mainlanders witnessed Puerto Ricans arriving in greater numbers during the 1940s, Puerto Rican bureaucrats had to defend their workers as nonthreatening, productive people. In New York City, a nativist "Puerto Rican Problem" campaign swept the city in 1947. Articles in publications ranging from conservative tabloids to the *New York Times* accused Puerto Rican migrants of aggravating already-existing problems of overcrowded housing, unemployment, communicable diseases, and crime. "600,000 PUERTORICANS COME TO DINNER — THEY FLEE DARK FUTURE IN THE SUN TO BECOME CITY'S PROBLEM BROOD," a *New York Daily News* headline blared. The next year, in 1948, the BEM created a "Migrant Division" to help facilitate Puerto Rican migration and adjustment to the "ethnologically alien" mainland.[40] Much like Mexican consuls and intermediaries tried to massage social relations between braceros and locals, Puerto Rican authorities institutionalized assistance to their hybrid citizen-guestworkers, who were deemed both social risks in public space and flight risks in the workplace.

The number of Puerto Rican guestworkers, and the grand total of their remittances, kept rising into the 1950s. The Puerto Rico Planning Board estimated that remittances doubled from $1,326,000 in fiscal year 1951 to $2,783,000 in 1954.[41] Motivated to keep the guestworker program churning safely and efficiently, the Puerto Rican government tried to protect workers from racial discrimination by circulating pamphlets to both migrants and employers. *Know Your Fellow American Citizen from Puerto Rico* (1950) was distributed to employers and community leaders in cities like New York and Chicago, and *How to Hire Agricultural Workers from Puerto Rico* was published in 1957. The BEM also sponsored public television shows, radio programs, and newspaper articles about topics ranging from migrants' labor rights to how to dress on the mainland to the US educational and tax systems. In January 1952, Puerto Rico's Department of Education announced English classes specifically geared toward prospective migrants. Lessons included how to order food, how to travel by train and bus, tidbits about culture and diet on the mainland, and how to obtain medical or legal help. Puerto Ricans paid eager attention to this media; the unemployment rate on the island had climbed to 17.8 percent in the 1954–55 fiscal year.[42] By 1956 the Migration Division had established twelve offices on the mainland, mostly in the Northeast. Its central office was in New York, with others established in Chicago; Boston; Hartford, Connecticut; Keyport and Camden in New Jersey; Rochester, Middletown, and Riverhead in New York; and Hamburg,

TABLE 1.3. Puerto Rican farmworkers placed on US mainland farms via the Farm Placement Program, 1955–1961.

State	1955–56	1957–58	1958–59	1959–60	1960–61
Connecticut	1,200	829	1,992	1,477	2,070
Delaware	210	591	863	1,127	1,284
Illinois	—*	—	—	—	20
Indiana	—	—	62	95	25
Maine	9	33	30	28	41
Maryland	106	161	175	164	252
Michigan	—	56	23	22	—
New Hampshire	46	101	84	78	100
New Jersey	6,704	6,503	6,619	6,476	6,882
New York	2,536	1,788	1,108	962	1,446
Ohio	—	—	4	7	6
Pennsylvania	1,903	1,600	1,443	818	875
Rhode Island	21	6	25	0	5
Wisconsin	—	—	6	26	12
Total	12,735	11,668	12,434	11,280	13,018

*Dashes represent no record of imported Farm Placement Program laborers in a given year in a given state.

Source: Data from Edwin Meléndez, *Sponsored Migration: The State and Puerto Rican Postwar Migration to the United States* (Columbus: Ohio State University Press, 2017), 204.

Pennsylvania. By this time there were close to 15,000 Puerto Ricans working for 96 US farmers.[43] In the Northeast, Puerto Ricans were working on farms in New Hampshire, Pennsylvania, and New Jersey; nurseries in Massachusetts and Rhode Island; and tobacco fields in Connecticut. During the late 1950s Puerto Rican labor was called to new places like Long Island, New York; and Bangor, Cape Elizabeth, and South Portland in Maine.[44] By the end of the decade, the vast majority of FPP laborers were employed under the umbrellas of large agricultural associations, including the Glassboro Service Association of New Jersey and the Garden State Service Association, a mega-cooperative of growers in New Jersey, New York, Pennsylvania, and Connecticut (see table 1.3).[45]

Though the Mexican and Puerto Rican guestworker programs appeared separate and unconnected—workers infrequently worked at the same site—they were both being used to satiate the appetite of US employers, and they were both being linked to the undocumented Mexican immigrant problem.[46] During the early 1950s, the Immigration and Naturalization Service (INS) conducted multiple raids, with one actually carrying the derogatory name "Operation Wetback." Because the Bracero Program had become more competitive and costly (ten or more men waited for every one contract available), this had created a parallel flow of undocumented migrants from Mexico who wanted to skip the line and contracting process. "The wetback is a hungry human being," the president's Commission on Migratory Labor wrote in its 1951 report. Undocumented migrants comprised a competing and vulnerable workforce that employers hired to undercut *all* agricultural laborers' (including citizens' and braceros') wages. INS officers sometimes mistook US-born Mexican Americans—and Puerto Ricans—for "wetbacks" and rounded them up during immigration sweeps, making these two populations feel doubly insulted when they were racially profiled and wrongly apprehended. Meanwhile, Puerto Rican authorities created a new office when they discovered that some undocumented Mexicans were fraudulently using Puerto Rican birth certificates.[47]

Another way that the plights of Mexican and Puerto Rican workers converged was in their food protests. Like Mexican braceros, Puerto Rican workers craved food that reminded them of home and experienced a level of "homesickness, loneliness, and, sometimes, depression" that resulted in everything from weight loss to psychological crisis. "Satisfying Puerto Ricans' hunger proved to be a sensitive but critical affair, key to maintaining an available labor force," Ismael García-Colón wrote.[48] Between the 1950s and the 1970s, Puerto Rican workers conducted their own actions regarding meals, confinement, and mistreatment in their labor camps. Workers complained about being charged $1.50 or more daily for cold sandwiches, milk, soggy rice, inedible fish, and unsalted beans. In larger camps, they walked out of mess halls in defiance and frustration. In smaller camps without dining rooms, workers pooled their money to buy food and cook meals in their own tiny bunkhouse kitchens but did not have easy access to grocery stores or the ingredients they wanted.

Since Puerto Ricans' US citizenship made them distinctive guestworkers, they felt more emboldened to complain and ask mainland and island authorities to visit their camps and conduct inspections. They also made sure to occasionally denounce their treatment on US East Coast farms in the island press, particularly the opposition newspaper *El Imparcial*.[49] The Service Section of

FIGURE 1.1. Puerto Rican officials visit farmworkers in their mess hall, ca. 1956. *Left to right, standing:* Puerto Rico department of labor secretary Fernando Sierra Berdecía, Governor Luis Muñoz Marín, Migration Division director Joseph Monserrat, and PRDL official Eulalio Torres. Offices of the Government of Puerto Rico in the United States Records, Center for Puerto Rican Studies Library and Archives, Hunter College, City University of New York, New York.

the Migration Division, tasked with investigating accidents and intervening in wage and health-care disputes, served 16,834 Puerto Rican migrant workers in the 1951–52 fiscal year, and numbers steadily rose to over 20,000 workers per year after that. New Jersey stood out as a state in the Northeast that violated guest-worker contract provisions to a noticeable degree; inspections found violations in half of its 2,668 labor camps during the fiscal year 1955–56.[50] This number alarmed authorities so much that in November 1956, Puerto Rico governor Luis Muñoz Marín, Fernando Sierra Berdecía, and other FPP personnel visited New Jersey. They found the worst conditions among "Boricua braceros" at Seabrook Farms. "The kitchen was horrifying. It was a nauseating spectacle with a grand production of flies every time someone came close. The stove did not work well and the cook had improvised one outside in the dirt," their report stated.[51] In a photograph from the visit (fig. 1.1), Puerto Rican workers show their government leaders trays of what appears to be bland white rice, gloppy beans, slices of white bread, and tepid coffee.

Across time periods, both Mexican and Puerto Rican guestworkers employed a politics of disgust to assert their needs as hungry workers who needed calorically and culturally adequate food. In anthropologist Hanna Garth's words, these guestworkers were asserting their right to "alimentary dignity." In post-Soviet Cuba, Garth explained, the state tried to introduce new foods into people's diets, such as soy and vegetable proteins, to make up for the scarcity of meat and dairy. "Certain foods may be consumed out of necessity to 'fill up,' but these foods are not placed in the same categories as dignified cuisine," Garth writes.[52] Puerto Rican officials had to be vigilant and constantly pressure farmers and employer associations to give workers adequate food, housing, and wages. During the 1960–61 fiscal year, Migration Division representatives made 1,113 complaint-related visits to labor camps. And according to its annual report from that same year, the Department of Labor recovered $157,299 in wage theft for Puerto Rican workers.[53]

Much like how Mexican braceros were racialized and stereotyped as sexually threatening masses of men, Puerto Rican guestworkers were disproportionately arrested and incarcerated for long periods in the Northeast. Migration specialist Jorge Colón had to visit the Birds Eye processing plant in Avon, New York, for instance, when local residents complained that Puerto Rican workers were "crossing their back yards" and "bothering . . . girls in the street."[54] Meanwhile, in New Jersey, the Farmworker Division of Camden Regional Legal Services noted several incidents of "the bail system . . . being used as a means of punishment" for Puerto Rican farmworkers. One farmworker spent three days in jail because he could not pay a taxi fare. Another worker spent two months in jail before receiving his preliminary hearing on auto larceny charges. Three men languished in jail for over three months on a questionable charge of possessing a concealed weapon. One farmworker spent over five months behind bars because he lacked his $500 bail.[55] When workers finally responded to this disproportionate policing by organizing demonstrations of resistance, it spooked those in power. In July 1966 in North Collins, New York, local authorities called the Migration Division when they believed Puerto Rican workers were about to "riot" against police. When Jorge Colón arrived in town and stopped into a bar, he overheard a group of Puerto Ricans "talking about the most effective way to burn" buildings, police cars, and businesses that refused to serve them. Some in the group already had guns, bricks, gasoline, and bats. Colón persuaded them to file formal grievances instead of using violence, and later that day 300 Puerto Rican workers gathered on Main Street to list their complaints (mostly regarding police harassment) to the mayor.[56]

These demonstrations of resistance by Puerto Rican workers are also found in the records of major northeastern vegetable processing factories such as Birds Eye in upstate New York during the late 1960s and 1970s. On the surface, Birds Eye's contract with Puerto Rican guestworkers seemed fair. Workers would either process vegetables or harvest and plant broccoli in the fields for a minimum wage of $1.60 an hour and $675 minimum for their entire contract term. If they did not reach that minimum pay, Birds Eye agreed to top off the amount. The company also promised to provide clean housing and bedding, water, light, and fuel at no cost. In exchange, workers would pay a maximum of $2.20 per day for three meals. If a cook was not hired at the camp, workers could use cooking and eating facilities and enjoy free transportation to grocery stores and food suppliers.[57] Almost immediately, Birds Eye violated this contract. In April 1968, for instance, the company stated it did "not want to" supply pillowcases because "the men didn't use them. They use them for laundry bags [instead]." This likely pointed less to workers' hygiene and more to a lack of hampers and laundry facilities at the camp. Workers also complained about clogged sinks, uncomfortable mattresses, dirty showers, nonexistent trash collection, and a lack of recreation.[58] The neglect of guestworkers' basic needs was revealed in one of Birds Eye's memos to a Department of Labor representative in Puerto Rico. The company commodified and dehumanized its expected workforce for the upcoming season, informing the addressee, "Here are the dates and numbers for each of our *shipments*."[59]

Anything but passive, Puerto Rican guestworkers made decisions to rebel at Birds Eye, or change their plans and leave the plant altogether. A sample of termination notices from a cohort of workers hired on the same day in July 1968, for example, illuminates workers' dissatisfaction with—or strategic use of—their guestworker contract. Several men worked for just a short time at Birds Eye before quitting to join family elsewhere on the mainland. Juan Serrano Rosario left on August 16 "to go to New York City with relatives," while Efran D. Rivera left on September 1 "to join [his] brother in New York City." Mario Velásquez made clear his plan to "visit [his] sister in Pennsylvania—then return to P.R." on September 12. A few days later, Regino Encarnación Vega "quit to go to Rochester with friends" and a few days after that, Rafael Ayala Laboy informed Birds Eye he was "leaving to get [a] job in Brooklyn."[60] Other workers claimed family deaths or problems as the reason they were returning to Puerto Rico.[61] By specifically naming next destinations and loved ones, workers communicated to Birds Eye that they had other, preferable options, and were fuller human beings than just "shipments." Other workers were sent back to Puerto Rico by Birds Eye for insubordination. Efraim Echavarría, for example, "misse[d] work, would not go to [his] work station, [and] would not do his work." Jose Hernandez exhibited a "refusal to work, [and] tardiness."[62] Several workers' termination notices read "to return to Puerto Rico," which could have signified the end to the harvesting and processing season, but the varying departure dates hint at other reasons cloaked by boilerplate language.[63] A batch of eleven workers' notices from August and September 1970 contained the phrase "*quit* to return home to Puerto Rico," which gave them a different flavor of dissatisfaction rather than mutually agreed parting.[64] Several others "quit for another job" or "quit without notice."[65]

These termination notices reveal how often guestworkers articulated their unhappiness—about not just the food served to them while working but also the conditions of food work in general. Like braceros, Puerto Rican guestworkers were highly frustrated with the real amount of their take-home pay. As citizens, they had wages subtracted for federal and state taxes, Social Security, the guestworker program's insurance policy, and miscellaneous deductions. After deductions, the net pay for one worker who earned $223 was $165.72. For others, $248.54 turned into $187.50, and $321.28 into $254.04. One way some workers increased their take-home pay was to accept full-time employment with Birds Eye after their contract term and convert their status from guestworker to regular employee.[66] For others, the idea of finding a job in a city like New York held the promise of a less isolating existence. "The Waldorf-Astoria could not run without its 450 Puerto Rican workers," the hotel's personnel director said in the 1970s. In New York, Puerto Ricans were working in hotels, restaurants, schools, dry cleaners, hospitals, and factories. They served as postal workers, doctors, dentists, lawyers, and police officers, and more than 4,000 of them owned grocery stores, barbershops, drugstores, and other businesses throughout the city. Connecticut experienced a 481 percent increase in its Puerto Rican population between 1960 and 1970, and counted a total of 88,361 of them by 1980, with the largest concentration living in Hartford. The economics of survival, however, would still be challenging in these cities. And if ex-guestworkers ended up raising families in urban public school systems, the food served to their children echoed their past labor camp meals. Lunches of bologna, peanut butter, or cheese sandwiches with "dry and curled up" bread, diluted and cold soup, and sour milk would provoke future protests—specifically by Puerto Rican women—for culturally desirable and nutritious food in school cafeterias during the civil rights era.[67]

The Ironic Rise of Mexican Food

Ironically, while Latin American guestworkers pleaded for better food between the 1940s and the 1960s, their food was becoming more and more available to mainstream America. The taste for this cuisine had fluctuated in previous periods. During the late nineteenth century, tamales (rolled and steamed corn-meal pouches stuffed with meat or vegetables) became a street food fad in Los Angeles, Chicago, and other cities in the US West. African American vendors introduced them to the South, and a pop-up restaurant at Madison Square Garden associated with William Cody / Buffalo Bill's "Wild West Show" tour sold them, as well as a Manhattan restaurant called The Tamale, which opened in 1893.[68] The magazine *Good Housekeeping* published its first tamale recipe in 1894, and in 1900, Otis Farnsworth opened an establishment named Original Mexican Restaurant in San Antonio, which featured a platter that allowed customers to combine enchiladas, tamales, beans, and rice on one plate. Though they would be met with incredulous sniffs today, canned tamales (consisting of a can lined with masa and filled with meat) sold successfully across the United States. This tamale obsession fizzled out in the mid-1910s, partly due to concerns about unsanitary street food. In San Antonio, Texas, a group of Mexican American women (nicknamed the "Chili Queens") who had sold chili, tamales, rice, beans, and coffee in open-air public markets since the 1880s, were targeted for cooking their food at home first before bringing it to market and reheating it. Citing unsanitary food preparation and a lack of washing areas, the San Antonio Department of Health banned the Tejana entrepreneurs from outdoor markets in 1936.[69] Notably racialized as "dirty," the Queens' demise stood in stark contrast to the commercial success of German immigrant and Texas restaurateur Willie Gebhardt, whose mass-produced "Gebhardt's Eagle Brand Chili Powder" became a bestseller in 1896. In the 1920s his company started selling Mexican food box kits for one dollar apiece that contained a can of chili con carne, a can of beans, a can of tamales, two cans of deviled chili meat, and a bottle of Eagle chili powder.[70] A few Mexican Americans succeeded in the canned good industry. Californian Emilio Ortega (who founded the Ortega Canning Company in 1899), sold canned peppers, salsa, beans, and menudo. Arizonan Pedro W. Guerrero started the company Rosarita in the late 1940s, and George de la Torre (who founded the Juanita's brand in 1946) enjoyed similar success.[71]

Mexican restaurants began opening in the Southwest and other parts of the nation in the 1920s. Founded in 1922 in Tucson, Arizona, El Charro Café is the nation's oldest continuously operating Mexican restaurant. El Cholo Spanish Café in Los Angeles became the second. Midwestern restaurants began serving chili on top of spaghetti and hot dogs, and a diner called Hot Shoppes in Washington, DC, sold tamales and chili during this decade.[72] While some Americans loved this emergent availability of Mexican cuisine, others could not reconcile their desire for Mexican cuisine with their distaste for Mexican immigrants. Thus, they decided to characterize the food as "Spanish" instead, lending it a European palatability. In a moment of high contradiction, while Great Depression–era deportation and repatriation campaigns were carried out against almost one million Mexicans and Mexican Americans in the United States, newspapers and magazines encouraged white middle-class families to try Mexican recipes in their kitchen and buy Spanish-Mexican home decor to create a "fiesta" look. The Federal Writers' Project of the New Deal encouraged "housewives anywhere" to try making tortillas for their families. "[They] can be made about as well in Maine as in Mexico," one contributor wrote, encouraging the use of cornmeal and chili powder to make the tortilla *masa* (dough). Meanwhile, reformers and churches instituted "Americanization" programs for people of Mexican descent who remained in the country in the 1930s and 1940s. Among other things, reformers tried to change Mexican families' diets by telling them to replace tortillas with bread, substitute lettuce for rice and beans, and stop eating fried food.[73] White diners' culinary adventuring with Mexican food continued in the meantime.

Mexican and Puerto Rican guestworkers likely had no idea that while they were asking for more culturally familiar ingredients and meals, the white American mainstream was receiving and enjoying them. During World War II, army bases in the United States served chili con carne to troops while military commissaries delivered Mexican food to soldiers in Europe. Then, during the immediate postwar period, tourism to Mexico increased exponentially (by 1953 Mexico was the most popular travel destination for US vacationers). Consumer interest in having Mexican food more readily available in US grocery stores inspired companies to develop prepackaged Mexican TV dinners and taco kits by the mid-1950s. The Old El Paso company, a Texas-based firm, spearheaded the national expansion of canned and prepackaged items like salsa, taco shells, frijoles, and enchiladas. Mexican food could be found on the road too. As Cecilia Márquez has described, 1950s and 1960s chain restaurants like the popular rest stop South of the Border along the East Coast Interstate 95 advertised "authentic" Mexican combo platters. By 1967 the total number of Mexican restaurants in the United States had risen to 135,000 nationwide, and the average American could experiment with southwestern or Tex-Mex ingredients and foodways.[74] Puerto Rican food did not become as popular or commercialized—consumers have shown relative disinterest in Caribbean food because it does not conform to the "spicy" or "fiesta" paradigms through which Mexican food is viewed. But for both Mexican and Puerto Rican guestworkers, the cruel indignities of begging for more desirable food and not receiving it were only amplified by the irony that they were likely the ones harvesting and processing the very vegetables that showed up in Mexican TV dinners or cans of beans and salsa at grocery stores.

From the Bracero Era to the Chicano Era

Both the Mexican and Puerto Rican guestworker programs declined for their own reasons. The Bracero Program was eventually terminated by Congress in 1964 due to continued labor abuses and louder protests from union, civil rights, and religious leaders. The FPP began to decline during the 1970s as US employers continued favoring noncitizens over Puerto Ricans. In Pennsylvania's mushroom industry, for instance, the American Civil Liberties Union (ACLU) reported "considerable friction" between Puerto Rican and Mexican workers. One Puerto Rican man complained, "What are we going to do about [undocumented] Mexicans? They take our jobs away, they don't have papers to be here. It's not right."[75] In other industries like apples, Puerto Rican workers witnessed farmers replacing them with Mexican and Jamaican pickers. The Puerto Rican government sued a group of apple farmers in New England in 1976 for refusing to hire Puerto Ricans, but by the time the Supreme Court ruled in 1982 that East Coast apple growers could be forced to hire Puerto Ricans, it was too late. The FPP had already withered away to 4,284 contracted workers by 1977.[76] Over the next two decades, guestworker wages rose at a snail's pace, which further discouraged Puerto Ricans from migrating under an official government program. Meanwhile, unchecked exploitation continued. In 1983, two investigative reporters found Puerto Rican blueberry pickers in Chatsworth, New Jersey, making one dollar an hour instead of the mandated minimum of $3.10. In 1990, food canning workers were making $3.90 an hour while being charged $5.97 per day for three meals.[77]

As Mexican and Puerto Rican ex-guestworkers skipped out on or overstayed their contracts and began new lives in the Northeast, they found other growing Latinx populations. Hundreds of thousands of people—including children airlifted in Operation Pedro Pan—had left Fidel Castro's Cuba and arrived in the United States in the 1960s. Pedro Pan children (and adults waiting to be reunited with their children) were dispersed around the country, including northeastern states like Rhode Island, where a "Cuban Club" was established to support these new refugees.[78] Political instability in Latin America—frequently influenced and even funded by the US government—drove other migrants north. Guatemalans fleeing internal violence began arriving in New England in the early to mid-1960s, with many finding employment as domestic workers or simply stopping through on their way to Canada to seek asylum. That same decade, New England lacework factories and textile mills began recruiting workers from Colombia. In the decades following dictator Rafael Trujillo's assassination in 1961, Dominicanos moved to New York in droves and established a presence in other cities like Boston, Salem, and Lawrence, Massachusetts; Waterbury, Connecticut; and Providence. By the early 1970s, the US consulate in Santo Domingo was processing 400 to 600 immigrant, student, and tourist visa applications per day. Even if one overstayed a visit, one researcher wrote, "It is fairly simple for Dominicans to identify themselves to English-speaking North American officialdom as Puerto Ricans" and start working.[79] Unlike their guestworker predecessors who were confined to labor camps, the Latinx communities that formed in northeastern locales found ways to procure and provide culturally desirable food for each other. A famous Dominican market in Providence called Fefa's provided one such space of nourishment. Josefina "Fefa" Rosario arrived in the United States from the Dominican Republic in 1949 and made her way to New York City to reunite with an older sister. She later met her husband Tony at a Connecticut restaurant, where he was working as a busboy and she as a "salad lady." The two then worked together at a hotel restaurant in New Haven, Connecticut, before moving to Rhode Island, where they worked as kitchen staff for hotels, restaurants, and country clubs. Tony expressed his desire to open his own grocery store and restaurant, and a close friend loaned the couple the money to do so. "We got the idea of opening a market . . . [because] we would often . . . drive to Connecticut in our blue station wagon to buy food for ourselves and for other Dominicans who were living in South Providence," Josefina remembered. "Things like platanos, yucca, café, cilantro. . . . [We would] sell it door to door." As more people learned of the couple's procurement services, Fefa and Tony settled on a large parking lot where people could pick up their orders. "[A] long line would be waiting for us when we arrived. . . . Those who did not order things would come anyway to see what we had. . . . That's how they would get their shopping done," she recalled. The couple finally opened Fefa's Market on Broad Street around 1960, and opened a kitchen and counter inside.[80] The bodega became a beloved place where Dominican customers could eat and drink their favorite things, read Dominican newspapers, play dominoes, and get help with English translation from the couple's three bilingual daughters. Fefa and Tony themselves gave several newcomers housing at their private residence and sponsored countless people in their immigration paperwork.[81]

Even though Latinx communities and food entrepreneurs were finding ways to feed themselves the things they loved, many food workers were continuing to starve. Though the flow of guestworkers had temporarily stopped, US farmworkers were still suffering from poverty-level wages and continued hindrances to their unionization. As the bracero era gave way to the "Chicano" era of the 1960s and 1970s in which Mexican Americans articulated greater ethnic pride and engaged in more noticeable civil rights activism and political militancy, the United Farm Workers (UFW) union of California became a touchstone for struggling and hungry farmworkers. Led by Cesar Chavez, the UFW would captivate and polarize the nation with its argument that one did not need to travel to the "third world" to find deprivation and malnutrition. Its labor strikes and national consumer boycotts of grapes, lettuce, and wine would mark a turning point in the average person's understanding of the irony that US food workers were going unnourished themselves.

CHAPTER TWO

The United Farm Workers' Northeastern Food Boycotts and Discourses of Hunger

It is unfortunate that the men, women, and children
who plant and harvest the greatest quantity of food
ever in this country don't have enough for themselves.
—Cesar Chavez, *Harvard Crimson*, April 6, 1979

The protests of Mexican and Puerto Rican guestworkers, who demanded better food for their laboring bodies, both foreshadowed and intersected with one of the most famous food boycott campaigns in US history.[1] Angered citizen farmworkers had watched as their employers hired guestworkers instead, and as federal protections like a minimum wage, overtime pay, and regulation of child labor protected the industrial sphere but not the agricultural one. Farmworkers earned the lowest wages of any group in the US workforce; in 1962 their average total annual income was $1,164 for only 137 days of work (due to waiting for weather, crop ripeness, or available jobs). This was far below the national poverty line of $3,000.[2] Moreover, since many farmworkers had to migrate around the country to follow different harvests, they lost residential eligibility for housing and food programs, stable education and health care, and voting rights.

Propelled by the ethos of the civil rights era and larger discussions of socioeconomic inequality in the United States, multiple media exposés of farmworkers' conditions were published in the late 1950s and 1960s in venues including *Commonweal*, *Newsweek*, *Time*, and the *New York Times*. In 1960 the National Association for the Advancement of Colored People published *No Harvest for the Reaper: The Story of the Migratory Agricultural Worker in the US*, and reports from eight individual states on farmworker conditions were published between 1959 and 1963.[3] CBS made the biggest waves when it aired the hour-long documentary *Harvest of Shame* the day after Thanksgiving in 1960. The special, which aimed to shock people resting after their holiday meals, graphically depicted the poverty of citizen farmworkers and their children. Viewers flooded CBS and members of Congress with emotional letters demanding greater rights and protections for this precariat class.

It was in this environment that the United Farm Workers Organizing Committee (UFWOC, shortened to UFW in 1972) began making a name for itself. The union was first established in California in 1965 as a merger between the Agricultural Workers Organizing Committee, led by Filipino labor activists Larry Itliong and Philip Vera Cruz, and the National Farm Workers Association, headed by Mexican American organizers Cesar Chavez and Dolores Huerta. Beginning in 1968 and continuing through the 1980s, the UFWOC led multiple worker strikes and national consumer boycott campaigns against California's nonunion grapes, lettuce, and wine. Many Americans felt inspired to picket grocery stores, fruit and vegetable stands, colleges and universities, military bases, and other food outlets in solidarity with farmworkers. Historically, boycotts have been a means of protesting economic, political, and social injustices in the marketplace, drawing on the concept of a "moral economy" in which people make economic decisions through an ethical and not just material lens.[4]

This chapter analyzes the United Farm Workers' multidecade and multisited food and drink boycott campaigns. Specifically, it details the efforts by Latinx, white, and Filipino UFW activists dispatched to the US Northeast to spread and translate a California-based union's message to other regions of the country.[5] It was important that Americans understood the UFW's fight as one for *all* farmworkers, rather than just California ones. In the Northeast and other regions, UFW organizers worked hard to make the average consumer feel that by making the simple choice not to buy certain items at their supermarkets, they could be allies to the farmworker cause without deviating much from their normal routine. The UFW succeeded in attracting supporters including other unions and Latinx-led organizations, religious leaders, college students, wealthy elites, artists, and civil rights icons like Robert F. Kennedy and Coretta Scott King. As the *New York Times* declared in 1969, "The grape strike has become chic."[6]

Though the media credited UFW president Cesar Chavez with galvanizing supporters nationally and internationally, the union's success would not have been possible without women union leaders and boycott participants. One of the union's most valuable contingents of supporters was housewives. Since they were entrusted with making the food shopping decisions for their families, the power of their purses was particularly salient. Women had led consumer boycotts in the United States since the nineteenth century, and working-class women spearheaded food protests in the Northeast during the early twentieth century.

In February 1917, rising food prices caused hundreds of women food shoppers in Brooklyn, New York, to overturn food pushcarts, set produce on fire with kerosene, take food without paying, and fight with police. Four hundred women then marched to New York City Hall shouting, "We want food for our children." The protests spread to other northeastern cities. In Philadelphia, women threw fish from stands and doused food with kerosene. In Boston, 300 people on the West End ransacked a grocery store before police suppressed them.[7]

The UFW targeted women very specifically in its literature and campaigns, and recruited them as organizers or volunteers. Many times, women were the key to getting entire families to move from California to organizing outposts elsewhere in the United States or Canada. If the woman of the household agreed to head a boycott committee elsewhere, her husband and children usually followed, and other women were inspired to work beside her. The UFW sent couples and families to cities like Buffalo, Boston, New York, Montreal, Cleveland, and Miami. Dolores Huerta, Jessica Govea, and Hope López are well-known exemplars of this traveling commitment, but many other women less visible in the historical record did the same. Whether they organized small local boycott committees, directed citywide campaigns, or picketed with their children in front of a grocery store for just a day, women were invaluable assets to the union struggle because of their ability to politicize the domestic act of food shopping, and to claim the moral authority to speak in support of deprived farmworker mothers and their children.

Along with encouraging women to be leading figures, the UFW strategically aligned the farmworker struggle with larger national and global discourses about hunger that were circulating during the late 1960s and 1970s. As Lana Dee Povitz has argued, it was as if the US government suddenly "discovered" hunger in the late 1960s. In 1968 after a fact-finding mission to the poverty-stricken Mississippi Delta, the Citizens' Board of Inquiry published a 100-page report titled *Hunger, U.S.A.* Shortly after that report, CBS aired the documentary *Hunger in America* and the White House held its first Conference on Food, Nutrition, and Health in 1969. Frustrated with many reports but a lack of real action on the issue of food inequality, some organizations took it upon themselves to provide food in their communities. The Black Panther Party began its free breakfast program for children in January 1968 "to build a well-fed, well-cared for, healthy black community." The Puerto Rican Young Lords Organization, originally founded in Chicago in 1959 to focus on issues of gentrification and displacement of Latinx communities, branched out to New York in 1969 and began a free breakfast program in East Harlem. The Young Lords collaborated with the Panthers on another free breakfast program in the city in October 1969.

Undoubtedly embarrassed, the federal government invested an unprecedented amount of money in food programs. By the summer of 1970, free breakfasts had been instituted in the Washington, DC; Chicago; and Cleveland school systems.[8] The UFW added its own spin on hunger discourse. Union literature used text and visuals conjuring underpaid and starving mothers, fathers, and children. Cesar Chavez fasted several times to bring attention to the farmworker cause. Hunger strikes were in the zeitgeist—people were conducting them for various causes in India, Ireland, Latin America, and elsewhere in the 1960s. Chavez and other UFW organizers, including women, publicly fasted for several days or weeks at a time to send a visceral public message about farmworker sacrifice and deprivation.

This chapter brings the UFW, and Latinx people, into the wider set of actors who addressed hunger and food injustice in the later twentieth-century. It chronicles the union's hunger discourses and fasting practices, women's leadership, and the Northeast's essential role in maintaining the union's power and traces them between the 1960s and 1980s. The structure of this chapter is somewhat tidal, as the union's struggles and tactics repeated themselves when it undertook new boycott campaigns against grapes, wine, and then lettuce. Constant effort in the Northeast was necessary to keep enough pressure on southwestern agribusiness to negotiate with the union. Arguably, without organizers, activity, and fundraising in the Northeast, the UFW would have enjoyed far fewer minutes of fame and less financial ability to remain in front of consumers and media. Despite its successes in the Northeast, however, the UFW did not achieve all its aspirations in the region. Though it tried to connect the plight of southwestern and northeastern farm laborers, the latter were never a contingent that the union made strong efforts to organize, and thus a transregionally vibrant UFW never manifested in the ways some of its leaders hoped it would.

The Boston Grape Party:
The UFW's Beginnings in the Northeast

Before it decided to launch its first national consumer boycott campaign, the UFWOC organized grape workers to strike in Delano, California, beginning in September 1965. At this time the nation's estimated 1.8 million farmworkers earned an average wage of $1.23 an hour. The union sought a $1.40 minimum wage, in addition to vacation and health benefits.[9] To amass strength, the UFW tried to collect as diverse a supporter base as possible in California, and the media took notice. In February 1966 the *New York Times* called the grape strike "a rather amorphous, highly ideological cause célèbre involving farm workers, churchmen, civil rights groups, zealous social activists, college students and leaders of organized labor." Journalists were fascinated by Chavez himself, and often made comments on his appearance. One article called the thirty-eight-year-old figurehead "swarthy" and "articulate," while another described him as "a stocky, sad-eyed, disarmingly soft-spoken man, [with] shining black hair trailing over the edge of a face brushed with traces of Indian ancestry. . . . To his followers he is a messiah who inspires utter devotion."[10] Religious overtones were indeed present in much of what Chavez and the union did. In the spring of 1966 the UFWOC led a 300-mile march from Delano to Sacramento designed to end on Easter Sunday in front of the state capitol building. Chavez and thousands of marchers walked the state's highways and dirt roads holding US and Mexican flags, tapestries of Our Lady of Guadalupe, and red banners decorated with the union's logo of a black thunderbird. This *peregrinación* (pilgrimage) ended with a crowd of 8,000 people in Sacramento who went unmet by Governor Pat Brown, who was advised to stay in Palm Springs with his family.[11]

Though this was a frustrating moment, the UFWOC earned some victories in its early years. It won contracts for about 5,500 workers across nine wine grape companies, including Schenley, DiGiorgio, Gallo, Christian Brothers, and Pirelli-Minetti, and the contracts gave workers minimum hourly wages of $1.65 to $1.80 an hour, some benefits, and hiring halls. Over time, through smaller campaigns, the UFWOC raised farmworker consciousness in other places including Arizona, the Rio Grande Valley of South Texas, Florida's citrus belt, Midwestern states like Wisconsin and Michigan, and the Pacific Northwest. The Northeast remained an essential region to hit—California grape growers who were avoiding UFWOC contracts were selling their product under different names and labels in major fruit markets in Boston, Philadelphia, and New York City. This was a flagrant violation of the Federal Fair Label and Packaging Act of 1967, and the UFWOC immediately filed lawsuits in New Jersey and Boston. Initial stirrings of UFWOC organizer activity in the Northeast appeared in 1967, when union field representative Frank Myers visited Providence on December 1, New Bedford on December 7, and Nantucket and Newport on December 12. Myers was likely visiting grocery stores to record nonunion grapes, and gauging locals' support for eventual boycott committees.[12]

In addition to keeping an eye on the Northeast, Chavez announced to the media that he was beginning a fast on February 16, 1968 to bring attention to the issue of farmworker deprivation. Fasting had been a political technique used before—Mohandas Gandhi had carried out a hunger strike to protest the British government's decision to separate India's electoral system by caste in the 1930s; college students called for wheat-less meals in schools to ease worldwide famine in April 1946; Irish Liberation Army leader and hunger striker Seán McCaughey died in May 1946; Japanese rail workers fasted for more pay in December 1949; French and Bolivian miners fasted in 1962 and 1963; and Vietnamese students in Paris staged an anti-Diem hunger strike in August 1963.[13] Medically speaking, fasts can last for thirty to fifty days, sometimes sixty, if enough water is imbibed. However, once a person's fat reserves are depleted, muscle protein becomes the source of amino acids that the liver draws upon to make glucose. Lethargy sets in and blood pressure drops, sometimes to the point that it no longer supports adequate circulation. Potentially fatal heart arrhythmias or organ failures can occur.[14] To Chavez (who worked and organized from his bed during his fast), the potential harm he was doing to his body represented the risk and malnutrition that farmworkers experienced every day. Three weeks in, Chavez's doctor ordered him to ingest bouillon, grapefruit juice, and some medications to stave off kidney damage. "Toward the end, I began to notice people eating," Chavez recalled. "I'd never really noticed people *eat*. It was so . . . so . . . Well, like animals in a zoo. I couldn't take my eyes off them." A thinning and weakened Chavez was an equally disturbing sight for supporters, who worried he would do long-term damage to his body. In the middle of one night, a drunk man entered Chavez's bedroom and tried to force-feed him tacos from his lunch pail. Chavez yelled for help, and several men pulled the intruder off him. Chavez eventually allowed the "hurt and dejected" force-feeder to return so he could explain his reasons for fasting to the tearful man.[15]

On March 10, 1968, more than 4,000 people gathered in Delano for a mass and rally marking the end to Chavez's twenty-five-day fast. Robert F. Kennedy even flew in to march in the procession headed by a large wooden cross and a figurine of Our Lady of Guadalupe. Chavez, who had lost thirty-five pounds, had to be physically supported by two men as he walked through the crowd and sat on an altar installed on a truck bed. Kennedy sat beside Chavez and broke the fast with him by sharing a piece of bread. It became one of the most famous photographs of the 1960s.[16] Though he denied his fasting was political theater, Chavez was no doubt trying to elicit more public sympathy and place greater pressure on growers to come to the negotiating table.

By the next month, the mayors and city councils of northeastern cities including New York and Pittsburgh had endorsed the UFWOC boycott, and non-unionized grapes were piling up in major national market centers. Producers who usually relied on selling in New York City scrambled to reroute their grapes to smaller cities like Rochester, Buffalo, and Syracuse.[17] Boston became a center-piece city of UFWOC protest during the summer of 1968. Centuries before, the Boston Tea Party of 1773 had been an early boycott of a commodity, followed

by abolitionists' sugar, rice, indigo, and cotton boycotts in the late eighteenth
and nineteenth centuries. A group of 900 farmworkers and supporters—who
included nuns, priests, and members of the Boston Typographical Union, the
United Packinghouse Food and Allied Workers, and the Meat Cutters Union—
reenacted the tea party and marched from the Boston Common through the
Freedom Trail to the docks. Chavez spoke to the crowd, invoking Tea Party and
old New England history. "I think of almost all the cities in America, Boston
excels in the tradition of dissent," he declared. Demonstrators dumped several
hundred pounds of grapes into the harbor, with each case representing a different
California grower refusing to negotiate with the UFWOC. The protest indeed
made a splash; soon after, Boston's mayor, Kevin White, released an edict prohib-
iting city departments from buying California grapes. A few days later, a group
of housewives, teenagers, and small children picketed at a First National grocery
store and asked shoppers to patronize the five other markets in town that had
agreed to take nonunion grapes off their shelves.[18]

Meanwhile, political battles over grapes were erupting in the halls of Congress. South Dakota senator and presidential candidate George S. McGovern
joined a UFWOC picket line (led by Cesar Chavez's brother Richard) in front
of a Greenwich Village supermarket and brought reporters and a cameraman.
California Republican member of Congress Robert B. Mathias distributed bags
of grapes to all members of the House, provoking Mexican American Representative Henry B. González (D-Texas) to call it "[a] contemptible strike-breaking
activity." President Richard Nixon ate grapes publicly and remarked, "I will continue to eat California grapes and drink the produce of these grapes whenever I
can."[19] Eating or not eating grapes became one's political statement—either one
was joining the UFWOC fight, or taunting it. Taking sides filtered down to the
smallest, youngest participants. When Cesar Chavez visited Philadelphia, "[a]
young girl with pale skin walked to him and gave him a tiny pink flower.... She
smiled and blushed and told him, 'I have not eaten a grape in a year and a half.'"[20]

Seeing how effective Chavez's first fasting campaign had been, the union
continued to use fasting to gain public attention. When hunger strikers planted
themselves in front of grocery stores, customers' natural curiosity was piqued,
and pickets had time to inform shoppers about the grape strike before they entered the store. Bill Jeffers and Tom Paruszkiewizo, two UFWOC volunteers
in Rochester, New York, conducted a two-week fast until a local chain store
stopped its orders of California grapes. On December 22, 1968, a day of fasting
was held on the Boston Common to show solidarity with farmworkers.[21] And
around the country, students of all ages conducted fasting days and other forms
of protests. In suburban Port Washington, Long Island, high school students

mobilized seventy people to picket in front of a Bohack's grocery store, which removed grapes from one of its locations four days later. The UFWOC benefited particularly from college students' support, as these young adults were eagerly looking for opportunities for political activism and expression. A Citizens' Committee for the California Grape Boycott established a headquarters on the Princeton University campus, the Harvard-Radcliffe Catholic Student Center invited Chavez to give a talk, Yale students convinced their dining facilities to stop serving grapes, and Trinity College students pressured an A&P store in Connecticut to remove its grapes. A picket line formed at Al's Fruitstand near Columbia University, and a group called Students for the Grape Boycott protested outside the Federal Office Building in Manhattan.[22]

Though they were fewer in number, Mexican American students living in the Northeast wrote to the UFWOC not only to get involved but also to feel closer to their familial and cultural roots. This became even more important where Chicano students felt in the minority, including at elite colleges and universities in the Northeast. In a letter to Cesar Chavez dated March 24, 1969, Rutgers graduate student Elma González wrote: "I come from a family of migrants from Texas. My parents started out from Jim Hogg County 15 years ago and went into West Texas to pick cotton. Two years later we joined a 'bonche' from Zapata County and went into Nebraska for beet thinning and into Wisconsin for cucumber picking. Through the years we harvested green beans, cherries, tomatoes, cotton and things I've forgotten about. . . . [But] we have not forgotten our past, and I would like to help my people."[23] Similarly, in a letter to Chavez from upstate New York in April 1969, Colgate University student Everardo García wrote about his background and a development at his school: "I thought I would let you know what has been going on here in this town, where I am the only Mexican-American from San Benito, Texas. Colgate University has discontinued buying table grapes, since the facts about the Huelga [Strike] and the conditions of our people were made known to them."[24] The national media began to identify the UFWOC's activity as part of the larger Chicano civil rights movement that was sweeping the Southwest at this time. In California and Texas, students were walking out of their schools to protest educational discrimination and demand a more culturally inclusive curriculum. A mass anti–Vietnam War protest called the "Chicano Moratorium" was disrupted by police violence in Los Angeles, Rodolfo "Corky" Gonzales was leading Chicano youth groups in Denver, and evangelical Reies López Tijerina led a campaign to take back New Mexico federal land that eventually involved the National Park Service and a manhunt for Tijerina himself.

Next to these other activists and causes, Chavez seemed like a less radical (and thus more palatable) figure of Mexican American civil rights protest. *Time* magazine named him Man of the Year in 1969, while the *New Yorker*'s Hendrik Hertzberg wrote, "Cesar Chavez . . . is the closest approximation of an American Gandhi we ever had in this country." When Chavez visited New York City on October 10, 1969, he attracted nearly a thousand pickets at the Veterans Administration to help him criticize the Army's increased shipments of grapes to Vietnam. Both Democratic and Republican politicians attended the protest along with garment workers, taxi drivers, hospital and hotel workers, teachers, and city employees. Chavez climbed on top of a car and delivered his remarks in both Spanish and English. Afterward, participants marched to a nearby Gristedes market to continue demonstrating. The next month, Chavez led several hundred people through the cobblestone streets of Pittsburgh's wholesale produce market. "It was a motley group. There were housewives in well-tailored slacks and students in faded jeans, priests in Roman collars and blacks with Afro hair-do's, a few businessmen in conservative suits and a barrel-chested union leader," the *New York Times* reported. The UFWOC's protests were taking place against the backdrop of other worker and anticorporate boycotts in the United States— the Oil, Chemical and Atomic Workers were boycotting Shell Oil products, the AFL-CIO was boycotting General Electric, and the Amalgamated Meat Cutters were campaigning against Iowa Beef Packers. Yet the UFWOC also had its vocal critics. A writer at the *Providence Journal* opined that most farmworkers did not want to be represented by the UFWOC, and that Chavez was forcing it upon them. An organization called the Farm Workers Freedom to Work group, which claimed a Latino general secretary, emerged as well but was likely set up by a growers' association.[25]

By the end of 1969, grape sales had decreased by more than 20 percent in forty major US cities, and the union had a noticeable northeastern network in place. Boycott offices had been established in Vermont, Connecticut, Rhode Island, and Maine. "The gains made by these farm workers could have a direct bearing on farm workers in our state . . . the potato pickers, the blueberry pickers, the apple pickers, and many other workers . . . [who] haven't even the most minor of voice in their occupational destiny," the *Maine State Labor News* encouraged its readers. In New Hampshire, residents picketed a grocery co-op for several weeks until it removed its grapes. Volunteers organized themselves in upstate New York and several cities in New Jersey. Denice Plunkett, a "soft-spoken girl" from Iowa, began organizing the Fall River–New Bedford area of Massachusetts.[26] Plunkett was one of several women who would contribute their time and energy to the union, and make an impact upon customers through their multifaceted rhetoric of motherhood, moral consumption, and female power.

FIGURE 2.1. A UFW volunteer pickets in front of the New England Produce Market, un-dated. Photo by Jon Chase. United Farm Worker Collection, Walter P. Reuther Library, Archives of Labor and Urban Affairs, Wayne State University, Detroit, Michigan.

Striking, Leading, and Starving:
Northeastern Women's UFW Activism

Though Chavez was admired as a charismatic union leader, the UFWOC movement's success would not have been possible without the work of women. When the union first sent California-based members to different parts of the country to organize boycott committees, it assigned couples and families to travel together. Alfredo and Juanita Herrera managed Denver, while Julio and Fina Hernández coordinated Cleveland. Andy and Looming Imutan led Washington, DC, and Baltimore; Maree and Juan Flores were sent to Buffalo; and Manuel and Marcia Sánchez organized Miami. The union even dispatched organizers over the border into Toronto and Montreal, as about 200 million pounds of fresh grapes were being exported to Canada each year.[27] By sending whole families, couples, or groups of women to boycott together in regions outside the Southwest, the UFW banked on women to be the glue that would hold these activist-units together and create new ones.

The union's biggest hub for northeastern boycott activity was New York City, not simply because of the city's size but because New York State was highly agricultural—the UFWOC could use conditions there to point out that farmworker mistreatment transcended region. New York was the seventh-largest employer of migrant labor in the nation, relying on a total of 48,000 seasonal workers per year. This workforce consisted of local and intrastate workers, interstate labor from the US Southeast, Puerto Rican workers, and migrants from Canada and the Caribbean. Farmworkers' housing in the state ranged from sparse dormitories to old bus shells, chicken coops, and barns. Random visits to thirty camps across the state by Columbia University researchers deemed the majority "uninhabitable" because they were overcrowded, underheated, lacked hot water and sanitary kitchen facilities, and had "filthy" outhouses instead of flush toilets.[28] New York needed a strong boycott organizer to determine the fate of the union in the Northeast, and UFWOC vice president Dolores Huerta was assigned to the helm.

Huerta arrived in New York City in January 1968 with forty-seven farmworkers (and three of her young children) in a caravan of cars and a yellow school bus. The Seafarers' International Union offered to feed and house the arrivals in Brooklyn. This logistical help relieved Huerta, but she still found herself on her own when it came to designing political strategy. "There were no ground rules," she said. "I thought, 11 million people in New York, and I have to persuade them to stop buying grapes." She began with picket lines where union volunteers passed out leaflets and participated in in-store demonstrations. Huerta's children joined picket lines after school and on the weekends, and her daughter Lori organized a teen group, Youth of Brooklyn, which sent delegations to grocery stores to pressure managers.[29] Huerta then planned something more ambitious—a grape blockade. Since she already had the support of the Seafarers' Union, Huerta succeeded at stopping the first grapes of the 1968 season from being transported across the Hudson River to New York City. The grapes rotted in New Jersey and reduced the quantity of available grapes in New York City by more than 75 percent. Huerta was forced to stop her blockade, however, when grape growers filed a complaint with the National Labor Relations Board (NLRB) and sued New York unions for $25 million in damages and losses. The UFWOC took this as an encouraging sign that grape interests were frightened. Indeed, in New York State—where California growers normally sold about 20 percent of their table grape crop—sales dropped by 90 percent at one point and shippers were forced to put their grapes in cold storage. In addition to the lawsuit, grape growers pushed their own media narrative that the UFWOC was encouraging Americans to engage in food waste.[30]

Huerta turned to other techniques to tackle large grocery store chains such as A&P, Bohack's, Waldbaum's, Hills, and Finast. A particularly controversial one was the "shop-in," in which undercover demonstrators entered a store (while pickets marched outside), stashed grapes at the bottoms of their baskets or carts, and then covered the fruit with several items. When they reached the checkout line, they exclaimed, "I am not a strikebreaker, I won't shop at this store!" and abandoned their carts, leaving workers to unload them and discover the smashed grapes. Dolores advised boycotters, "A brown or black [picket] line in an all white area is extremely effective," and that they should enlist two to four women, "preferably the house wife type," to approach people before they went into the store. Huerta's organizing style captivated some shoppers but provoked ire or discomfort in others. The United Food and Commercial Workers (UFCW) expressed concern because its members feared the UFWOC's shop-ins and picketing would threaten their own livelihoods as store employees. The UFWOC responded by making it clear to shoppers that they were boycotting certain *products* and not entire grocery stores, and the two unions supported each other's strikes after that.[31]

Like Chavez, Huerta attracted a wide range of religious, civic, ethnic, student, civil rights, consumer, and labor allies. An early supporter was Huntington Hartford, an heir to the A&P fortune, who participated in a UFWOC picket line. Huerta also won the endorsement of the New York City Central Labor Council, which then obtained Mayor John Lindsay's support and a ban on the city's annual purchase of fifteen tons of grapes for prisons and hospitals.[32] Huerta also mobilized college students, unions, and Latinx organizations to participate in a massive letter-writing campaign to father-son grape growers Victor Joseph and Joseph Giumarra. Several letters were connected by a common discourse about the "feudal" or "medieval" working conditions of farmworkers, hinting at Huerta's coaching. Dan Pellegrom, the Student Council president of Columbia University, wrote to the Giumarras, "We had thought that serfdom was dead, yet the conditions under which your employees worked seem truly feudal. We are urging the students and faculty of Columbia University (some 20,000 people) . . . not to buy any California grapes *this year, next year, or any year,* unless a contract a signed." Writing from Brooklyn College, where students had been boycotting for two years, student body president Michael Novick concurred, "We will not buy grapes until your medieval attitudes are changed." Local 89 of the Chefs, Cooks, Pastry Cooks and Assistants Union of New York—which represented 10,000 people and 900 restaurant kitchens—called the Giumarras a "medieval employer" with "medieval working conditions" in its letter.[33] The Latinx organizations that wrote included migrant hometown associations like the Asociación Arroyanos Ausentes (connected to Puerto Rico); veterans organizations; civil rights groups; civic and social clubs like the Hijos de Camuy, Bohio Borincano Social and Athletic Club, and Círculo Social Cubano; a chauffeurs' association called the Asociación Nacional de Choferes Puertorriqueños e Hispanos; and church youth groups.[34] Though Latinx and Black communities were not mutually exclusive, Black-led organizations also joined UFWOC efforts, placing pressure on grocery store managers in Brooklyn and Harlem. The New York City UFW flirted briefly with an alliance with the Black Panther Party, but this association fizzled when five grocery stores across Manhattan, Brooklyn, and the Bronx were firebombed and many suspected this was the work of the Panthers.[35] This was too radical a tactic for a union whose leader proclaimed a philosophy of nonviolence.

Despite this lost partnership, Huerta felt overall that the New York boycotters were making progress. In a December 29, 1968 memo, Huerta lauded their collective achievement of getting the major chains of A&P, Waldbaum's, and Shoprite to take grapes off their shelves, along with smaller stores including Food Fair, King Kullen, IGA, Key Foods, and Met Foods. Long Island was the "cleanest" area in New York State, and suburban towns in New Jersey had been smoothly organized. It was bigger New Jersey cities like Newark, Jersey City, and Hoboken that were still "dirty" with grapes.[36] In February 1969 Huerta returned to California to organize workers there, but New York activities continued. Boycotters visited fruit stands with leaflets and "gentle threatening" of a picket line if the vendor did not comply. A riot and demonstration took place at SUNY Stony

GRAPH 2.1. The UFWOC boycott's effect on the California table grape industry's 1968 and 1969 seasons.

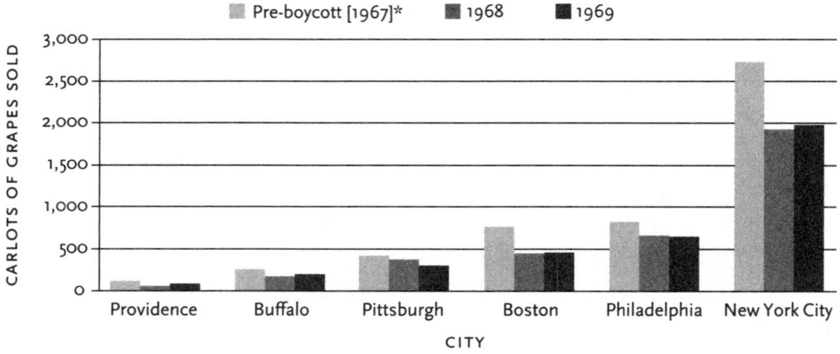

Source: Data taken from UFWOC Boston Correspondence files, box 5, folder 17, Walter P. Reuther Library, Archives of Labor and Urban Affairs, Wayne State University, Detroit, Michigan.
*The pre-boycott data is likely from 1967. In the original document, this data was simply labeled "pre-boycott."

Brook, and in various towns upstate people wrote to the UFWOC for literature and buttons to start their own boycott committees.[37] Across the Northeast, the replicable boycott model allowed people in smaller cities to be political (see graph 2.1).

Though Huerta had returned to the West Coast, equally impressive but lesser-known women organized the UFWOC in other cities. Of the forty-two other UFWOC boycott coordinators in major North American cities in 1969, four were women. Jessica Govea led Toronto and then Montreal; María Saudado headed Indianapolis; Peggy McGivern oversaw Buffalo; and Hope López became a powerhouse in Philadelphia. Born in California in the 1920s, López had been a child farmworker before attending college in Fresno. She worked as a community organizer and in an antipoverty program before she became involved in the UFWOC and agreed to direct the Philadelphia boycott. López arrived there in February 1969 as a forty-one-year-old widow with two of her five children in tow. Antonia Saludado and Carolina Franco accompanied López as her assistants. Saludado was the daughter of migrant Mexican parents, had worked in fields throughout California, and served in the UFWOC's Los Angeles and New York boycotts. Franco, a woman of Mexican and Cherokee heritage, had harvested crops with her family as a child. She began working for the UFWOC at twenty-two, marched to Sacramento with Chavez, and had boycotted in Los Angeles, New York, and Boston.[38]

López, Saludado, and Franco were tasked with building on the work of their Philadelphia predecessors, Frank Díaz and Eric Schmidt, who had both returned to California. The office's female support staff, however, remained to help the incoming trio. Jean Hunt managed the boycott office, Ruth Yarrow conducted boycott workshops for local women's groups, and Temple University sophomore Lilli Sprintz was a stalwart volunteer. These three women helped López, Saludado, and Franco move into what they affectionately called "The Grape House" in Philadelphia's Kensington neighborhood. Dozens of people visited the house to give the women gifts, clothes, furniture, money, alcohol, and moral support. "Can anyone please send us some chiles, jalapenos?" Hope López joked in a letter to Cesar Chavez. "This city discriminates, no Chicano food to be found." Saludado began organizing college students to boycott grapes in their dining halls, and López acquired donations from other unions including the Meatcutters Union, American Federation of Teachers, Paper Mill Workers, Brewery and Beer Distributor Drivers, and Bookbinders and Bindery Women. Meanwhile bricklayers, garment workers, auto workers, and retail clerks in Philadelphia all picketed for the UFWOC.[39]

By using the language of motherhood and female morality, the women leaders of the Philadelphia boycott were able to attract middle-class white housewives to the farmworker cause. At other times, they deployed feminist rhetoric to attract "women's libbers" interested in social justice.[40] This mixed-class and multipolitical makeup helped lend more credibility to what otherwise might be viewed as a marginal or niche Chicana group. In her speeches, López made appeals to housewives, benevolent maternalists, and feminists by describing farmworker women's arduous lives. Children were consistently conjured up in UFWOC literature related to farmworker hunger and suffering. One flyer—which was reproduced and co-opted several times for different UFWOC campaigns—depicted a young, weakened girl in a shabby dress sitting on a bed alone in an empty room, with a bare light bulb hanging overhead. "Juanita is Hungry," it read. "Her mother and father—and thousands more—earn a dollar an hour in the vineyards of Delano, California. They have been on strike for years against the millionaire growers." A Spanish-language flyer with the same photo invoked more menacing images: "Miles de niñas como esta, mal alimentadas, viviendo amontonadas, con su familia, en chozas que resultan ser como campos de concentración" (Thousands of girls like this one, malnourished, live piled up with their family in shacks that look like concentration camps).[41]

The UFWOC knew what it was doing with these flyers—this was an era in which the US government was paying greater attention to the problems of child hunger, poverty, and malnutrition. A report titled *Hungry Children* was published in October 1967 after government representatives visited the Mississippi Delta and reported on their observations. One year after this trip, the Senate Subcommittee on Hunger and Malnourishment was created. A White House Conference on Food and Nutrition took place over three days in 1969, and hosted 5,000 participants, including activists and community organizers, nutrition scientists, and food advertising executives.[42] The media also tackled the topic of child hunger. A December 1972 NBC broadcast, *What Price Health*, featured a child of farmworkers who weighed the same at six months as she did at birth due to malnutrition. Nicknaming her "Juanita," a doctor said of the baby and others like her: "We saw hunger and poverty and human misery to a degree that we had not dreamed possible in affluent America. . . . Malnutrition since birth has already impaired them physically, mentally, and emotionally. They do not have the capacity to engage in the maintained physical or mental effort which is necessary to succeed in school, learn a trade, or assume the full responsibility of citizenship in a complex society such as ours."[43]

Back in Philadelphia, Hope López did not shy away from identifying as a concerned mother with five children herself. By using the rhetoric of motherhood, family, and food justice, she was able to convince working-class mothers to join her team as boycott volunteers. López and her assistants made the conscious decision to emphasize their gender over their Mexican American identity because they wanted to draw in a multiracial set of white, Black, and Puerto Rican Philadelphians. By this time, Philadelphia claimed the third-largest Puerto Rican population in the United States (27,000 people) after New York City and Chicago. López drew explicit parallels between southwestern farmworkers and their counterparts on the East Coast. "Many of the farm workers in South Jersey and Pennsylvania are Blacks or Puerto Ricans suffering from the same lousy wages, lousy housing and lousy conditions as we have in California," she said. María Lina Bonet, the president and founder of the Fraternidad Puertorriqueña, offered the use of the organization's hall and donated a refrigerator to the Grape House. Mary Rouse, the head of the Kensington Council on Black Affairs and the editor of a Black newspaper called the *Informer*, gave López space to publicize the boycott in Spanish and English. Spanish-language newspapers and radio programs also helped to spread the UFW's message, and a few bodegas (out of the eighty that existed in the city at this time) acted in solidarity by refusing to stock grapes. López and her boycotters decided to target five large supermarket chains in the area. Acme claimed sixty stores, followed by A&P and Food Fair with thirty-five apiece, Penn Fruit with twenty-six, and Great Scott with eleven. There were also forty-five independent markets. López invoked the power of women's purses to threaten grocery store management. "May I remind you," she wrote to one store manager, "that 99% of your customers are women. The ladies put you in the position of strength that you now hold and these same ladies can knock you right off that pedestal."[44] By the mid-twentieth century, housewives were not just preparers of food but the shoppers who held the purse strings. Elsewhere in the Northeast, women were using their roles as mothers and food shoppers to take a stand. In response to an August 1969 article in the *Hartford Courant* that featured grapes in a recipe, Jane K. Dixon wrote in, "My entire family was distressed upon seeing the [recipe]. . . . Grapes are an immoral buy. The migrant workers who pick those grapes live under conditions that no American should have to endure." Women fought on the other side of the grape fight too. One woman said to pickets in Newport, Rhode Island, "I have the right to buy anything I want to buy. It's my money." Antiboycott women's groups funded by growers, such as the Housewives United to Protect Food Supply, leafleted in several cities and characterized the UFWOC as communist.[45]

In addition to mobilizing pickets, López decided to conduct her own hunger strike in front of an A&P store on May 26, 1969. Her fast, which lasted seven days, was likely the first conducted by a woman in the UFWOC. Flyers that picketers handed out to spectators emphasized López's farmworker background and the fact that she was a mother of five.[46] Compared to Cesar Chavez's fast, López's might have been more disturbing to onlookers. If a woman and mother refused food, it violated gendered expectations that she would maintain enough strength to be a good caregiver. It may also have appeared more shameful for a grocery store owner to let a woman starve herself outside his doors. A captioned photo of López in the *Philadelphia Evening Bulletin* reinforced her connection to children and humble desires: "Still smiling, Hope Lopez . . . chats with youngsters who stopped by . . . [and said] when she finally gets to eat will probably ask for a bologna sandwich."[47] As López's body weakened, an interdenominational candlelight service was held around her, followed by a mass a few days later. After delegations of women visited the offices of A&P, Penn Fruit, and Food Fair, all three chains agreed not to stock grapes. Acme, which was still holding out, received a delegation of boycotters shortly after. "Bring the kids and the babysitter. They should be involved in changing history too," the call for a delegation read. Children's presence would not only attract more attention and sympathy but also soften women boycotters' image and counteract impressions that these women were neglecting their families.[48]

During the late summer, however, chain stores in Philadelphia took advantage of middle-class housewives' vacationing or lack of availability and began to stock grapes again. The UFWOC boycott committee reignited their effort with more hunger strikes. In September 1969, twenty-five-year-old Carolina Franco and twenty-year-old Lilli Sprintz began fasting outside the offices of Food Fair Stores. Their fast lasted nine days and ended with Food Fair stopping their grape purchases. The next month, Antonia Saludado, sixty-year-old Black civil rights activist Wally Nelson, and upper-class white mother Tavia Fielder began a three-week fast to force Acme to stop selling grapes in suburban Pennsylvania, New Jersey, and Delaware. Acme complied with the boycott on July 29, and Great Scott followed two days later. Thus, five months after arriving in Philadelphia, López's volunteers could declare that all the city's major chain stores had stopped selling grapes.[49]

Elsewhere in the Northeast, people fasted for the union. In Paterson, New Jersey, in mid-September 1969, Tina Best conducted a sit-in at an A&P store with her thirteen- and twenty-year-old daughters Carolyn and Christina. All three were arrested when they refused to leave the store at closing time. Tina later performed a solo fast at the A&P store, and Cesar Chavez made a personal phone call to share strategies on how to keep herself well. A few days later in East Providence, twenty-three-year-old Jesuit seminarian Gary Hemelin sat himself to starve in the parking lot of Almacs Market. By the sixth day of his fast, 2,000 customers had signed a petition of support. Hamelin fasted for eighteen days and broke his fast with a piece of tortilla in Manning Chapel at Brown University in front of numerous supporters. Though these fasts seemed random and scattered, the union had a strategy that it shared with volunteers who wanted to take on a hunger strike. "If anyone wants to use the fast idea, it has to be very well organized," a memo read, and emphasized. "The person who is fasting should *look* weak and sit in a chair (preferably rocking) and *stay sitting down all the time*." The memo added that a candlelight service should take place three or four days into the fasting.[50]

Along with attracting women volunteers, the UFWOC needed to keep collecting allies who could offer their outrage, presence on picket lines, and financial support. Off the ground and up in the air, the union convinced Trans World Airlines to remove grapes from its fruit bowls in June 1970.[51] And crossing lines of class, the UFW reached upward to the very wealthy and elite on the East Coast. As William F. Buckley Jr. wrote in the *Boston Globe* in August 1970, "Non-California-grape-eating was indisputably the single most important thing that . . . eastern seaboard blue bloods . . . [could do] during 1969–1970." Similarly, Steven V. Roberts wrote in the *New York Times*, "The grape strike has become chic. You aren't really 'in' the New York liberal scene until you've been to a fund-raising party for the union." Tom Wolfe wrote about "Radical Chic

FIGURE 2.2. UFW volunteers picket in front of an A&P store at Christmastime. United Farm Worker Collection, Walter P. Reuther Library, Archives of Labor and Urban Affairs, Wayne State University, Detroit, Michigan.

evenings" in New York, where wealthy white people invited the Black Panthers and UFWOC organizers to their house parties, which featured white servants for racial inversion. Meanwhile, some of New York's most celebrated graphic artists, including Paul Davis, created posters for the union.[52] Describing these culturati or "limousine liberals," Wolfe qualified their activism as remaining in a particular comfort zone: "Radical Chic invariably favors radicals who seem primitive, exotic, and romantic, such as the grape workers, who are not merely radical and 'of the soil' but also Latin; the Panthers, with their leather pieces, Afros, shades, and shoot-outs; and the Red Indians who, of course, had always seemed primitive, exotic, and romantic.... All three groups had something else to recommend them, as well: they were headquartered three thousand miles away from the East Side of Manhattan."[53]

Wolfe identified the first big Radical Chic party as a UFWOC fundraiser hosted by twenty-four-year-old New York assemblyman Andrew Stein on his father's estate in the Hamptons in late June 1969. The guest list included Ethel Kennedy (making her first public appearance since her husband's assassination), track star and actor Rafer Johnson, and Filipino American UFWOC organizer Andy Imutan with his wife and three sons. When the fundraising began, Imutan took the microphone and asked everybody to close their eyes and pretend they were a farmworker in California eating tortillas and baloney sandwiches for breakfast at 3 a.m. before heading out into the fields.[54] As guests were holding their glasses of champagne and plates of hors d'oeuvres, Imutan wanted to remind them how luxury-less farmworkers' daily lives and meals had to be.

The UFWOC also sought out environmental activist support, given that farmworkers suffered from toxic pesticide exposure. In an appearance before the Senate Subcommittee on Migratory Labor on September 30, 1969, Chavez accused growers of "systematic poisoning" and termed pesticides *la muerte andando*, or the walking death. Farmworkers had died from being sprayed with pesticides from helicopters, their children had been born with birth defects, and both children and adults were part of "cancer clusters" in agricultural communities that used high levels of pesticides. The toxins were being stored in humans' fatty tissues, producing everything from dizziness to muscle pain to neurological disorders and cancers because of abnormally proliferating cells.[55] Chavez's antipesticide testimony was made in service of farmworkers in all regions, including the Northeast. In Massachusetts, for instance—where about 7,000–8,000 Puerto Rican migrant farmworkers were being imported into the state every year to join US Black and Cape Verdean migrant workers in cranberry bogs—three Puerto Rican migrant farmworkers sent to spray Parathion in Cape Cod without protective gear collapsed after their fourth day of doing so. They were all declared dead on arrival at the hospital. Despite nationwide environmental protests, treatises, and media exposés on the negative health effects of pesticides, US growers doubled their pesticide use between 1966 and 1976. When American chemical corporations exported banned or restricted pesticides like DDT abroad, pesticide residue often came back into the United States via food imports.[56]

In July 1970, to much fanfare and relief, the UFWOC finally obtained contracts with twenty-seven grape growers in California. The contracts offered workers between $2.10 and $2.20 an hour, banned the use of hard pesticides, and provided health and welfare benefits. More contracts were signed after that, and the union won wage increases, paid vacation days, medical insurance plans, and pesticide protections for many of its members. Across the country in Philadelphia, organizers threw a fiesta at a local church to celebrate. Dozens of clergymen, student volunteers, and union members and their families sat down to a communal dinner of enchiladas, beans, and wine made with union grapes. Soon after, Hope López returned to California to administer the new contracts, Saludado left to return to her previous job, and Franco married farmworker-organizer Miguel Vásquez and moved with him to Connecticut. Sprintz joined the UFWOC as a full-time organizer and directed the lettuce boycott in Cleveland, and California couple Doug Adair and Harriet Teller took charge of Philadelphia when the union organized a lettuce boycott there next.[57]

Other women kept or took on director and organizer posts in the Northeast during the early 1970s. Eighteen-year-old Celia Saludado (who became a farmworker at the age of nine and a grape picketer by fourteen) became the new organizer for North New Jersey.[58] Charismatic organizer Marilu Sánchez visited Puerto Rico at the beginning of 1971 to drum up support, speaking to both agricultural workers in the countryside and to urban hotel kitchen staff. Nora Casillas and couple Eva and Ruben Reyna took over the boycott office in Buffalo. In Queens, New York, seven women organizers shared a three-bedroom apartment paid for by the Brooklyn Catholic Diocese, the International Longshoremen's Association, and the International Union of Electrical, Radio, and Machine Workers. Like other UFW staffers, each woman received an ascetic union salary of ten dollars a week (five dollars for personal expenses and five dollars for food). The oldest of the group, sixty-seven-year-old Amparito Vásquez, transformed their pooled groceries into creative Mexican dishes and made life at this other "Grape House" more beautiful and nourishing.[59] Without women's power, commitment, and care, success in the Northeast and other regions outside California would have quickly flamed out.

Tying Together the Southwest and Northeast

Almost immediately after its victories in the grape industry, the UFWOC had to take on the lettuce industry. Growers in California's Salinas Valley had signed "sweetheart contracts" with the Teamsters union to prevent the UFWOC from organizing their workers next. In response, Chavez and Huerta called for a workers' strike in Salinas on August 24, 1970, and a new national consumer boycott of lettuce. The UFWOC also started boycotting other products owned by the holding corporations of lettuce companies, including Smirnoff vodka, Jose Cuervo tequila, McMaster's Scotch, A-1 sauce, Grey Poupon mustard, and Ortega chiles.[60]

To get the new message about lettuce out to the American public, exchanges took place between farmworkers in the Salinas Valley and UFWOC boycott committees in the Northeast. Hilario and Leonor Izaguirre, both from Salinas, moved to Queens to organize New Yorkers. And in early October 1970, a group of Salinas Valley farmworkers came to Manhattan to march on the Upper West Side and canvas supermarkets. Picketers used the days before Thanksgiving to demonstrate at grocery stores, and Chavez spoke at a morning service in Riverside Church to 2,000 people. The next month, when Chavez was jailed in Salinas, California, for violating a picketing injunction by lettuce grower Bud Antle, New Yorkers rallied in protest at 5:30 a.m. outside Bud Antle's operation in Hunt's Point Market in the Bronx. In January 1971, union supporters picketed in front of Fort Dix Army base in New Jersey to protest the military's purchase of Bud Antle lettuce.[61]

During the lettuce boycott, the UFWOC (shortened to UFW in 1972) kept many tactics consistent, including its grocery store demonstrations. Volunteers leafleted outside, asked managers to inspect cold storage rooms for nonunion lettuce, phoned and wrote to store executives, and held fundraisers like concerts, wine-tastings, and car washes. Meanwhile, counterprotesters who believed the union was trampling on the freedom of consumer choice became more aggressive. At some markets, they sat directly in front of UFW marchers and defiantly ate bunches of grapes. Others called the pickets "Russians" and tore up boycott literature. A common tactic among supermarket managers was to remove their stocks of grapes while picketers demonstrated but place them back on shelves as soon as they left. Some managers believed the grape boycott helped them to sell *more* grapes to shoppers annoyed by the UFW.[62]

The UFW was, of course, not the only organization fighting for farmworkers' rights. There were overlapping struggles in the Northeast playing out as well. On Long Island, New York, the Suffolk County Human Rights Commission investigated migrant potato workers' labor camps after multiple farmworker complaints. The camps' occupants, who were mostly US-born Black, white, and Puerto Rican workers along with Jamaicans and other Latin American workers, were paying sixty-five cents a day for unsanitary housing on a salary of under two dollars an hour. Across the Long Island Sound, young Puerto Rican organizer Juan Irizarry—who founded the Asociación de Trabajadores Agrícolas (ATA) during his time as an asparagus picker in Delaware—was trying to organize tobacco workers in Connecticut. Irizarry hoped the ATA could negotiate directly with agricultural employers instead of the Puerto Rican government, which he considered ineffectual and too lenient on employers. The ATA tried to mobilize workers in the tobacco fields of Connecticut and Massachusetts, mushroom fields of Pennsylvania, potato fields of New York, and blueberry and tomato farms in New Jersey, but no contracts resulted from these early efforts.[63]

A landmark legal case regarding farmworkers' rights, however, emerged in New Jersey in 1970. The state was home to famous canneries like Seabrook, Campbell's, Hunt, Del Monte, and Progresso, where about 25,000 Black, Puerto Rican, and Mexican American migrant workers lived in camps that were virtual "fire traps" lacking ventilation and indoor toilets. Exacerbating this confinement, it was common practice for New Jersey farmers to intimidate antipoverty officials, health-care workers, educators, or labor advocates who wanted to enter labor camps to speak with workers. By segregating their employees from the outside world, bosses were also preventing workers at different camps from comparing notes about their wages and conditions. A breaking point came when Peter K. Shack (a lawyer for Camden County Legal Services) and Frank Tejeras (a caseworker for the Office of Economic Opportunity–funded Southwest Citizens Organization for Poverty Elimination) were attacked by a farmer and arrested for trespassing at a New Jersey camp. The UFW experienced similar treatment in New Jersey the following month when organizer Gilbert Padilla was violently ordered off a farm.[64] As Shack brought his case to court, the UFW focused on New Jersey as an organizing priority. José Gómez, a twenty-seven-year-old from Laramie, Wyoming, was appointed to direct the lettuce boycott there. He visited churches to speak and take donations, and inspired several residents to picket grocery stores.[65] A victory finally came on May 12, 1971, when the New Jersey State Supreme Court ruled in *State v. Shack* that farmers could no longer keep visitors out of migrant farmworker camps. The case cited the Economic Opportunity Act of 1964, which ensured farmworkers' right to the "opportunity for aid available from federal, State, or local services." A similar case in Michigan, *Folgueras v. Hassle* (1971), established a federal right of visitors' access to workers, complementing *State v. Shack*'s state-level verdict.[66]

With this new privilege in place, northeastern farmworkers continued to protest for other improvements, including their food. In June 1972, a group of fifty Puerto Rican migrant workers produced written complaints of being overcharged for cold, meager portions of food; improper paycheck deductions; no weekend day of rest; a lack of laundry facilities and hot water; and dangerous transportation and insecticide exposure. Then, in April 1973, tobacco workers at Camp Windsor in Connecticut conducted a work stoppage until they were given better food and three hot meals a day. They claimed cooks gave them rotten meat, cold dinners, and an inedible chicken and rice dish. "We're not animals," striker José Santiago declared in Spanish. "This isn't food for a person who works eight, nine hours a day."[67]

Meanwhile, the UFW continued to use food in political moves as well, either by providing it or taking it away. The Pittsburgh boycott committee sold enchiladas to fundraise, advertising them as "DELICIOUS Mexican morsels, hot from the UFWOC kitchen" for four dollars a dozen. Boycott committees in New York and Los Angeles held benefit dinners, or *sopas*, around the Thanksgiving and Christmas seasons. In Hauppauge, Long Island, people could attend UFW wine and cheese parties for $3.50 a person. Other UFW committees decided to make their statement through the *absence* of food. During Thanksgiving 1969, organizers decorated tables on the Boston Common with white tablecloths and china, but no food. The Philadelphia office sponsored a "Farmworkers' Thanksgiving Day *Non*-meal," charging donors three dollars per empty plate.[68] Food and drink protests remained in the zeitgeist. Food prices had jumped by 14.5 percent in 1973 alone, and housewives' meat boycotts took place that year across various US cities. Meanwhile, Chicano consumers in the Southwest were boycotting Frito-Lay, which had debuted a "Frito Bandito" ad campaign featuring a sleepy, sombrero-wearing, criminal Mexican character. Those engaged in the concurrent boycott against Coors Beer (which aimed to change the company's discriminatory hiring and employment practices) teased "Mexican American sellouts" to stick to their "vendido diet" of Coors, grapes, and Fritos.[69]

To show once more the effects of food deprivation, Chavez engaged in a riskier fast in May 1972. This fast lasted twenty-four days and, during its penultimate week, the *New York Times* ran a photo of the forty-five-year-old Chavez wincing, "face hollowed and drawn," and being wheeled on a stretcher to the hospital for dehydration. His weak appearance resulted in several telegrams of support from people in the Northeast, and even from across the ocean by a farmworkers' union in Orléans, France.[70] Chavez ended his fast at a memorial mass for Robert F. Kennedy in Phoenix attended by more than 5,000 people including folk singer Joan Baez and Kennedy's eldest son Joseph Kennedy III. The mass, assisted by eleven priests and ministers, featured 100 loaves of bread and wine made with union grapes. Jerome Lackner, Chavez's doctor of seven years, sat at his feet, concerned about the "distant and mushy" sounds in Chavez's heart and the "instabilities and abnormalities" in his electrocardiograms. Still wearing his hospital bracelet, Chavez told the assembled crowd, "What is a few days without food in comparison to the daily pain of our brothers and sisters who do backbreaking work in the fields under inhuman conditions. . . . What a terrible irony it is that the very people who harvest the food we eat do not have enough food for their own children."[71]

Many believe this particular fast shortened Chavez's life, but his family and supporters took up the baton. On July 23, 1974, Cesar's forty-five-year-old brother Richard began a fast in front of Hills supermarket in Huntington, Long Island, sitting in a canvas chair and drinking only water and lemonade (and smoking cigarettes) as pickets marched back and forth in front of him. When the Young Americans for Freedom, a right-wing organization, taunted him by eating lettuce and grapes next to him, Chavez read the Bible.[72] Chicano students at schools like Cornell, the University of Pittsburgh, the University of Pennsylvania, Princeton, and Villanova continued to protest on behalf of farmworkers. Multiple food co-ops across the Northeast, including Brooklyn's famous Park Slope Food Co-op, provided support to the UFW by holding benefits and donating their leftover produce to union members. The Loisaida Social House on the Lower East Side, a social hub for the Nuyorican community, held a "United Farmworkers Benefit Night" for $2.50 a ticket.[73] Contrary to one *New York Times* reporter's opinion that "the rad-chics from New York's Sutton Place to San Francisco's Nob Hill are bored with [the UFW]," it seemed the union was still having an impact. A 1975 nationwide poll showed that 17 million American adults were boycotting grapes, 14 million were boycotting lettuce, and 11 million were boycotting Gallo wines. Additionally, on May 10, 1975, "National Farm Workers Week" was observed in seventy cities in the United States and Canada.[74]

The mid-1970s were a period in which the US government decided to become, as Felicia Kornbluh puts it, a "nutritive welfare state," especially for children. The Black Panthers' free breakfast program was, in food historian Mary Potorti's words, "one of the most devastating, forceful, and potentially revolutionary critiques of the American food system to emerge" during the twentieth century. The US government gave permanent status to the Special Supplemental Nutrition Program for Women, Infants, and Children (WIC) in 1975, and free school breakfasts were established by the Child Nutrition Act that same year. Yet activists still had to work hard to bring this food out of theoretical legislative existence and into reality. Meanwhile, the organizers of a "Food Day" headed by the Washington-based Center for Science in the Public Interest asked Americans to boycott the "terrible ten" food products of 1975, which included Wonder Bread, Coca-Cola, candied breakfast cereal, bacon, Gerber baby food desserts, and—to the UFW's delight—table grapes.[75] High on this publicity, the UFW kept holding benefit dinners and dances with Mexican food and folk singers, or sacrificial nonmeals. The Toronto UFW chapter even created *The Lettuce-Less Salad Book*, which contained recipes for a "coconut-carrot salad" featuring mandarins, lemon juice, and mayonnaise; a "tuna-pineapple salad" with rice, sour cream, and chutney; and a "frankfurter supper salad" of hot dogs, cucumbers, peas, and French dressing.[76]

Ten years in, the union's grocery store boycotts were still going strong in the Northeast, and women and children were central to their optics and success. In a coordinated series of demonstrations at multiple Waldbaum stores in Long Island suburbs and upstate New York, participants refused to leave stores, formed human chains and sat in the aisles, chanted and lit candles, and shouted "Waldbaum's approves of child labor," "Waldbaum grapes have blood on them," and "If you shop in Waldbaum's you are killing children in the field." At some stores, women used other picketing techniques. In New Hyde Park, Long Island, Carmen Blanco—along with other adult women and small children—conducted a "Liberty March" in front of a Waldbaum store. They dressed in red, white, and blue clothing, and children carried musical instruments and American flags. When the police were called by the store manager, one officer told Blanco's group that they were behaving like "ladies," and he was pleased with their conduct.[77] Waldbaum ownership tried to sue the UFW and get an injunction, but they were unsuccessful in the face of customer testimonies that complimented the picketers' civility and called their protests "lady-like," "extremely peaceful," and "a most gentle form of picketing." Knowing their audience, women organizers in different locales used a variety of tactics—from the militant to the maternal— to earn customer support.[78]

Cesar Chavez continued touring the Northeast in the late 1970s, giving talks in New York City and Providence, Rhode Island; holding two rallies in Waterbury and Bridgeport, Connecticut; and making visits to Boston and to Portland, Maine.[79] The union also decided to show up in unconventional spaces. It hosted two concerts in Madison Square Garden in 1976 with headliners including singer-songwriter Melanie, Gil Evans (who had worked with Miles Davis), and Otis Blackwell (a founder of rockabilly). The concert programs' sponsored advertisements—which came from the staff of *Ms.* magazine, Audre Lorde, Mexican restaurant owners, postal workers, the National Lawyers' Guild, and the Corset and Brassiere Workers Union, among others—showcased the

UFW's diverse supporters.[80] At the finish line of the 1979 Boston Marathon, UFW members held up a large banner that read "STRIKING FARM WORKERS SALUTE THE BOSTON MARATHON / BOYCOTT CHIQUITA" and handed out leaflets. United Brands, which sold Chiquita bananas, was the parent corporation of the lettuce company SunHarvest, which the UFW was still trying to unionize. Bananas were likely being offered to runners at the finish line, making it opportune for the union to spread its message about corporatism and greed.[81]

The UFW's Tensions and Declensions

Despite this continued momentum, there were noteworthy tensions and problems that signaled a decline of the union as the 1980s approached. First, Filipino members felt they had lost positions of real power in the union, and that their concerns were going unaddressed by a Mexican American–dominated organization. This resulted in a significant number of departures. Chavez was also critiqued for his treatment of undocumented Mexican migrants, whom he viewed as blocks to citizen farmworker unionization because employers could use them as strikebreakers. "In abolishing the bracero program, Congress has but scotched the snake, not killed it. The program lives on in the annual parade of thousands of illegals and green carders across the US-Mexico border to work in our fields," Chavez told a Senate subcommittee. He and other UFW members picketed at Immigration and Naturalization Service branches and reported undocumented people to the INS, and Chavez launched an "Illegals Campaign" in 1973 that tracked and reported undocumented immigrants, though some UFW field offices refused to cooperate.[82] A few months later, Chavez established a "wet line" in the citrus orchards of Yuma, Arizona, to patrol 125 miles of border and prevent undocumented migrants from entering. In response, a coalition of Chicano groups based in the Southwest confronted the union with a public statement insisting that all workers, including undocumented workers, had rights. In the Northeast, members of the Syracuse UFW support committee resigned and stopped picketing during the last week of August 1974. "Many people in the upstate committees were very concerned that the union took the position of the 'illegals' that they did," their letter read. UFW organizer Fred Ross mentioned this tension when training Brooklyn volunteers a few years later, blaming infiltrators who "disrupted the hell out of" Syracuse because "all they wanted to talk about was the aliens."[83]

After being criticized by other Mexican American activists, Chavez modified the union's call for stricter immigration control to emphasize the suffering of both groups, and used a discourse of hunger to articulate that common suffering.

A 1973 UFW leaflet read, "The farmworkers on strike under the flag of the UFW do not blame the illegal workers . . . but rather collusion (between growers, labor contractors, the Western Conference of Teamsters, and the Border Patrol) that allows one group of powerless people—work-hungry people from Mexico—to be used by California's giant growers as pawns in a battle against another struggling group, the farm workers who have worked so hard to build their own union."[84] This language of hunger continued in 1979 in the UFW Boston newsletter: "We saw hundreds of people brought in from the poorest states of Mexico to be used to break the strike, the hungry pitted against the hungry." A few years later, in an interview with the *Boston Globe*, Chavez reiterated, "We have a difficult problem because there's massive unemployment in Mexico, hunger, and workers wanting to come across to be able to feed their families, and we don't want to be judges as to who eats and who doesn't eat in this world."[85] Chavez still, however, wanted US citizen workers to be considered first for agricultural jobs.

In a way, Chavez's views about the perils of uncontrolled undocumented immigration echoed other Americans' anxieties at the time. A 1976 Gallup poll asked, "What problems, if any, result from the presence of illegal aliens in this country?" (About 28 million Mexicans entered the United States without papers between 1965 and 1986). The majority of respondents mentioned that migrants took jobs away from residents.[86] The 1980s were characterized by more immigration from Central America and Mexico, and debates over the "amnesty" bestowed upon certain undocumented immigrants by the Reagan-era Immigration Reform and Control Act (IRCA), which legalized certain categories of immigrant workers. Others worried that the undocumented would abuse the welfare system and drain public resources. In reality, undocumented migrants barely utilized welfare services because they feared detection and apprehension by applying. Moreover, only citizens and legal residents had access to public federal assistance programs such as Aid to Families with Dependent Children, Medicaid, and food stamps. In 1980, an International Conference for the Full Rights of Undocumented Workers was held in Mexico City, signaling the urge to connect workers across the Americas. Under Chavez's leadership, the UFW missed an opportunity to be a more inclusive union, hindered by the fear—that Chavez felt was constantly being proved right—that it was already hard enough to obtain rights and protections for US citizen farmworkers.

As far as organizing farmworkers in the Northeast, UFW leadership was aware of the labor problems that the Southwest and Northeast held in common. Substandard housing, wage theft, verbally and physically abusive crew leaders, and high pesticide exposure were prevalent in both regions. Early on in the grape strike, after a 1966 labor camp fire in Fredonia, New York, that killed two wine workers, the union's newspaper *El Malcriado* proclaimed, "In the not-too-distant future, the eagle of the Farm Workers will be flying over the big wineries in New York."[87] In the 1970s the UFW briefly joined forces with Juan Irizarry's 6,000-member Asociación de Trabajadores Agrícolas (ATA) and even named Irizarry the UFW's new Northeast regional coordinator in 1977. Soon into the partnership, however, the ATA and UFW began disputing tactics. Irizarry was more open to direct and violent confrontation, while Chavez wanted to continue pursuing nonviolent strategies. Chavez's support for ATA decreased, and the UFW eventually stopped paying the salaries of ATA organizers. A frustrated Irizarry left both organizations. Some UFW organizers had hoped for a truly interracial and transregional union for farmworkers. Speaking of Puerto Rican farmworkers, organizer Marilu Sánchez wrote in a letter to a fellow organizer, "Together with our California workers, it could be a beautiful thing—and . . . with the black Southern workers . . . out-a-sight!!!!!!!!"[88] Ultimately, working through the challenges of actual mergers with Eastern farmworker organizations was not a priority for top UFW leadership.

As the 1970s ended and the 1980s began, the UFW operated out of offices in California and Seattle in the West; Texas and Florida in the South; Chicago, Detroit, and Cleveland in the Midwest; Washington/Baltimore, Philadelphia, Pittsburgh, New York City, Newark, and Boston on the East Coast; and Montreal and Toronto in Canada.[89] At its zenith in the late 1970s, the UFW boasted a membership of 50,000 people. By 1985, that number had fallen to around 6,000. The union's difficulties persisted when the hard-won contracts of the past came up for renewal and growers evaded renegotiation by signing contracts with the Teamsters instead, changing their firms' names, or splitting up and selling parts of their businesses. Meanwhile, the Agricultural Labor Relations Act was, in historian Christian O. Paiz's words, "toothless and glacial" in securing actual rights for farmworkers.[90] Chavez's desire to control the UFW from the top down clashed with members' demands for more input and power on the local level. Chavez increasingly purged allies, lawyers, and valuable union leaders.[91] Paiz has pointed out that Chavez and the UFW's declension was not unusual in this political context. "Nearly *all* unions and progressive movements collapsed under the weight of reactionary politics and economic transformations. . . . By then [the 1980s], like most US unions, the UFW found itself with dwindling resources, a disgruntled and vulnerable workforce, an even more hostile political context, and an ineffective labor law."[92]

As the UFW reinvigorated its grape boycott to begin again on July 11, 1984, Chavez toured the East Coast once more, hitting key cities like Washington, DC; Philadelphia; Pittsburgh; and New York City. He continued to use the technique of the hunger strike and began a "National Fast for Life" in the summer of 1988 that became a fasting chain with activists and celebrities. After fasting for thirty-six days, Chavez passed the fast to Rev. Jesse Jackson. Others involved included actors Martin Sheen, Emilio Estevez, Edward James Olmos, Lou Diamond Phillips, Danny Glover, Whoopi Goldberg, and River Phoenix; singer Carly Simon; Sierra Club executive Michael Fischer; and Robert Kennedy's daughters Kerry and Rory. Other Americans conducted fasting chains in solidarity, including Chicano students at all nine Ivy League schools. In the summer of 1989, the New York City Council endorsed the grape boycott and proclaimed July 3–9 to be "Grape Boycott Week," complete with electronic billboards in Times Square. By the end of the 1980s, however, New York was the only northeastern stronghold left—there was no evidence that any other boycott offices still existed.[93]

The Northeast is certainly not the only region that should be examined more deeply to create a more complete history of the UFW, but it is an essential one for understanding how a California-based union translated its message across different spaces and eras. The union had the task of keeping its name *in* the mouths of the American public, while making sure certain food and drink stayed *out* of them until farmworkers' physical and political hungers were satisfied. Countless people in cities and suburbs in the Northeast helped make this happen, including many dynamic but lesser-recognized women activists.

While national attention to the UFW faded by the late 1980s, the number of US Latinx and Latin American food workers across the nation had only increased. This was largely due to demographic and economic shifts produced by IRCA, civil wars in Central America, the North American Free Trade Agreement of 1994, and internal migrations of people of color around the United States. While many of these food workers would remain tucked away in fields or factories, the 1980s and 1990s were a time when some Latinx food entrepreneurs became more visible in the United States through their culinary businesses and innovations. Emerging restaurateurs, bodega and taquería owners, and street vendors brought a wider variety of Latin American food to US consumers, who were delighted to taste it all. The next chapter discusses how a fascinating range of food entrepreneurs brought new knowledges of Mexican food to the Northeast in particular, and expanded people's palates to embrace a wider range of complex, regional cuisines.

PART II

How Latinx Newcomers Transformed Foodscapes, 1980–2011

CHAPTER THREE

Changing Mexican Foodscapes and Food Entrepreneurs in New York City

At the beginning of April 1981, the *New York Daily News* published an article titled "Tex-Mex Fever Hits Manhattan." Relying heavily on flour tortillas, meat, red chiles, cumin, pinto beans, and melted cheese, Tex-Mex cuisine was New York's latest obsession.[1] There was a larger cultural ethos driving diners' interest in Tex-Mex—chili contests were taking place across the country, *Dallas* was a popular television show, more people were listening to country music, and young professionals from the US West were moving to New York and craving dishes that reminded them of home.

On a national scale, this fascination with Mexican food had taken some time to develop; during the late nineteenth and early twentieth centuries, middle-class and elite diners in both the United States and Mexico circulated negative stereotypes that Mexican food was unhealthily spicy, the cuisine of poor indigenous peoples, or unhygienically prepared. During the mid-twentieth century, however, more US citizens were visiting Mexico for tourism and bringing home cravings for the cuisine. Mexican food eventually became part of the "TV dinner" revolution, with kits and plates first debuting in Texas and California. The Ashley Company sold a taco dinner kit for $1.89 in 1955 that came with canned tortillas, beans, taco sauce, and a handheld taco fryer. That same year, Los Angeles shoppers began seeing TV dinner combination plates consisting of an enchilada, tamale, refried beans, and Spanish rice in their grocery stores.[2] By the early 1960s multiple companies were selling Mexican TV dinners across the Southwest and Midwest. The marketing and packaging decisions of corporate food producers were no doubt influencing consumers' ideas of what Mexican meals should be—cheap, convenient, and plentiful. Meanwhile, more restaurateurs came onto the scene. Luis Silva, an immigrant from Guadalajara, opened the Spanish Gardens Taco House in Kansas City, Missouri, in 1958 and offered an Italian-Mexican mashup of fried tacos topped with a ketchup-like sauce and parmesan cheese. Fast-food chain restaurants like El Torito (founded in 1954) and Taco Bell (1962) steadily increased their number of franchises. In South Carolina, the rest stop South of the Border drew high numbers of motorists in the 1950s and 1960s with its billboard mascot "Pedro," a short, chubby, dark-skinned Mexican man who beckoned travelers to stop for "authentic" Mexican food, souvenirs, and mixed Mexican-Confederate atmospherics.[3] Internationally, Mexican food was trending as well, informed by people's actual tourism in Mexico or the desire to participate in a fiesta fantasy. A "Taco Bill" opened on Australia's Gold Coast in 1967, "La Cucaracha" restaurant opened in London in 1969, Café Pacífico debuted in Amsterdam in 1976, and a Tex-Mex restaurant named Le Studio opened in Paris in the early 1980s. Budapest had an Acapulco Restaurant, and the former Soviet Union claimed a Cowboy Bar and Tequila House.[4]

Those who consider New York City ahead of the culinary curve might be surprised that in the early 1980s Mexican food was hard to find there. It lagged behind other cities like Chicago, San Antonio, and Los Angeles, which had larger Mexican-origin populations and a longer history of Mexican restaurants. At this time, only a sprinkling of Mexican restaurants existed in Manhattan. In 1959 Spaniards Louis Castro and Manuel Vidal opened El Charro in Greenwich Village, and Mexican restaurateur Carlos Jacott debuted El Parador in Midtown East. Mexican Village, a restaurant owned by a Mexican woman, had served the New York University area since the mid-1960s, and two Irish businessmen opened the Tex-Mex establishment El Coyote near Astor Place in 1981.[5]

Contrary to the assumption that "ethnic" cuisines immediately appear in a place after immigrant populations do, Mexican food took time to become a part of New York's culinary landscape. Still, there was no doubt that New York was already a Latinx city. Spaniards had settled there centuries prior and were followed in the 1800s and early 1900s by Cuban and Puerto Rican political exiles, many of whom worked in the cigar factories of lower Manhattan. Pan-Latino enclaves formed in East Harlem and Chelsea in Manhattan, and Greenpoint, the Navy Yard, and Red Hook in Brooklyn. The Puerto Ricans who moved to East Harlem coexisted with Italian residents and added their own food into the neighborhood. White-tablecloth Puerto Rican establishments in this new "Spanish Harlem" included San Juan, Ponce de Leon, and Victor Café. By the late 1920s, more than 125 Puerto Rican bodegas and restaurants existed in the Big Apple. In the borough of Brooklyn, Puerto Rican photographer Justo Martí remembered being "so happy to pass . . . the bodegas along Atlantic Avenue, bananas hanging on the windows."[6]

Mexican-origin people migrated to New York in the early twentieth century, arriving directly from Mexico by ship or train, or after previous work stints in the cotton fields of Texas, the stockyards and factories of Chicago, or the auto assembly lines of Detroit. By 1930 about 3,000 people of Mexican origin (three-quarters born in Mexico, the rest second-generation Mexican Americans) lived in New York City's boroughs, with the majority settling on the Upper West Side of Manhattan and in Queens. An early Mexican food entrepreneur of the 1930s was Juvencio Maldonado, who owned a Mexican grocery store on the Upper West Side and a restaurant called Xochitl in Times Square. During the 1940s, when commercial travel became more affordable between San Juan and New York, more Puerto Rican migrants increased the city's Latino demographic. Though it was surely an undercount, the 1940 Census counted 134,250 Hispanics (61,463 Puerto Ricans, 25,283 Spaniards, 23,124 Cubans and Dominicans, 19,727 Central and South Americans, and 4,653 Mexicans) in the city.[7] Then, during the 1950s and 1960s, Colombians and half a million Cubans fleeing revolutions came to New York in growing numbers. Chino-Latino restaurants owned by Chinese Cubans and Chinese Peruvians, such as La Caridad 78, La Dinastia, and Flor de Mayo opened in Manhattan from the 1960s on and enchanted diners. After Dominican Republic dictator Rafael Trujillo was assassinated in 1961, an exodus of Dominicans made New York their home. They opened more bodegas in the city and formed organizations like the Metro Spanish Food Wholesalers (founded in the Bronx in 1967) to purchase goods in bulk. Ecuadorian and Peruvian migrants followed during the 1960s and 1970s and settled on Long Island and in Queens.[8] As *New York Magazine* declared in the summer of 1972 to describe the impact of Latinx migration upon the city, "Botanicas have come to Flushing and arroz con pollo to Woolworth's."[9]

Though many histories can be written about Latin American food diasporas in the United States, this chapter tells the story of how Mexican food became more desired and accessible in New York City from the 1980s onward. There was a citywide and nationwide fascination with Tex-Mex and Mexican food in the late twentieth century unlike any other. (Cuban food attracted attention, spurred by tourism and tropical fantasy, but did not reach the heights of consumer obsession that Mexican food did.) This chapter focuses on the specific career of Zarela Martínez, an immigrant Mexican chef who—in the words of *Bon Appétit*—"single-handedly changed New York's Mexican food scene" during the late 1980s and 1990s by serving haute regional Mexican dishes. Martínez rose to celebrity through a confluence of circumstances and connections, and spent her career as a restaurateur confronting racialized expectations that Mexican food was inherently simple and cheap. She argued instead for its elevation as a complex and refined global cuisine. The 1980s and 1990s marked huge waves of migration from Mexico to Manhattan and other places around the Northeast and wider United States. Martínez took advantage of this demographic shift and the growing national appetite for Mexican food to build her career. Her eponymous restaurant, which operated in Manhattan from 1987 to 2011, attracted an elite clientele and food critics' attention. Historian Natalia Molina has described ethnic restaurant entrepreneurs as "place-makers" who help define neighborhoods as ethnic spaces and leave an indelible cartographic mark.[10] As a culinary placemaker for New York, Martínez's story helps to map several histories, including those of Mexican food's spread in the Northeast, Latinas' food-related labor and creativity, and immigrant entrepreneurship in the United States.

This chapter weaves discussion of Martínez's career with the demographic and cultural shifts of the late twentieth century that transformed New York into a home for many kinds of Mexican food and Mexican people. During the 1980s and 1990s, an influx of Latin American immigrants fleeing political and economic chaos in their home countries arrived in the city. Many opened food businesses including bodegas, bakeries, taco trucks, and tortilla factories. While Martínez certainly enjoyed more career and class privilege than these migrants—she had been supported by influential white men and achieved success in the food world very quickly—it can be productive to place their histories on the same plate. Whether haute or humble, food makers mutually constituted a blossoming Mexican foodscape in New York, with each making the other's food more interesting to consumers. In the 1980s, Martínez helped usher in an exciting age for Mexican food and educated customers on regional differences in the cuisine. This primed diners to embrace other Mexican restaurants and street food enterprises when they came onto the scene in the 1990s and early 2000s. In turn, these humbler food businesses kept the public's interest in Mexican food piqued, and higher-end restaurants like Martínez's remained relevant and special. Food entrepreneurship and success crossed class lines, and invigorated New York's culinary landscape.

Martínez is unlike most of the food workers discussed in this book. The inclusion of her trajectory as a restaurateur might seem jarring, but she fits in as a provocative figure and businesswoman around whom a bigger story about Mexican food and food labor can be told. "Relatively little attention has been paid to Latino entrepreneurship, perhaps because Latinos . . . tend to be perceived as labor migrants," anthropologist Laura H. Zarrugh has argued.[11] As in other groups, Latinx people exhibit a diversity of statuses, solidarities, and political outlooks. Martínez intentionally presented herself as a Mexican chef from an elite background and did not align herself with a "Chicana" identity. Though Martínez was not working class, and did not take up the political causes that some might expect, she was still a Latina immigrant food entrepreneur with her own hunger for respect and recognition.

What Martínez did spend effort on, that has lasting ripple effects today, was speaking up for the value and depth of Mexican cuisine. Long before cultural critics like Anthony Bourdain, she asserted that Mexican food was elegant and deserving of respect. This message was her attempt to counter a spreading and discouraging discourse about Mexican food as inherently casual and inexpensive. The long colonial and exploitative relationship the United States had enjoyed with Mexican land and labor since the 1800s, and increasing US citizen tourism in Mexico, undoubtedly shaped perceptions of Mexico as an exotic vacationland where things like sex, alcohol, and spicy food could be consumed cheaply.[12] As more Mexican people migrated north over the twentieth century and took jobs on US farms and in factories, restaurant kitchens, and street vending, their food-related labor became coded as "immigrant" and low-wage work. Latinx food and Latinx labor were thus devalued together. No matter her class background, Martínez realized, she and her business were not immune to a spreading public opinion that "real" Mexican food should be cheap. In this way, her business and the enterprises of her more modest immigrant counterparts were similarly impacted and bound up together.

Becoming the Hot Tamale of Manhattan

Maria Zarela Martínez Gabilondo was born in 1952 in the town of Agua Prieta in Sonora, Mexico. Her parents José Martínez Solano and Aida Gabilondo hailed from Arizona but moved to a ranch in Mexico after getting married. "My mother cooked all sorts of foods," Zarela remembered of her family's formal candlelit dinners. "We would have rabbit provençal one night, [then] Chinese almond chicken, lasagna, curry." The family's recipe book indeed shows that Aida made everything from pork tamales to lamb curry to chop suey.[13] Aida's experimentation and openness to other cuisines was likely influenced by her experiences eating different diasporic cuisines in Mexico, including Chinese food and Lebanese immigrant-influenced *tacos al pastor*.[14] Like others living in the Texas-Mexico borderlands, the Martínez family had a transnational domestic routine, often crossing the border into El Paso to go to banks, doctors' offices, and supermarkets. What distinguished them from many Mexicans, however, was their financial comfort and social networks. "We moved in very different circles. We basically hung out with high society people from Juarez," Martínez said. After obtaining a university degree in mass communications in 1971, Zarela moved to El Paso, where she became a social worker for the Department of Welfare and met and married widowed parole officer Adolfo Sánchez. Adolfo brought three children to the marriage, and when Zarela became pregnant with twins, this created a financial strain. To make extra money she began baking for friends and family, cooking for private dinner parties, and established her own catering business.[15]

As a social worker and caterer, Martínez exposed herself to two different communities living in El Paso—those desperately in need of resources and social services, and those who employed servants and hired her to cook for glitzy gatherings. Her catering clients often asked her to stay away from Tex-Mex fare. "Everybody already had a maid who would make the enchiladas and burritos; they wanted something else," Martínez said.[16] As her catering business gained steam, Zarela craved moral support from her husband but found the opposite. He became emotionally and physically abusive, turning to alcohol and extramarital affairs. Zarela's mother decided to intervene and gift her daughter a series of private cooking classes in California to encourage her culinary development. Zarela left Adolfo in the fall of 1980 and began traveling with her mother to take cooking classes around the country. In New Orleans, the duo ate at the famous Cajun restaurant K-Paul's. Aida pressured Zarela to approach chef Paul Prudhomme, who was standing near their table and checking dishes emerging from the kitchen. Immediately charmed by the women, Prudhomme invited them to cook in his kitchen for the rest of their stay; he educated them on Cajun cuisine, and they taught him Mexican dishes in exchange.[17]

Soon after this encounter, *New York Times* food critic Craig Claiborne asked Prudhomme to recommend a Tex-Mex chef for an April 1981 event hosting 130 French chefs at Tavern on the Green. Claiborne wanted to showcase various American regional cuisines—from Chesapeake seafood to Kansas City barbecue—for the European guests. Prudhomme promptly suggested Zarela and Aida, and flew to El Paso to help the shocked pair plan their menu and ingredient transport. They ended up shipping nine crates of food to New York, including 1,000 homemade tamales. Cooking on such a public stage was nerve-wracking but confidence-building for Zarela, whose menu included crab enchiladas, *ropa vieja* (marinated and shredded beef), and picadillo (a spicy meat stew). Instead of serving the food on conventional silver plates, she used Mexican ceramic dishes adorned with crepe paper and flowers. "Everyone went wild," she remembered, and at the end of the event she received a standing ovation.[18]

The exposure that Martínez gained through this event was career-launching. Shortly after the dinner, Claiborne wrote a profile on Zarela for the *Times*, deeming her a rising star in New York's food scene. This feature won her more catering clients, and she began flying back and forth between El Paso and New York. In April 1982 she convinced Tavern on the Green owner Warner LeRoy to let her cater one of his private parties, where guests like Lauren Bacall and Yoko Ono tasted her food. Zarela served *puerco manchamanteles* (pork with a sauce of to-matoes, ancho chiles, and dried fruits) and shrimp with green and red chiles, but the menu went underappreciated—Warner and his guests were disappointed by the lack of Tex-Mex staples, and Zarela had to make "some hurried nachos" to appease them. This was an early sign that New Yorkers were still quite attached to a US southwestern style of Mexican cooking. A few months later, however, Claiborne invited her to cook at a party for himself and other prominent cook-book authors, including Diana Kennedy (a white expat in Mexico who published the best-selling *The Cuisines of Mexico* in 1972), Penelope Casas (who wrote about Spanish food), Marcella Hazan (Italian), Madhur Jaffrey (Indian), and Florence Lin (Chinese). They, along with guests like food critic Gael Greene and chefs Jacques Pépin and Alice Waters, were incredibly valuable networking contacts for Martínez.[19]

While Tex-Mex food could easily be found in prepackaged form or in casual restaurants in the Southwest and Midwest, it was trickier to find in the North-east. Mexican TV dinners took longer to appear on the region's supermarket shelves, and Mexican restaurants were still rare. The Old El Paso company, a Texas-based firm, made its canned goods sporadically available in northeast-ern supermarkets and bodegas by the 1950s. Southern California native Rosa-lind Oliva, who moved to Worcester, Massachusetts, recalled that the scarcity of Mexican ingredients forced her to buy canned tortillas out of desperation. "[They] were thick and grainy and fell apart at the ends when I rolled and fried them," she remembered.[20] New Hampshire welcomed its first Mexican restau-rant in 1970; Portland, Maine, claimed two establishments in the 1970s and one in the 1980s; and Boston boasted a few successful eateries over the ensuing years. Of the 2,500 Mexican restaurants that existed in the United States by the early 1980s, only 150 were located in the Northeast.[21] Restaurant owners were trying to accommodate customers' desire for heaping Tex-Mex combination platters, but this style garnered harsh critique from prominent food writers. "The public is paying for an awful lot of stomachache and heartburn," chided Diana Kennedy, while *New York Times* food critic Bryan Miller characterized early Mexican food in New York as "one gastronomic Alamo after another." "Mush, more than magic, is the way of New York–Mex," agreed a critic in *New York Magazine*.[22] It was the perfect time for Zarela to carve out her niche in Manhattan as a chef who focused on regional Mexican dishes.

In 1983, Martínez moved with her sons Aarón and Rodrigo to Manhattan, aided by $10,000 from her mother. She booked a steady stream of catering gigs and received positive press, including an article that highlighted her "fill-your-own-taco" party option that encouraged diners to try unfamiliar things like *huitlacoche* (a fungus that grows on corn) and squash blossoms. She catered cocktail parties, buffets, and seated dinners at which she impressed celebrities including Paul Newman, Glenn Close, and Meryl Streep. She also threw parties at her townhouse on the Upper West Side to expand her network. At these gatherings, where chefs and food critics mingled with jazz musicians and artists, Zarela made sure her guests saw her two young sons roving around the apartment, a pointed reminder of her single motherhood.[23] Meanwhile, Craig Claiborne recommended Zarela to be a chef for President Ronald Reagan's May 1983 Economic Summit Conference in Williamsburg, Virginia. There, she cooked a lunch of chili con carne and cornbread, pork and fish tamales, and stuffed beef filets and poblano chiles that was enjoyed by world leaders including Margaret Thatcher, François Mitterrand, and Pierre Trudeau (see fig. 3.1). Soon after, *USA Today* deemed Zarela the "newly crowned high priestess" of Mexican regional cooking and *Cuisine* called her "a culinary star preaching the gospel of *real* Mexican food, distinct . . . from the muddy, searingly hot Tex-Mex version Americans know."[24] Zarela gained a stronger foothold in Manhattan's food scene the following year when she agreed to serve as a consultant for restaurateur David Keh's new Mexican venture, Café Marimba. Zarela was responsible for developing sixty new recipes and guiding the kitchen staff in testing them, and would receive a percentage of total restaurant sales in return. When it opened in December 1984, one reviewer stated that Café Marimba could stand alongside the restaurants Cinco de Mayo and Rosa Mexicano (both owned by Cuban-born and Spanish-raised chef Josefina Howard) to "signify the beginnings of a long-overdue coming-of-age of Mexican cuisine in New York City."[25]

"Amigos: The city is gripped by Mexican madness. Never before has there been such passion for Mexican food, or so many places to enjoy it," declared *New York Magazine* in 1983. By this point, Fort Worth natives June Jenkins and Barbara Clifford owned the popular Tex-Mex restaurants Juanita's and the Yellow Rose Café, respectively, and eateries with names like Santa Fe, Pancho Villa's, Margaritas, and Tortilla Flats dotted the city.[26] Martínez chafed at being lumped in with Tex-Mex chefs in the press, but she knew she needed to spin herself within the genre to stay on diners' radars. While Martínez and others thought Tex-Mex was greasy and unrefined, its proponents believed it to be historically complex regional cookery. Passionate Tex-Mex chefs strove to distinguish their cuisine from the "tide of slushy green margaritas, sustained by gooey cheese nachos" that led some to imagine Mexico as a "country-as-theme-park." Tejana entrepreneur Ninfa Laurenzo, for example, gained renown for her restaurant, Ninfa's, which opened in 1973 on Houston's East End and grew to a chain of thirteen restaurants across Texas by 1980.[27]

FIGURE 3.1. Zarela Martínez meets President Ronald Reagan at the May 1983 Williamsburg Economic Summit. Photo used with permission of Zarela Martínez.

No matter their specialty, successful Latina food entrepreneurs were very rare in the United States. In Los Angeles, Mexican immigrant single mother Natalia Barraza became known for her restaurant El Nayarit, which offered regional western Mexican cuisine and drew working-class Latinos and Hollywood celebrities alike during the 1950s and 1960s.[28] In the Northeast, Josefina Howard and Zarela Martínez were high-profile Spanish-speaking women in the food industry. Interestingly, though she was a Mexican immigrant, Martínez never portrayed herself as someone struggling with barriers related to citizenship, race, or gender. This strategy and mindset differentiated her from most women chefs in America who were trying to climb the ladder of fine dining and speaking out about the inequalities they experienced. Rampant sexism in the industry had created vast disparities in professional advancement between men and women; even chefs' jackets, kitchen stoves, and knives presumed a taller and larger male body.

In an October 1985 *Town and Country* article, "America's Great New Women Chefs," Zarela was featured alongside pioneers like Anita Lo and Alice Waters but vehemently denied that she experienced any sexism in the industry. "There is no discrimination," Martínez often told reporters. "I'm a Mexican. I'm a woman. I'm short. And sometimes I'm fat. Don't tell me you can't make it."[29] Though she had clearly benefited from the early support of influential men like Prudhomme and Claiborne, Martínez created the impression that a woman's success in the food world simply depended on her strong will and self-advocacy.

Martínez further distinguished herself from other women chefs in the United States by embracing food critics' exoticization and sexualization of her. One review, for instance, called her "a hot tamale. Sassy, sexy, small, dark-eyed, dark-haired, she's always prepared to party." Another reviewer called her "notorious for the bravura of her cleavage." Instead of being bothered by the "hot tamale" trope historically used to stereotype Latinas as fiery, volatile, and sexually available, Zarela seemed flattered by it and even created a flyer for her catering business that read, "Have Your Next Affair with Zarela: The 'Hot Tamale' of Mexican Food."[30] This breezy acceptance might have been due to her upbringing in Mexico and perceiving the phrase as more humorous than harmful. Or, as Madeline Y. Hsu has argued, Martínez perhaps saw the strategic value of capitalizing on the stereotype: "To attract a broader range of customers . . . purveyors of ethnic foods may adapt ingredients, cooking techniques, decorative schemes, and even their own personas to present some manner of the recognizably exotic. . . . Gaining recognition and visibility often accompanies, perhaps inescapably, self-exoticization."[31] Rather than wearing chefs' whites for press photos, which most chefs used to communicate their authority in the kitchen, Martínez circulated glamour shots of herself in off-the-shoulder blouses or dresses, surrounded by flowers and fruit, and wearing heavy makeup and jewelry (see fig. 3.2). Instead of smothering the sexy Latina stereotype, Martínez played it up out of vanity, business strategy, or both. Deciding not to wear chefs' whites was also a way for Zarela to establish her identity as a public-facing restaurateur, rather than a cook confined to the back of the house.

Martínez's identification as a Mexican woman with an elite upbringing invites interrogation of how inter-class relations operated in the advancement of her career. Indeed, she owed much of her restaurant and cookbook success to lower-income women food makers in Mexico who shared their techniques and inspired her recipes. A long-standing and problematic dynamic in the world of food and cookbook writing, the capitalization on the knowledges of lesser-privileged food makers is also present in the careers of Latinx food creatives. In the summer of 1985, Zarela took two months' absence from Café Marimba to travel with her

FIGURE 3.2. Press photo of Zarela Martínez in her signature off-the-shoulder dress. Photo used with permission of Zarela Martínez.

mother Aida and photographer Laurie Smith through Oaxaca, Yucatán, and Veracruz. The trip's purpose was to gather new recipe ideas for the restaurant and a cookbook that Zarela eventually wanted to publish. She took copious notes in a travel diary about the food and dishes she ate, musing upon how she would alter or improve them. Reflecting upon the trip's first meal, which was cooked at a friend's home in Mexico City by a woman named Luz Barrera, Martínez wrote: "[Luz] is a quietly assertive, self-possessed, amiable woman who though quite still the 'servant' as is traditional in Mexican homes is self assured and proud of her position." Zarela took Barrera's dessert that night—a mango pudding made with condensed milk, lime, and rum—and duplicated it for Marimba's menu. Another dish that became a Zarela trademark—a red snapper hash made with cinnamon, cloves, scallions, tomatoes, cumin, and jalapeños—was in her words "immediately appropriated" from a *botana* (cocktail snack) at a bar in Tampico that used crab. As Janet Floyd and Laurel Forster have pointed out, recipes "exist in a perpetual state of exchange" and, conventionally in the food world, an alteration of just one ingredient or technique can make a recipe one's own.[32] At Mexican markets and festivals, Zarela persuaded local women—from market sellers to restaurant owners—to share their recipes and techniques, but first showed an interest in their personal stories to earn their trust.

On the one hand, these exchanges might have felt flattering to the Mexican women offering their personal recipes and cooking techniques to be shared with US dining audiences. On the other hand, Martínez would be the one to shape the narrative of the recipe and profit from it in her restaurant and future cookbooks. Furthermore, Martínez's customers or readers would enjoy the feeling of "knowing" a Mexican foodseller without ever having met her or tasted her creations firsthand. Martínez was certainly not the only cookbook author to engage in this practice. Many of Diana Kennedy's recipes in *The Cuisine of Mexico* were "based on the meals the . . . maids cooked for her," while Border Grill restaurant co-owners Mary Sue Milliken and Susan Feniger learned several dishes from a Mexican employee's mother who, in their words, "would walk us through all of it." Philosopher Lisa Heldke concedes that "cuisines are always a patchwork of borrowing and lending, undertaken at various conditions of liberty and bondage."[33] Yet the more mediation and distance that comes between a less-privileged source of a recipe and a prestigious and profitable food venture, the more likely "culinary colonialism" is to occur. Martínez affirmed that she paid homage to these women's labor by attributing recipes to them in her cookbooks, sending them copies of the books, and staying in touch. Indeed, her three cookbooks cited her sources—while her first was heavily influenced by women she knew while attending school in Texas, California, and Guadalajara, her next two credited the friends, cooking instructors, and market vendors who enlightened her about the cuisine of Oaxaca and Veracruz.[34] These women were invaluable to Martínez, not only for their recipes but because they offered her an intimate experience of Mexico that strengthened her knowledge of the country and her self-presentation as an "expert" to customers and the press.

By late 1985 Martínez had been promoted from consultant to executive chef at Marimba, but she struggled with leading a kitchen and meeting the demands of a 180-seat restaurant. She preferred being the face in the front of the house rather than working on the production line. Unluckily, in March 1986, *New York Times* reviewer Bryan Miller noticed this and critiqued Martínez for not tending enough to her kitchen crew. This injurious review was compounded the next month when Diana Kennedy ate at Café Marimba and told the *Times* it "lacked Mejicanidad" and needed "a good Mexican palate behind it."[35] Due to ongoing conflicts between Keh and Martínez over their menu and financial matters,

Zarela left the restaurant and Keh shut down his Mexican experiment. Financed by a $20,000 loan from an aunt, Zarela opened her eponymous restaurant on October 1, 1987 and convinced all of Marimba's staff to follow her, including head chef Gary Jacobson, pastry chef Edward Bonuso, and every runner and busboy. Martínez initially experienced skepticism from others, including bank lenders, that she had enough resources to open her own business. "At that time most people in this country thought of Mexicans as migrant field laborers and restaurant dishwashers and rarely came in contact with legitimately wealthy Mexicans," she remarked.[36]

Located in a former tavern in Manhattan's Midtown East near the United Nations building, Zarela's new restaurant featured dishes such as chicken tamales with mole sauce, a chile relleno with walnut cream and pomegranate seeds, *cochinita pibil* (Yucatan-style pork shoulder marinated with achiote and sour oranges and served in a banana leaf), and a margarita cheesecake. Almost immediately, Zarela's restaurant was favorably compared to Josefina Howard's Rosa Mexicano in Manhattan, Rick Bayless's Frontera Grill and Topolobampo in Chicago, and Milliken and Feniger's Border Grill in Santa Monica. Critic Bryan Miller returned to visit Zarela and declared it "arguably the best Mexican restaurant in New York City." The more intimate sixty-seat restaurant was packed every night with customers, with musicians performing on the staircase.[37] To this point, Gotham's trendy 1980s food scene had been dominated by steak houses, Italian or Continental establishments, and French restaurants like Indochine, Le Colonial, or Le Cirque, but Martínez's and Howard's Mexican restaurants offered a different ethnic cuisine that also intersected with the emerging "seasonal" and regional food movement seen in Alice Water's Chez Panisse or Danny Meyer's Union Square Cafe.[38]

The 1988 Zagat New York City restaurant survey—which covered 740 restaurants and 3,500 participants who dined out an average of 3.6 times per week—illuminates more about how diners perceived Mexican food establishments. Diners' top Mexican and Tex-Mex restaurants were El Parador (a more established "pacesetter") and Rosa Mexicano ("stylish Mexican" with beloved guacamole made-at-the-table), followed by Santa Fe, Cinco de Mayo, and Albuquerque Eats. The language in the survey showed what diners expected and praised when it came to Mexican food. Albuquerque Eats, where dinner and a drink cost twenty-two dollars on average, was complimented for its "casual atmosphere, plentiful portions, and lethal margaritas." The phrases "lethal margaritas," "casual feel," "fun and festive," and "reasonable prices" were used by diners to characterize multiple Mexican restaurants. Prices for dinner ranged from fifteen dollars at the "deliberately tacky" Exterminator Chili in Tribeca to thirty-six dollars at

Arizona 206 and Café on the Upper East Side. Whether it was over a plate of nachos at a kitschy dive bar or a candlelit dinner in a restaurant with a terracotta and pastel palette, diners wanted big drinks, plenty of food, and a transporting experience that would make them forget they were in New York. A newcomer to the guide, Martínez was praised as "one of the best Mexican cooks north of the border" in her restaurant's blurb.[39]

Mexican food establishments in New York City, 1988

Albuquerque Eats	Rosa Mexicano	Tortilla Flats
El Coyote	Border Café	Caramba
Mike's American Bar/Grill	Exterminator Chili	Lucy's Retired Surfers
	Santa Fe	Zarela
Arizona 206 and Café	Cadillac Bar	Cinco de Mayo
El Parador	Home on the Range	Lucy's Surfetería
Pancho & Lefty	Southern Funk Café	Zona Rosa
Blue Moon	Cantina	Cottonwood Café
El Río Grande	La Fosse aux Loups	Mexico Next to Texaco

The festive atmosphere at Zarela was powered by the hard work of a diverse and largely immigrant staff. "That kitchen was rocking," recalled Brooklyn-born Italian American pastry chef Ed Bonuso, who transitioned to the culinary profession in his forties and worked at Zarela until its closure. In the small kitchen in the back of the house, dishwashers worked in heat and steam, prep cooks cleaned and chopped food, line cooks worked under pressure, and sous-chefs supervised plates and managed inventory. In the front, busboys cleared and replenished tables, waitstaff attended to customers, and hosts greeted and ushered patrons. Though one might assume Martínez's workforce was mainly Latino, this was not yet the norm in New York's restaurant scene. Filipino chefs Romy Dorotan and Amy Besa, who owned and operated the highly acclaimed restaurant Cendrillon, remembered that in the late 1980s New York restaurants employed mostly white, Asian, and Haitian workers in their kitchens. In the early days of Zarela's restaurant there were a few Latino employees—a dishwasher/porter named José was of Mexican descent, and a Dominican employee named Hilario worked his way up from being a dishwasher to a line cook and then a chef—but the majority of the back-of-the-house employees were immigrants from Bangladesh. In the front of the house, bartenders and waitstaff (who had the privilege of visibility, tips, and interacting more directly with customers) were mostly young US-born men and women who wanted to break into a career in show business. A Black bartender named Winston was a longtime employee, and a French manager named Claude oversaw overall operations. When asked to reflect on her employees' treatment and wages, Martínez asserted she paid them all very high salaries and held an annual party for them in which she and her friends did all the cooking. This, of course, was her own personal memory and opinion; workers could have felt differently about their compensation and benefits. Outside the restaurant, Martínez also had the help of Latinas who cared for her sons while she was working. If she had to stay at the restaurant and was not able to greet her children after school, she left them food to reheat or asked their Salvadoran nanny Adella to cook for them. Adella's cooking was so impressive that Zarela later hired her to work at the restaurant, and one employee recalled that Adella was put in charge of making all the restaurant's coveted tamales.[40]

With its "roaring house party" feel, Zarela's restaurant crossed borders of clientele and attracted a mob of young midtown professionals, curious foodies, international visitors associated with the United Nations, and celebrities including Paul Newman, Bette Midler, Richard Gere, Mick Jagger, Salman Rushdie, Brooke Shields, Warren Beatty, and Diane Sawyer.[41] The restaurant also frequently catered private events and parties for well-known figures including Joan Didion, Martha Stewart, and Linda Ronstadt. Zarela regularly offered gossip about her famous patrons to newspapers back in El Paso or to Spanish-language publications like *Hoy* or *Vanidades*. This was a way for Martínez not only to stay connected to her former homes but also to keep her image and reputation circulating beyond New York to the bilingual media of the US-Mexico borderlands.

The Southwest also figured heavily into the restaurant's ingredient procurement during its early years of operation. Martínez and her managers often shipped in tortillas from Texas or California because tortilla producers in New York were quite scattered. Casa Moneo, a store in Chelsea owned by Spanish immigrants since 1929, was reputedly the only place in Manhattan where one could find tortillas, chiles, and other Mexican ingredients alongside other Latin American items, including "Argentine cider, paella pans, prefab mole sauce, [and] frozen blocks of coconut milk." A tortilla factory named Mayab Happy Tacos was established in Bushwick, Brooklyn, in 1976 but did not survive for long. Cousins Félix and Fernando Sánchez, who migrated together from the Mexican state of Puebla to New York in the 1970s, opened their own tortilla businesses—Félix founded Puebla Foods in Passaic, New Jersey, in 1978 and Fernando opened El Gordo Tortillas in Bushwick in 1986. The latter would become the bigger factory Tortillería Piaxtla. These places were likely too far away for daily pickup and delivery, and a lack of geographically convenient suppliers surely frustrated

Martínez and other Manhattan chefs. Meanwhile, food critics lamented that New York's Mexican culinary scene was stagnating because "relatively few Mexicans have chosen to make their home here."[42]

More Newcomers, and More Mexicos

The next decade, however, changed everything. Along with Central Americans fleeing civil wars in their home countries, Mexican migrants began settling in the United States in greater numbers during the late 1980s and 1990s due to a series of events. The Mexico peso suffered devaluation, and a 1985 earthquake devastated the states of Michoacán and Guerrero, pushing people to migrate north for work. Then, the 1986 Immigration Reform and Control Act (IRCA) bestowed a path to citizenship and permanent legal status to certain categories of undocumented immigrants in the United States (including 1.2 million farmworkers and other "Special Agricultural Workers"), which gave more people the freedom to move about the nation. Finally, in 1994, the North American Free Trade Agreement flooded the Mexican market with US agricultural surplus crops, which sunk the price of Mexican foodstuffs so low that 2 million Mexicans working in agriculture felt compelled to migrate north for their economic survival. In particular, migrants from the state of Puebla moved to New York through word-of-mouth and chain migration. Whereas the US Census counted 23,761 Mexican New Yorkers in 1980, there were 61,722 by 1990, making Mexicans the fastest-growing Latinx population across all five boroughs.[43]

Unlike previous waves of migrants that settled in the Bronx or Brooklyn, the Mexicans and other Latin Americans who arrived in New York in the 1990s overwhelmingly gravitated to Queens for affordable homes within commuting distance to Manhattan. By 1990 there were an estimated 381,120 Latinos living in Queens, including 100,410 Puerto Ricans, 63,224 Colombians, 52,309 Dominicans, 35,412 Ecuadorans, 18,771 Cubans, 14,875 Peruvians, 13,342 Mexicans, 10,893 Salvadorans, 4,050 Panamanians, and 3,607 Hondurans.[44] Many of these newcomers took jobs in factories, construction, domestic service, and restaurants, and were often exploited by employers who assumed these workers would accept low wages out of desperation or their undocumented status. Restaurant work, for instance, demanded twelve hours a day, six days a week, for a total weekly salary of $200 or less. In construction, it was common for Mexican workers to be paid about forty or fifty dollars for two or three days' work. Though employers believed wages in US dollars far surpassed what these migrants could earn back home, restaurant worker Luis summed up the dilemma: "Sure, I'm making dollars, but I'm spending dollars too. You have to pay your bills, your rent, you have to buy your food, you have to wash your clothes. You know, everything you have to do in Mexico you have to do here."[45]

Some Mexican migrants decided to go into business for themselves as food makers and sellers. They opened taco trucks and tamale pushcarts in Brooklyn and Queens, *panaderías* and bodegas in East Harlem and the Bronx, and hole-in-the-wall restaurants in Midtown Manhattan. Informal producers sold their specialties to bodegas, neighbors in the know, and restaurants. Damiana Bravo, for instance, cooked and sold her twenty-ingredient mole. Augustín Juárez, who worked in a kitchen of a Manhattan Italian restaurant, supplemented his income by planting seeds from his native Oaxaca on an acre-and-a-half plot on Staten Island.[46] Additionally, a tortilla "boom" occurred between 1990 and 1993, as more than twenty new factories were established. The neighborhood of Bushwick, Brooklyn, became known as the "Tortilla Triangle" for its three major tortillerías (Buena Vista, Chinantla, and Piaxtla—all named after towns in Puebla), which churned out millions of tortillas a week. Tortillería Piaxtla's owner, Fernando Sánchez, experienced such success with his Brooklyn factory that he established a grocery store and tortilla factory in Providence as well.[47] Providence was becoming a more Latinx city in its own right. Extant communities of Dominicans, Colombians, and Cubans were being joined by Guatemalans seeking political asylum in the 1980s, and a contingent of K'iche'-speaking Mayans by the 1990s. The beloved Fefa's Market, the city's first Latin American market, was joined by Sanchez Market (another outlet for Latin American groceries) and Antillas Restaurant, which served Puerto Rican and Dominican food. Antillas owners and brothers Roberto and José González often bought Latin American ingredients from New York City's Hunts Point produce market for their and others' restaurants, and even resold the produce to individual customers who could not make the same trip.[48]

As historian Andrew Sandoval-Strausz has argued, Latinx migrations revitalized many US urban spaces during the twentieth and twenty-first centuries, and street food vendors have played an important role in that process.[49] *Ambulantes* change the visual, olfactory, and auditory landscape of a neighborhood through their presence and goods. They can—through quick and affordable food provision—literally influence someone's taste. Additionally, food cart or truck vending is one of the first occupations a new immigrant entrepreneur can enter, due to lower startup costs. Food studies scholar Krishnendu Ray explains, "It requires relatively little money or credit or social or cultural capital to get into the business of selling food, most often by the poor to the poor."[50] By offering food out in the open, street food vendors challenge traditional ideas about where food should be seen, sold, and eaten. Both Mexican women and men became street food sellers in New York City. With their pushcarts and big steaming aluminum pots, they enticed passersby with one-or-two-dollar tacos, *elote*, tamales, and *paletas* and fruit cups in the summertime. Vendors often moved in accordance with the rhythms of citygoers, stationing themselves throughout business and tourist districts during weekdays, moving outside churches and nightclubs on weekends, and setting up near parks during soccer season or on Mexican holidays.[51] In neighborhoods like Astoria and Jackson Heights, Queens, where diverse immigrant populations already lived, Mexican ambulantes sidled up alongside other ethnic food purveyors on the streets, or sold underground in subway stations. These vendors—along with the bodegas, panaderías, and tiendas that imported Mexican products—began making neighborhoods that had previously been Italian, Greek, or Chinese into Mexican ones as well.

In addition to mobile food trucks and carts, culinary change happened in New York as fledgling Mexican restaurants became fixtures in unexpected places. In East or "Spanish" Harlem, a longtime Puerto Rican neighborhood, Mexican Mario Olmedo opened a taco stand in 1987 followed by a bodega and taquería in the 1990s. Initially nervous from witnessing "a lot of Puerto Ricans chasing Mexican guys down the street to beat them up," Olmedo's business paved the way for other Mexican enterprises to open amid Puerto Rican ones. On Manhattan's Upper West Side, businessman Arthur Cutler financed his former domestic workers Gabriela and Miguel Hernandez in opening their restaurant Gabriela's, which became a neighborhood hit. In Sunset Park, Brooklyn—a neighborhood known for its mix of Scandinavian, Irish, Chinese, and Vietnamese residents— Puebla immigrant Jaime Oliván opened a taquería named Tequilita's in 1990 that still exists today. Other restaurants found strategic locations to serve both non-Latinx consumers and Mexican workers who longed for the taste of home. When Mario and Estella Ramírez opened their restaurant Rinconcito Mexicano in Manhattan's midtown Garment District in July 1993, it drew in eager Mexican customers who worked in the district's sweatshops. Mario knew these workers' struggle. He had migrated from Puebla in 1973 and washed dishes in New York hotels before working as a sous-chef at the Russian Tea Room. He eventually purchased a fifty-acre farm in upstate New York, where he grew the chiles, tomatillos, squashes, cilantro, and corn he used for his restaurant's menu. "When New Yorkers taste my cooking they know the real Mexico . . . and they don't want unreal Mexico anymore," Ramírez told then-twenty-seven-year-old National Public Radio reporter Maria Hinojosa.[52] The proliferation of Mexican food establishments in the 1990s not only excited New York's dining public but brought comfort to Mexicans living in a metropolis that did not always feel comfortable.

Meanwhile, the 1990s marked a new peak in the US obsession with Mexican food. In 1991 salsa surpassed ketchup as the best-selling condiment in the country, a fact mentioned in an episode of *Seinfeld*. President Bill Clinton extolled cheese enchiladas as his favorite meal, and the number of Mexican restaurants in the nation rose from 13,034 in 1985 to 20,600 in 1994.[53] Pace Picante was America's most popular brand, due in part to its famous commercials that poked fun at the impossibility of New York actually knowing its salsa:

> Cowboy no. 1: This ain't Pace Picante sauce!
>
> Cook: What's the difference?
>
> Cowboy no. 1: Pace is made in San Antonio . . . by people who know what picante sauce is supposed to taste like.
>
> Cowboy no. 2 (reading the label of the cook's sauce): This stuff's made in New York City!
>
> All cowboys: New York City?!
>
> Cowboy no. 3: Get a rope.

Between 1980 and 1990, tortilla sales quintupled from $300 million to more than $1.5 billion. Even Wonder Bread developed its own tortillas, called Soft-Wraps, and encouraged Americans to begin wrapping tortillas around hot dogs, spreading peanut butter and jelly on top of them, or layering tortillas in "cross-cultural" lasagnas. Historically denigrated as poor field-workers' food, tortillas had now become a desirable and fun item that could be rolled, folded, and fried into various configurations and dishes. Restaurants like Taco Bell (4,000 franchises strong by this point) and McDonald's won the public over with soft tacos and breakfast burritos. By the mid-1990s, Chipotle was gaining fans with its customized burrito-making options. By the end of the decade, a few behemoth corporations had grabbed a huge share of the Mexican prepackaged food market. Pillsbury Inc. owned the Old El Paso Brand, the Campbell Soup Company had bought Pace Picante sauce, PepsiCo owned Tostitos salsa and chips, and Kraft had won the rights to sell Taco Bell products in supermarkets.[54]

Though it was safe to say that the United States was obsessed with Mexican food, it was becoming clear that assumptions about "authentic" and "street"-style food and immigrant labor were beginning to result in a monetary devaluation of this cuisine. By 1993, Zarela restaurant was six years old and Martínez found herself struggling against popular notions about the expected price point of "authentic" Mexican food. *Forbes* remarked that Zarela's "a-la-carte prices [were] steep for fiestas," while another review lamented, "When the check came, alas the Mexican fantasy faded, and I was jolted back to high-priced Manhattan. For a casual restaurant, Zarela is pretty pricey."[55] Zarela charged for rice, beans, and guacamole, and held its entrees between fifteen and twenty dollars to meet the costs of labor and the procurement of high-quality ingredients. Even though Martínez's food was far from casual, her restaurant had the fiesta-style atmosphere that many American diners assumed came with low prices. In a letter to Martínez, a customer scolded her for charging $4.75 for a side dish of rice with sour cream and asked, "Why can't beans and rice come as part of the meal, as they do in Mexico or anywhere else? How do you charge so much money for your inauthentic Mexican food? As someone who lived in Mexico for four years and travels there often on business, I was very disappointed in your food and your prices."[56] In this letter, the accusation of inauthenticity was specifically tied in with the cost of the items. From Zarela's perspective, the reason that rice and beans did not come with a meal was because she believed the "combination platter" itself was an inauthentic thing. Critics' reviews and diners' comments were alarming to Martínez. No matter how refined she believed her food to be, customers balked at or questioned her prices because of assumptions about the price ceilings for "real" Mexican cuisine. As Mexican food historian Jeffrey Pilcher lamented in his book *Planet Taco*, "Very few Mexican restaurants can command prices comparable to those of French restaurants, even when using the same fresh ingredients and, in many cases, the same Mexican workers. Customers have simply refused to consider the two cuisines as equals." Zarela affirmed the same thing a decade earlier by telling the *New York Times*, "Mexican food is just as elaborate as French or Italian cuisine, but it's still perceived as something that's cheap. I use exactly the same ingredients as Le Cirque does, the duck, the sushi-quality tuna!"[57]

Arguably, this late twentieth-century devaluation of Mexican food happened in tandem with continuing Mexican immigration to the United States. As smaller immigrant-owned food enterprises such as taco trucks, street carts, and taquerías became more visible in New York and other places around the United States, this reinforced consumers' ideas that Mexican food was inherently casual, fast, and low-priced. Speaking about Chinese cuisine's valuation over time, Krishnendu Ray observed that the *New York Times* gave peak attention to Chinese restaurants in 1965, but then decreased coverage considerably once that year's Hart-Cellar Immigration Act resulted in an influx of Chinese immigration to the United States. Ray suggests "an inverse relationship between the prestige of a cuisine . . . and the number of immigrants."[58] The already low pay that Latino food workers were receiving (highly incommensurate with their skill and ingredients) decreased even more as consumers equated immigrant food labor and service with cheaper wages. In essence, US consumers began believing that the price of the food should match the price of the people. This made it more challenging for *everyone* along the Mexican food-providing chain—whether immigrant or citizen—to persuade diners that their ingredients and labor deserved certain compensation.

Determined to keep a high position in New York's Mexican food scene, Zarela tried to keep innovating with her restaurant. In 1993 she began featuring special state-specific menus inspired by the food of Quintana Roo, Sonora, Tlaxcala, and Jalisco. For Day of the Dead in 1995 she offered a Oaxacan menu, and other restaurants quickly followed her lead.[59] Martínez also kept pursuing the publication of a cookbook for a general audience. Her breakout in the cookbook world finally happened when she published *Food from My Heart* (1992) and *The Food and Life of Oaxaca* (1997), to glowing reviews for the latter.[60] Zarela kept her name in the press by writing several guest pieces for *Saveur, Food and Wine*, and the *Los Angeles Times* and consulting for Goya Foods (headquartered in Secaucus, New Jersey), where she helped write copy and recipes for their canned food labels.[61] By this point, her mother Aida had also published her own cookbook, *Mexican Family Cooking*, which was praised as a resource for "young Mexican-Americans . . . who are losing touch with the foods, literature, and songs of their Mexican heritage."[62] Zarela did not strive to reach that same Mexican American audience. In fact, recalling a lunch she had with feminist icon Gloria Steinem, Martínez recalled how Steinem mentioned she had just been with Dolores Huerta. "Who's that?" Zarela asked. "WHO is THAT?" Steinem replied, aghast. "She's with Cesar Chavez and the United Farmworkers union. How could you not know that? She's Mexican." "No, Gloria, she's Mexican American. And I'm American Mexican. It's a huge difference," Zarela replied.[63] While Steinem was expecting Mexican-origin people to have the same emotional affiliations and political solidarities, Martínez was not invested in this cause. Her Mexicanness was instead refracted through a kind of "American" ignorance and distance from a Chicano demographic (though ironically, many white Americans knew a great deal about Huerta and the UFW by this point).

Martínez upheld her belief that the United States was a place where immigrants could succeed, but this perspective did not square with the very real economic exploitation, discrimination, and violence experienced by other Latinx people in New York during the 1990s. An infamous "Operation Bodega," led by INS special agent Joseph Occhipinti, conducted a series of raids on Dominican bodegas in Manhattan during 1989 and 1990 (Dominicans owned 80 percent of the borough's 9,000 Latinx bodegas and grocery stores at this time). Claiming that Dominican *bodegueros* were funneling illegal immigrants and using their stores as "fronts" for illegal gambling, money laundering, food stamp violations, and drug dealing, the raids arrested twenty-five people and deported forty-three more. Bodegueros protested in newspapers, calling the raids racist and corrupt since Occhipinti did not have proper search warrants and even stole money (deeming it "evidence") from the businesses' cash registers. Occhipinti was eventually jailed.[64] Meanwhile, Mexican and Central American day laborers were being harassed, beaten, and even killed by white residents in the suburbs of Long Island. This region had claimed a significant Latino population since World War II, when an influx of Puerto Rican families became homeowners via the GI Bill and filled a glut of new jobs at the Pilgrim psychiatric hospital. Long Island churches and immigrant advocates had also participated in the Sanctuary Movement and welcomed a significant number of Central Americans during the 1980s.[65] In the 1990s and early 2000s, however, groups of immigrant day laborers waiting for work on street corners became more conspicuous. Residents became extremely hostile, despite knowing that many of their neighbors were hiring these very day laborers for landscaping and construction. As the Southern Poverty Law Center wrote of Latinx immigrants living on Long Island, "They are regularly harassed, taunted, and pelted with objects from cars. They are frequently run off the road while riding bicycles, and many report being beaten with baseball bats and other objects." An infamous hate crime occurred in Patchogue, Long Island, in November 2008 when a group of seven white boys—who bragged their weekend pastime was "beaner jumping"—stabbed Ecuadorean immigrant Marcelo Lucero to death at a train station. Lucero's murder led the Civil Rights Division of the US Department of Justice to investigate police discrimination against Latinx people on Long Island and indifference to crimes committed against them.[66]

Meanwhile, in the restaurant world, sexual harassment and wage theft were common forms of violence toward Latina workers. In May 1994, a group of Mexican immigrant workers protested in front of the popular Times Square restaurant México Mágico to demand that their boss Raymond Posadas pay them $100,000 dollars in back wages. Female employees complained of being sexually harassed and assaulted by Posadas and restaurant manager Javier Alcalá. Spanish-language media covered another story about waitstaff at the Manhattan Mexican restaurant Selena. Cristina Pinzón, a twenty-year-old immigrant from Guerrero, worked as a waitress there for twelve hours a day, six days a week, for about $100 a week (the equivalent of $1.39 an hour) and endured sexual harassment on the job. Another waitress who had been fired by the restaurant corroborated Pinzón's account.[67] Despite their labor contributions to multiple sectors of the city's economy, Mexican migrants in New York City still lagged behind other residents financially. Though they could make a higher average annual income in New York than in Puebla ($10,231 versus $4,133), they still made far less than the average Hispanic/Latino household in the city ($12,206) and New

York households overall ($22,402).[68] Along gendered lines, the average Mexican man (who tended to work in food service/retail, construction, or manufacturing) earned $15,631 annually, about half of the typical male New Yorker ($29,155). Mexican women, for whom domestic service and factory work were common occupations, earned on average $11,731 a year, less than half of female New Yorkers ($24,469).[69] These lower earnings could be partially explained by lower educational attainment levels and a lack of proficiency in English, but anti-immigrant discrimination was certainly a factor. Employers who preyed on the desperation and vulnerability of undocumented workers saved thousands of dollars by paying them subminimum wages and counting on their silence and fear of deportation.

By 2000, the total number of Americans who identified as Hispanic in the US Census had risen to more than 35 million. Parallel unauthorized migration added another 5 million.[70] All five of New York City's boroughs had undergone striking Latinization between 1990 and 2000, and Mexicans experienced the highest rate of growth in every borough. In the Bronx, Mexican immigrant residents increased by 180 percent and the overall number of Latinos increased by 21.3 percent, making up almost half of the borough's total population. Manhattan's Mexican population increased by 178 percent, and Spanish Harlem became predominantly Mexican instead of Puerto Rican. The total Latino population of Staten Island, long an Italian or "ethnic white" borough, increased 64 percent, and its Mexican population shot up by 566 percent. This was likely because—in addition to a steady flow of Puebla migrants—a significant number of migrants from Ciudad Nezahualcóyotl, a city of more than 2 million people just outside Mexico City, were forming a settlement in the Port Richmond neighborhood. These newcomers transformed a ghost town that had been in economic decline since the 1970s into a bustling "Neza York," with new bakeries, flower shops, taquerías, and supermarkets. In Brooklyn, Mexicans increased by 218 percent and clustered in the Sunset Park and Bushwick neighborhoods. In Queens, Mexican residents increased by 334 percent and gravitated toward the Elmhurst, Corona, and Jackson Heights neighborhoods. Citywide estimates counted 300,000 residents of Mexican descent living alongside 830,123 Puerto Ricans, 579,269 Dominicans, 250,000 Colombians and Ecuadorans, and others who made up a total of 2.2 million Nueva Yorkers.[71]

Thanks to continuing Mexican migration and a concurrent increasing demand for Mexican food, the culinary landscape of New York by 2000 was completely different from the one Zarela Martínez found upon her arrival in the city in the 1980s. "Now a Mexican mother can go to the store, pick up a bag of tortillas made in the Bronx, fill them with chorizo from a factory in Queens or chicken . . . and follow them with panque (Mexican poundcake) made in a big panadería in Park Slope," declared the *New York Times*.[72] Against this backdrop,

MAP 3.1. Mexican enclaves in New York City's boroughs by the early 2000s. Map prepared by Alejandro Falchettore / R Software. US CENSUS TIGER data, 2020.

Martínez felt confident she could open another Mexican restaurant, Danzón, this time focusing solely on the coastal European- and African-influenced cuisine of Veracruz. Martínez also published a companion Veracruz cookbook and acquired her own thirteen-episode, half-hour television show, *Zarela! La Cocina Veracruzana*, on PBS. Much to Zarela's dismay, Danzón went unfavored by critics and only survived until May 2002. Meanwhile, her son Aarón's career as a Nuevo Latino fusion chef and television figure was on the rise. By 2003 he had published the cookbook *La Comida del Barrio* and appeared on Food Network shows including *Melting Pot, Iron Chef: America, Chopped,* and *Master Chef.*[73]

Motivated by her son's success, Zarela pivoted to designing a "Casa Zarela" line of housewares that included table linens, bedding, bath accessories, and cookware decorated with vibrant Mexican heart, flower, *lotería*, and chili pepper ico-nography. She pitched this line of "aspirational" products to Walmart, pointing out that Walmart Mexico already exposed Mexican immigrants to the brand long before they arrived in the United States. Taking citizens and immigrants together, the Latino population in the United States was estimated to be 41.3 million, with 65 percent being people of Mexican birth or heritage. By February 2005, the Casa Zarela line was being carried in hundreds of stores across the nation, most prominently at Walmart and Bed Bath & Beyond.[74] During this time of her multiplatform celebrity, however, Martínez began experiencing bodily tremors that resulted in a diagnosis of Parkinson's disease. During her nightly visits to her restaurant, she recalled, her face and mouth would become so rigid that she could not give her customers her usual smiles and smooth con-versation. "Nothing has been as humiliating and I suffer deeply," she wrote as she processed her experience.[75] She even drafted a treatment for a television program that, by following her own journey and interviewing expert guests, would shed light on how people with Parkinson's could battle their depression, isolation, and physical pain. Arguably, Zarela's pursuit of the media limelight demonstrated her immense, continuing need to tell her story and be in conversation with others.

In the autumn of 2006 the *New York Daily News* proclaimed, "New York is finally a city with great Mexican food." People could easily find tamales, *cemita* sandwiches, Mexican candies, medicinal herbs, and other beloved items in Bronx bodegas or street carts in Queens. On the weekends, Latino and non-Latino cus-tomers alike swarmed the weekend taco stalls along the soccer fields of Riverside Park in Manhattan and Red Hook in Brooklyn.[76] Concurrently, more Latinx social spaces opened, including sports leagues and pan-Latino nightclubs. The club Montezuma, which was managed by a Dominican in the Bronx, boasted a neon sign emblazoned with the phrase "Tu México en New York" (Your Mexico in New York) and spun a mix of cumbia, bachata, ranchera, and reggaeton. In Queens, the club Chibcha featured a similar variety of music such as "a strap-ping Mexican ranchera starlet one night, a Venezuelan folk ensemble another, followed the next night by vallenato music from Colombia's northern coast." Nueva Yorkers had indeed created a *México de afuera*, or a Mexico outside of Mexico, and they were being helped along by other Latin American and Carib-bean communities. By 2010 the greater New York City metropolitan region was home to over half a million people of Mexican origin (and 3.4 million Latinos in total), with significant numbers of Mexican-origin people living in Westchester and other Hudson Valley counties. Poughkeepsie had even been termed a "little Oaxaca" for its Mexican immigrant demographic that had infused the deterio-rating downtown with new businesses, shops, and restaurants.[77]

Amid these demographic shifts, a small pantheon of highly regarded Latina chefs and restaurateurs had emerged in New York City. Sue Torres, Julieta Ballesteros, and others acknowledged that their work would not have been possible without their culinary *madrina* (godmother) Zarela, who—in the words of Torres—"has been trying to make Americans and New Yorkers understand the cuisine for so many years." Zarela had been not just a place *maker* for the Mexican community of New York but a place *taker*, unafraid to stake territory in a competitive city and industry. Zarela's restaurant finally closed its doors in February 2011. Its rent had skyrocketed to $20,000 a month and, as Martínez lamented to the media, "There are six Mexican restaurants nearby, most of them fast-food. And the young people would rather go to a taco truck instead of out for a Mexican meal."[78] Though there was sadness in shutting down after almost twenty-five years in business, this was a rare milestone for any New York restaurant to reach. Zarela's lasting legacy would be the flourishing of more Mexican restaurants around the country; an estimated 40,000 of them existed nationwide by the 2010s. This decade witnessed a "taco awakening" in the United States, as diners clamored for tacos filled with everything from barbacoa to bulgogi to lobster.[79]

Another lasting but problematic legacy has been the continued devaluation of Mexican food, and Latinx food labor, through a rhetoric about "authenticity." Much like Chinese food, Mexican food has been unable to escape the idea that it should be cheap. The review site Yelp, whose average users are disproportionately young and white, has been "an essential venue for urbanites . . . to negotiate their ideas about Mexican-ness." Yelpers, as Dylan Gottlieb argues, "are searching for one thing above all else: 'authenticity.' Reviewers are constantly assessing the alleged verisimilitude of a restaurant's food, atmosphere, and even the ethnicity of its employees." Customers look for nonwhite patrons, humble or nonexistent decor, and cheap menu prices to affirm the "realness" of a Mexican restaurant. A textual analysis of 2016–17 Yelp reviews for the top twenty Mexican restaurants in New York City revealed that commenters considered cheap prices, dirty floors, plastic chairs, and Latinx customers eating within to vouch for a Mexican "authenticity" they imagine exists.[80] For more recent years, data mining of Google reviews would perhaps show the same. As scholars across many disciplines have agreed, there is really no stable or monolithic authenticity when it comes to food. "Authenticity is historically contingent and constantly defined and redefined," historian Monica Perales states.[81] Cuisine is constantly being altered depending on geographies of access to ingredients, technology, and transport. Additionally, what is deemed authentic can change across regions, generations, and time.

Yet powerful tropes about authenticity have made it incredibly difficult for Latinx restaurateurs to charge higher prices to cover their ingredients and labor.

Many consumers might be unintentionally freezing Mexican food in a "traditional" state of being, produced in a climate of humility or poverty. This can lead to, as Perales puts it, "these ideas [fusing] onto the people."[82] Thus, owners and workers become frozen as ever–working class and encounter pushback if they charge prices that allow them to be financially comfortable and their businesses profitable. This pushback is even stronger for undocumented immigrants trying to operate their own businesses. Meanwhile, elevated Latin American cuisine can exist unquestioned in the hands of white chefs who rarely have to qualify their decisions to charge a certain price. Indeed, some white chefs have earned authority and renown by crafting their image as "discoverers," "translators," and "experts" of a particular cuisine for a fine dining experience. And even if they decide to make street food, historian Mark Padoongpatt explains, "their whiteness 'elevates' cuisines and makes them fashionable, trendy, and award winning."[83] In 2011, the same year that Zarela closed, the *New York Times* profiled Alex Stupak and his "brave new Mexican restaurant" Empellón more than once. A pastry chef with no experience in cooking Mexican food, Stupak joked, "I guess you could say I have no business opening a Mexican restaurant." He then told the *New York Times*, "I like that [Mexican food's] an underdog. I like that it's undervalued." His menu items, which included scallop-cauliflower tacos, attempted to disabuse diners of their assumptions about Mexican cuisine, but he did not make a similar statement about the respect that Mexican food *laborers* deserved from the public.[84]

Over the last decade, some high-end chefs and restaurateurs from Mexico have gained fame in the United States. Enrique Olvera, the owner of Mexico City's restaurant Pujol, opened Cosme in New York City. Daniela Soto-Innes, who previously served under Olvera as a pastry chef at Cosme, was the youngest person to be named "World's Best Female Chef" at under thirty years old. In Chicago, Carlos Gaytán was the first Mexican American chef to win a Michelin star. Meanwhile, worker-owned restaurants like Cosecha in Oakland or South Philly Barbacoa in Philadelphia have gained cult followings via social media.[85] While buzz around Mexican cuisine may not seem like anything new anymore, the longer history of when and how Latinx chefs and restaurant owners earned recognition in the United States remains spotty. Zarela Martínez is an example of an important figure in food and business history who helped raise New Yorkers' consciousness about Mexican regional cuisine. She pushed back against the idea that "authentic" Mexican food should be cheap, fast, and free-flowing with complimentary guacamole, chips, and salsa. Over the course of the late twentieth and twenty-first centuries, Martínez and other food entrepreneurs created "multiple Mexicos" that people could ingest on a regular basis in New York and elsewhere.

While a particular echelon of Latinx chefs and food celebrities achieved commercial success, there was still vast and invisible labor being performed by US Latinx, Latin American, and Caribbean food workers across the nation. During the late twentieth century, this became increasingly noticeable in states and regions where residents did not expect large contingents of newcomers to arrive. The next chapter moves to Maine to explore what happened when Latinx food worker populations tried to stop being "temporary" people passing through for harvest seasons, and instead make more permanent, year-round lives for themselves in the far Northeast.

CHAPTER FOUR

Not Everybody's Vacationland

The Lives of Latinx Food Workers in Maine

D riving across the state of Maine, one cannot miss the highway signs and license plates with the slogans "Vacationland" and "The Way Life Should Be." During summers full of sun and sparkling blue water, hikers take on the mountains of Acadia National Park and tourists pack coastal cities like Portland and Rockland to eat lobster rolls and wild blueberry pie. During the fall and winter, foliage tours sell out and people bring the intoxicating smell of pine into their homes with Christmas wreaths and table centerpieces tied up with flannel bows. Things like seafood, blueberries, and wreaths are the products of multitudes of laborers who not only live and work year-round in Maine, but who migrate from places as varied as Mexico, Nova Scotia, Honduras, and Haiti.

Many might not know about this multicultural Maine because, demographically, Maine remains the whitest state in the nation. In 2001 the *Bangor Daily News* ran an article titled "Maine 97% White, Least Diverse in Nation." In 2010, 95.2 percent of the state's inhabitants identified as white, and in 2020, 90.8 percent did.[1] In the popular imagination, work in Maine is performed by hardy, white locals whose families have lived in the state for generations. Yet Maine has, for many centuries, absorbed a variety of migrants. After its initial population by the Wabanaki and then its founding by Anglo-Americans in 1786, the city of Portland participated in the West India trade. Ships full of lumber, bricks, salted fish, and ice sailed from Maine to the Caribbean islands and returned with sugar, molasses, and rum. Wealthy Cubans sent their children to study in Maine or moved there together as families. Some Maine towns even changed their names to honor Latin American countries and their independence struggles from European empires. Holmanstown changed its name to Mexico in 1818, and Partridgetown became Peru in 1821. The federal census recorded twenty-five people from Mexico, Cuba, and South America living in Maine in 1860, and a "Sociedad Litteraria Espanola" was founded in Portland by 1881.[2]

During the twentieth century, Maine's agricultural, seafood, and forestry workforces were all augmented by African American migrant labor from the US South, Mi'kmaq and Passamaquoddy tribal members, and French Canadians. More Cubans came to the state either as middle-class exiles from the Castro regime or as airlifted Pedro Pan children during the 1960s, and refugees from Afghanistan, Vietnam, Peru, and Czechoslovakia arrived in the 1970s. During that same decade, Maine began importing Jamaican guestworkers to fill a labor void in its apple industry, and over the next twenty years other workers who traveled "the Eastern stream" of migratory agricultural labor began coming to Maine for work. Usually starting in Florida in the late winter to pick citrus, tomatoes, and bell peppers, these Eastern Streamers move up to Georgia to pick peaches; North and South Carolina to pick tobacco; New Jersey for high-bush blueberries; and then Maine for apples, broccoli, and wild blueberries at the end of summer. During the fall and winter months they can either choose to stay in Maine to work in the egg, forestry, and seafood industries, or move back down to Rhode Island to work in cranberry bogs, New York to pick apples, or Virginia and North Carolina to harvest Christmas trees.[3] By the 1990s more Mexican American and Puerto Rican citizens, as well as Mexican- and Central American–born migrants, joined the Eastern Stream and Maine's mix of seasonal workers. The range of immigration statuses in Maine—citizen, legally contracted guestworker, and undocumented—shows how even the far Northeast emulates the rest of the nation in its food worker demographic. More refugees from Africa (coming from Congo, Ethiopia, Somalia, Sudan, and other countries) arrived in Maine during the 1990s. By 1997 Maine claimed 1,244,048 residents, with 27,962 of them being people of color (8,283 Asian, 5,643 Black, 5,503 Native, and 8,533 Hispanic). And in 2008, according to the Maine Department of Education, eighty-six languages other than English were being spoken in the homes of Maine students.[4]

This chapter sketches out Latinx food workers' experiences in multiple Maine industries over a calendar year—eggs (year-round), blueberries (summer), apples, broccoli, and potatoes (autumn), and sea cucumbers (winter)—to illustrate several points. First, Latinx food labor in Maine—as in other northeastern states—is often invisible by design. Workers are hidden from view as they care for egg-laying chickens in barns, rake in vast blueberry barrens, process potatoes in warehouses, or process seafood in cold factories near the water. The infamous DeCoster Egg Company, for example, abused its migrant employees for decades and left consumer illness, worker injury, and death in its wake. Much like the chickens they tended, DeCoster workers felt trapped in hazardous and substandard conditions. As well as being tucked away in a laboring sense, Latinx communities' invisibility in Maine is compounded by the imagined absence of Latinx people living this far North.

The second point this chapter makes is that Latinx labor in the food chain has replenished, and at times completely saved, economies that maintain Maine's touristic image and income. Outside of Portland and wealthier coastal communities, the landscape of the rest of the state is remote, rural, and lonely. Latinx and Caribbean workers have filled in numerous labor gaps in this terrain over the past five decades. In stark contrast to the thoughtless phrase "unskilled labor," these migratory workers come with a high degree of skill, nimbleness, and resilience that they use to move between different seasonal jobs and employers. It is nothing less than athletic. Migrant workers expend an immense amount of physical, financial, and emotional resources as they try to make a year-round living. In addition to separating from home and family for unanticipated amounts of time, many migrants go into debt obtaining guestworker visas and plane tickets, or paying smugglers, to get to the United States. If recruited by US labor contractors, they become trapped in cycles of debt to these brokers, who promise high wages only to surprise them with low piece rates, isolated and substandard housing, unsafe transportation to and from work sites, and deductions of countless things like blankets, tools, and food from their paychecks. Socially, migrant workers experience discrimination and segregation from local residents, and long distances prevent them from easily reaching resources like medical care and legal aid. In the blueberry industry in particular, Latin American and Caribbean communities have participated in a combination of lawsuits, strikes, and community-building efforts to improve their working conditions.

Finally, as more Latinx people have decided to try living permanently in Maine, this has been met with surprise and sometimes hostility among locals. This phenomenon was part of a national trend in the late twentieth century. During the 1980s and 1990s, Latinx populations (both citizen and migrant) boomed in "non-gateway" states away from the US-Mexico border. For example, the Latinx population of Wisconsin grew by 400 percent, Utah by 645 percent, Alaska by 1,000 percent; and in North Carolina, Tennessee, and Alabama by 1,800 percent. The 2000 census of the six New England states counted 871,000 Latinx people, a 60 percent increase between 1990 and 2000. There were 427,340 in Massachusetts, 318,947 in Connecticut, 90,452 in Rhode Island, 19,910 in New Hampshire, 9,226 in Maine, and 5,316 in Vermont.[5] When a new wave of Latin American migrants arrived in Downeast Maine in the 1990s and took jobs in sea cucumber processing and wreathmaking, they faced racism and economic resentment. In response to this rejection, Latinx people tried to build networks and create spaces where they could feel a sense of community. These spaces—which often involved food and ranged from mobile food trucks to bodegas to restaurants—also happened to draw in Mainers hungry for culinary diversity despite their wariness about ethnic diversity.

What ties together many Maine industries is that they have been boosted by flexible Latinx and Caribbean laborers who have been willing to stay year-round and stitch together different seasonal jobs, or return at the same time every year. When it comes to commodities like eggs, blueberries, potatoes, and seafood that are shipped beyond Maine to other parts of the United States and world, these workers prove their value to state food systems as well as to regional, national, and global ones. Labor and immigrant advocates in Maine have tried their best to claim rights for these underappreciated workers. Getting workers politicized and mobilized, however, is a tall order. Understandably, migrants have reservations or a lack of enthusiasm about participating in labor strikes or legal battles. If strikes or court cases take too long to ripen and bear fruit, workers have little choice but to move on to other jobs or states to maintain a livelihood. For this reason, the rare moments of victory in which workers not only change conditions for future waves of workers but also are able to stay and claim Maine as their home too, are truly significant. Positioned at the far reaches of the Northeast, Maine is a US-Canadian borderland that is often storied to be a white space. In reality, it has been home for contingents of US-born Latinx, Latin American, and Caribbean people who have pushed back against being treated as temporary.

The Egg before the Worker:
Year-round Injustices at DeCoster Farms

One of Maine's most notorious and lawbreaking businessmen is Austin "Jack" DeCoster, who grew up in Turner, Maine, and began his chicken and egg business in 1949 at the age of sixteen. His early start was due to a family tragedy—his father, a logger, collapsed and died suddenly in front of him as the two were returning from a day of work. To help his mother and siblings make ends meet, Jack took responsibility for the 125 hens on his family's farm, and within a year had grown the flock to more than 1,000 birds. He founded the company Quality Egg in 1961 and by 1973 had 350 employees and chickens laying 1 million eggs per day. Named "the undisputed egg king of New England" and "one of the largest egg producers in the world," with annual sales exceeding $35 million, DeCoster ingratiated himself with Turner authorities by building a Baptist church, fire station, and two baseball fields; donating eggs to church and community events; and paying a vital amount of taxes.[6]

When it came to his own employees, however, DeCoster skimped as much as

he could. In 1975 he employed nineteen young male Vietnamese refugees resettled from New York, housed them in three trailers, and paid them about two dollars an hour for work in the chicken barns and egg facilities. It was not long before the men began complaining about high paycheck deductions for things like
bedding, furnishings, and heating oil that they were rarely able to access. They
sought help from the legal aid organization Pine Tree Legal Assistance (PTLA),
founded in 1966 with Office of Economic Opportunity funding, to fight for
a cash settlement. The next year, the Maine State Legislature mandated that
DeCoster (and any other farm with more than 300,000 birds) had to pay every
worker a minimum wage. DeCoster immediately began to look for additional
property in other states, a sure sign he was not willing to comply. In the late 1970s
when his Maine workers tried to unionize and walk off their jobs, DeCoster fired
all of them (a judge later ordered him to restore their positions). He was also notorious for hiring children as young as nine to perform jobs involving hazardous
machinery, and subsequent injuries of teenagers at his farm prompted Maine
lawmakers to ban such employment. In 1980 the US Department of Labor filed
a civil action suit against DeCoster for violating several provisions of the Fair
Labor Standards Act, forcing DeCoster to pay workers $200,000 in back wages
in February 1985.[7]

Despite these numerous cases and punishments, DeCoster kept neglecting
the beings that helped create his fortune, whether they were human or animal.
In February 1987 a henhouse fire killed 100,000 of his birds and, instead of
promptly burying them, DeCoster left their dead bodies in the open air so long
that his neighbors filed a lawsuit. These unsanitary conditions extended to his
egg consumers as well. In June 1988 New York State embargoed DeCoster eggs
after three salmonella outbreaks were traced to his companies. During one of
these outbreaks, 500 New Yorkers were hospitalized and 11 died. Then, at the
beginning of 1992, DeCoster paid a $165,000 fine for violating several waste, air,
and water control laws. These multiple lawsuits and fines did not stop DeCoster
from becoming the nation's largest brown egg producer by 1992 and establishing egg and hog farms in Maine, Iowa, Ohio, and Minnesota. He also sold his
eggs abroad, sending millions to Hong Kong's "wet markets" from the docks of
Portland.[8]

Today, if one drives down Plains Road, which bisects the old DeCoster
chicken barns and egg-processing complexes (now owned and operated by another company), one can sense how huge DeCoster's operations were in the late
1980s and early 1990s. Imposing 700-foot-long buildings are interspersed with
smaller ones, and large silver funnels of chicken feed punctuate the landscape.
Donald Hoenig, who served as a field veterinarian for the Maine Department of

Agriculture from 1986 to the early 1990s, and then as Maine's state veterinarian from 1995 to 2012, recalled that DeCoster's chicken barns contained cages four or five tiers high, and the chickens were confined their entire lives to less than eighty square inches of space. They had no place to perch or scratch, and the eggs they laid immediately rolled down onto a conveyor belt to processing workers who washed, candled, and packed the eggs into cartons and boxes. DeCoster often stuffed many more chickens to a cage than the limit mandated by the Department of Agriculture, which resulted in the chickens' emotional distress, fighting, and unsanitary living conditions. A Guatemalan worker tasked with cleaning out dead chickens daily from the cages revealed to PTLA that DeCoster would then sell the tortured carcasses to the Campbell Soup Company.[9]

DeCoster treated his workers almost exactly as his chickens. In addition to hiring local white residents from Turner and a small number of Vietnamese workers, DeCoster employed non-English-speaking Czech and Latin American immigrant workers who were desperate for jobs and feared deportation. By the late 1980s, one-third of DeCoster's workforce was Latinx. They had been lured from Mexico, Central America, and states like California, Texas, and Florida with radio advertisements promising $500 or more a week and comfortable housing. In South Texas, which suffered one of highest unemployment rates in the country at 15 to 19 percent, DeCoster labor contractor Homero Ramirez offered Mexican American and Mexican recruits a minimum wage of four dollars an hour, a promise of a twenty-five-cent raise every six months, and free housing. The trip from the Texas-Mexico borderlands to Maine, as one young Mexican couple who worked at DeCoster Farms described it, was "almost three days, around 2,800 or 2,900 miles." After this arduous journey, workers were met with disillusioning conditions. Like the chickens they oversaw, workers were cramped into decrepit dwellings by the dozen without space, clean air, or privacy. Workers complained that DeCoster management sometimes placed several Mexican families into one trailer while giving white families their own dwellings. Trailers often lacked potable running water, electricity, heat, stoves, and proper winter insulation, and were infested with raw sewage, rats, and roaches.[10]

In an echo of the circumstances that led to New Jersey's *State v. Shack*, DeCoster's workers were hidden from visitors and public view. DeCoster posted a "No Admittance" sign at the entrance to the employee trailer park to prevent lawyers, social workers, health specialists, labor organizers, and teachers from visiting his employees. He also prevented workers from engaging in religious worship if priests wanted to come minister to workers in their camps. DeCoster argued he was entitled to sequester his workers because they did not pay rent or utilities and thus did not have tenants' rights to visitors. DeCoster made an exception to his no-visitors rule when IRCA passed in 1986 and he wanted law-yers to help legalize his undocumented employees.[11] Another likely reason for DeCoster's hostility to visitors was his fear of being raided by immigration au-thorities. In 1987 the Border Patrol and the Immigration and Naturalization Service (INS) arrested nine Mexican and Guatemalan workers at his farm and fined DeCoster $32,850 for a lack of paperwork. Then in mid-May 1992, more than a dozen federal agents raided the farm and arrested seventeen more Mexi-can workers. Farm manager and labor recruiter Homero Ramirez was charged alongside the DeCoster Company for harboring "illegal aliens" and served ten months in federal prison.[12] In May 1992, PTLA decided to bring a lawsuit against DeCoster's sequestering of workers. The case rose to Maine's supreme court, which ruled in January 1995 that visitors' access to farm tenants was guar-anteed by state law.[13]

As a result of this ruling, legal teams were able to interview DeCoster employ-ees and file several complaints and compensation claims against the company. These filings, in addition to a powerful 1995 exposé of DeCoster's health and safety violations by a local newspaper, compelled the US Occupational Safety and Health Administration (OSHA) to begin a thorough investigation of the company in 1996. OSHA representatives asked a man named José Soto to serve as a volunteer interpreter for DeCoster's Spanish-speaking workers. Born in Puerto Rico, Soto had worked as a police officer in Atlantic City and then lived in New Hampshire, where he worked at a wool mill and volunteered at Manchester's Latin American Center before he and his family moved to Maine in 1984. Soto surely witnessed many disturbing things during this OSHA in-vestigation, because in early 1996 the administration's final report counted 1,161 violations of workers' health and safety and fined DeCoster $3.8 million, one of the highest fines it ever issued.[14] These violations included "unguarded machines" and exposed live electrical parts; worker overexposure to noise, contaminated air, chicken manure, pesticides, and other toxins; a lack of protective equipment and clean water in the factory; and substandard employee trailer housing. In a settlement with OSHA, DeCoster agreed to pay $2 million of the original fine in exchange for a surprise inspection within a year. If he scored more than ninety abatement points on that inspection, he would not have to pay the remainder.[15]

News of the OSHA settlement provoked public outcry and led three large grocery store chains in Maine and Massachusetts—Shaw's, Shop 'n Save, and Stop & Shop—to initiate a boycott against DeCoster eggs in the summer of 1996. Soon after, the grocery store Hannaford declared it would also stop buying DeCoster eggs.[16] Unlike the United Farm Workers' boycotts of previous decades, these boycotts were consumer-initiated rather than union-created. According to an opinion poll at the time, 78.6 percent of people surveyed supported the DeCoster boycott, and 92 percent had an unfavorable view of the company. The federal government, however, did not bat an eye while giving DeCoster more than $14.3 million in subsidies in 1996, which helped him to sell his eggs to buyers in Saudi Arabia and elsewhere in the world, often repackaging them under different names.[17]

DeCoster continued to look for other loopholes. To rid himself of his 368 OSHA housing violations, he began moving employees out of his trailer park into dilapidated apartments in the nearby town of Lewiston. This town was already absorbing an African refugee population from Somalia and Sudan, and Latinx egg workers found themselves in a place where white locals were expressing unhappiness about influxes of foreign newcomers. Though DeCoster workers were promised free housing when they were recruited, they were now expected to pay rent for apartments that were barely furnished with few functioning utilities. Additionally, DeCoster maneuvered to make it virtually impossible for his workers to bring legal cases against him or to unionize. Though the Migrant and Seasonal Agricultural Worker Protection Act (AWPA) existed in federal legislation to enforce minimum housing, safety, wage dispensation, and transportation standards for migrant workers, DeCoster characterized his business as a "year-round" operation so that his workers and their advocates could not invoke it. In 1997, when Maine passed a law permitting workers at large-scale agribusinesses (with more than 100 employees) to unionize, DeCoster immediately split his company into eight smaller companies, leaving only two of them large enough to be eligible for unionization.[18]

In response, the United Paperworkers International Union (UPIU) began conducting membership drives at those two companies. The UPIU campaigns were a unique moment in which Chicano activists from the US Southwest tried to help Maine workers with their labor struggles. Ruben Solis, an organizer for the Southwest Workers Union out of San Antonio, flew to Maine and spoke at a solidarity rally for DeCoster workers. "Everybody's watching what's happening here," Solis said to the forty attendees and the media. "Maine is on the cutting edge of addressing the exploitation of workers in the poultry industry."[19] By this time, several Mexican and Central American migrants were working for poultry companies in the Carolinas and other mid-Atlantic states, as well as in the Northeast. Not long before the UPIU union drives in Maine, the INS had arrested fourteen undocumented migrants at Poultry Products Inc. in Manchester, New Hampshire, and estimated that over 1,000 undocumented migrants from Mexico, Canada, Guatemala, Honduras, and Brazil lived in New Hampshire, in addition to tens of thousands of US Latinx residents.[20]

Meanwhile, surely influenced by the worker mistreatment he witnessed during DeCoster's OSHA investigation, José Soto founded the nonprofit Maine Rural Workers Coalition (MRWC) in 1998 with DeCoster workers and community volunteers. Its membership consisted of Chicano, Latin American, and Caribbean agricultural workers from places as varied as Texas, California, Mexico, Guatemala, Honduras, El Salvador, Colombia, Puerto Rico, and Jamaica. Local community members and area college students joined as well. Initially sponsored by grants from the Catholic Campaign for Human Development and the National Council of La Raza, the MRWC tried to educate DeCoster workers about their labor rights and available community resources. The organization fielded daily requests for assistance with English translation, finding doctors and health care, negotiating with landlords, acquiring workers' compensation and food stamps, and navigating the court system. The MRWC also conducted private meetings with Latinx DeCoster employees at their trailer park to hear their grievances about low pay and DeCoster's expectation that they keep working through illness or injury.[21] In May 1999 the MRWC welcomed Farm Labor Organizing Committee (FLOC) leader Baldemar Velásquez for a visit. Velásquez had organized thousands of migrant farmworkers in Ohio and Michigan, and was eager to persuade DeCoster employees to unionize.[22] In the end, after eight months of organizing efforts, workers at the two DeCoster spinoff companies voted 52–21 against union representation, but multiple employees later reported that DeCoster supervisors had shown them anti-union videos and threatened them with termination if they voted for the union.[23] The United Paperworkers brought an NLRB complaint against DeCoster, but he responded that his workers were agricultural workers who did not have the federal right to collectively bargain in the first place.

After this attempt at unionization, DeCoster made cosmetic changes in hopes his workers would quiet down. He bought them new trailer homes complete with wallpaper, tile floors, and new furniture. Additionally, he changed just enough—turned on fans, installed some showers, and placed bilingual signs around the farm—to earn enough points at his OSHA abatement inspection in the spring of 1998 to meet his legal settlement's requirements.[24] Moreover, by splitting his one large company into six smaller ones, record-keeping about injuries got diffused and his numbers did not look so damning. A group of angered employees responded by revealing details about their work hazards at a press conference in June 1998, at which an OSHA representative was present. Many of them affirmed that "[DeCoster] treats us like animals" and gave testimony about fainting in barns from overexposure to ammonia and other chemicals, and being denied medical attention for serious injuries. In one horrific case, Puerto

Rican worker Carlos Cordova lost several fingers in an accident at the plant, and instead of packing the severed fingers on ice so they could be reattached at a hospital, a supervisor tossed them into a trash can filled with chicken manure. It took half an hour for someone to call an ambulance.[25]

Meanwhile, the lawsuits against DeCoster continued. A major one—brought by three plaintiffs on behalf of about 3,000 employees—concerned overtime pay. Plaintiffs contended that they worked up to sixty hours a week as mechanics, cleaners, egg candlers, and packers at DeCoster without extra pay. In response, the company's lawyer argued that state overtime laws did not apply to agricultural workers. Superior Court Justice Nancy Mills ultimately ruled that workers employed by DeCoster from November 1991 to 1997 (some of whom were his own relatives) were eligible for compensation ranging from a few hundred dollars to $60,000 each. A law firm worked aggressively to find former DeCoster employees scattered across multiple states and countries. It contacted the departments of labor in each state, took out television and newspaper ads, and enlisted the help of the Mexican government and twenty community volunteers who phone-banked twice a week for two months. Many of DeCoster's former employees were found in Mexico and Texas, while some were in Europe. By late May 1999, 1,275 past and present DeCoster workers had filed overtime pay claims and a total of $5 million in backpay was distributed.[26]

The second major lawsuit came from a surprising source to the south. Through its consul in Boston, the Mexican government had become aware of the mistreatment occurring at DeCoster. It sent a vice-consul and investigator to the farm and subsequently filed a class action suit with fourteen employees against DeCoster and his companies. A national government had not become involved in agricultural labor this way since the Bracero and Migration Division program eras, but Mexican Embassy officials declared that Mexico had a legal right to protect its citizens in a foreign country.[27] This landmark suit, filed in the US District Court of Portland, claimed racial discrimination against Mexican-origin workers and contended they were subjected to worse housing and working conditions than white employees and less medical care and workers' compensation. In March 2000 Portland federal judge D. Brock Hornby dismissed the Mexican government as a plaintiff and ruled that each individual worker had to prove that they were the victim of discrimination. DeCoster eventually settled the suit in March 2004 and paid $3.2 million divided among almost 700 claimants.[28] The Mexican consulate in Boston was likely inspired by this case to pay more attention to Mexican Mainers, because in April 2004 it organized a "Consulado Móvil" (Mobile Consulate) in Turner to provide support and services. DeCoster proceeded to pay other OSHA fines and settled multiple back wage and overtime lawsuits over the course of the early 2000s. It was simultaneously clear and baffling that DeCoster preferred to pay legal fees, fines, and settlements rather than pay his workers fairly from the start. Yet by settling so many cases before they went to trial, he kept his lawbreaking less visible to the public. In the end, there could have been many more eligible recipients of DeCoster settlement money, but many workers' migratory lifestyle prevented them from being notified of their compensation.[29] In 2017 DeCoster and his son Peter were each sentenced to three months in prison—not for any labor-related offenses but for their responsibility in a 2010 salmonella outbreak that made thousands of people ill. While consumer suffering was very visible in this sentencing, worker suffering remained unseen. The elder DeCoster is out of prison and rumored to still have a heavy hand in the egg industry, even though he has legally turned over the ownership of his plants to other companies.

Though the MRWC viewed the DeCoster settlements as victories and helped many people claim their overdue earnings, its leaders lamented the migratory nature of its membership. Farmworkers were constantly joining and leaving the organization, neglecting to pay their dues, or using the MRWC to file their settlement claims but not joining the coalition after it helped them. Though the organization made a genuine effort to have migrant farmworkers serve as active leaders, the inescapable reality was that these workers would have had to stop being the kind of migrants they were. Crises in Latin America also took up their mental and emotional energy. In November 1998, for instance, many workers were absent from an MRWC meeting because Hurricane Mitch—which had devastated Central America the week before—had left them grieving for the dead or struggling to find out what happened to family and friends.[30]

Amid frustration about the itinerancy of its membership, the MRWC tried to create spaces of belonging and community. According to the *Maine Times*, the state's Latinx population had increased to 8,700 people.[31] In the summer of 2001, José Soto opened a small Hispanic goods market called Bodega de Coquí near the MRWC office in downtown Lewiston. The bodega sold Goya products, masa for arepas, *aguas refrescas*, tropical produce like mangos, avocados, and plantains, and a small selection of Central and South American beers. The 1,200 Latino families who lived in Lewiston at the time were thrilled about the food selection, as well as their ability to make phone calls and send emails and money orders to Latin America. Bodega de Coquí became a beloved hangout for Latinos, Jamaicans, and other people of color.[32] Meanwhile, in Portland, other cultural brokers emerged. Dominican migrant Juan González opened La Bodega Latina, which became a social hub for Latinos and African migrants.[33] Cuban native Armando Vives, who had moved to Maine in 1970, operated a shoeshine and cobbler stand

and helped new Mainers navigate negotiations with landlords, acquire federal food aid, and other facets of daily life. In 1997 Dominican artist Rafael Clariot and others founded the Portland-based Latin Community Council of Maine, which offered English translation services and health care education.[34] Other organizations of the late 1990s included the Agrupación de Defensores de Obreros Migratorios (Association of Defenders of Migrant Laborers) and the Network Hispanos de Maine. The MRWC officially disbanded in 2005 due to a lack of consistent funding and interpersonal conflict. If it had lived longer the organization would have surely mobilized workers in other industries, including timber, seafood, and blueberries.

Summer Blues

High-bush blueberries are the ones most abundant in our supermarkets. They can thrive easily in multiple states, and grow on bushes that are four to eight feet tall. Wild low-bush blueberries from Maine, in contrast, have a distinct and bright flavor and grow low to the ground, often on top of a glacial rock layer. The wild blueberry season begins in late July or early August and lasts two to four weeks, depending on how fruitful the harvest is. Wild blueberry raking is one of the most physically painful forms of agricultural work, as it requires harvesters to bend at an uncomfortable angle with a short-handled rake. Shaped like a dustpan with tines, the rake needs to be pulled quickly and repeatedly to collect enough berries for a twenty-three-pound box. Motivated by a piece rate per box, workers move up and down huge blueberry barrens that can cover hundreds of square miles. It takes a seasoned worker about ten minutes to fill one box. Over the decades, Maine has come to produce millions of pounds of berries per year, but wages for the state's wild blueberry workers have stayed disturbingly static at $2.25 to $3.00 per box.[35]

Wild blueberry raking in Maine was previously performed by a blend of local white residents; Mi'kmaq, Penobscot, and Passamaquoddy Indians from Maine and Canada; and Nova Scotians. These groups came to work for Wyman's and Cherryfield Food, the two largest harvesting companies in the state since the nineteenth century. Seasonal workers viewed this summer money as supplemental income to pay for school supplies, toys, and household expenses, and often brought their children to work with them.[36] During the 1970s, however, the living and working conditions of these workers began concerning some state authorities. In August 1974 Maine's Human Rights Commission spent a week investigating Mi'kmaq and French Canadian workers' temporary housing in the blueberry barrens. Head investigator Terry Lunt-Coin ultimately declared to the media that blueberry workers' conditions were "an abomination and an affront to even the most minimal standards of human dignity." The commission's report detailed labor camps without bathing facilities and flush toilets, and an absence of drinking water for workers in the fields. Wyman's owner responded, "The workers don't complain," but blueberry workers were not as satisfied as their bosses liked to imagine. A few years later in 1978, a protest erupted when Wyman's began using larger boxes but did not raise workers' piece rate per container. Indigenous Canadians and Mainers ended up forming the first picket line the company had seen in its 100-year history. Just as it had done for DeCoster's egg workers, Pine Tree Legal Assistance came to blueberry workers' aid and joined a Maine Civil Liberties Union lawsuit claiming interference with workers' right to associate and negotiate. The company eventually provided $100 back pay for each day the pickets had missed work, and went back to its smaller boxes the following year. Through the 1980s, the wild blueberry harvest drew new seasonal workers—from retirees to teenagers, to unemployed Pittsburgh steel workers, to oil workers from Louisiana. Yet because housing had not improved much in a decade, workers would sometimes set up their own tents, or sleep in their cars.[37]

Around 1990, Maine's blueberry workforce became more Mexican and Central American. Much like DeCoster's labor recruitment, blueberry companies targeted Mexicans and Mexican Americans living in impoverished South Texas border towns like McAllen and Weslaco and promised them $600 per week. Problems immediately arose. In August 1990 a group of South Texas workers decided to leave Allen's Blueberry Freezer Company when they observed that Tejanos were being assigned to less productive rows in the barrens and being given fewer hours than they were promised. "We came here because men told us we were going to make a lot of money. That's baloney," said worker José Padilla, who had come from the border town of Eagle Pass, Texas. Another caravan of Mexican and Texan workers from Eagle Pass who worked the 1991 season decided to file two lawsuits in the US District Court in Bangor in 1993 against the Maine Wild Blueberry Company of Machias and its labor contractors for misleading them about wages, working conditions, and housing. Contractors had told these workers they would be picking berries off of "high bushes" for $100 a day when workers actually had to pay more than $21 a day for transportation to and from their stoop labor in the blueberry fields. They also lived in "unsafe, unsanitary, overcrowded" housing that lacked enough beds, hot water, and kitchen facilities. The eight plaintiffs sought $500 for each violation of the Seasonal and Agricultural Worker Protection Act, as well as their unpaid wages and legal costs.[38] Despite these legal actions taken by their compañeros, US-born Latinos and Latin American migrants kept coming to Maine's blueberry barrens in hopes they could make a large sum of money in a short period of time. They wanted to believe accounts from people like José Ignacio Guijón, a twenty-seven-year-old Mexican working in Maine with his four brothers, who told the *Bangor Daily News* that he made as much as $1,700 a week. Jasper Wyman & Son reported that even though Mainers and First Nations from Nova Scotia and New Brunswick continued to account for the bulk of their rakers, the number of their Mexican migrant employees more than tripled (from 68 to 238) between 1991 and 1994.[39]

Apart from wages and housing, another struggle that blueberry workers faced was the damage wreaked on their bodies by the poor ergonomics of the short-handled rake that they used for blueberry bushes no more than sixteen inches off the ground. Very much like the *cortito* or short-handled hoe used in the Southwest, low-bush blueberry rakes caused chronic and debilitating musculoskeletal injuries of the back, knees, wrists, arms, and shoulders. The Maine Migrant / Mobile Health Unit (MMH), a van operation founded in 1991 that traveled to different migrant camps in the evenings, treated many people with this affliction with medicine and physical therapy. When the unit asked blueberry workers to name their top health priority, the community answered that they wanted a redesign of the rake. Unit site coordinator Blanca Santiago, a Puerto Rican woman who had lived in Maine since 1987, believed other issues such as dehydration and toxic pesticide exposure were more pressing, but she listened to the community's request. Like their counterparts in the egg industry, blueberry workers' bodies were being strained and endangered by their labor, and their cramped housing conditions only worsened their discomfort. Companies seemed to expect workers to accept a future of inevitable disability. MMH took on a four-year project to reduce injury in the raker population and succeeded at getting extensions for blueberry rakes in the early 2000s. It also diagnosed and treated migrant and seasonal farmworkers of all kinds in Maine who suffered from eye conditions, tuberculosis, skin conditions created or aggravated by pesticides, dental problems, hypertension, malnutrition, diabetes, and mental health issues originating in Maine or by witnessing violence in their home countries.[40]

Much like DeCoster workers, Latinx blueberry workers quickly found out they were expected to remain invisible lest they be surveilled, ostracized, and criminalized. Adrián Bravo Chávez, an undocumented migrant who traveled the Eastern Stream from Georgia to North Carolina and up to Maine, remembered that white locals would promptly call immigration authorities on him and other Latinos under the assumption that they were "illegal aliens." After one incident in which locals chased him and some coworkers out of an abandoned trailer where they were sleeping, Chávez and his friends resigned themselves to living in the woods in plastic tents and under tarps. After long days of picking blueberries, they tried to swim at local beaches, only to have white beachgoers stare, yell at them to get out of the water, or run over to chase them out. Having migrated from one country to another, and then one state to another, these workers still felt hounded in Maine and never able to rest. "Immigration [officials] . . . were behind us, nonstop," Chávez said. Indeed, the US Border Patrol conducted frequent sweeps in blueberry barrens. It apprehended and deported eighty Mexican and Central American berry rakers in the 1992 season; forty Mexican migrant berry rakers during the 1993 harvest; forty-nine in 1995; twenty-nine in 1996; twenty-one in 1997; and at least sixty-eight in 1999.[41] In a letter to the editor of the *Bangor Daily News*, Mainers Karen and Michael Foley expressed what other locals felt about Latino migrant workers but acknowledged that Wyman's and other companies were to blame for the tension: "There are many Mainers who are working in the blueberry field side by side with these migrants who are not at all happy with them being there. In a state where unemployment is out of control . . . we need all the jobs we can get. . . . Obviously, this is why Jasper Wyman and Sons is so happy to see migrant workers. . . . Without them, the growers would have been forced to pay decent wages to Maine people."[42]

In 1998, however, in a noteworthy moment of multicultural labor mobilization, more than 700 employees (Latinx, Native American, white Mainer, and Nova Scotian) staged a strike at their labor camp against Wyman. About 500 workers lived at the company's small blue cabins in the town of Deblois, while 200 others lived offsite. One morning in mid-August, workers refused to enter the barrens and told their foremen they needed higher pay because the crop yield was so bad (high temperatures had caused berries to burn, shrivel, and fall off the bushes). They also demanded functioning toilets at their camp. Later that morning, several workers at the blueberry-freezing factory in Deblois walked off their jobs too. In a matter of hours, the Wyman company agreed to increase rakers' pay from $2.25 to $2.75 per twenty-two-pound box after meeting with raker representatives and Juan Perez-Febles, the Cuban-born director of the Maine Department of Labor's Migrant and Immigrant Services Division. Donato de Santiago of Mexico, the representative for the Spanish-speaking worker contingent, expressed his gratitude for how "both the Native Americans and other American rakers joined with their Hispanic co-workers" to create a successful outcome.[43]

In an echo of Mexican and Boricua braceros' food complaints and demands of the past, blueberry rakers also asked for culturally familiar food near their dwellings. The Wyman company accommodated this demand by allowing Latina food vendors to set up at workers' campgrounds. Tomasa Flores was one of the earliest food vendors who served blueberry rakers. She sold salsa, gorditas, *sopa de mariscos* (seafood soup), and rice and beans.[44] Another popular food business was run by Romana Vásquez, who had worked in the food industry in Guanajuato, Mexico. She moved with her children to the United States in the 1990s to join her husband Gosafat, who had been working as a migratory worker in multiple crops and states. In 1998 a friend urged the Vásquezes to move to the small town of Milbridge, Maine, to work in the blueberry and sea cucumber industries. Over the next few years, Romana and Gosafat came to see Maine as a safer and more tranquil place to raise their children. Noticing a lack of Mexican food available to residents, Romana began selling her home-cooked food out of an old bus parked on a back road in Deblois, and moved the vehicle into Wyman's fields during the months of July and August. In 2013 the family bought a dilapidated house on Milbridge's Main Street and renovated it into a restaurant named Vazquez Mexican Takeout (see fig. 4.1). Festooned with multiple American flags and garlands of *papel picado* (decorative Mexican paper), Vasquez's sells tostadas, tamales, burritos, and combination platters along with special weekend items like menudo and American summer standards like burgers, hot dogs, fries, and ice cream. Even on the coldest and wettest of days, local Mainers flock to the restaurant alongside migrant workers. The Vásquezes' children branched out to offer other services to the Milbridge community; one opened an auto shop, another opened a painting business, and another established a daycare.[45]

By the early 2000s, 8,000 to 10,000 Latinx blueberry workers were coming to Maine every summer. "They know if we're going to have a good crop. They're well-informed. They have a network, and I don't know how it works, but it does," Wyman & Son's vice president remarked in 2002. To meet the needs of this seasonal community, enterprising Latinx families opened food trucks, restaurants, and convenience stores that offered money transfer, phone, and mail services to Latin America.[46] Meanwhile, Juan Perez-Febles established a Rakers' Center in the town of Columbia that offered a one-stop shop for blueberry workers to obtain free services such as canned goods and clothes, an education office, legal advice from PTLA, and access to health care. The center is now located in Harrington and continues to be a pop-up resource for the blueberry workers who arrive every summer. In 2004, the Maine Department of Labor estimated, the blueberry workforce in Maine was comprised of 45 percent Latinx, 45 percent Native American, and 10 percent white rakers or processors.[47]

Over time, more Haitian workers have been absorbed into this blueberry labor pie. During the 2010s, a group of them ended up as central plaintiffs in legal cases against Maine blueberry companies. In *Antoine v. Paul*, a lawsuit filed in US District Court in July 2014, the PTLA represented eighteen Haitian blueberry workers against labor recruiter Carol Paul, the Coastal Blueberry and Hancock Foods companies, and several housing providers. The worker-plaintiffs claimed

FIGURE 4.1. Vasquez's Mexican restaurant, Milbridge, Maine. Photo by the author, 2018.

the defendants had underpaid them and provided substandard housing in violation of the Migrant Seasonal Agricultural Worker Protection Act (AWPA). The worst details emerged when workers Solange Estinvil, Dieuseul Francillon, Lenord Damisse, and Henriquez Polycarpe described the "housing" that Paul had given them upon their arrival. Estinvil and Francillon were assigned to two separate trailers. One already had thirty Hancock employees living in it, while the other had eighteen inhabitants but no mattresses or beds. One worker remembered having to sleep on a scrap of carpet in the living area, while other workers slept in the kitchen or hallway. Horrified, Estinvil decided to sleep in a vehicle on the property with three other workers, while Francillon lived in his own vehicle with one other worker. As for Damisse and Polycarpe, Paul "housed" each of them in a vehicle for their first night in Maine. Though the AWPA did not require farm labor contractors of agricultural employers to provide housing to migrant workers, it imposed minimum standards on employers who did. The workers' lawsuit sought $204,969 for statutory damages and lost wages, and an unspecified amount for their "humiliation, inconvenience, physical discomfort, emotional distress and mental suffering." US Chief District Court judge Nancy Torresen found enough evidence of Paul's and the companies' intentionality (and multiple violations of AWPA and OSHA regulations) to determine that all the plaintiffs deserved restitution.[48] Haitians held an interesting place here— through their lawsuit they invoked a long history of African American workers being exploited in Maine, and drew notice to Caribbean migrants becoming a greater share of the state's agricultural workforce.

If one drives by the Wyman workers' camp in Deblois today, one sees rows of freshly painted small blue houses, shaded by tall thin trees (see fig. 4.2). Portable toilets and showers remain in the middle of the campground, laundry hangs from lines or tree branches, and workers simply cross the road to reach the blueberry barrens. A "No Trespassing" sign, however, keeps one from looking inside the bunkhouses to see if their interiors have really changed since the 1970s. Advocacy organizations like PTLA, the Maine Mobile Health Program (MMHP), and Mano en Mano are still making a difference for workers in Maine. MMHP, which serves seasonal and settled workers regardless of immigration status, uses roving medical trucks as miniature doctors' offices. Doctors, nurses, social workers, and community health workers provide primary and acute care in the vans during the daytime and evenings, and can also help workers make appointments with specialists like dentists, eye doctors, and gynecologists. MMHP also offers telehealth appointments with a Haitian Kreyòl–speaking social worker for people who need them. Mano en Mano operates the Blueberry Harvest School, a three-week program serving the children of migrant blueberry workers.[49]

Meanwhile, the wild blueberry industry itself is undergoing transition. Harvest gluts some years have led to berries being frozen and waiting to be sold on the market. That, coupled with some summers of poor yield, has resulted in the price of wild berries dropping drastically. Some growers, foreseeing no profit, have decided to destroy some of their fruit rather than harvest it. Other blueberry companies are experimenting with using machines instead of people to rake berries. A machine can harvest in an hour what fifty people can do in a day, but the glacial rock underneath can pose complications to machines that lack the observation power of eyes and the delicacy of hands. If the blueberry yield continues to be disappointing, employers will cease to hire crews and migrant workers will stop relying on Maine for a summer income. In the summer of 2021, the usually busy hiring day at Wyman's resulted in only recruiting 35 to 40 workers for the season. In past years, between 400 and 500 workers had been needed.[50] Even if

FIGURE 4.2. Wyman's blueberry workers' camp, Deblois, Maine. Photo by the author, 2018.

major blueberry companies decide to eliminate human rakers over time, Latin American, US Latinx, and Caribbean communities will continue to perform the agile patchwork necessary to creating a full year of work in Maine.

Autumn Work

When the blueberry season ends in September, the harvested barrens turn a deep shade of red and workers move on to other places, such as apple orchards in midcoast and western Maine, or broccoli fields and timber forests in far northern Aroostook County. Over the last quarter of the twentieth century, Caribbean workers helped these sectors immensely. In 1975, Maine apple growers imported 211 Jamaican laborers to augment their local Mainer and seasonal Canadian workforce. After a flight to Miami and a thirty-eight-hour bus ride up to Vacationland, the Jamaican workers picked apples seven days a week for nine hours a day. Apple pickers must be prepared to carry, set, and reset forty-pound ladders and descend and hoist thirty-pound buckets of apples. A very experienced picker could average 75 to 120 bushels of apples a day and earn up to $385 per seven-day workweek. Over time, Jamaicans supplanted other workers in the orchards, a phenomenon influenced by the 1986 passage of IRCA. At this time, most Jamaican agricultural workers in the United States were working in the sugar industry, but sugar was deemed a nonagricultural "dessert," making these Jamaican workers ineligible for IRCA legalization. As a result, many turned to other crops like apples in the Northeast. Maine welcomed this new labor force, as very few locals wanted to pick apples and preferred to be crew bosses and tractor drivers instead. In 1990 apple growers in Maine brought more than 600 Jamaicans for the harvest. During the late 1980s and 1990s, Latin American workers arrived in apple work, while contingents of California Filipinos and Tejanos migrated to harvest in the broccoli fields.[51]

As with eggs and blueberries, similar forms of exploitation occurred in autumnal crops. In 1986 PTLA filed a complaint against Caribou broccoli farm owner (and Maine state representative) Forest "Bud" Ayer for having Black and Latinx employees work fifty to sixty hours a week for a take-home wage of ten to twenty dollars after various deductions for things like bedding and laundry, and imbalanced meals of pigs' feet, rice, and bologna. Additionally, Ayer's company housing lacked proper heating and hot water, showers, and toilets.[52] Though organizations like the PTLA have accomplished significant gains in Maine, the US federal government still refuses to establish national protections for agricultural laborers. As long as individual states are left to make their own decisions about workers' rights, piecemeal lawsuits and court cases will take too long to benefit those who have already migrated through those states.

Compounding this problem is employers' increasing reliance—not just in Maine but across the United States—on the H-2 visa program, the longest-running guestworker initiative in the history of North America. Instituted soon after the Bracero Program's end, the H-2 program is a federal guestworker program split into two kinds of visa categories: H-2A for agricultural workers (with no visa cap) and H-2B for nonagricultural workers performing one-time, seasonal, peakload, or intermittent labor (capped at 66,000 per year). The H-2 program has been criticized as a copycat successor to the Bracero Program. Its workers—who are recruited from all over the world and employed in industries including agriculture, forestry, seafood, food service, construction, and hospitality—often do not earn the wages promised to them due to piece rates or wage theft and are bound to one employer for the entirety of their contract. Meanwhile, employers use labor contractors to muddy the waters of their liability. Like the Bracero and Migration Division programs before it, the H-2 program lacks the proper infrastructure and funding to enforce labor and safety regulations. As a result, H-2 guestworkers often experience similar forms of precarity as undocumented laborers and fear speaking out because of blacklisting or deportation. With multiple guestworker streams coming into the United States from places as varied as Eastern Europe, the Caribbean, and Southeast Asia, it is becoming ever more difficult to monitor these worker flows. Similar problems regarding guestworker programs exist along the northern border as well. Some Latin American migrants now bypass the United States altogether and head straight to Canada to work in tomato greenhouses or cherry orchards but encounter similar forms of mistreatment.[53]

Both Maine's potato and forestry industries are currently using H-2A and H-2B laborers. During the coldest half of the year, Mexican, Central American, and Jamaican H-2A workers move to isolated northern Maine towns to process potatoes in warehouses. Because of the weather and roads, the workers' transportation options are limited, and it is also hard for advocates like the Migrant Mobile Health unit to reach them for wellness checks. State Monitor Advocate (and Colombian migrant) Jorge Acero opined that even though potato workers' housing was remote and lonely, it appeared warm and well constructed. Unlike other states like Texas and New York where there are multiple state monitor advocates, Acero is the only one in Maine and must traverse the entire state checking for employers' compliance with H-2 program regulations. In forestry, Latin American and Caribbean H-2B workers have followed in the footsteps of previous waves of European migrants, French Canadians, Nova Scotians, Anglo-Americans, and Native Americans who have felled and replanted trees since the 1700s. In other forestry hubs like Alabama or Oregon, Latin American and Caribbean men have been working as *pineros* for a few decades. In addition to timber cutters and planters, there are also Latinx and Caribbean wreath workers in Maine. Male "tippers" scale trees and cut the uppermost branches to deliver to another group of workers (mostly women) who labor in factories to create holiday wreaths and centerpieces. Workers usually arrive in mid-to-late October and work into mid- or late December. Some come to wreath work from earlier stints in the apple, broccoli, blueberry, or lobster and seafood industries, but increasing numbers of migrants are coming to Maine specifically for wreath work. Whether they are laboring in the woods or in factories, forestry workers maintain not only the literal Maine landscape by replanting seedlings as they thin and cut trees but also a cozy, touristic, and thus profitable Maine by creating holiday wreaths that adorn homes all over the country.[54]

The public-facing story of Maine products like blueberries, lobsters, and balsam holiday wreaths still conjures an imagined lineage of white Mainer labor.

This narrative obscures the historical reality that the labor behind these commodities has been, for decades, truly global. There is the opportunity to better inform consumers about the varied people who really make these items, if Maine is willing to update its cultural narrative. Elna Osso, a Peruvian-born public health nurse in Portland, observed, "The fact that now I speak Spanish on a daily basis says a lot about how the face of Maine has changed. . . . [But] I also think it makes a lot of people nervous."[55] Restaurateur Romana Vásquez's daughter Juana (who worked in wreaths for some years) added, "I don't think locals realize how much migrant workers bring to the community and economy here. The stores here sell a lot and migrants are contributing a lot to the economy, and they don't realize that. They just see negativity around their arrival. Blueberries, lobster, wreaths, Bar Harbor restaurants and tourism, hotels . . . people don't realize how much it affects them if migrants are not able to come."[56]

Despite grumblings by locals, migrants are essential to the smooth workings of the state's food economies and touristic appeal. While some programs have been created to cultivate agricultural entrepreneurship for workers of color in Maine (the New American Sustainable Agriculture Project, for instance, encouraged Latin American and African immigrants to farm their own pieces of land and sell the produce at farmers' markets), most continue to labor under a simultaneous hypervisibility and invisibility.[57] To these unappreciated laborers, Maine certainly does not feel like Vacationland, or The Way Life Should Be.

The Sea Cucumber and Winter

When the calendar flips to the cold winter months of December through February, Maine workers who have toiled outside all year long move indoors to seafood processing factories. A vital seafood hub is Downeast Maine, a counterintuitive moniker for the far eastern coastal region of the state that extends from the town of Ellsworth to near the Canadian maritime provinces. Hundreds of sardine canneries existed in this region during the 1950s, and then decreased to only a few by the end of the twentieth century. In the mid-1980s the export of sea urchins from the New England coast to Asia began, and the town of Milbridge (an hour's drive north of Bar Harbor and Acadia National Park) opened a sea urchin operation to begin selling to Hong Kong. Due to overfishing, however, the urchins were depleted almost to extinction. Sea cucumbers became the hot new commodity of the 1990s for the price they could fetch in Asian markets. Milbridge became the site of Maine's first major sea cucumber processing plant, and by 1999 a dozen boats around the state were dragging up to 1 million pounds of sea cucumbers per week.[58]

Arguably, the reason that Maine's sea cucumber industry skyrocketed in size and profits during the 1990s was because of increasing Latinx migration to the state during that decade. Without a contingent of migrant workers willing to serve as processing employees in the months between other seasonal jobs, this particular seafood sector never would have flourished. The next chapter delves into sea cucumber labor in Maine and fish processing in New Bedford, Massachusetts, to show how Latinx labor has helped to boost and even save not only northeastern food economies based on land but also those based on water.

PART III

Food Labor Flows and Futures, 1990–2024

CHAPTER FIVE

Latinx Seafood Workers
on the New England Coast

F rom the Chesapeake Bay to the Gulf Coast to Alaska to New England, Latin American and Caribbean workers in the US are helping cod, crawfish, crab, scallops, and lobster get to restaurants and markets around the globe. Like the migrations of the sea creatures they process, the migrations of many of these seafood workers are long and arduous and rhythmic in their seasonality. Just as this book honors Latinx history as fundamental to US and northeastern history, this chapter affirms the sea as fundamental yet understudied in Latinx history. For centuries, Latin American and US-born Latinx people have had deep and intimate histories with coasts and water. They have sailed seas as traders, explorers, and members of the military; they have come to shores as pleasure-seekers, beachgoers, and tourists; and they have seen and smelled oceans as they process its creatures into food inside of waterfront factories. Water-related events such as hurricanes, flooding, and droughts have also pushed people to become climate migrants to the United States.

In his book *The Human Shore*, John R. Gillis writes about the differences between people who live on and enjoy coasts, and people who have a different working relationship to them: "Every summer I am made painfully aware of just how different my relationship to the sea is from that of my Maine neighbors who make their living from the ocean. I have come to appreciate the difference between living *on* coasts and living *with* them, and have learned to make a sharp distinction between people located on coasts and coastal people whose historical relationship with the coastal environment goes beyond mere residence."[1] Coastal living implies privileges like property, intergenerational wealth, and a schedule that allows year-round living or summer vacations in a picturesque setting. Under these circumstances, the coast and sea are beautiful and restorative. Yet for those who rely on coastal economies to make their income, the sea is a capricious, moody entity that either creates fortunes or takes them away. Depending on their previous lived experience, Latinx seafood workers might find themselves feeling at home, lonely, or continually surprised by a coastal existence. If one is coming from a landlocked country, or from work experience in land-based industries, seafood processing requires a whole new language and skill set. Many Latin American migrant workers remark on the time it takes to learn the names of different fish in English—*flatfish, cod, yellowtail, flounder, dabs, grey sole, haddock*—and to adjust to cold, wet, pungent work.[2] This chapter focuses on the coastal communities of Milbridge, Maine, and New Bedford, Massachusetts, as two examples of northeastern locales where Latinx people have found a foothold in the seafood industry and become essential to processing commodities that end up in fish markets and restaurants. It asks what seafood work felt like, in both a sensory and social sense, for Latinx people in New England during the 1990s and 2000s. Did laboring in a coastal community make a difference in their ability to integrate with residents? Did living by the water offer a sense of space and peace for migrants who fled climate disasters, economic scarcity, and civil wars? Or did seafood work constitute an isolated or lonelier daily experience?

In Maine, sea cucumbers became a prized commodity for international export beginning in the 1990s. Central American and Mexican laborers filled this important labor niche in seafood and brought new profits to the state at the turn of the century. Yet many white locals still regarded them as shadowy laboring bodies or threatening figures of illegality and cultural change, especially if Latinx families wanted to establish a more permanent year-round life in the state. Meanwhile, down the coast, the town of New Bedford, Massachusetts, is the highest-value fishing area in the United States. Along with people of Norwegian and Portuguese descent, French, Vietnamese, and Cape Verdean immigrants called New Bedford home before a significant number of workers from Mexico, Central America, and the Dominican Republic joined the mix in the late twentieth century. As seafood companies and boat captains became accustomed to hiring Latin American workers long-term, they expressed gratitude that this workforce stepped in just as many local white youth no longer wanted to inherit seafood work as their occupation. Though both Maine and Massachusetts have centuries-long histories of international maritime and fishing communities, New Bedford residents expressed more acceptance toward Latinx and Caribbean people as a seafood labor force out of economic pragmatism. The fact that many of these workers are undocumented, however, means that New Bedford has been a site of surveillance by immigration authorities.

This chapter ends by zooming out from the Northeast to briefly discuss H-2 visa seafood processing workers in other US regions, such as the Chesapeake Bay and Gulf Coast, reinforcing how hidden and understudied Latinx seafood labor histories continue to be.

Consider the Sea Cucumber

The sea cucumber is a slimy, grayish-green, oblong cold-water animal—closely related to sea urchins and starfish—that has a small orange "flower" or tentacle cluster at one end. Sea cucumbers have slippery collagen-filled skin, no limbs or eyes, and reside in frigid waters on the bottom of the ocean floor, where they help recycle nutrients and purify water for other sea creatures. While sea cucumbers are considered oddities in the United States, they are desirable commodities elsewhere in the world and have long connected people from Maine, Central America, Europe, the Pacific Islands, and East Asia through their harvesting and trade. They are particularly prized in Asia for their culinary, ceremonial, aphrodisiacal, and medicinal properties. Purported to prevent blood clots and high blood pressure and ease joint pain and arthritis, sea cucumbers can be eaten whole or their skins can be processed into powder to fill medicine capsules.[3] According to one Chinese specialist, "The sea cucumber nourishes the blood and vital essence (jing), tonifies kidney qi (treats disorders of the kidney system, including reproductive organs), and moistens dryness (especially of the intestines). . . . Common uses include treating weakness, impotence, debility of the aged. . . . Hence, the popular Chinese name for sea cucumber is *haishen*, which means, roughly, ginseng of the sea."[4]

The Northeast was tied to the Pacific World through the sea cucumber trade in previous eras. As historians Edward Melillo and Nancy Shoemaker have separately detailed, traders from Salem and Nantucket, Massachusetts traveled to Fiji between the 1820s and 1850s to cash in on prized sandalwood and sea cucumbers (also known as *dri* in Fijian or *bêche-de-mer* in French) that they could ship to China. Inside bêche-de-mer houses, Fijian workers pickled the animals in iron cauldrons (originally used in New England for boiling maple syrup) before drying them in the sun or in smokehouses.[5]

More than a century later, another plentiful supply of sea cucumbers was discovered—this time along the rocky coast of Maine. Initially, when they swept sea cucumbers up from the ocean in the 1980s, Maine fishermen considered them to be "trash fish" devoid of value. Yet Asia was demanding sea cucumbers as a culinary delicacy, and some European pharmaceutical companies were interested in the animal's chemical properties to treat arthritis and cancer. By the early 1990s, a few seafood traders in Maine began to export and sell sea cucumbers at a high price to Hong Kong, from which they were distributed to other markets in East Asia. Soon, sea cucumber harvesting and exporting became a full-blown industry in the state. According to the Maine Department of Marine Fisheries, the cash value of sea cucumber landings grew from almost $0 in 1990 to more than $700,000 in 2007. This might pale in comparison to the soft-shell clam industry ($10 million to $15 million) or the lobster industry ($200 million to $300 million), but profits from sea cucumber exports were far greater because they were divided between only a few companies versus thousands of commercial licenses for lobster catching.[6]

Sea cucumber processing is hard and nasty work, and not for the faint of stomach. In Maine, after the cucumbers were collected in drag nets, fishermen stored them in plastic tote bags and sold them to a buyer from a processing facility, who was often waiting on the docks. Employees at the processing plant then had to work quickly to slice the animal open and clamp its body to a board with vise-grips to scrape out the meat. In a defense response known as auto-evisceration, sea cucumbers eject their innards on their attacker, covering workers (who were supposed to be wearing heavy rubber aprons, boots, gloves, and goggles) in poisonous pinkish slime. Some sea cucumber species even discharged toxic chemicals into the air, causing workers to suffer respiratory issues termed "sea cucumber asthma." Workers quickly scraped out sea cucumber meat to drop in one bin to be flash-frozen and vacuum-packed, and reserved the skins to be washed, boiled, and spin-dried in machines until they reached a beef jerky-like texture. The skins and meat were then driven from Maine to New Jersey for transport to Asia. On average, workers could produce 60 pounds of processed meat and skins in a ten-hour workday, while the fastest workers could produce 100 pounds. To give a sense of wages, in 2008 workers were being paid $1.75 a pound, meaning one could earn between $100 to $175 a day.[7]

Lawrence and Drusilla Ray were the first to open a sea cucumber processing plant in Downeast Maine, in the sleepy coastal town of Milbridge in the late 1990s. The Rays initially believed that white Mainers would be eager to work at their new business. "Washington County had the highest unemployment rate in the state. We figured people would be beating down the doors," Drusilla said. In contrast to wealthier coastal Maine communities to the south like Belfast, Rockport, and Portland, the Downeast region is a more economically depressed zone where desirable work opportunities are hard to come by. As regional writer Sanford Phippen put it, "This Maine is frustrating; it is hard on people. It is a life of poverty, solitude, [and] struggle." The 1990 census classified 52.5 percent of Maine residents as rural, and Department of Commerce figures revealed 13 percent of the population was living below the poverty line, the highest figure for New England and higher than the national average of 12.4 percent. To the Rays' dismay, local Mainers were not interested in sea cucumber processing work. "It was dirty. It was cold. It was wet. It was repetitive. It was smelly," Drusilla admitted.[8]

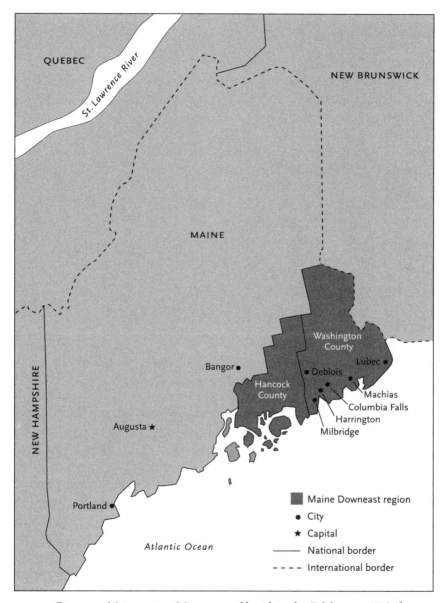

MAP 5.1. Downeast Maine region. Map prepared by Alejandro Falchettore / R Software. US CENSUS TIGER data, 2020.

Arguably, the only reason that the Maine sea cucumber industry became highly profitable in the late 1990s was because this was an era of increased Latin American migration to the state. After a bad blueberry harvest in the summer of 1998, a foreman asked Drusilla Ray if she would accept some of his work-hungry Latino employees. Ray jumped at the opportunity, and the first group of twenty-five men—who hailed from Mexico, El Salvador, and Honduras—moved into a barn next to the sea cucumber plant. Over the next few years, these workers returned with their families, and brought along other migrants who planned to process sea cucumbers from January to June, harvest blueberries in July and August, and cut trees or make wreaths during the autumn months. The Rays eventually provided workers with trailer housing in a gravel lot behind the factory and charged them $100 per adult per month in rent, with heat and utilities included. At its peak, the plant employed seventy-five Latino workers, mostly from El Salvador and Honduras. The prospect of settling in Milbridge and making it a year-round home where they could patch together seasonal jobs was appealing. Edith Flores and her parents were among the first who came to work for the Rays. At first, Flores said, life in Milbridge "felt very isolated. But it was sort of like the town where I come from in Mexico, where everyone knows each other. It was calm, peaceful." Argentine migrant Santiago Rave remembered that when his parents visited cousins in the nearby town of Ellsworth, Maine, "they fell in love with the fact that you didn't have to lock your car doors, your house door." Seeking a greater sense of tranquility and safety, many Latin American and Caribbean migrants started coming directly to smaller US towns in the late twentieth century instead of making their initial stop in a bigger city. Noticeable numbers of US Latinx citizens tired of metropolitan life did the same.[9]

As the sea cucumber industry took off in Maine, the Maine Rural Workers Coalition (MRWC) kept an eye on Latinx processors' working conditions. Coalition organizer José Soto, who had seen atrocious working conditions at the DeCoster egg company years earlier, decided to conduct interviews with some sea cucumber workers in the spring of 2000. One of his most memorable interviewees was sixteen-year-old Honduran orphan Ángel "Geovanny" Nufio. After both of his parents died, Nufio migrated to the United States without papers in 1997 and received a temporary work visa, perhaps through the Special Immigrant Juvenile program. In his interview, Nufio explained that he spent up to ten hours a day processing sea cucumbers on the coast. Every time he had to cut one of the animals open, it squirted poison all over his hands, clothes, and face. "After four months, my eyes began to feel like a cloud was coming over," he said. "They would sting. Always." Nufio claimed the company never gave him any protective gear and never paid for a doctor visit even though he repeatedly asked for one. Finally, a friend took him to the hospital. By that point, he said, "I lost my eyesight practically completely. The doctor said I have to stop work. I cannot see." Geovanny took the hospital bill back to his employer, but the company refused to pay the $200 cost. "They just ignored me like I didn't exist," Nufio said. He had to start wearing eyeglasses, which were eventually paid for (along with his medical bills) by the MRWC. Soto then shared Nufio's story with the *Maine Times* to bring more attention to the plight of sea cucumber workers.[10]

White employers were not the only ones turning a blind eye to workers' precarity in the sea cucumber industry; some Latin American intermediaries were as well. Luis and Yasmin Centeno Pérez, who had originally moved to Maine to work in blueberries, owned several businesses targeted toward Latino customers. They initially operated a food truck that sold mobile meals to agricultural workers in fields and camps, and then opened a convenience store in 2000. "The Mexican Store" sold clothing and CDs; food items like tortillas, chorizo, avocados, and mangoes; and offered money transfer, fax, phone, and mailing services. Yasmin minded the store while Luis worked in Milbridge's sea cucumber plant and made drives to Boston twice a month to stock up on specialty Latin American foods. People came to rely on the couple, and Luis also presided over Sunday Pentecostal services for a tiny congregation of Spanish speakers in the town of Columbia Falls. For workers who could not reach the Mexican Store themselves, Luis drove a "traveling bodega" vehicle to sell goods at remote broccoli farms or lumber camps. Later, Yasmin and Luis opened a restaurant on US Route 1 that served Mexican and Central American food to a mixed clientele of migrant workers and local Mainers. The pair's final venture was contracting and transporting sea cucumber workers. A new plant had opened in Lubec, a small town at the easternmost point of the United States. In 2005, the plant's owner paid Luis and Yasmin $400,000 to act as labor contractors—they would recruit and house the workers, pay their wages, and transport them daily between Milbridge and Lubec. In January 2006, during one of the crew's commutes, their windowless cargo van broke down on a snowy road. The workers had been instructed by Luis and Yasmin to hide in the woods if this ever happened, but they feared the freezing temperatures and waited for help instead. When police arrived and questioned the workers, they notified ICE and the Border Patrol, and the undocumented workers were turned over to deportation hearings and proceedings. Luis and Yasmin were charged with visa fraud, transporting and harboring illegal immigrants, and conspiracy to hire illegal workers.[11]

On the one hand, Yasmin and Luis had facilitated some ease and comfort for Mexican and Central American migrants in Downeast Maine, but on the other they had knowingly put a vulnerable crew at risk of detection and deportation.

Other truths emerged during their court trials about their own labyrinthine immigration stories. Yasmin claimed many times in immigration documents that she was Honduran, while Luis told the media that he and his family had fled the Guatemalan civil war when he was twelve. In reality, the couple was Mexican (their "Mexican Store" hinted at their true nationality) and had entered the United States without papers in the late 1980s. They knew being Mexican was not the preferable nationality if one wanted to be considered a humanitarian exception to immigration restrictions. Luis applied for asylum in 1991 using a false Guatemalan birth certificate with the surname Centeno Pérez. Meanwhile, Yasmin used the name Doris Centeno to claim asylum from Guatemala, and then Temporary Protected Status as a citizen of Honduras with the surname Escalante. She used yet another name, Amanda Ayala Centeno, to obtain immigration documents, a Social Security number, an alien registration number, and a green card in 1993. Both were indicted by a federal grand jury in September 2007, and Luis fled the country shortly after. A convicted Yasmin served a jail sentence of fourteen months, and Luis—who used the aliases Juan Lorenzo Hernández López and Abraham Gallardo Paredes in Canada—was eventually arrested at the Toronto airport. He returned to Maine and was sentenced to two years and nine months in federal prison.[12]

This confusing case reminds us of the reversals and shades of nuance in the expected story of US employer-villain and Latin American worker-victim. It also highlights the gradations of vulnerability that Latin American migrants knew existed in the United States. Yasmin and Luis hoped that by posing as Central American asylum-seekers, they would have a better chance of being able to stay than if they identified as more easily deportable Mexicans. Their false stories were their own survival tactic. Unsurprisingly, the Lubec sea cucumber company itself evaded any punishment, as it had sloughed off responsibility by hiring Yasmin and Luis as its labor contractors. These incidents were not the only immigration-related arrests in Maine's sea cucumber industry. In April 1998 INS agents raided the Rays' sea cucumber processing plant in Milbridge and arrested four Mexican workers and one Honduran worker. In March 2000, Border Patrol agents arrested sixteen people (twelve Mexican, four Guatemalan) who had been hired through a contract labor company in Connecticut to work at a sea cucumber processing plant in the town of Beals.[13]

Even though Central American and Mexican laborers had filled a labor niche in seafood and brought new profits to Maine, they were hidden from view in various ways, leading many Mainers to either regard them as shadowy laboring bodies or threatening figures of illegality and cultural change. Immigration-related incidents became the way that many Mainers generalized about a "Latino threat" at the turn of the twenty-first century. In 1990 the census recorded 1,303 residents in Milbridge, with only 1 person claiming Hispanic origin. By 2000, it recorded 1,279 residents and 84 Hispanics.[14] As they watched these families settle in their small town during the first decade of the 2000s, a significant constituency of white residents became flustered by the idea of Latinos residing in Milbridge long-term, sending their kids to school, and buying or renting homes.

Then, after 9/11, a dramatic uptick in border apprehensions occurred within both the southern and northern border zones of the United States. Since almost the entire state of Maine fell within the Border Patrol's 100-mile jurisdiction, patrol stations could be found in the towns of Houlton, Calais, Fort Fairfield, Rangeley, Houlton, and Van Buren, while an INS office was established in South Portland. In 2004, Border Patrol agents descended on Portland in particular, raiding Latino and Somali businesses, factories, and a shelter for unhoused people. Their rough treatment and racial profiling of brown residents ruffled enough feathers that the *Portland Press Herald* asked a Border Patrol assistant chief in Maine to answer for his colleagues' conduct. "A lot of our agents are just off the southern border and there's a different atmosphere down there.... Things are more aggressive," the assistant chief admitted. Ten people were arrested during these street sweeps, and another eleven employed at a Chinese restaurant (two Chinese nationals, nine Mexican) were arrested and detained for deportation proceedings. At this time, Maine's total population was 1,274,923 people, with 9,360 of them identifying as Hispanic, but this was surely an undercount that missed undocumented migrants. For some time after the raids, Latin American migrants refused to leave their homes or go to work. La Bodega Latina owner Juan González remarked on how many customers called him during the time of the roundups, asking if it was safe to come shop. As Rev. Virginia Marie Rincón observed, the silver lining to the raids was that Latinx leaders and communities became more active and united. They organized meetings and a march that city officials and sympathetic Portlanders attended. Immigrant rights activists and allies in Maine later participated in the "Day without an Immigrant" or "Immigrant Spring" of 2006, where between 3.5 million and 5 million people in more than 120 cities across the nation called for a path to citizenship for the millions of undocumented people already living and working in the country. Another series of raids followed in Maine in 2011, with restaurants being the targets. Ten men (nine from Latin America, one from China) working at an Asian restaurant in Portland were apprehended while the restaurant owners, a Chinese couple, were arrested for hiring, transporting, and housing unauthorized employees.[15]

Latino business owners were also caught up in immigration authorities' roundups. Héctor Fuentes, the owner of three beloved Mexican restaurants in

Maine, was charged with harboring and employing undocumented immigrants. Interestingly, his arrest sparked outcry from patrons on social media. Along with deeming Héctor a hardworking and generous man, customers complained they were losing good food and service at low prices. Support was so strong that some locals came to the restaurant to fill the void left by the restaurant workers. Alek Fortier, a thirty-one-year-old insurance agent who worked next door to the restaurant, came to wash dishes on a Friday and Saturday night. "Everybody loves Hector," he told reporters. "People were walking in all night and saying, 'What can I do?'"[16] Apparently, the desire to keep Mexican food in the area was so strong, and Héctor himself was such a nonthreatening figure, that locals rallied around him as a community member instead of a lawbreaker.

Though some Mainers might equate the words *Hispanic* and *Latino* with "foreign," "illegal," and "threatening," others are aware that this population has boosted—and perhaps even saved—the economies of the towns in which they settled. As *Down East* magazine declared of Latinos in an August 2008 article titled "Invisible Mainers," "There are major Maine companies that would go out of business without them." Younger on average than white residents, Latinx Mainers counter the socioeconomic effects of the state's demographic "graying." In 2014 almost one in five Mainers was older than sixty-five. That year, Maine immigrants paid $126 million into the state's Social Security coffers and $34 million into Medicare.[17] By 2017, Maine's Latinx population was conservatively estimated at 21,375, and a growing number of Latinx-owned businesses were contributing varied goods and services. Ángel Ortíz, born in Spanish Harlem to a Puerto Rican father and Chilean mother, moved to Maine during his time in the Navy and started a plumbing company. Miriam Curtis, a native of Ecuador who met her husband during a visit to her sister in Maine, began a small organic chicken and egg farm and worked as a nurse for the Maine Migrant Health program. María and Alejandro Rave, who migrated from Argentina, started as a grocery bagger and doughnut shop employee but eventually opened their own restaurant. Mónica Elliott rushed to Maine from Peru when her husband—who was working at a salmon hatchery—experienced a medical emergency. Mónica struggled with the language barrier and finding a job in the faraway town of Lubec, but began making Peruvian-inspired chocolate and received $26,000 from supportive local residents to rent some storefront space. In 2005 she opened Monica's Chocolates, which still exists today.[18] Personal connections, whether in the form of neighborly friendship or love and marriage, could determine everything for an immigrant to Maine, including the beginning of their own food-related businesses.

If one reflects on the long history of seafood labor in North America and the

US Northeast, a contingent of immigrants and newcomers is nothing strange. As Portland fish processing company Arctic Pride's president Spencer Fuller commented to the *Portland Press Herald*, "This waterfront wouldn't happen [without immigrants]. . . . If you go back in history, it was Irish, Italians, Germans and Scandinavians. Historically, there's really nothing different than what we see now." Yet the specter of Latinx permanency in Maine, coupled with the fact that some Latinx families started achieving upward economic mobility through owning their own businesses, was jarring enough to stir up xenophobic backlash. Mexican-born Victor Flores, who moved to Maine in the late 1990s and married a white woman who worked beside him at the Rays' sea cucumber plant, remembered one incident outside the town's supermarket. After he parked next to a white man's car, Flores recalled, "He thought I was too close to him, so he started getting mad. And the first thing, he's like, 'Go back to Mexico! Go back to where you came from! You don't belong here!'" Some incidents of racial conflict also occurred at the Milbridge elementary school—some children taunted others to "go back to Mexico," no doubt mimicking the adults around them. In response, local Milbridge officials organized diversity-awareness workshops, potlucks, and community meetings. One outcome of these meetings was the creation of Mano en Mano, an organization that aimed to bridge the gap between newer and older Milbridge residents. While it helped Latin American residents access English classes, student tutoring, and health care, it offered Spanish classes to white Milbridge residents and held events to build awareness and appreciation of Latin American cultures.[19]

This cross-cultural outreach came to a halt, however, when Mano en Mano won a $1.2 million federal grant in 2008 from the Department of Agriculture to build a six-unit apartment complex for low-income workers. Many white residents assumed the housing units would only be given to racial minorities, migratory workers, or undocumented immigrants. Mano en Mano's director, Ian Yaffe, tried to assure people at town meetings that the units would only be given to US citizens or residents working in a farm or sea occupation. White residents ultimately voted 68–49 to block the project and place a six-month moratorium on the complex. Mano en Mano filed a federal lawsuit alleging discrimination under the Fair Housing Act and the Equal Protection Clause of the Constitution. It won the case and built a six-unit complex. The apartments went to three Latinx, two mixed-race, and one white household, but this housing fracas remains a sore spot in the community.[20]

Other spots of racial "soreness" developed in the Northeast around this time between white residents and Latinx newcomers. An infamous anti-immigrant campaign occurred in the former coal mining town of Hazleton in northern rural

Pennsylvania. After 9/11, a number of Latinos—Dominicans, in particular—moved from New York City to Hazleton for respite, and other immigrants arrived to work at the Cargill meat processing company. At one point, 70 percent of Cargill's workers were Latin American. Alarmed, Hazleton's mayor Louis Barletta instituted an "Illegal Immigration Relief Act" in 2006 that proposed to make English the city's official language and punish landlords and businesses that rented to or hired undocumented immigrants.[21] Put into context, 2006 was the year Congress tried and failed to pass comprehensive immigration reform; Minutemen had stationed themselves along the US-Mexico border; and "A Day without an Immigrant" rallies and walkouts were taking place in several cities. The Hazleton city ordinance read, "Illegal immigration leads to higher crime rates, contributes to overcrowded classrooms and failing schools, subjects our hospitals to fiscal hardship and legal residents to substandard quality of care, and destroys our neighborhoods and diminishes our overall quality of life." The glaring xenophobia of the ordinance brought national media to Hazleton. The CBS television news magazine *60 Minutes* filmed in the town, and at one point zoomed in on a small Dominican bodega, where a handwritten poster read "Plátanos Verdes 8 x 1.00." Changing food was shorthand for demographic and linguistic change, not to mention the success and proliferation of Latinx-owned businesses. As anthropologist Leo Chavez wrote in his book *The Latino Threat*, xenophobia becomes apparent when Latinx people "are no longer flesh-and-blood people; they exist as images" of illegality.[22] In this case, the *plátanos* served as the symbol of threat. The City of Hazleton was sued by the ACLU and others, and the case went to trial in March 2007. In a 200-page decision, US District Court judge James Munley found Barletta's employment and rental prohibitions unconstitutional under the Fourteenth Amendment.[23] During the first decade of the 2000s, anti-Latinx xenophobia that was heightened by the "border threat" and "national security" rhetoric of 9/11 had to be fought in courts by immigrant advocates nationwide.

Sea cucumber processing ultimately ended in Maine in the early 2000s due to overharvesting. Latinx workers are still working in Maine's seafood industry today but as lobster and fish processors instead. Much like sea cucumbers, lobsters were originally considered a "trash" food in the nineteenth century that was served to animals, the impoverished, and the incarcerated. Lobster only became a desirable delicacy and status symbol in the 1920s when railroads began serving whole cooked lobsters in train cars. As the newly wealthy began buying land for vacation cottages in Bar Harbor and Kennebunkport, lobster became bound up with images of luxurious summers in Maine.[24] Today, lobsters remain priced out of reach for much of the working class, including the Puerto Rican,

Mexican, Haitian, and Honduran workers who process them in factories.[25] As Maine lobstermen working on boats continue to be predominantly white, the notion persists that seafood labor does not include migrants or people of color. This myth is easily overturned, however, once one pays attention to the seafood commodity chain past the moment of catch.

Latinx Fish Workers in New Bedford, Massachusetts

A few chapters into *Moby Dick*, the narrator Ishmael takes a stroll through 1840s New Bedford, Massachusetts. He observes the mix of Europeans, Indigenous residents, and New Englanders from Vermont and New Hampshire in the town, all looking to make their fortune in fish work and whaling. Cod fisheries in this region were among the first European business ventures in this area, as well as porpoise-hunting and whaling for blubber to make oil. During the nineteenth century whaling ships made stops in the Portuguese colony of Cape Verde, situated off the coast of West Africa, to bring back salt, supplies, and hired workers. Eventually, some of these Cape Verdean laborers acquired their own ships, returned to the colony, and shuttled additional people to New Bedford. Soon, Cape Verdean workers had branched out to other sectors, including the cranberry bogs of South Massachusetts and Cape Cod.

After the whaling economy disappeared, Massachusetts fishing fleets owned primarily by fishers of Italian, Portuguese, and Norwegian ancestry became the most sophisticated in the world. Since the Johnson-Reed Act of 1924 limited certain European migrations, Portuguese migrants came to Massachusetts undocumented. Immigration authorities began tracking them when angry New Englanders complained they were taking too many fishing jobs. "Aliens of the Portuguese race [are] said to be illegally in the United States and members of the crew on Gloucester fishing vessels," Boston's District INS director wrote to his superior in March 1935.[26] New Bedford became even more diverse as a smattering of French and Vietnamese migrants arrived and entered seafood work. Meanwhile, a germinal Puerto Rican community emerged in the 1970s and took work in the town's textile mills. Debra Kelsey, who moved with her family from Puerto Rico to New Bedford in the 1970s, remembered that "all the Puerto Ricans . . . lived in the south end of New Bedford. . . . [It was a] little Puerto Rico."[27]

During the late 1990s and early 2000s, a noticeable number of Mexicans, Dominicans, and Central Americans began arriving in New Bedford and taking processing work in haddock, cod, flounder, yellowtail, and scallops. As we have seen in the case of Maine, Mexicanos were already traveling labor circuits that would bring them to the New England coast. Meanwhile, more Dominican immigrants were bypassing bigger urban destinations like New York or Providence and moving to smaller locales like Paterson, New Jersey; Lawrence, Massachusetts; and New Bedford by the turn of the twenty-first century. Meanwhile, Central Americans were being pushed northward by political turbulence and economic desperation. One woman seafood processer from Guatemala recalled the civil war and violence that affected her family. "They took my dad and I no longer knew where my dad had gone. . . . They took my aunts and uncles and cousins. We saw them thrown out in the street . . . dead."[28] In El Salvador, hurricanes and earthquakes affected the usual production of exports like coffee, sugar, and corn, and struggling campesinos moved to cities for jobs. Yet even industrial labor was financially unsustainable, and this worsened when El Salvador converted to the dollar in 2001. Several migrants recalled that many times all they had to eat were rolled tortillas with a pinch of salt, as even beans were not always readily available. Additionally, the implementation of the Central American Free Trade Agreement (CAFTA) in 2006 had effects similar to those of NAFTA. US food exports flooded Central American markets, and native-grown farm products lost their profitability. The United States seemed to offer the promise of bigger and faster earnings. One migrant woman living in New Bedford observed, "The people who . . . come back [to Central America after migrating] and have cars, they live better. They have big shops like you see here called minimarkets. . . . That is how one becomes curious and wanting to come here [to the United States]." Needing to cross multiple borders, Central American migrants' journeys were harrowing. One woman described her twenty-two-day experience of traveling from El Salvador to Guatemala by bus, from Guatemala to Mexico in an open motor boat (*lancha*) for fourteen hours, then from Mexico across the border to Houston before going to Boston and ending up in New Bedford.[29]

Word of mouth from existing kin networks in New England was the way most Latin Americans chose New Bedford. Jaime Rivera, who migrated from Puerto Rico in 2006 at the age of seventeen, already had family in Massachusetts. He found a job at the NORPEL (Northern Pelagic) plant in 2007 as a fish packer, and eventually worked his way into becoming a nightshift supervisor. He married a local woman, and his parents ultimately joined them in New Bedford.[30] Tomás Calil, a Maya K'iche' man from Guatemala, moved to Massachusetts in 2000 to join his brother in seafood processing. He started working at a plant called Bergie's Seafood in 2002 and by 2017 was serving as a supervisor preparing orders for customers in other northeastern cities. Calil described his workdays as often beginning before sunrise and consisting of unloading fish from boats, cutting fish and putting it through a skinning machine, and then packing the products on pallets for delivery. Because he had worked with twenty-five other workers at the plant for almost fifteen years, he felt the crew was like his family. Compared to his former agricultural labor in Guatemala, Tomás said—with a smile perceptible in his voice—that he far preferred seafood work. He looked forward to the days that he could drive products to New York and Boston; not only did this allow him to see more of the Northeast, but he could feel like an important figure in a bigger network of food provision.[31]

Meanwhile, women found work as cutters and cleaners in fish processing plants. Rosa Herrera grew up in San Sebastián, El Salvador, but migrated to the capital of San Salvador at fifteen to find a job as a domestic worker. Raising three daughters as a single mother, her salary was not enough to support all of them. She made the excruciating decision to leave her daughters in 2004 for the United States. In New Bedford, she gained experience separating and packaging scallops and cleaning fish by hand. While male fish processors are mostly tasked with cutting fish and wrapping pallets carrying about 1,000 pounds apiece, women are given the more delicate job of skinning, descaling, and deboning fish with very sharp knives, tongs, and tweezers. They also use wire brushes to clean fillets for market sale. Preserving as much of the fish as possible (while not injuring oneself in the process) requires a high degree of skill, and a high tolerance for repetitive motion. Rosa worked the night shift, focused on processing cod, in a crew of about forty people. Though she remarked that her supervisor was very patient with new hires, she said in Spanish, "You have to be fast and thorough with your work. And if you do a bad job of cutting the fish, you're mistreating the fish too." Christmastime and Easter, being holiday seasons with fish-centric meals, are the busiest times for women fish cleaners. Then, during summers, calamari production and scallop processing take over. When asked if seafood work exhausted her body, Rosa replied, "Sí, [estoy] más cansada" (Yes, I am more tired), and pointed out that the icy environment in the processing warehouses creates more pain in her bones and joints. Other women workers mentioned seafood work's physical toll on the body. "Your hands get swollen, it hurts," said another Salvadoran woman who had experience in herring, mackerel, scallops, and clams. "I had to wear three sweaters, three pants, gloves because of the extreme cold." The woman described removing clam meat from shells, and being paid only $1.90 per bucket (which held forty pounds of clam meat), requiring a fast pace to earn enough for the day and week.[32]

It soon became clear to New Bedford locals that Latin American immigrants would be the new heirs to fish processing work. While some locals waxed nostalgic for a European-immigrant fishing past, others were pragmatic and knew that changing waves of workers had always kept the seafood industry flowing. Portuguese-born Virginia Martins, a co-owner of a fishing vessel fuel and supplies business, reflected on the demographic change in New Bedford's fishing workforce. "You had all Portuguese . . . [and] now you have your Spanish, your Mexicans, your Guatemalans. They basically took it over," she said.[33] Martins's use of the phrase "taking over" could be matter-of-fact acceptance, or it could connote disappointment, resentment, or nostalgia for an old New Bedford. Jim Mercer, a diver of English, Irish, and French Canadian descent who swam beneath boats to resolve mechanical problems or obstructions, observed that there were now Guatemalan captains of some fishing boats, and that others had several crew members from the Dominican Republic. Mercer laughed as he commented on these Latin American immigrants' quick adjustment to an English-dominant culture: "There's only a handful of guys that don't know English. . . . I'll pop up out of the water and, you know, I'll give [them] a 'Buenos días!' and they'll laugh, they think it's funny, they're like, 'Yeah, good morning.'" Cindy Pettway, born in New Bedford to French and Portuguese parents, remarked, "Young kids just don't want to do this [fishing] work anymore. They want to go to work somewhere where they can sit at a computer all day."[34] While residents of Milbridge, Maine, reacted negatively to Latinx workers settling long-term, New Bedford residents acknowledged—whether ruefully, neutrally, or gratefully—that Latin American workers stepped into the seafood industry just as the children of seafood workers were rejecting their occupational inheritance.

Receiving support and concrete training opportunities from supervisors has been essential to helping Latin American immigrants advance within New Bedford seafood companies. Alexander Chavis, who migrated in 2006 at the age of sixteen, had been helping his mother in El Salvador with a small restaurant she ran out of her home. Alexander had hopes of becoming a professor but saw working in the United States as the only way he could save up money for his university tuition and book costs. Friends and relatives already living in New Bedford helped him acquire a job packing fish at Bergie's. Chavis's first boss was a Portuguese man who spoke some Spanish and trained him closely in skinning, cutting, and packing fish during his first months at the plant. Now in his thirties, Chavis is the one who teaches new Salvadoran and Guatemalan workers how to cut and pack fish. He remarked on how complicated it becomes in the workplace when employees are speaking Spanish, Portuguese, English, and K'iche' (a Mayan language of Guatemala) all at once. Four of Chavis's siblings eventually migrated from El Salvador to join him in Massachusetts. "Todos trabajamos en pescado" (All of us work in fish), he said. Sebastián Ayala, another Salvadoran immigrant, began working at NORPEL and moved his way up to foreman, a role in which he supervised machinery and trained new employees.[35] Some Mexican, Dominican, Salvadoran, and Honduran men have obtained work outside the plants as fishing boat crew members, braving the moody and stormy conditions of the open sea.

Though it is relatively rare, some Latin American migrant men have branched out from working for a seafood employer to starting their own fishing-related businesses. Maya K'iche' migrant Héctor Grave came to New Bedford from Guatemala with his mother in 1998. Though he was only fourteen, Héctor immediately sought work on the waterfront and found a job packing scallops and loading fish at a seafood plant. During that time, a friend showed him how to make fishing nets, and he quickly picked up the skill. When designed for fishing in federal waters, nets are huge and measure up to 300 feet long and 20 feet wide. Héctor worked for several years at gillnet companies before he started his own net-making and repair business. He developed a customer base in New Bedford, Rhode Island, and Maine through word of mouth, and hired other migrants to help him make nets during high-demand periods. "Now all the gill netmakers in New Bedford are Guatemalan," he remarked with pride.[36] Though some men have moved up the ladder in the seafood industry, others struggle to know whether the same will happen for them. Guatemalan migrant Valeriano García came to the United States at the age of thirty and lived in Providence briefly before moving to New Bedford in 2007. He began working in the fishing industry in 2012, and his responsibilities included managing the storage of fish, squid, and shrimp bought at auction. At the time of his interview in 2017, he hoped to be promoted to supervisor because of his deep knowledge of the *helaría* (warehouse freezer) but was still waiting for management's decision. "If it doesn't happen, I'll accept that," he said in Spanish.[37]

Meanwhile, women contend with a lack of advancement in fish processing plants because of gendered differences related to pregnancy and childcare. Some women reported that once their pregnancies became visible, they were told they could no longer work because of slippery floors. A woman named Guadalupe, who possessed a degree in health sciences and had worked as a phlebotomist before the Salvadoran civil war and earthquakes pushed her to migrate to New Bedford in 2002, spoke of women workers' frustrating experiences. They felt immense pressure—particularly if they were mothers—to not fall short of production quotas. During busy processing seasons, she added, showing up for early morning or late-night overtime hours is difficult for parents who must drop off and pick up their children at school or pay a babysitter. Guadalupe recalled a particularly traumatic scolding by her supervisor for her unanticipated lateness to work one day. He publicly accused her of leaving her whole crew in the lurch but was noticeably easier on his "favorites" and paid them higher wages. Speaking in Spanish, Guadalupe said, "They [bosses] need to understand that I can't just work and work. People get sick, but their only concern is work and work and work.... [Companies] think immigrants are not educated and they think they can treat them like this."[38] The question of gendered differential treatment was one that emerged in other women workers' interviews. Many were uncertain if their hourly wage rates differed from their male counterparts, showing how closely guarded this information was by management (and by the male workers themselves). Additionally, none of the women interviewed occupied supervisory roles, implying a continued patriarchy in seafood work. (Interestingly, some white women in New Bedford have taken over their fathers' roles as the new heads of seafood businesses in town.)

In speaking of their general satisfaction levels about living and working in New Bedford, workers' responses to oral historians run the gamut from strained to content. Many had lived landlocked lives in Central America or Mexico, and New Bedford was their first experience living and working in a coastal community. When asked about how she felt about her new life by the sea, one woman responded about her initial impressions:

> I thought [New Bedford] was beautiful and thanks to God he gave us the sea and that is why we have work. Sometimes ... when I go to the shore with my husband I think, "Oh Lord so many fish and thank God for them we have our jobs, how beautiful is the sea, it gives us a life and allows us to buy shoes, clothes, right?" You can even buy a handbag to match your clothes. In my country you couldn't even buy a pair of shoes, and now [we have] all of those things. Here we feel very delighted.[39]

By contrast, another woman spoke of her disillusionment because of how she had held the United States in her imagination:

> Cuando uno está allá y ve la T.V. y dice, "Wow, Los Estados Unidos de maravilla," pero ya cuando una viene y tienes que vea la realidad.... Aquí nunca se sabe cuándo es verano porque aquí todo el tiempo está frío.... No es un trabajo que se diga "qué trabajo muy bonito ... o se siento muy orgulloso." ... "Dónde trabajas?" "En pescado." "Uyy!" ... es el peor pero ... uno se queda por necesidad.
>
> (When one is over there and watches television one says, "Wow, how marvelous the United States seems," but when they come they have to see the reality.... Here [in the fish plants] one never knows when it's summer because it's cold in here all the time.... This is not a job where one can say, "It's a lovely job," or "I'm proud of my job." ... [Someone asks,] "Where do

you work?" "In fish." "Uyy! [they respond in disgust.]" ... It's the worst but
... one stays out of necessity.)[40]

Meanwhile, migrants who had lived and worked in fish processing for many
years seemed to accept or express contentment with their lives, despite missing
their families in Latin America or struggling to send significant remittances
every month. When asked about the most difficult part of his job, Sebastián
Ayala replied, "I think [it's] the cold. ... The winter's cold, very terrible," but on
the whole expressed satisfaction with the life he had created in Massachusetts
with his wife and children. "I like New Bedford. I feel comfortable here," he
said. At the time of her interview, Rosa Herrara was in her mid-fifties and had
worked thirteen years in the fishing industry. She felt she had adapted her whole
life to the United States and had no plans to return to El Salvador. In Maine,
Massachusetts, and other coastal locales, Latinx workers-by-the-sea are having a
multitude of sensory and emotional experiences with the water. Some might feel
hard limits upon their ability to really take pleasure in the coastline, whether
those limits are because of laboring in a cold and unpleasant smellscape, or because of poverty and anxiety about their immigration status or families back
home. Others, like the woman above who walked the shore with her husband,
spend moments taking in the sea as beautiful, and even giving. Latinx seafood
workers' varied relationships to coastal environments are fascinating, sparse in
the historical record, and important to study further.[41]

Though increasingly xenophobic rhetoric about migrant workers has pene-
trated New Bedford as much as other places in the United States in recent decades, seafood industry figures—including fishermen themselves—push back on
the idea of criminalizing and deporting seafood workers. "We are now strangling
an already struggling industry. I recommend that we start thinking holistically
before we bring this community as we know it to an end," wrote a commenter
named "Fisherman" on the *New Bedford Light* website. He was responding specifically to an article about a long-running nonprofit in New Bedford named the
Immigrants' Assistance Center (IAC), and some comments beneath that called
for apprehending immigrants. To the fisherman, the "ending" of New Bedford
would not come in the form of a racial or demographic shift but in residents' de-
nial of a much-needed immigrant workforce for fish processing. Similarly, Irish
immigrant and NORPEL plant manager Eoin Rochford remembered responding to a colleague who commented to him over lunch, "It's wrong having all these
immigrants in there in the fish business." "I says to him, 'What are you talking
about?' I says, 'I'm an immigrant ... nobody else will do the job. ... [Americans]

don't want to do it,'" he said. Rochford continued, "The Guatemalans here, they love working with fish, and they have a great attitude towards it, personality-wise, you know?. . . . They never complain about anything, you know?"[42] Seafood company supervisor Kevin Hart made similar comments: "[Will we] take this regular white guy over here [who's] going to do nothing but piss and moan and complain the whole time. . . . Or am I going to take this Mexican over here who's going to get on a boat and ain't going to say a word, but do everything I tell him and work his ass off the whole time?"[43]

Though Rochford's and Hart's views supported the presence of immigrants in New Bedford's seafood industry, the common refrain that Latin American newcomers do the jobs no one else wants to do should be considered with caution. Immigrants appear as "hard workers" with a "good work ethic" precisely because they are more desperate and vulnerable. They need to acquire and keep a job, and thus often push themselves to exhaustion because of the sacrifice, risk, and debt they incur by migrating in the first place. And even if they maintain a certain pace and temperament in the workplace, migrants might not earn the wages they deserve compared to seafood workers of the past. João Bernardo, a Portuguese upholsterer in his sixties, observed that Portuguese fish workers in New Bedford used to earn "at least fourteen, fifteen dollars an hour." He continued, "They payin' them [Central Americans]—what—six dollars, seven dollars an hour? So they put two people there workin' on the price of one. So that's why they hire them. . . . They using these people."[44] Nothing about fish processing work has been deskilled or become easier, but this Latin American workforce is being paid less overall because of their overwhelmingly noncitizen status. Several fish processors pointed out that their eight-dollar-an-hour wage for twenty to thirty hours a week could barely cover rent, bills, babysitter, gas for a car, and remittances to family members abroad.

And though seafood companies would not want to be exposed for this phenomenon either, there is also noticeable child labor in seafood processing. This is due to three things—an uptick in unaccompanied minor migration to the United States, a lack of Department of Labor oversight, and the prevalence of labor contracting agencies that ignore children's ages and false documents. In December 2023, the US Department of Labor (USDOL) began investigating Atlantic Red Crab and Sea Watch International, two seafood processors in New Bedford. It also began looking into Workforce Unlimited and B. J.'s Service Company, two staffing agencies that operate in New Bedford and Rhode Island. According to the USDOL, more than 300,000 migrant children had entered the country unaccompanied since 2021. These solo minors had either lost their guardians or coyotes along their migration journeys, or had been intentionally sent alone by desperate parents who hoped their child would be paired with a relative or sponsor and start earning money for the family. One such child, New Bedford seafood worker Faviola, immigrated from Guatemala when she was fifteen and began working at Sea Watch six days a week from 6 a.m. to 6 p.m. She sorted clams and extracted their meat for packaging, and cleaned processing machines with a hazardous chemical solution. Four other Guatemalan children between fifteen and seventeen years old were interviewed by the *New Bedford Light* and described similar working days. Each felt responsible for supporting their families in Guatemala and New Bedford, and had forged paperwork to claim they were older than eighteen. Some tried to attend school, but the demands of work won out over their education. Lázaro, a girl who began working at a fish processing plant at thirteen, confessed, "I would go to school, but I would be so tired that I would sleep through my classes." Lázaro tweezed bones out of salmon and whitefish five nights a week, from 3 p.m. until 3 a.m., until she paid off a $5,000 loan from a Guatemalan bank that she used to pay a smuggler. When her mother eventually joined her in New Bedford, Lázaro started attending New Bedford High School.[45] Some community organizations have become vital for Latinx seafood working communities, and particularly children. The Immigrants' Assistance Center, a nonprofit established in 1971 to serve all immigrants in New Bedford, connects newcomers with food, shelter, jobs, English classes, and help with completing their citizenship applications. When the New Bedford school system contracted IAC to work with unaccompanied youth from Central America, IAC facilitated greater funding for language instruction and mental health support to help young people process their migration traumas.[46]

In recent years, Latinx seafood processors in New Bedford have spoken out more about their laboring conditions. "You have to speak up for yourself with confidence and get rid of the fear because if you don't, someone will walk all over you, because that is life in the United States. . . . If they [employers] need us, why do they treat us so poorly? I don't understand," said one woman who had to fight for her vacation days despite working for three years straight.[47] Protests seemed even more necessary when seafood processors began dying on the job in disturbing ways. One such victim was William Couto, a sixty-three-year-old processor for the clam company Sea Watch International who died in 2019 after his clothes became entangled in machinery.[48] In the spring of 2023, seafood workers attempted to organize for raises to sixteen dollars an hour and improved safety conditions, but their mobilization was met with massive layoffs at processing plants. The companies claimed they were cutting ties with staffing agencies and rechecking all workers' eligibility to work legally, but workers suspected it was also a move to stifle their labor activism. After a law firm filed a complaint with the NLRB on behalf of the workers, the Boston and Providence field offices of the USDOL visited New Bedford in July 2023. The result of this visit was a formal alliance between OSHA and the Centro Comunitario de Trabajadores, a center that advocated for "immigrant and low-wage workers in southern New England." The agreement initiated labor rights education and hazard training programs for workers but did not appear to demand higher wages from the fish companies.[49]

Panning out to the national scale, Latinx seafood processors are laboring in other US regions like the Chesapeake Bay and Gulf Coast, where employers use the H-2B visa program to import Mexican, Central American, and Caribbean workers. While employers justify their use of the program by claiming a lack of interested citizen workers, others believe these companies are intentionally replacing citizens with a lower-paid immigrant precariat. Up until the 1980s, crab processing was dominated by US-born Black women, but under the H-2B program the workforce has changed to a Caribbean Black and Latina one. The older group of workers is now pressured to meet the higher production quotas set for the newer generation of workers in order to keep their jobs.[50] The same problems that plague H-2 workers in other industries carry over to seafood. These visa holders earn lower wages than are promised to them, live in substandard housing in remote and isolated areas, and experience a lack of occupational safety. This isolated existence certainly echoes guestworker programs of the past, and neither the United States nor Canada show signs of stopping seafood guestworker programs. In British Columbia seafood processing plants, old waves of workers have been swiftly replaced with foreign labor. In New Brunswick fish plants, low-paid workers from the Philippines are now the majority.[51] Employing an immigrant precariat in seafood is, in one way, a reverberating legacy of the world's oldest whaling economies. In other ways, this is a particularly late twentieth- and early twenty-first-century phenomenon of accelerating ethnic succession to undercut wages for citizen workers.

Moving from water to two more liquids, the next chapter interrogates the social, financial, and culinary geographies of Latinx laborers who work in milk and wine. By examining dairies and vineyards in Vermont, upstate New York, and Long Island—all places in which the border and immigrant policing is salient—it explores how physical constrictions of mobility affect workers' bodies and emotions, diets, and their levels of alienation from the drinks they help to keep flowing in America.

CHAPTER SIX

Empty Cups

Latinx Dairy and Wine Workers in Vermont and New York State

[If] everybody wants their milk when they have their
breakfast in the morning, they want to have their cheese
on their cheeseburgers, and they want their powdered milk
and they want their WIC formula and WIC free food programs,
they'd better support immigration, is my thinking.
—Ben Dykema, Vermont dairy farmer, 2007

Some wine lovers might protest that . . . dredging up colonial
history is a buzzkill, a weary intrusion on our enjoyment of
wine. . . . For once, can we leave politics aside and just drink
wine? . . . [But] wine has never been apolitical, and . . . the
colonial context in which wine was first created has inflected
its production and consumption into the twenty-first century.
—Jennifer Regan-Lefebvre, *Imperial Wine*, 2022

Milk and wine are frequent accompaniments to our meals. We take milk in our coffee and tea throughout the day, serve milk with school lunches, and look forward to relaxing with wine at happy hour gatherings, dinnertime, and celebratory moments. These drinks would not flow so easily into our cups without immigrant labor, and specifically Latinx labor. While Latinx communities have been helping the nation eat, they have also been helping the nation drink.

In the Northeast, the dairy industries of Vermont and upstate New York profit from a pastoral image that attracts tourists as well as long-term residents. When one thinks of Vermont, one imagines red barns and green rolling hills, white fences and dairy cows, and vivid autumn leaves with apple- and pumpkin-picking. Vermont is the US state with the highest dependence upon a single commodity for its agricultural revenue. Around 80 percent of Vermont farmland is dedicated to producing or supporting dairy, and 70 percent of the state's agricultural sales comes from more than 321 million gallons of milk produced each year. In total, the dairy industry provides 6,000 to 7,000 jobs and $360 million in wages.[1] Meanwhile, the upstate (and specifically Hudson Valley) region of New York, known for its apple orchards and cideries, also produces a large amount of milk that makes its way into cartons or is turned into cheese and Greek yogurt.

Since the 1980s, US dairy farmers have been complaining about their harder jobs and smaller profits. Cow feed costs keep rising, federal subsidies have decreased, milk prices are unstable, and weather patterns keep changing, affecting grasslands and herds. Moreover, much like in New England seafood, dairy farmers' children are showing waning enthusiasm for inheriting family businesses. During the 1940s about 11,000 dairy farms operated in Vermont, but as of 2024 only about 500 remain, due to consolidation and people leaving the farming profession. To stay operable and profitable, many dairy farmers have increased the size of their herds and number of milkings from two to three times per day. This has radically changed the nature of milking work, requiring overnight shifts and a workforce that is available at unconventional hours.[2] Thus the dairy industry, like many other sectors of the US food industry, has become reliant on people divorced from a family or social life—in this case, solo male Latino migrants. Between 2000 and 2010, the Latino population in Vermont grew twenty-four times faster than the overall population, and as of 2019 about 1,000–1,200 Latin American migrants (90 percent undocumented) sustained the state's dairy industry. In total, 68 percent of Vermont's milk (and 43 percent of New England's milk) comes from farms reliant on immigrant workers.[3] Though this chapter will focus more on Vermont dairy, it includes complementary information on upstate New York, as employers there have also hired a substantial Latinx workforce. In 2011, 2,600 undocumented immigrants from Mexico and Central America worked in the milking parlors of upstate New York, and that number has only increased over time.[4]

Meanwhile, in the world of wine, Long Island's North Fork is a young wine-producing region that holds great appeal for tourists. Though the wines of New York's Finger Lakes are better known, the North Fork is comprised of interesting terroirs that used to be dedicated to cauliflower, potato, and other vegetable cultivation. Today, the North Fork Wine Trail boasts miles of vineyards, pumpkin and sunflower patches, and farmstands. The wine produced here travels down to supply the restaurants and hotels of the Hamptons, a series of villages along Long Island's southeastern coast. In both the North Fork and the Hamptons, a Latinx wine, food, and hospitality workforce lives and labors among year-round locals and summer vacationers.

To stay attractive and romantic to consumers and tourists, both the dairy and wine industries hide truths about how their products are made possible by vulnerable immigrant laborers who do not enjoy their own economic, health, or food security. Dairy and wine workers often make long and perilous journeys to the United States, risking their lives and paying large sums to smugglers to begin working in dairy barns or vineyards. Moreover, because both Vermont and portions of New York State are within the 100-mile radius of heightened Border Patrol surveillance, migrant workers live in fear of apprehension and deportation. This anxiety constricts many of their waking hours. In the dairy industry, it is even common for employers to grocery shop for their workers so they can remain hidden in milking barns or their employer-provided housing. Geographically and physically constrained in their daily movements and decision-making, many dairy workers interviewed for oral history projects in the 1990s and early 2000s described feeling *encerrado* (enclosed, hemmed in, imprisoned), leading geographer Susannah McCandless to characterize Vermont as a "carceral countryside."[5]

That being said, Latinx dairy and wine workers are not passive victims. They experience varied dynamics along the worker-employer relationship spectrum, from benevolent paternalism to genuine human connection. They mindfully arrange their working situations, negotiate with employers about their treatment and conditions, and create comforting solutions to what they lack or long for, including food procurement. One way that Latinx wine workers have become connected with dairy workers, at least in New York State, is through their struggles to enforce the recently passed Farmworker Fair Labor Practices Act. Dairy laborers and their advocates tried and failed several times during the 2000s to convince state legislators to approve the act. When it finally passed in 2019 and went into effect in January 2020, it was a group of Latino wine workers on Long Island who first tested the law's promise by unionizing. Their attempt to create the first recognized collective bargaining unit of agricultural workers in New York State is a giant and continuing feat.

Migrating to Milk

The havoc NAFTA wrought by exporting cheap commodities to Mexico (including, ironically, powdered milk) which then depressed the market prices of local Mexican agricultural products resulted in rural Mexican citizens, and later Central Americans, migrating north for *migradólares*. Between 1993 and 2007 an estimated 2.3 million Mexicans left agriculture, another 3 million migrated internally within Mexico to work in tomato and strawberry fields owned by companies like Driscoll's, and half a million people per year began migrating to the United States. Many people wanted to migrate into dairy because, unlike other agricultural jobs, milking cows can offer year-round employment. Over time, migrants began heading straight for Vermont, oftentimes prearranging a job in dairy by taking a friend or relative's place at a milking parlor while the other returned home. Currently, the most frequent sending states to Vermont dairy jobs are Chiapas, Tabasco, and Veracruz in Mexico and Guatemala, El Salvador, and Honduras in Central America. The vast majority of migrating dairy workers are undocumented young men. There are far fewer women in dairy because, some speculate, employers fear they will get pregnant and need higher-quality housing, nutrition, and medical care.[6]

Interviews conducted with Vermont dairy workers in the early 2000s reveal how economically desperate they felt in their home countries, and how dangerously their initial migrations played out. Fabián Martínez, who worked in supermarkets and Walmart in Tabasco, Mexico, made 1,000 pesos (about $100) per week. He was attending university but felt forced to leave because of financial stress. Since Martínez had a compañero from Tabasco already working in Vermont, he decided to join him.[7] Pedro (also named in his interview as Leonel) came to the United States from Chiapas at the age of eighteen. He already had a father and two siblings working in poultry and construction on the East Coast. Pedro/Leonel worked in Michigan, Florida, and California before going to Vermont. Freddie Hernández García, who made the equivalent of $300 a month working for a supermarket in Chiapas, migrated to the United States because his mother needed money for an operation. Freddie traversed the perilous Arizona desert and ate mayonnaise when he ran out of food and water. His cousin Miguel led him to a job in Vermont.[8]

Freddie was not alone in this dangerous journey through the Arizona-Sonora borderlands. In 1994, then president Bill Clinton's "Operation Gatekeeper" tried to deter migrants by installing lights, physical barriers, and higher numbers of Border Patrol agents at key entry points, such as the Tijuana / San Diego border. All this did, however, was funnel migrants to more dangerous terrain such as the Arizona desert to evade detection. Temperatures in the Sonoran Desert reach 110 degrees during the summer and drop well below freezing in the winter. Over the next fifteen years, which geographer Joseph Nevins termed "the dying season," more than 5,000 bodies were recovered in the borderlands, and many more have never been found.[9] Tabasco migrant Raoul, who walked for two days and two nights to cross the border, said of the Arizona desert, "I don't want to remember that. It's very hard, very ugly. It's not easy. *Arriesgas la vida*" (You're risking your life). From Phoenix, he went to Vermont with directions from friends already working there.[10] Inocente, a planter and harvester in Tabasco, decided to migrate at seventeen but was caught by immigration authorities on his first crossing attempt. He made a second attempt eight days later, and walked fifteen days in the desert with a group of sixty people. He was lucky enough to make it to Phoenix, but others died along the way. "They ran out of water, got sick in the desert, had a heart problem. . . . There were 20 in our group at the end," he remembered. Inocente worked in New York and Texas before arriving in Vermont. On average, undocumented crossers were apprehended three times and had to cross the border six times before making it into the United States. Smugglers charged desperate Mexican migrants higher and higher fees, which shot up from $500 to $1,000 a trip in the early 1990s to $1,500 to $1,800 in 2005 to $4,000 today (and the fee is even higher for Central Americans).[11]

Migrants are well acquainted with geographies of risk when migrating to and within the United States. For example, if they succeed at crossing, many migrants band together to pay a taxi driver several hundred dollars to take them to their final destination instead of traveling by public transportation. They already know that immigration officials board Greyhound buses to ask for papers. As sociologist Julie C. Keller has written about Latin American migrants in midwestern dairies, workers are intentional and intelligent about facilitating their work arrangements and mobility. If they become a trusted employee of a dairy farmer and want to return to their home country for a period, they will sometimes ask their employer to loan them the money to make the return journey back to the farm later. In essence, workers ask their employers to pay their future smuggling fee.[12]

Meanwhile, dairy farmers made their own calculations. Between 1993 and 2006, farmers' share of milk profits fell from 40 percent to just 15 percent of consumer sale price because of profits taken by processors and distributors. Depending on the product into which their dairy was diverted—milk, cheese, or yogurt—the profits could be even lower. In New York State, for instance, Greek yogurt brings in a lower profit than cheese and milk, but farmers have no control over what product their milk will ultimately make. To stay competitive with larger dairy farms, smaller enterprises needed to intensify their milking schedules and find a workforce to perform overnight shifts.[13] At first, Vermont dairy farmers were wary of hiring Latin American migrants, but they quickly saw the benefits. Jason Hatch, a seventh-generation dairy farmer in Ferrisburg, hired three Mexican workers to augment his existing staff of his uncle, brother-in-law, and cousin. When asked if he was nervous about hiring them, Hatch responded, "Oh, yeah, very nervous. Yeah. But it was the best decision I've ever made, by far.

Super people. Really good people." Kevin Cahart, who had been farming since 1969 with a citizen workforce, began hiring Latin American workers in 2000. "They're a godsend for us," he said. "They're just dependable, reliable people and great workers. Absolutely great workers." As in other economic sectors, dairy farmers expressed that citizen workers could no longer be trusted to show up and perform consistent work. Upstate New York farmer Kevin Acres recalled how he and his wife Phyllis had to work the night of their twenty-fifth wedding anniversary when his expected worker did not show. Vermont farmer Ben Dykema, who was at first hesitant to hire a Latin American worker, recalled a colleague asking him, "Why don't you try one?" This refrain of "try one" echoed in upstate New York. Doug Moser, who sold milk to Kraft for cream cheese, was asked by a colleague, "Well, why don't you try a Hispanic[?]" in answer to his labor woes.[14] As a result, many Vermont and upstate New York dairy farms were employing Latino workers by the early 2000s.

Milking the Body Dry:
Vermont Dairy Workers' Lives and Isolations

In the autumn of 2019, I toured a Vermont dairy farm classified as large, with about 1,600 milking cows. The first things I noticed upon walking up to the milking barn were Spanish-language music playing on a speaker and two trash cans filled to the brim with empty energy drink bottles. The milking parlor was spacious, clean, and well ventilated. Two automated rows of milking stalls flanked the building, and three Mexican workers—two younger, one older— milled around the space. A system of gates directed cows, wearing transponders around their necks, into specific positions in the milking parlor. Before the machines latched onto the cows' teats, the workers took a laundered rag, dipped it in a dark red iodine solution, and wiped the teats to kill bacteria and prevent mastitis infection in both the cow and the milk. The workers then squeezed some milk by hand to make sure the stream was clear before they attached the mechanical milkers to the cow. The machines extracted the milk rapidly; multiple gallons appeared on the counting machine in a matter of seconds. As the cows stood and waited, workers walked up and down the rows, spraying the floor if the animals were urinating or defecating. They had to evade kicking hooves to keep from getting splattered or injured until the machines unlocked and fell back, waiting for the next phalanx of cows.

When I asked about workers' shifts, the farm's owner said the first workers of the day arrived at 5 a.m. to milk all 1,600 cows, a process that lasts until 2 or 3 p.m. The next shift arrives at 5 p.m. and stays until two or three in the morning.

FIGURE 6.1. Mexican dairy worker spraying cows in line for the milking machines, Vermont. Photo by the author, 2019.

This parallel night and day shift system seemed to be the norm. At another Vermont dairy farm, workers arrived at 1:15 a.m. and milked until noon, and then another shift took over from 1 p.m. until midnight. On average, dairy workers labor for seventy to eighty hours per week. At some operations the hours were split differently—at one dairy barn where the crew worked six days a week, workers had shifts of four hours in the morning, then a break, and five or more hours in the afternoon. A survey of Latinx dairy workers in New York in the late 2010s revealed that the average daily work shift was 11.3 hours, similar to Vermont's.[15] In addition to milking, workers are expected to complete other tasks, including cleaning out stalls and wiping down equipment, scraping manure, and feeding cows. In some cases, employers said, workers decide to work both shifts of the day and just use the one or two hours in between to eat, sleep, and shower. "They're willing to work 7 days a week. . . . These guys, they have nothing to do or no place to go, so they're willing to work to earn that extra money to send home," one farmer said. This double-shift decision takes a massive toll on workers' bodies and cognition. Speaking from a farm in upstate New York, a journalist said of one man, "The daily work routine on this industrial dairy was literally milking his body dry, leaving only enough energy to drift like a *sonámbulo* [sleepwalker] between the milking parlor and the trailer after his shifts."[16]

For this intense milking and maintenance work, dairy workers in Vermont are paid an average hourly wage of between $7.50 and $9.75. This salary, employers quickly point out, does not have to go toward any rent. Dairy employers often provide year-round housing to their immigrant workers that they consider "built into" their wages, and which is often located next to or directly across from the milking barns. Employers also provide utilities such as heat, electricity, and cable television, and coordinate trips for workers to go grocery shopping or perform other errands. Despite these benefits, many workers felt their pay still fell short. A worker named Geraldo, who was paid $500 a week for working on a small, eighty-cow dairy, calculated that his hourly pay hovered between $5.95 and $7.94 per hour, which averaged below the state's $7.25 minimum wage at that time. Moreover, Geraldo said, his employer frequently paid him many weeks late. "I never told them that the pay was not right, because of fear. Because I really need the work, and if they fire me, where will I go?" he said. A survey of 172 Vermont farmworkers conducted by the organization Migrant Justice in 2014 revealed that 40 percent received less than minimum wage and no days off; 30 percent suffered a work-related injury or illness; 29 percent regularly worked seven or more hours without a food break; and 20 percent had their first paycheck illegally withheld. Meanwhile, at New York's state capitol building in January 2018, farmworkers gathered to share testimony regarding their working conditions. Antonio Jasso, who had milked 2,400 cows a day at a farm in eastern New York since 2010, reported that during his first three years he worked an average of eighty-five hours a week for $7.50 an hour. Unlike his citizen coworkers, who took water breaks without issue, Jasso testified he was scolded by his boss for taking a short water break after working thirteen hours straight. More than three dozen worker deaths had been recorded on New York dairy farms between 2007 and 2014, but only five were investigated by the Occupational Safety and Health Administration, since farms claiming ten or fewer nonfamily employees were exempt from OSHA oversight.[17] Though it might be true that migrant workers make higher wages in the United States than they would in their home countries, this does not cancel out the hardships, indignities, and risks they experience on the job.

Several dairy employers voiced admiration of Latino workers' skills in comforting and connecting with animals, an ability bordering on veterinary expertise. At the Vermont farm I visited, the adult cows were eager to interact—they pushed their way forward in the pens to nudge their heads and noses toward us. Their big, round eyes pleaded for attention. Meanwhile, calves relaxed in little hutches with a pleasant view of the surrounding mountains and green fields. Workers at Vermont farms often help birthing cows by pulling their calves out and giving them necessary shots. Working with animal bodies that can grow up to 1,800 pounds, workers need to be calm and authoritative. "Sometimes animals understand too," Pedro/Leonel said while speaking of his habit of talking to agitated cows to calm them. Farmer Philip Livingston said of his employee Ulysses López, "Louie was an *excellent*, excellent cow person . . . he could give IV bottles, like, better than a veterinarian, or as good," and recalled how Louie had once deftly lassoed a runaway cow.[18] This valuable skill set, if performed by a US citizen, might have earned someone the ability to strike out on their own and offer their consulting and expertise to multiple dairy farms. Because they are constricted to their employer's barn and fearful of immigration authorities, however, Latin American immigrant men do not feel free to demand compensation for these extra skills. Not all dairy workers had positive experiences with the animals they tended. Antonio Jasso was injured in 2015 when a cow kicked him in his left knee. Another New York dairy worker, Crispin Hernández, was injured when a cow stepped on his hand. Even though Hernández asked for medical help, the farm's owner did not take him to a doctor, likely out of fear that both he and Crispin would be reported to immigration authorities.[19]

There are certain jobs on dairy farms that employers consider off-limits for their Latin American employees due to anxieties about immigration authorities seeing them. "They all want to drive the tractor and they all want to mix feed and they all want to do everything [outside], but the reality is it's the danger, the risk, the hazard level goes up dramatically," said Ben Dykema. Mark Akins agreed, "The immigrants milk. They don't get outside the barn. They do chores in the barn. . . . That is all that they do." Local citizens are given the outdoor tasks instead, and Akins implied citizens were entitled to more socialization anyway. "They do not want to be in a parlor for 8 or 9 hours a day. They want to be outside, they want to be communicating with other people, they want to have different priorities than just milking cows," he said.[20] Depriving undocumented workers of open-air jobs is a very conscious decision employers make, rooted in both fear for their own enterprises and beliefs about what citizens deserve more. Informal labor contractor Nancy "Mama" Sabin—who spent part of her youth in Puerto Rico and sometimes translated or obtained medicine and food for migrant workers in Vermont—gave another striking rationale for keeping dairy workers tucked away from citizens. She believed the latter would resent immigrants for their stable jobs and salaries. "Take the teller at the bank and she sees a check coming in for $550 or $600 . . . and she gets very pissed off because her boyfriend is working 40 hours a week and only getting $300 or $400. . . . They're very, very jealous over the Mexican, so the best place for the Mexican is to stay *hidden* on the farm," she argued. This perceived economic resentment is disturbing and noteworthy, as it surely parallels some of the xenophobia found in other rural working-class communities in the United States that have absorbed a noticeable immigrant workforce.[21]

Overwhelmingly, migrant workers feel very much like cows—penned in their housing, with little control over their radius of movement. Though employers are comforted by being able to keep an eye on their workforce, migrant men do not enjoy any separation between work and home. Their employer-provided housing also varies in quality. If workers are fortunate, their dwellings are equipped with bunk beds, multiple refrigerators, laundry machines, and insulation for cold winters. Kevin and Phyllis Acres spoke of the housing they provided their Guatemalan employee Levi: a private dwelling valued at $40,000 with radiant heat, insulation, and tile floors. At the other end of the spectrum, Ferrisburgh dairy worker Víctor Díaz reported living in a trailer where sewage had leaked into the drinking water. In a 2014–15 survey of eighty-eight dairy workers in New York State (mostly undocumented Mexican and Central American men), 58 percent reported insect infestations in their housing and 32 percent claimed inadequate ventilation. In a 2015 episode of the National Public Radio broadcast *This American Life*, a tour of upstate New York dairy farms yielded one house where thirteen workers shared seven beds in a two-bedroom trailer. As one cohort of men returned from a shift, the other cohort gave up their beds and switched places. Black mold had grown in the cabinets, and one worker had elected to sleep on a platform placed on top of the bathtub for some privacy. If a friend or sexual partner visited one man, the rest crammed into the only other bedroom.[22]

Encouraged to stay hidden in barns or their housing, migrant dairy workers inevitably feel lonely. Mary Mendoza, a professor and Vermont resident who volunteered to teach English to dairy workers between 2006 and 2008, recalled joining the men in the dairy barns at the end of their shifts and walking them home so that their English lessons would not infringe too much on their sleeping time. She taught them English farm vocabulary (such as "iodine" and "mastitis"), but also felt compelled to teach them the rules to poker so that their bosses could not swindle them out of their wages in the evenings. In describing the worker housing she saw, she recalled one house with a large communal living room, laundry room, and three refrigerators. Several small bedrooms had been built down a hallway, and then more had been constructed on a lower level. Some bedrooms had bunk beds or two twin beds. "They would love it when I would come over. . . . It was nice to have . . . a human in their house that wasn't talking to them necessarily about work all the time," she said. Some workers trusted Mendoza enough to hand her money to buy international calling cards so they could contact their families.[23]

Unknowingly, almost all the Vermont dairy workers interviewed for the Golden Cage oral history project used the same word, *encerrado*, to describe their lives. Though some expressed that they liked Vermont because it was *tranquilo* and *bonito* (peaceful and pretty), sadness and isolation overwhelmed their narratives. "After 10 months in the United States I felt alone, I felt depressed, I was in the house walking around alone, del trabajo a la casa [from work straight home] to my bed to sleep to eat. . . . Es una vida encerrada," said Freddie, who spoke to his wife every eight days. Another concurred, "Encerrado . . . no puedes salir [you can't leave]. . . . I miss my family, mis novias [girlfriends] [*laughs*], comida [food], diversiones [fun activities]." Workers feel they have very little space to move, and experience boredom and helplessness. Raoul spoke about his monotonous daily routine. "Every day is the same. We can't leave, we can't go anywhere different. . . . If we go to the [grocery] store, we [get apprehended and] go back to Mexico . . . porque somos ilegales, no tenemos papeles [because we are illegal, we do not have papers]. . . . Estoy encerrado. Estamos encerrados." Fabián Martínez characterized his life as "encerrada—se me aburro" (closed in—I get bored). The farthest he dared to go was a fifteen-minute walk out of his house to buy something or play soccer. When asked how his limited mobility affected him, he replied, "Te estresas. Te estresas. Porque todos los días, todos los días lo mismo" (It stresses you, it stresses you. Because every day, every day is the same). "My reality and the reality of all the others who live here is that we are trapped both in the house and in our work," he concluded in Spanish.[24] The "Invisible Odysseys" art project—which provides paint, wooden boxes, and mixed media materials to Mexican farmworkers in Vermont to make three-dimensional representations of their migration journeys—captured the words of some female migrants. In one diorama titled *La belleza puede ser engañosa* (Beauty can be deceiving), a woman wrote in her accompanying text in Spanish, "My first impression when I arrived in Vermont was that everything looked so green and beautiful. . . . As the years have gone by . . . [because] I can't go out and travel around freely. . . . I began losing my love of what everyone else saw as beautiful."[25]

Some employers were attuned to their workers' isolation and tried to create trusting and respectful relationships with their workers. Family-like rituals such as sharing meals or leisure time figured heavily in cultivating such dynamics. "They really are [like family] to me, they are. If they have a problem . . . I'd have 'em up for dinner with my family and talk things over and, you know, they think the world of that," Jason Hatch said.[26] Rob Hunt started a communal calendar for his workers on which they wrote not only the daily business of the farm but the birthdays of employees and their children. "It makes a huge difference," he said, and continued, "The cultural differences are the—that's the hardest part. You know, knowing, or not knowing how easily you can offend them or disrespect them just completely unintentionally. . . . [I thought that] you don't need to visit about your wife and kids; you don't need to visit about whether you had a good sleep. . . . I learned that pretty quickly, if you don't show interest in them as a person you don't get much cooperation."[27] Hunt's milking crew demanded to be treated like fuller people with families and concerns outside of work. Hunt himself admitted that if he did not pay attention to that reality, he would encounter surlier and less cooperative employees.

Other farmers concurred about the importance of connecting with family. Dustin Bliss, a farmer in upstate New York, babysat one of his employee's daughters over Easter weekend when the employee had to tend to his wife in the hospital. "My Hispanic employees, right along with local employees, were at my wedding," he added. "We have them over for dinner. We celebrate birthdays, we buy each other gifts." Philip Livingston said of his employee Louie, "If my daughter was out there playing in the yard he'd make sure . . . [to] play with her for a few minutes. . . . He has four kids [back home] and I think that was part of his kind of healing." In many dairy farmers' families, the children and grandchildren of the farmers are the brokers or bridges between their elders and the milking workers. "My grandchildren think the world of [my employees], you know? And some of them are taking Spanish right now, so that they can communicate a little more," one farmer said.[28]

Other employers shared play and leisure time with their employees, and learned their longer life histories. In outings with his employees to swim at a local pond, Blake Gendebien learned, "Carlos meditates, he is into metaphysics [and] was a college student in Puebla in Mexico. . . . Chris came from Chicago. He worked at a restaurant; he is like a gourmet chef. . . . Tony . . . is in his mid-40s, he's been here much longer and he was paying for his daughter to go to nursing school. He has a home also they are slowly chipping away at." Mark Akins, who employed a mix of citizen workers and immigrant workers from Guatemala, took it upon himself to help his employee Pascual with immigration issues. After Pascual's wife Francesca was apprehended at a Vermont Walmart and deported, Pascual was left raising two young daughters. "We were required to go to Buffalo every six months to check on his citizenship applications. We have hired an attorney and a consultant to help him along in that process," Akins said. There are also cases of workers who do not feel humanized by their bosses. A worker named Inocente, for example, remembered his employer "didn't let me rest or do anything for me" when he was experiencing appendix pain. "I ran away," he said. "The boss thought of me as nothing more than someone who's supposed to work."[29] Some workers run away without notice, or threaten to leave a farm, if conditions do not improve.

Procuring Food

Motivated to keep a reliable workforce, Vermont dairy farmers try to offer other perks such as helping workers acquire computers, internet, cell phones, and groceries. Rob Hunt affirmed the essential task of building trust with his workers and proving his own reliability.

> Hunt: They've been mistreated by every white person they've ever met and they do not trust *at all*.
> Interviewer: How do you try to build it?
> Hunt: Paying 'em on time. Doing what I say. . . . If I tell them we're going to go shopping on Wednesday, we'd better go shopping on Wednesday.[30]

Being driven to grocery stores for food shopping is incredibly important to Vermont dairy workers, as it is one of their only experiences of autonomy outside the workplace. They are not satisfied with minimal gestures of "gifted" or "bonus" food, such as being treated to the occasional pizza, doughnut, or fast food meal by their boss. Some employers offer to make the grocery runs themselves by collecting lists from their employees, but errors in translation result in mistaken orders, missing products, and frustration. Workers look forward to their grocery shopping trips not only as a break from a monotonous routine but also as a moment of control over what they get to eat. During her English tutoring sessions with workers, Mary Mendoza made sure to teach them phrases related to food shopping and interacting with store employees, such as "How much does that cost?" or "Do you have any jalapeños/cilantro/beans?" to help them feel able to navigate store interactions.[31]

Unfortunately, at times these shopping trips become frightening experiences or get derailed altogether. Almost all of Vermont falls within the 100-mile radius of the border where Border Patrol officers (and post-2003, Customs and Border Protection) have the authority to stop and search people and vehicles. Through the presidential administrations of Bill Clinton, George W. Bush, Barack Obama, Donald Trump, and Joe Biden, the United States has committed to a "crimmigration" system in which immigration violations previously treated as noncriminal misdemeanors have become categorized as crimes, and the border has become even more militarized.[32] Vermont farmer Blake Gendebien, speaking of the "gung-ho" Border Patrol agents brought into Vermont from Arizona, said, "All they want to do is pick people up." Agents circle farm properties, sometimes parking their cars within sight of milking parlors. The heightened chance of being detained and deported keeps both workers and employers on edge. Freddie Hernández García remembered a traumatic incident in which his employer left him and a relative to fend for themselves: "We went to Wal-Mart to buy stuff— clothing and stuff to eat . . . immigration came inside the store. I was there with my brother in law. . . . The boss was waiting for us in the car. We were taking two carts of food, and went to the car, and the boss wasn't there. And immigration asked us for our papers. We didn't have any, and were detained for several days . . . it was horrible."[33]

While some workers are detained and then released, others are deported. Farmer Ben Dykema remembered of one Sunday evening, "We came home from church and the barn and house lights weren't on and we thought, maybe they overslept. . . . We got a phone call about 20 minutes later from St. Albans Correctional, [and the workers] said, 'You need to milk your own cows 'cause we in jail.' [*laughs*]." INS officers, who had found a paycheck stub with Dykema's address at another farm, had simply walked into the house and taken the men out of it. "We were all really upset when they left," Dykema said. "We did receive a letter from one of the guys who said, 'I always wanted an airplane ride, but not this way'" [*laughs*].[34] While it is possible that Dykema's laughter reflects the actual wry humor the workers used at the time of their communication with him, Dykema did enjoy the privilege of being psychologically distanced from the actual consequences the workers experienced. Though it is hard to know how the men processed their jailing at the time, "You need to milk your own cows" was a resigned if not sarcastic statement. Apprehensions and deportations of dairy workers occurred elsewhere in the Northeast. In Clinton, Maine, four Mexican dairy workers were arrested in July 2008 when a tip to the sheriff's department led ICE officials to the workers' trailer. The men, who had been working at the farm for eighteen months, pleaded guilty in US District Court to document fraud, while their employer evaded charges. In Vermont, to this date, no farmer has been prosecuted for hiring undocumented workers; the employees have borne all the punishment. In May 2012, Vermont began participating in the Secure Communities Program, which allowed local law enforcement to share information with ICE until it was suspended by President Barack Obama in November 2014.[35]

As word of each apprehension spread, workers became more fearful. Describing workers' hemmed-in condition, anthropologist and Vermont resident Teresa Mares has written of the "ongoing fear and anxieties of living and working in a border region where one is invisible in the workplace yet hypervisible in public."[36] In being deprived of what many people consider a mundane practice of grocery shopping, dairy workers do not get to see or purchase the products they help to produce, such as milk, cheese, yogurt, and ice cream. Their dread of deportation further alienates them from the community and nation in which they labor. It does not help matters when employers bring up deportation as a threat or joke. When two of his Mexican workers got into a physical altercation, for instance, one farmer threatened, "You guys ever have a fistfight again and I'm calling immigration and you guys will be out of here in a heartbeat."[37] That leveraging of an uneven power dynamic, in a mere moment, undoes prior social and emotional bonding between employer and employees.

One way that migrants respond to their limited food procurement options is buying desired foodstuffs from mediators. A network of entrepreneurs drives vans of Latin American items from Boston, New Jersey, or New York City and stops at workers' houses to sell items like tortilla masa mix, banana leaves and corn husks for tamales, phone cards, and piñatas. Some migrants rely on friends or relatives living elsewhere in the Northeast to send them packages of herbs and candy.[38] On the transnational scale, an entire industry now exists for Latin American package pickup and delivery. *Paqueteros*—informal couriers who facilitate the transfer of goods between family members divided by borders—transport food items, handicrafts, and medicinal remedies from south to north, and consumer goods like sneakers and electronics from north to south (see fig. 6.2). The most requested food items by migrants in the United States are dried chiles and herbs, festive breads associated with certain holidays, fruit preserves, seeds, corn, teas, dried flowers, and sweets. *Paqueteros* travel by vehicle or airplane with multiple suitcases, and charge customers by package weight.[39] Sending packages is one way that people in the home country can maintain a connection with their loved ones in *el norte* and maintain migrants' nostalgia and tastes for home. Lidia Ruis, a woman in Chiapas who had three sons working in Vermont, expressed distress that her sons returned to her with different manners of speaking, dressing, and eating. "It's as though they had a different face. What they were before, they aren't now. . . . They don't want to eat what we have. There's a lot of change related to food . . . they don't like it [our food] very much anymore."[40] Food care packages are one way family members at home try to keep their loved ones from changing so drastically during their absence.

Northeastern community advocates have fought to ensure that dairy workers

FIGURE 6.2. *Paquetero* service van, Brooklyn, New York. Photo by the author, 2021.

do not experience food insecurity amid their isolation. Defined as a lack of access to a reliable daily supply of nutritional and culturally desirable food, food insecurity affects about 15 percent of Americans and almost 1 billion people worldwide. When it comes to Latinx (citizen, immigrant, and mixed-status) households in the United States, about one-quarter are classified as food insecure compared to one-tenth of white households. If one is a farmworker, the rate of food insecurity triples or quadruples the national average.[41] In addition to a lack of access to grocery stores, Vermont dairy workers do not have enough time and energy to eat properly during their work days because of their long shifts. Bladimir Santiz Cruz observed, "At work one comes out too tired to cook food. And you are so tired because of lack of sleep, you don't have time to cook food. Only one meal for all the day and night. At work your stomach is screaming from hunger."[42] In New York's Hudson Valley, Antonio Valeriano remarked that the dishes he and his colleagues made after work were simple and minimal: "Something that we can put together quickly. More than anything we want to rest." An example of one dinner was warmed tortillas, heated cans of tomato sauce, and shrimp-flavored ramen noodles.[43] As Alyshia Gálvez and others have shown, a migrant's time in the United States is connected with poorer health outcomes due to factors like stress and eating greater amounts of inexpensive processed foods and sugar. Studies have proved that the longer a Latin American immigrant spends in the United States, the higher their risk is for diabetes and obesity. "Diabetes is the disease of the migrant. . . . Not just because migrants change the way they eat, but because it is the somatization of pain, trauma and depression," said one priest in Puebla, Mexico.[44]

To give workers a greater sense of pride and control over their food supply, the University of Vermont project Huertas has helped people plant and maintain kitchen gardens since 2012. "This form of agency is extremely rare in the lives of workers whose labor is devoted to feeding others rather than attending to their own physical, spiritual, and cultural hungers," Huertas advocate and University of Vermont anthropology professor Teresa Mares remarked. In their gardens, workers can plant things that remind them of home, such as chiles, squash, and epazote, or other useful items like garlic, watermelon, and cucumbers. Huertas has helped build and maintain gardens for dozens of dairy farms, and gardens can serve as personal refuges and spaces of food sovereignty.[45] Another foodways project in Vermont is Viva el Sabor, a culinary collective of Mexican and Guatemalan cooks who sell plates of homemade food to local communities. At an inaugural pop-up dinner in the college town of Middlebury in the summer of 2021, the collective sold plates of tamales, tacos, Veracruzan chicken empanadas, and *pellizcadas* (gordita-like griddled cornmeal cakes topped with beans or meat) to more than 1,000 eager people. One of the cooks, Magnolia González, was married to a dairy farmworker and had lived in Vermont for thirteen of her fourteen years in the United States. Matilda Fuentes had been a calf-feeder on a dairy farm herself, and before moving to Vermont had cooked in restaurants in Florida, Kansas, and North Carolina. After this successful event, these women and the other cooks were contacted for catering other events, a potential jumpstart to their own future food businesses.[46]

Brown Grains in White Rice: Migrant Dairy Workers' Hypervisibility

Despite the ways they try to feed themselves, or the ways others support their culinary desires, migrant dairy workers still do not feel free because of the US crimmigration framework and deportation regime. After several years of net zero migration from Mexico (2009–19), a combination of growing violence and a worsening economy led to a spike in 2020. When the Biden administration began and the COVID-19 pandemic increased anxiety about national borders, Title 42 (which limited immigration based on public health concerns) justified more enforcement at the US-Mexico border. Biden and Vice President Kamala Harris also focused on curbing migration from Central America into Mexico, providing billions of dollars to Mexico's and Central American governments in hopes of keeping people from crossing their borders.[47] This national anti-immigration paradigm trickles down to the local level and influences residents' beliefs and behavior. Seeing brown-skinned people or hearing Spanish has disconcerted some white Vermonters so much that they immediately call police and immigration authorities upon seeing such a person in their neighborhood. Many locals judge Latin American migrants as having come into the United States the "wrong" way, when in reality current immigration laws and visa ceilings have made it nearly impossible to immigrate the "right" way with proper documents, which take years or decades to obtain. The discursive trauma that comes of relegating Latin American people to the immigration or crime blotter sections of Vermont newspapers only magnifies the sense that these people will never belong to the wider community. As a Latina migrant worker observed,

> This countryside is really quite enchanting. . . . But I think that for us, as immigrants, seeing the landscape no longer matters so much to us if we feel ourselves to be such prisoners, and so shut in. . . . I know the river, the lake, and it's absolutely lovely, I mean, you can't find a thing wrong with it. The community is very clean, the towns are very clean, wherever you look, everything is in order. . . . [It's as if] they don't even want a single brown grain in the rice.[48]

Vermont's manicured pastoral image has come at the cost of migrants feeling *they* are the brown grains in the rice, too conspicuous in their difference and not integrated into the whole.

Some Vermonters have accepted the presence of Latin American migrant labor, but mostly for economic reasons. "The sheriff always waves to workers when he sees them, he doesn't do anything," said dairy farmer Rob Hunt. "This is an extremely conservative community, but they are readily accepted." Vermont's governor, James Douglas, even said, "I respect the laws of the United States, of course. But the cows have to be milked."[49] Mentioning that his father had been a Dutch migrant worker in Montana's potato fields, farmer Ben Dykema said, "Without the labor, the Hispanic or, you know, migrant labor of any sort, the agricultural industry, you know, is gonna either fold or the American people will pay for imported food . . . if they . . . moved to Vermont because it's beautiful, they have to . . . [accept] the Hispanic labor that's coming in here."[50] Farmer Rob Hunt agreed: "Let 'em in. . . . Are we worried about the influx of illegal aliens that are coming to Vermont to milk cows? Is that a real threat to our homeland security?.... Tell the truth, that if it weren't for illegals in this country our Social Security System would be in the *minus* numbers.... The reason that we don't seriously close the border is because lettuce would be $10.00 a head . . . tomatoes would be $50.00 a package."[51]

When asked what *they* would say to US citizens and politicians if they had the opportunity, Vermont migrant dairy workers sought to emphasize their humanity and hard work. "We are here for nothing more than to work.... We didn't come here to conduct ourselves poorly, or to do bad things.... We are helping you in your jobs, with your land. We are not bad people," said Raoul in Spanish. "We are doing work that they wouldn't want to do. Standing in the shit of cows," agreed Inocente. "More than anything I would say give us our papers," said Freddie Hernández García. "I love this country but there is not much fun here.... Living illegally I feel alone, depressed, and distanced from my family.... If I was legal, I could buy a car, go places, go to the store, go to work, the hospital."[52] When asked what he did for fun, Pedro/Leonel laughed and replied in Spanish, "Nothing fun here, the only fun I have is talking to the little cows." "And what do the cows say?" asked the interviewer. "*Ya!* [Enough!]," he replied, laughing in both amusement and obvious commiseration with the animals.[53]

While dairy employers might praise migrant workers for their work ethic, the reality is that migrant workers become unavailable to other things and people in their lives because of the labor regime of dairy work, and the deportation regime of the United States. As much as a deportation nation keeps people out, historian Ana Minian and others have argued, it also keeps people trapped within. By postponing their returns home for months or even years because of fears they might not be able to enter the United States again for future work stints, migrants and their loved ones experience an elongated form of time and a slower velocity of life. Some workers describe creating their own mental escapes and daydreams to tolerate the pain. "When I work I put on music, and my mind is on the other side [in Mexico] when I'm with the cows," Inocente said. One project that seeks to address Vermont migrants' mental health is the participatory comics project called El Viaje Más Caro (The Most Costly Journey). By asking migrants to share their personal life stories and turning them into graphic narratives by local artists, El Viaje Más Caro aims to serve as "graphic medicine" that acknowledges the risky experiences and bravery of migrants who come to work in the United States. More than twenty interviews with migrants have been transformed into bilingual comics that address topics such as traumatic US-Mexico border crossings, substance abuse, and domestic violence.[54]

Some workers experience such profound depression and anxiety about their confinement and undocumented status that it keeps them from seeking out essential medical services. "They really tried to avoid going to the doctor," Mary Mendoza said, "because they didn't want to be deported. They only went if things got really extreme or scary." Employers are also wary of driving workers to a hospital because of immigration authorities' surveillance. This forces some workers to pay *raiteras*, or Spanish-speaking women drivers, to drive them instead. When he experienced stomach pain so severe that "I felt like I would die," forty-eight-year-old Salvadoran worker Manuel paid a raitera thirty dollars for a ten-minute ride to the hospital when no one at his farm agreed to drive him.[55] In a survey of 120 Latino workers in Vermont's dairy industry from 2009 to 2011, 93 percent of men surveyed exhibited anxiety and depression linked to social isolation, fear of immigration enforcement, and physical pain. Twelve other workers revealed they only left their house every three or four weeks to buy groceries or attend church and medical appointments. In another study, one worker admitted he had not set foot beyond the perimeter of his farm for two years. Another had not left his workplace, except for emergency medical care, for *ten* years. When asked to draw maps of where they go in Vermont, some workers were only able to draw home and one other place.[56] During the COVID-19 pandemic, the social quarantine these workers were already experiencing transformed into a public health–related one as well.

In terms of legislative change, the Vermont Migrant Farmworker Solidarity Project (VMFSP), later renamed Migrant Justice, has fought for strengthened worker protections and rights. The VMFSP was founded out of a tragedy in late December 2009, when twenty-year-old Mayan migrant José Obeth Santiz Cruz died after getting tangled and caught in a gutter cleaner on a dairy farm. Eighty more people from Santiz Cruz's hometown in southwestern Chiapas worked on Vermont farms, and his mother had already lost three other sons. Shortly before his accident, Santiz Cruz had confided to her, "The new year is coming and I haven't been paid. Our pay is always delayed." In addition to calling for stronger safety mechanisms in the workplace, the VMFSP supported three farmworkers the next year (one woman and two men) in filing a formal complaint with the Vermont Department of Labor to collect $4,494 in unpaid wages from the owners of Mack Dairy Farm in Charlotte, Vermont.[57] During the mid-2010s, Migrant Justice focused on leading the "Milk with Dignity" campaign, which modeled itself on the Fair Food Program of the Coalition of Immokalee Workers (CIW). Milk with Dignity called for a farmworker-authored code of conduct for employers (that included fair wages, paid sick days, health insurance, and adequate housing), a third-party enforcement body, and financial incentives to farmers and companies that complied with the code. The campaign's major victory has been an agreement with Ben and Jerry's Ice Cream (signed in April 2017), but one high-visibility company's commitment can only take the campaign so far.

Meanwhile, in New York State, farmworkers and their advocates were trying to pass the Farmworkers Fair Labor Practices Act during the 2010s. Sponsored by state senator Jessica Ramos, a US-born descendant of Colombian coffee and avocado farmers, the act proposed to establish an eight-hour workday for farmworkers (whether citizen, guestworker, or undocumented), provide overtime pay after eight hours, guarantee one day of rest per week, and grant farmworkers the right to organize and bargain collectively. A senate committee held three hearings throughout 2019 to hear from both farm owners and farmworkers. Even though agriculture was a $226 million industry in New York State, farmers argued they could not give farmworkers extra overtime pay during harvest seasons. Using the refrain that they were "price takers rather than price makers," almost every farmer at the hearings testified that they operated on razor-thin profit margins. Several dairy farmers asserted that since they already provided workers with housing, utilities, workers' compensation plans, and occasional bonuses of food or money, those things made up for a lack of overtime pay.[58] Fox Hollows Farms owner Jeff Rottkamp warned the end was nigh if one more cost was added to farmers' long list of bills and expenses. "I treat my help very, very well, and they have a beautiful home that I provide for them. I pay more than minimum wage.... And when we have crops on the farm, they're free to help themselves to whatever they would like ... asparagus, strawberries, sweet corn, tomatoes, melons, string beans.... If we don't make a profit, the end is close." In response, proponents of the act pointed out that farmworkers should not bear the brunt of farmers' operating costs. Lisa Zucker, an attorney with the New York Civil Liberties Union, remarked, "This is a false choice. If farmers are struggling, State of New York, you, Senators, Governor Cuomo if you're listening, do more for them. Do more for these farmers. Maybe they need more tax credits. Maybe they need some kind of subsidies ... but don't do it on the backs of farmworkers."[59] Herbert Engman, the director of Cornell University's Migrant Program, concurred and pointed out that all the farmers' arguments had been heard at previous points in history: "When drinking water in the fields was required in 1996, they said it would put them out of business. It didn't. When access to toilets was required in 1998, they said it would put them out of business. It didn't. When equal minimum wage was passed in 2000, they said would it put them out of business. It did not.... Farmworkers should not bear the burden of bad public policy."[60]

Farmers responded by turning to other tactics. First, they warned senators about their colleagues' well-being and mental health. Palestinian farmer Zaid Kurdieh, a former agricultural economist for the US Department of Agriculture (USDA), pointed out, "Suicide rates among farmers is at an all-time high." Indeed, farmers' cooperatives in the Northeast and elsewhere were sending dairy farmers their milk checks and information about suicide prevention hotlines. "Not to be morbid or use someone as a prop, but a family friend yesterday hung herself from the barn," added upstate farmer Dustin Bliss. He agreed that farmworkers—particularly undocumented ones—deserved greater protections and visibility, but he suggested this could be achieved with drivers' license programs and more freedom of mobility instead of passing the act itself.[61] Second, many farmers argued that their workers would rebel or leave if they could not work as many hours as they desired. "They will leave if I don't give them at least 60 hours a week," one insisted. Another agreed, pointing out that since H-2A visa workers made the same regional rate of $13.25 an hour, they could easily decide to leave New York and work in another northeastern state. A smattering of workers gave testimony supporting this claim, affirming they wanted to earn and send as much money back home as possible. Lupareo Pérez-Carbajal said, "We make [a] promise back home, that we're going to come back with money, and give our kids what we can't give them over there." Leandro Mateos-Gaytán, a thirty-year employee of a vegetable farm, testified that he was accustomed to working seventy to eighty hours a week during the harvesting season and wondered how he would be able to pay his daughter's college tuition if the act was passed. While it is possible these workers were coerced into giving this testimony by their employers, it is equally possible that they rejected the act and how it would change their working lives and financial futures. A 2007 survey of farmworkers in New York's Hudson Valley found that 79 percent wanted to work as many hours as possible.[62]

Ultimately, after much debate, the act passed in 2019 and took effect on January 1, 2020. For the first time in New York's history, farmworkers were legally guaranteed overtime pay, a day of rest each week, disability and paid family leave, unemployment benefits, and the right to organize and join a union. Yet though the act was on the books, the real test would be how it would play out in reality. Almost immediately after the act was passed, for instance, New York farm bosses wanted to change the definition of "overtime" from over forty hours a week to over sixty hours. A test case for the act came soon, led by another group of drink workers—wine workers on Long Island's North Fork.[63]

Wine Meets Dairy: The Fight to Enforce
the Farmworkers Fair Labor Practices Act

During the twentieth century, Long Island was fertile agricultural land dominated by potato, cabbage, corn, pea, and bean cultivation. Beginning in the
1970s, ambitious grape growers began turning over the soil and planting vineyards. Breezes from the Atlantic Ocean, and summer evenings cool enough to
allow grapes to ripen slowly, made the area hospitable terrain. Today, the North
Fork's "Wine Trail" has expanded to about 2,000 acres and fifty tasting rooms.
In addition to farmstands and pick-your-own sunflower and pumpkin patches,
the North Fork is becoming a hotspot for hops cultivation. In total, wineries,
breweries, and cideries have brought 1.3 million visitors and $99 million in tour-
ism spending throughout the region.[64]

Both citizen and immigrant Latinx workers, who began working in Long Island vineyards in the 1980s, have shaped the North Fork's wine and tourism industries into what they are today. The amount of skill required for wine work—
in terms of mental acuity and physical work by hand—cannot be understated.
From spring to autumn, vineyard workers arrive in the early morning to plant
and graft vines, irrigate the land, apply pesticides, manage canopies of leaves,
tend fruiting vines to make sure they receive adequate sunlight and ventilation,
and carefully harvest grapes at the right time for fermentation. Close and thorough training is required for each task, requiring workers to put in long hours
and maintain sharp attention through cold, fog, or extreme heat. A wrong graft
or clip of a vine, or a wrong call of grape clusters' ripeness and flavor profile at
harvest time, could ruin an entire vintage and year's work. During winters, when
vines are bare, vineyard workers prune them to remove the previous season's
growth and decide how many buds should remain. Pruning vitally influences
the next year's crop. In this sense, vineyard workers—not just the winemaker and
designer—shape the final wine in the bottle.[65] Winery owners depend on having
reliable and knowledgeable employees, and vineyard workers are in turn grateful
for open-air jobs (in high contrast to dairy jobs, for example). Ramón González,
the foreman at Lebanese-owned winery Paumanok Vineyards in Aquebogue,
migrated from Guatemala to New York in 2007. "Out here [in the vineyards],
everything is amazing and beautiful," he said. Guatemalan migrant Olivia far
preferred vine clipping to working in a factory back in her home country, and
another worker named Jennifer agreed that it felt vastly better to work in the
fresh air compared to sitting at a cash register all day in Honduras.[66]

Long Island wine workers became the first group of laborers to test whether the Fair Farmworker Practices Act would ensure their rights in the case of a workplace grievance. A dozen farmworkers at Pindar Vineyards in the town of Peconic (organized by Local 338 of the Retail, Wholesale, Department Store Union / United Food and Commercial Workers Union) were recognized in September 2021 as New York's very first agricultural labor union. They asked Pindar to begin negotiating a new contract with them that would include paid sick days and holidays, as well as workers' compensation and health-care benefits. The workers, who made between fifteen and seventeen dollars an hour, also wanted a raise. In a visit to Pindar's tasting room in October 2021, I had a brief conversation with an employee that signaled trouble ahead. The union was a great thing for the workers, the employee remarked, but the vineyard ownership did not feel the same. The employee had even tried to encourage the owners (who were immigrants themselves, from Greece) to play up an immigrant narrative "because it's a beautiful one," and added, "If we didn't have them [the workers], we wouldn't have all this." Every weekend from the fall of 2022 into the spring of 2023, members of the local demonstrated outside Pindar's winery. They were asking customers not to boycott the winery itself but to advocate for workers' right to negotiate a contract. During the busy tourist month of October, the company tried to use tractors to block customers' view of the demonstrating workers. In November the workers moved to the sidewalk outside Pindar's tasting room in the town of Port Jefferson, but the company responded by closing the tasting room on those days. As of spring 2024 Pindar's owners had refused to come to the negotiating table to discuss the workers' proposed contract. "They are using delaying tactics at this point. It looks like we are going to have to ask a third party, a mediator to join," said Noemi Barrera, a union representative for Local 338 of the UFCW's Retail, Wholesale, and Department Store Union. New York state senate Labor Committee chair Jessica Ramos condemned Pindar, saying, "We did not pass the Farm Labor Fair Labor Practices Act as a suggestion."[67] Richard Witt, the executive director of longtime farmworker advocacy organization Rural and Migrant Ministry, commented that Pindar's peers might be influencing the lack of negotiation. "I think that there's probably pressure on Pindar by the wider farming industry, and by New York Farm Bureau, to not negotiate, because that would be the first negotiated union contract in New York State. And once the workers see that this is possible, then they will know in other farms, other vineyards, that they too, can be treated with dignity." As of 2024, New York farmers were still trying to freeze collective bargaining activity by asking to revise the act in various ways, including asking for a secret ballot provision for union votes and for employers to be able to issue temporary injunctions that would halt a union's strike activities.[68]

Crimmigration and Culinary Havens

Like Vermont, Long Island is a region surveilled by immigration authorities; it has been a regular destination for Latin American migration since the Sanctuary Movement of the 1980s. One of the biggest ICE cases that impacted Long Island's wine world was the 2018 apprehension of then thirty-one-year-old sommelier Luis Marín-Castro in the Hamptons. A native of Cuenca, Ecuador, who had emigrated with his family in 1997 at the age of eleven, Marín-Castro graduated from college before getting a job at the famous East Hampton restaurant Nick & Toni's. He worked his way up from busser to dining room captain and then sommelier. Luis split his time between Nick & Toni's and the wine store Wainscott Main Wine and Spirits. During his April 9, 2018 morning shift at Wainscott, Luis was unloading a case of wine outside when three ICE officers apprehended him. Marín-Castro was four days away from his biometrics appointment for a green card (his wife was a US citizen) and less than a month away from completing his three-year probation for a drunk driving charge in 2015. Wainscott's manager Chimene McNaughton told media, "Luis has been working for the shop and the New York wine community for the past year.... He has a brilliant wine mind." Marín-Castro was not given a chance to speak with an attorney and was detained for thirty-six hours in an ICE private prison facility in Hackensack, New Jersey. At 4 a.m. an ICE plane airlifted him for a transfer to Cibola County Correctional Center in Milan, New Mexico.[69]

Marín-Castro's case was unusual because of the amount of support he received from Hamptons locals. This could have been because he had a citizen wife already, but more likely because he had made an impression on social networks in food and wine. McNaughton collected more than fifty letters of support and other evidence of Marín-Castro's deep ties to East Hampton, and retained a leading immigration law firm in Texas. Two other friends established a GoFundMe page to pay for Luis's legal expenses and raised more than $57,000.[70] Wine importers donated $1,000 apiece and longtime customers of the wine shop and Nick & Toni's were generous as well. "Imagine all the resources you need to deal with all the steps along the way, and how few people in Luis's position have them," McNaughton lamented. Stuck in a system designed to be chaotic and disorganized, an average of 30,000 migrants are held in detention per day across hundreds of facilities in the United States. As of July 2023, 90.8 percent of people detained by ICE were held in detention facilities owned or operated by private prison corporations, which profit off of every bed and commissary meal filled. On average a person is held for more than a month, if not several months if they are fighting a legal case. After his hearing in the Southwest, Luis was bonded out and released back to the East End of Long Island.[71] Though his case was eventually resolved, many undocumented food and wine workers on the island continue to labor with anxiety. For those who depend on protection under Deferred Action for Childhood Arrivals (DACA), the question of the program's continuation hovers over their heads.

It is important to note that the wider wine worker community of Long Island also includes those who labor in the hospitality realm of the Hamptons, a series of villages located on the southeastern fork of the island. Though there are year-round residents in the Hamptons, the area completely changes in the summer. An influx of wealthy, mostly white summer vacationers fills beach houses, resorts, hotels, and restaurants. In large part, Hamptons hospitality employers rely on the H-2B visa program to bring in workers from Eastern Europe, the Caribbean, and Latin America to serve as waitstaff, hosts, cleaners, and cooks. While there is a Latinx population who lives year-round in the Hamptons, they are often invisible to other residents beyond the expectation that they are gardeners and landscapers, day laborers in construction, cooks and dishwashers in restaurants, valets, or house cleaners. Because real estate values have soared and affordable rentals are few, Latinx enclaves have developed in certain pockets of the Hamptons such as Riverhead, Hampton Bays, and an East Hampton appendage called Springs that is more mixed in resident profile and income. While summer occupations from April to September can provide enough income for a Hamptons worker to afford a room or a couch in a shared house, when winter comes some people decide to relocate to the North Fork for vineyard work or to other states to make money. For those who try to remain in the Hamptons year-round but who are left unhoused by poverty, encampments in the woods are sometimes the only option available. Cooking food over open fires and shivering in the cold temperatures, storms, and snow, these encampment inhabitants suffer—and some even die—while waiting for regular work to come again.[72]

If one looks for them, there are culinary havens in the Hamptons that try to nurture Latinx residents as well as other locals. Damark's Deli, founded in East Hampton in 1949, acknowledged its growing Latin American population around 2000 when Bruce Damark inherited the business. "It seemed like the entire population of Cuenca, in Ecuador, [had] moved to East Hampton. . . . I decided to see it as a market to be served," he said. Damark hired Julia Sangurima, a Cuenca woman, to begin making homestyle food including *guisado de puerco* (pork stew), *frijolitos con carne* (red beans with meat), and *mote pillo* (chewy dried hominy scrambled with eggs and peppers). White locals quickly immediately made their feelings known about this culinary change. "They said that if I started giving the Latinos their food, they would never leave," Damark said. He also observed some of his female white counter employees exhibiting open hostility to Spanish-speaking customers, sending them to the back of the line or pretending not to understand their orders. With time, however, locals adjusted, and now Damark's parking lot fills with both Range Rovers and construction vans. Meanwhile, more Latinx-owned restaurants have been established on the East End and serve both a Spanish-speaking and non-Spanish speaking clientele. Juan Hernández, an owner of Southampton restaurant La Hacienda, has an English-language Americanized menu that includes hard-shell tacos and burritos, while photographs for a Spanish-speaking customer base hang over the counter, featuring items like birria stew and *tortas ahogadas*, or stuffed sandwiches smothered in spicy tomato sauce and topped with onion rings. Chiquita Latina, a bakery and grocery store on Montauk Highway in East Hampton, offers a daily hot lunch of "comida Latina" that includes plantains and corn, rice and beans, and daily *guisados*. The Colombian establishment Brasa y Sabor in East Hampton sells rotisserie chickens, tropical paletas (ice cream popsicles), and guava-stuffed pastries. "I keep the menu 60–40, 60 percent American and 40 percent Hispanic," owner Robert Gonzales said.[73] In addition to restaurants, grocery and general stores are places where one can see a Latinx population's influence and desires. In its preprepared food case, the Springs General Store (which closed its doors in 2022) offered platters of red chicken tamales in red mole sauce next to more "American" items like grilled salmon and quinoa salad (the tamales often sold out by lunchtime). Moving throughout the store, Latin American provisions and snacks were mixed in all the sections. A spinning display tower held snack-sized bags of *tostones* (fried plantain chips), *chicharrones* (fried pork skins), and a "mofongo party mix" of plantain and cassava chips with pork skins and chile and lime. Bottles of Jarritos filled the soda case, and Goya tortillas and packages of chorizo were placed near cartons of eggs. In Southampton, the DeJesus convenience store is situated off the main drag, a few blocks before one approaches high-end restaurants and boutiques. Its front display window features embroidered Mexican dresses, painted pottery, and Virgin of Guadalupe statues. Inside is a wide range of dried chiles, beans, snacks, and household items. The owners of DeJesus also have a *paquetero* business that delivers Latin American goods to people around Long Island, echoing the procurement strategies of Latino dairy workers in Vermont.

In his essay "Wine and Milk," French thinker Roland Barthes wrote, "It is true that wine is a good and fine substance, but it is no less true that its production is deeply involved in . . . capitalism."[74] Both the dairy and wine industries, in seeking continued profits, have joined other food industries in recruiting and relying on immigrant labor, much of it undocumented. Though these workers develop significant expertise to create two important drinks for the public, they often feel excluded from this public, or policed within it. Their efforts, and their allies' efforts, to create spaces for food security, gastronomic creativity, and cultural community are ways of filling these workers' cups while they continue asking for a seat at the proverbial table.

CHAPTER SEVEN

COVID-19 and the Food Labor Chain

The COVID-19 pandemic transformed the nation in innumerable ways, forcing people to think more critically about systems we take for granted, including schools, consumer product supply chains, and the food and service industry. Major metropolitan thoroughfares like New York's Fifth Avenue were left empty and ghostly as city dwellers escaped to quieter locales and tourism ceased. Restaurants, bakeries, and bars were left shuttered and dark, indefinitely closed. Shelves in grocery stores were bare, with only a few undesirable items left. Farmers plowed their crops under because schools and businesses stopped purchasing in bulk. People died in such numbers that refrigerated trucks had to be parked outside hospitals to serve as temporary morgues. When it came to death and illness along lines of race, class, and citizenship, COVID-19 reemphasized the inequalities of certain groups' access to health care, social distancing, and remote work. In New York City, Latinx and Black populations were twice as likely to die from the virus because, as then governor Andrew Cuomo admitted, they made up more of the public workers "who don't have a choice, frankly, but to go out there every day and drive the bus and drive the train." In California, about 61 percent of COVID cases and 49 percent of deaths were among Latinx people, though they made up only 39 percent of the state's population. In Texas, Latinx residents made up 40 percent of the state but 48 percent of COVID deaths.[1] And because undocumented migrants shy away from seeking medical help because of exorbitant hospital bills and possible deportation, they struggled with the infection for longer or died from it.

As Americans stocked up on food for weeks of isolation, then vice president Mike Pence deemed food workers part of "critical infrastructure" and said that they had to "show up and do their job."[2] Like health professionals, the bodies of food workers were put on the line. Deemed "essential," these workers were contradictorily treated as disposable and replaceable if they got sick or died. This final chapter toggles between the Northeast and the wider nation to describe how six groups—farmworkers, food processors, grocery workers, restaurant employees, street vendors, and food delivery workers—were forced to serve the public while being denied protections such as the personal space to stay well and transparency about health risks while working. Moreover, in a repeating pattern from history, many of these food workers experienced food insecurity during the pandemic. In response, Latinx communities and their allies developed mutual aid strategies that provided culturally and nutritionally nourishing food to each other in a traumatic context.

COVID and Farmworkers

In the spring of 2020, the estimated 2.7 million farmworkers in the United States were some of the first to be designated by the federal government as essential and told to keep working despite their heightened risk of contracting the virus. In addition, Donald Trump raised the ceiling on H-2 visa migrant labor recruitment, going above the 205,000 visas dispensed for seasonal farmworkers and 98,000 for seasonal food processing and other workers the previous year.[3] This influx of guest labor crowded farmworkers' workplaces even more, as untested people were thrown together in buses to be shuttled to worksites, and housed in crowded bunkrooms, motel rooms, or other employer housing that lacked ventilation and enough bathrooms for large groups. The wages that farmworkers earned added insult to injury—the average annual salary for a farmworker family in 2020 hovered at around $20,000–$24,000 a year, and a third of farmworkers lived below the poverty line.[4]

At first, no proper quarantine periods were enforced to mandate COVID testing of farmworkers. In some states, advocates pressed officials to test people before they began working, but for those people already bussed or placed in dormitory-like housing, it was too late. Twenty-six H-2A agricultural workers at Champlain Orchards in Vermont tested positive for COVID-19 in October 2020. In Maine, clusters of COVID-19 cases were found among guestworkers at three different blueberry processing companies within a week. There, the organizations Mano en Mano and Maine Housing partnered to provide hotel rooms as quarantine shelters for farmworkers who had tested positive or been exposed to the virus. This hotel-shelter was staffed by Spanish and Haitian Kreyòl speakers who also lived in its rooms, and Maine Mobile Health made rounds to provide medical care. Workers were given three meals a day, which included homemade Jamaican, Puerto Rican, Haitian, Mexican, and Colombian food made by community members. Those in quarantine also received access to art supplies, herbal medicinal care packages, and English classes. During the more than six weeks of the blueberry harvest, 100 workers stayed at this community-created COVID shelter.[5]

Accounts of immediate contagion kept other Northeastern farmworkers away from their usual harvesting sites. A fifty-two-year-old Latina mother scheduled to ride a bus from Florida to New Jersey to pick blueberries, for instance, decided not to put herself and her daughters through the journey. Her instinct was right. President of the New Jersey Blueberry Industry Advisory Council Denny Doyle declared sans sensitivity, "This crop comes in, virus or no virus," and the Atlantic Blueberry company simply gave each worker two bandannas to cover their nose and mouth. Workers in crowded dormitories were separated only by hanging blankets. Meanwhile, others outside of agriculture implied that laborers should be blamed and ostracized for their own sickness. In May 2020, when a quarter of the workers at a large agricultural greenhouse in Oneida, New York, contracted COVID, community backlash manifested on social media and in angry telephone calls. The next month Florida governor Ron DeSantis remarked, "You don't want those folks mixing with the general public if you have an outbreak," further marginalizing a worker population upon whom his state was obviously dependent.[6]

If cleared to begin working, farmworkers encountered more obstacles to staying safe. A disturbing percentage of farmworkers still did not have access to basic toilet and hand-washing facilities in the fields, and were ignored, ridiculed, or overcharged when they requested masks and hand sanitizer. The Centers for Disease Control (CDC) finally issued safety recommendations for farmworkers in June 2020, but the Labor Department declined to make them mandatory; it was left up to individual states to issue farmworker protection regulations. By December 2020, only eleven states—California, Colorado, Michigan, New Mexico, New York, Oregon, Pennsylvania, Vermont, Virginia, Washington, and Wisconsin—had done so. For farmworkers who felt they could not afford to walk away from jobs, the prospect of testing positive and having to quarantine for several days without pay was frightening too. Many farmworkers around the country tried to evade testing, or continued to go to work despite testing positive, due to financial worries. If they worked in large crews, they also feared that revealing their sickness would force everybody to quarantine and lose income.[7]

By March 2021, half a million agricultural workers in the United States had tested positive for COVID-19 and at least 9,000 had died from it. When vaccines finally began to be developed, there were initial barriers to access. In Florida, people had to prove residency to get a vaccine, which deterred the undocumented. In Nebraska, where immigrants were the backbone of the meatpacking industry, officials stated that people without legal status would be vaccinated last.

Farmworker communities spoke out against being placed on the back burner. In California, where vaccine drives for farmworkers were prioritized, bok choy worker América Aguilera said to the *New York Times*, "With all due respect, it's about time we got the opportunity to be first at something." In a separate op-ed for the *Times*, Guatemalan migrant and farmworker Alma Patty Tzalain wrote, "I am one of the thousands of farmworkers across the country making sure there is still food to put on your tables. I have cleaned cabbage in a packing shed, milked cows on dairy farms, trimmed apple trees in orchards and wrapped and pruned tomatoes in a greenhouse."[8] Through reminding the public of their essential role in producing food and drink, farmworkers tried to close the distance between complaining consumers and the people toiling in the first link of the food supply chain.

Food Processing Workers

On April 26, 2020—in what some deemed an overly dramatic move—Tyson Foods chairman John Tyson bought ads in the *New York Times* and other newspapers declaring that the food chain was "breaking" and that the meatpacking industry needed more accommodations to keep running smoothly. Trump believed Tyson and issued an executive order to prevent shortages of pork, chicken, beef, and other products. The bulk of meat, poultry, and seafood workers in America are people of color, including a large percentage of immigrants from Latin America, Asia, and Africa. Animal processing workers are 34.9 percent Latinx, 34.5 percent white, 21.9 percent Black, 6.8 percent Asian American / Pacific Islander, 1.3 percent "other," and 0.7 percent American Indian / Alaskan Native. A whopping 71 percent are noncitizens, and a worker's average annual salary is $30,485.[9] Meat processing and packing was already a hazardous profession in the United States, with serious injuries occurring within its workforce at an average rate of twice per week due to overwhelming production quotas and a lack of thorough and multilingual safety training. When COVID-19 began spreading, slaughterhouses and chicken plants became hot zones for contagion precisely because of how they were designed. Workers were forced to stand shoulder to shoulder on an assembly line cutting and deboning animals at a fast pace. At Tyson chicken plants, for example, workers stand on the line for up to eighteen hours a day, processing 140 chickens per minute. Deprived of regular bathroom breaks, many poultry workers feel pressured to wear diapers instead of getting punished for disrupting workflow. In addition, many workers develop respiratory problems from exposure to chlorine and peracetic acid that are used to disinfect chicken meat. These lung issues were only exacerbated if one contracted COVID as well.[10]

Fifteen years prior to the COVID-19 outbreak, during the H1N1 pandemic, the White House had gathered agriculture, infectious disease, and business experts to plan models for safely sustaining food processing plants in a future pandemic. The meat industry neglected all this strategic advice in 2020.[11] Just like farmworkers, food processing workers were given little or no access to personal protective equipment or social distancing in the workplace, and numerous outbreaks resulted. Between March and April 2020, 6,500 COVID-19 cases and 20 deaths occurred among meatpacking workers, and a 2020 CDC report found that 87 percent of those infected were people of color. Within Tyson, which owned 123 plants across the United States and was the largest processor of chicken in the world, COVID-19 outbreaks and deaths were troublingly common. Companies essentially tried to pay workers for risking their lives. Tyson offered a bonus of $500 if people showed up at work for three months without missing a shift, incentivizing people to come to work even if they felt sick. Primex Farms, a nut-packing facility in California, offered a bonus to workers with perfect attendance. "It felt like they were trying to buy my life for an extra $100 a week," one worker said. By the early summer of 2020, the coronavirus had spread to more than 550 meatpacking plants across the country, infected more than 50,000 workers, and killed 255. The plants in question were owned by well-known companies including Tyson, Perdue Farms, Case Farms, Pilgrim's Pride, Smithfield, and Butterball. Latino workers were disproportionately affected. In fact, the first worker to die at a JBS beef plant in Colorado was Saul Longoria Sánchez, a seventy-eight-year-old Mexican immigrant who had worked at JBS for more than thirty years. The United Food and Commercial Workers (UFCW) union, which represented 70 percent of beef workers, 60 percent of pork workers, and a third of poultry workers, pushed for higher hazard pay at several plants, increasing workers' wages to a minimum of eighteen to twenty dollars an hour.[12]

Due to a lack of federal inspectors on the ground, food processing companies were allowed to evade pandemic precautions. During fiscal year 2018, there were only 1,815 OSHA or OSHA-approved inspectors (752 federal and 1,063 state) to evaluate 9.8 million workplaces and 143,860,530 workers. By this math, there was only one inspector per 79,262 workers. Federal OSHA inspectors would only be able to tour a particular workplace once every 165 years, and a state-level inspector would tour one every 108 years. Under Trump in June 2020, the total number of OSHA-approved inspectors fell even more to 862, the lowest number recorded in any presidential administration. Even if a company was deemed to be a violator, the median penalty for a worker's death was $7,761 at the federal level and $2,700 at the state level. On September 10, 2020, OSHA slapped Smithfield and JBS on the wrist, fining the companies $13,494 and $15,000 respectively for their worker deaths and infections. Meanwhile, in seafood, workers experienced similar precarities and neglect. In New Bedford, Immigrants' Assistance Center (IAC) employee Helena DaSilva Hughes said that the center received 10,000 phone calls per month from immigrant fish processors who needed help applying for unemployment benefits and food stamps. The center also partnered with fish houses to make sure employees were testing and receiving the vaccine. It arranged for a vaccination van to park outside of churches, and asked doctors and nurses who "looked like the community" to vaccinate 1,700 people. Meanwhile, to make up for lost income and soaring rents, New Bedford immigrants began finding plots of land on the edges of New Bedford to grow tomatoes, squash, and herbs and sold dishes from their home countries to locals via word of mouth or social media.[13]

Food Distributors and Grocery Workers

After harvesting and packaging, food gets placed onto trucks and is driven by another group of food workers to grocery stores. Fearful of not having enough provisions for an indefinite period of "shelter in place," Americans rushed out to grocery stores to sweep the shelves of all food—healthy, junk, and everything in between. What used to be a casual and predictable run for a household item or meal ingredient became a nerve-wracking and often disappointing venture if one found empty shelves. Middle- and upper-class consumers' usual assurance of finding what they wanted in stores, regardless of season, was gone. Facing unprecedented complaints, food distributors tried to perform logistical miracles by redirecting truckloads of food from closed schools, businesses, and restaurants to grocery and convenience stores. My stepfather Richard Rocha, an independent bread distributor with a large route in rural South Texas, could not unload his pallets fast enough for queued-up and desperate customers at his thirty delivery stops that included large chain grocery stores like H-E-B, fast food chains, and smaller convenience stores. At the latter, owners asked him to place the bread behind their cash registers so they could monitor and dispense their rations more calmly. Rocha remembered, "I had customers getting upset, bread was in high demand. All our bakeries were running on all gears, but there could be a day that we [distributors] would get no product. We had to miss some deliveries, but it wasn't anything I could control. I let go of an account at a gas station because the owner was just letting me have it [about the lack of bread], embarrassing me in front of everybody. I told him, 'I'm not coming back anymore' and left him with his mouth hanging open."[14] Though he was already losing crucial income because of school shutdowns, Rocha sacrificed even more of his earnings to avoid disrespect from buyers who did not understand his place in a longer supply chain.

Wholesale produce markets were also sites of chaos and pressure. At New York's Hunts Point Produce Market in the South Bronx—the largest wholesale produce market in the country, serving 22 million people—1,400 employees (largely immigrants and people of color) demanded higher wages for harder pandemic work. Management initially offered a raise of thirty-two cents an hour, which prompted workers to go on strike for a week to demand a dollar-an-hour raise. US member of Congress Alexandria Ocasio-Cortez skipped President Joe Biden's inauguration to join the picket line, bringing more visibility to the cause. Workers eventually agreed to a $1.85 wage increase over three years.[15]

Meanwhile, workers in grocery stores or chain stores that carried food and pharmacy items felt unsafe and mistreated by the public. Customers often disrespected proper mask-wearing and ignored plastic dividers when asking questions and paying for purchases, or even became so hostile that they yelled or spit at cashiers. According to the UFCW, which represented 835,000 grocery store employees in the United States and Canada at the end of 2020, 109 of its members had died and more than 17,400 had been infected with COVID. Compounding this, a significant number of grocery store workers were already being paid less than minimum wage and not paid for overtime. "Hero pay" ordinances for grocery workers passed in some parts of the country. The Los Angeles County Board of Supervisors, for example, voted to give grocery workers a short-term five-dollar-per-hour pay raise. Several national chains distributed "hazard pay" early in the pandemic, but many of these bonuses petered out in the spring and early summer of 2020. Some stores like Trader Joe's tried to maintain hazard pay for longer to retain their employees, raising an initial two-dollar hourly bonus to four dollars in February 2021. Often forgotten in the mix of grocery workers were bodega proprietors running their stores sometimes twenty-four hours a day, with a mix of food and convenience items. Some stores (either willingly or under pressure) created listings on food delivery apps to cater to the neighborhood's residents. Considered essential workers, bodega owners and employees endured similar risks of interacting with stressed customers in confined spaces.[16]

Street Vendors

Food truck operators and ambulantes with pushcarts mattered during COVID because they provided an alternative to restaurants; they broke up the monotony by offering quick, open-air meals that allowed people to socialize outside if they wished.[17] COVID brought a particular set of challenges to these mobile food businesses. One of the "epicenter[s] of the epicenter" of the pandemic was Jackson Heights, Queens, a dense patchwork of immigrant enclaves in New York City that recorded more than 7,000 cases in a matter of weeks.[18] These frightening statistics converged with a new labor pattern. Latinx people laid off from other jobs tried to become ambulantes for the first time and sold produce, tacos, masks, and other items. This economic pivot, however, was met with a crackdown and criminalization by the city. Concerns rose about health and sanitation in the street vending realm, especially if the food or items offered were homemade. More vendors were ticketed for operating without a license and health permit, or shut down altogether by police and health authorities. Until recently, in New York City a mere 2,900 food vendor permits have been issued per year, making it impossible to vend legally. The waiting list for a city permit is ten to twenty years, and permits sold on the black market are priced anywhere from $6,000 to $30,000.[19] Similar caps exist in other major cities. A lack of new permits not only shuts new immigrant entrepreneurs out of the street vending system but reinforces public associations between Latinx people and illegality. Another way the classed and raced nature of street vendor surveillance was underscored was the relative lack of policing of "ghost kitchens" among the hipster and more economically privileged classes. Ghost kitchens are either people's private homes or discreetly rented kitchen spaces for people who cannot afford to own and operate a full-time restaurant or bakery. COVID-19 circumstances made it possible for ghost kitchens to sell food and take orders through social media platforms like Instagram and arrange payment by Venmo for pickup or delivery.

Before and during the pandemic, several organizations advocated for street vendors. In New York, the Street Vendor Project, founded in the early 2000s, works with vendors to explain their rights, fight ticketing, and ask the city for higher permit ceilings. In late January 2021, the New York City Council voted to increase the 5,100 total vendor permit cap (including but not limited to food) by 4,000 permits, raising the number for the first time since the early 1980s. The new permits were supposed to be phased in beginning in 2022, with 400 more added every year for ten years. Enforcement switched from the New York Police Department to the Department of Consumer and Worker Protection, which decriminalized permit ticketing but also made vendors responsible for answering to different and more city agencies.[20] Street vendors had to conduct marches and protests into 2023 because the city did not dispense the extra permits at the speed it promised.

FIGURE 7.1. Street vendor permit protest, New York City Hall. Photo by the author, March 16, 2023.

Restaurant Workers

During the first three months of the COVID-19 pandemic, over 8 million restaurant workers in the United States lost their jobs. Restaurants either shut down completely or pivoted to becoming dry goods stores or providing takeout. While some fired restaurant workers could claim unemployment benefits, undocumented workers were abandoned, even though they comprised 10 percent of all restaurant employees in the country and as much as 40 percent in cities like Los Angeles and New York.[21]

When restaurants did open back up, both front- and back-of-house staff were nervous about what it would mean for their health and safety. Counterintuitively, the workers entrusted with handling and serving our food were the ones most pressured to come into work even if they felt sick. The fear of contracting COVID made many restaurant workers quit nationwide; they did not want to return to a workplace that dismissed their health concerns while paying them atrociously low wages. The federal minimum wage for restaurant workers, who are considered "tipped workers," has been frozen at $2.13 an hour for decades. It is assumed that customer tips will help a worker reach the federal minimum wage of $7.25 (which has stayed the same since 2009). If tips do not cover that difference, the employer is technically supposed to top off salaries, but many evade doing so.[22] Additional wage gaps exist in restaurant work between men and women, white people and people of color, and citizens and immigrants.

A common worker complaint when restaurants began to reopen was customers' expression of entitlement. "It's obscene to me the way people are acting," said one worker. Another remarked, "My job has never been more absurd, more political, and more dangerous." Many customers refused to wear masks or became hostile when asked to give staff more personal space. Because diners sought the feeling of normalcy, restaurant workers were expected to create that illusion by acting unbothered by a lack of mask-wearing. Moreover, women servers and bartenders experienced sexual harassment. "Take off your mask. I want to see your beautiful smile," multiple woman servers recalled male customers demanding.[23] Customers who continued to avoid restaurants out of discomfort and a fear of getting sick turned to another group of food workers living in precarity: food delivery workers or *deliveristas*, who were hit with virtually impossible expectations during COVID.

Deliveristas

Before the rise of delivery apps, food delivery workers were usually employed by one or two restaurants, and their delivery radius stayed within a certain neighborhood. Managers could certainly exploit a worker's immigration status by paying them low wages, but those workers would still be allowed to do things like sit in the restaurant, use its restroom, eat some free staff meals, and be given the occasional holiday bonus.[24] Today, delivery workers on bikes or in cars who are gigging for DoorDash, Grubhub, Postmates, UberEats, Instacart, and other companies are bound to apps that dispense rewards and penalties. They are expected to cover much larger areas than before and are often left in the dark about their next stops and the real amount of their tips. "I used to have a human boss. Now it feels like I work for a ghost on my phone," said Guatemalan migrant Gustavo Ajche, who worked for fifteen years in Italian restaurants before beginning to work for delivery apps around 2019.[25] On apps, workers receive higher scores for timeliness, which give them priority for future desirable orders and neighborhoods. "It's always so nerve-wracking waiting to see my ratings at the end of the day," said Carlos, a Zapotec courier. "Not knowing exactly what can bring them up or down keeps you scared all the time." Also unnerving for deliveristas during the early days of the pandemic—when it was not clear how one contracted the virus—was that they were touching food bags handled by others, and then encountering sometimes unmasked customers at their front doors. The "contactless" delivery culture instituted during the pandemic has stayed in place, and this makes delivery workers even more anonymous to a customer who can forget to humanize them when deciding on a tip. Instacart shoppers in particular complained en masse about "tip-baiting," where customers promised large tips at the beginning of their order to entice a worker, and then lowered or canceled them altogether after their delivery was completed.[26]

Even if a food delivery worker earns a tip, there are obstacles to fair payment because of the delivery apps themselves. An app can either take a large commission and lie about the amount of money that the worker really made, or wait weeks to dispense tips, which disorganizes workers' memories of their daily money earned. This lack of transparency eventually led to worker lawsuits against the apps Relay and DoorDash. The latter had to change its policies so that it properly informed customers how their tips would be distributed. Without a baseline minimum wage, deliveristas risk their lives to go fast and complete as many orders as possible. And as convenience and home items got added to delivery app options during COVID, deliveristas found themselves balancing heavy bags of dog food, toilet paper, and cases of wine on their bikes. During the year 2020, when the demand for food delivery was particularly intense, delivery workers accounted for nearly half of New York City cyclist fatalities.[27]

Deliveristas are also extremely vulnerable to robbery, particularly if they use an electric bike. A new e-bike usually costs $1,800 plus spare batteries ($600 each), chains, locks, and maintenance. The branded thermal bags for delivery apps can cost workers anywhere from $40 to $120. Losing a bike is devastating for a delivery worker, and being robbed at gun- or knifepoint only worsens the trauma. Many times, police do not follow up on the "minor" crime of bike robbery, even if a delivery worker can show them their bike's location via a GPS tracking device. For undocumented deliveristas, filing a police report is not even an option, for fear that providing details about themselves might lead to deportation. One way that workers have tried to help each other recover stolen property, compare wages, or discuss neighborhood safety is through texting and social media apps like WhatsApp and Facebook. Anthony Chávez started posting his videos of his delivery work to a Facebook page called Chapín en Dos Ruedas (Guatemalan on Two Wheels). César Solano, a nineteen-year-old deliverista from Guerrero, Mexico, created a Facebook group called El Diario de los

Deliveryboys en la Gran Manzana (The Deliveryboys Daily in the Big Apple) where workers could share their experiences and offer help or advice if they got robbed and the police were unhelpful. WhatsApp groups exchange information about open parks where deliveristas can safely wait for their next pickup, or restaurants that will allow them to use their bathrooms. At one bridge connecting Manhattan and the Bronx where many deliveristas had been getting robbed and attacked—as one worker put it, where "wildebeest [were] trying to cross with the crocodiles"—deliverista activists used social media to arrange a guard line of bikes. They helped form groups to cross together, and offered sodas and plates of tacos and beans to the crossers.[28]

Social media groups were also used to organize more formal worker protests. On October 15, 2020, more than 1,000 people showed up at New York's City Hall for a deliverista demonstration denouncing robberies, poor wages and working conditions, and a lack of resting stations and restrooms. In April 2021 another protest drew thousands, including representatives from the Service Employees International Union, the same union that had backed fast food workers' fight for a fifteen-dollar minimum wage. Later, the New York City Council passed a package of bills crafted with deliveristas that established minimum pay, tip protections, and transparency, and gave workers restroom access, delivery distance limits, and more control over their routes without app punishment for rejecting faraway orders. Senator Chuck Schumer also directed some federal infrastructure funds to create rest and device-charging hubs. Other cities have not passed bill bundles as significant as this one but might follow suit. Even if the deliverista movement wins in more cities, however, vigilance will be required to ensure tipping transparency and to control the exorbitant service fees that delivery apps or restaurants are now charging customers to cover the minimum wages they should be providing. Additional tensions in the deliverista landscape have arisen as the Republican governors of Texas and Florida have bussed Venezuelan and other migrants to Northeastern locales in massive numbers. Housed in shelters and hotels and waiting long periods for legal work permits, migrants in limbo in New York City and Washington, DC, have bought e-bikes and delivery app accounts on the black market to begin delivering food for money.[29]

Mutual Aid and Food

As in other eras, food workers experienced a high rate of food insecurity during COVID-19. In part, this was due to structural inequalities. Public transportation dwindled, as did free school meal and community food programs. As stores closed, new food deserts emerged. (The USDA classifies an urban area as a "food desert" if at least 20 percent of the population lives below the poverty level and there are no grocery stores selling fresh and nutritious food within one mile. The metric is ten miles for rural areas.) Meanwhile, undocumented workers who were ineligible to receive federal stimulus checks found themselves unable to afford or acquire food. In April 2020, recognizing that he led a state of 2 million undocumented workers, California governor Gavin Newsom allocated $125 million to give $500 apiece to undocumented individuals and $1,000 to families with undocumented members. This aid quickly dried up by July 2020. In New York City, the Excluded Workers Fund allocated $2.1 billion to provide financial help to New Yorkers who lost income during the COVID-19 pandemic and were excluded from federal relief programs. Applications closed in December 2021 and the final round of payments was dispensed at the end of 2022.[30]

In response to food workers' diminishing access to affordable and desirable food, a variety of mutual aid efforts emerged. One type of effort was food box provision. In Maine, which claimed the highest rate of food security in New England at 13.6 percent of households (28 percent in households of color), Presente Maine's Food Brigade began assembling and distributing food boxes in March 2020. Thousands of pounds of beans, bananas, limes, and fresh herbs and vegetables were given to thousands of people in Portland and surrounding towns. Mano en Mano distributed 150 food boxes of nonperishables and fresh eggs, vegetables, and culturally relevant items. Another organization, Wayside, packed an average of 449 boxes a month for Asian, Angolan, and Congolese communities that included recipient-requested items like dried salt fish, cassava leaves, potatoes, and jasmine rice. Meanwhile, Wabanaki Health and Wellness ran a "Traditional Foods Mobile Pantry" to distribute heritage food to tribal communities.[31] Community fridges also emerged in greater numbers, with local businesses such as restaurants, delis, and bodegas supplying the electricity. In one community fridge in Philadelphia—a city where one in five people suffered from food insecurity—items like apples, corn, tomatoes, Thai eggplant, jalapeños, summer squash, onions, Italian peppers, beets, and mint were on offer.[32] These food box initiatives and community fridges stitched together geographies of food access for struggling people, and helped Latinx food workers feel cared for when other modes of help seemed closed to them.

During the height of the COVID-19 pandemic, it finally seemed that the American public had realized how essential workers in the food chain really were, not just to the routines of their daily lives but also to their leisurely moments of socializing and celebration. Unfortunately, that realization did not last long enough to bring long-term federal legislation for greater compensation, rights, and health security for food workers. The investment in such protections

FIGURE 7.2. Community fridge, Brooklyn, New York. Photo by the author, 2023.

has returned to the food worker community itself and its allies, and it is unclear what other watershed moment ahead might trigger sympathy again, if this pandemic did not. One would think that being deemed "essential" would give food workers more political leverage, but two reasons this has not manifested might be that this workforce has been designed to stay so out of public view and that workers in each link of the food chain have become increasingly more atomized from each other over time.

In Aimee Bender's novel *The Particular Sadness of Lemon Cake*, a nine-year-old girl can taste in food the emotions of the person who made it. If we all had that ability, what emotions would we taste in the items created by food workers, not only during the COVID-19 years but also before and beyond them?[33] Most likely, we would taste exhaustion, depression, anxiety, longing, hope, fear, and loneliness. This kind of empathy, and action upon that empathy, should not be confined to magical realism. It is true that the food chain seems so interlocked with profit-seeking systems that it would take unprecedented cooperation and communal investment to make the food industry a healthier one. Yet in various ways, consumers can interrupt patterns of unsustainability in the food system. Though this book has focused on the lives and labors of Latinx food workers, it concludes with words for those wondering "What can I do?" or "What should I pay attention to?" when thinking of all food workers in the United States.

Food Is Pleasurable *and* Political

A significant part of the pleasure of eating is
in one's accurate consciousness of the lives and
the world from which food comes.
—Wendell Berry, "The Pleasures of Eating"

The phrase *food justice* envelops a wide range of issues including farm-workers' rights, the corporatization of the food system, food insecurity within communities and between nations, and environmental damage and sustainability. Though theoretically we produce enough food around the globe to feed everybody, the reality is that millions of people go malnourished and hungry every day. And as this book has shown, communities of US food *workers*—throughout history and still today—cannot afford or access the very food they help to produce. In the words of *MIT Technology Review* editor Gideon Lichfield, "The food system is not actually designed to feed people. It's designed to turn a profit."[1]

To think about solutions or methods that could foster more food justice in the United States, we can return to the questions posed at the beginning of this book: *Why must we bring politics into food? Can't we just enjoy this pleasurable thing without analyzing it?* We have long divorced the pleasurable from the political when it comes to food. Many assume that if one is consuming food, the experience should be simply pleasurable. Yet as David Foster Wallace has mused about in "Consider the Lobster," it is a fiction that food items—especially living, breathing ones—are totally pleasurable and void of ethical questions.[2] We as consumers often leave food-related politics up to the food *worker*—if they are unhappy, *they* are responsible for filing the complaints, forming the unions and organizing the protests, and speaking up about what is wrong in the food system. Yet the food worker deserves to experience food as a pleasurable thing too. Despite not having the privileges or resources they deserve, Latinx laborers have found ways to make and fight for food as a remedy for racism, depression, and homesickness, and as a strategic technique to capture public attention or achieve upward mobility. They have spoken back to power by halting their own work at strategic moments; using food or fasting to challenge power relations; or becoming food entrepreneurs themselves to nourish their community or avoid being exploited by other employers. At many times, Latinx communities have acted politically to keep food a pleasurable thing in their lives.

The dichotomy of the pleasured but apolitical food consumer and the pleasureless political food worker needs to be eliminated to create a crisscrossing model that affirms the humanity of the people on both ends of the food chain. As Lisa M. Heldke writes, we must move toward a relationship of "coresponsibility" that "will work toward the elimination of the pathological asymmetry that characterizes many of those [food] relations."[3] Similarly, in *The Omnivore's Dilemma*, Michael Pollan writes of efforts "to redeem that ugly word [*consumer*], with its dismal colorings of selfishness and subtraction."[4] Workers should be allowed to experience food as both a political and pleasurable thing, while consumers should bear more political responsibility as they enjoy food made by others.

As food workers have become increasingly commodified and invisible in our society, ethical questions about their treatment have disappeared from our view. This invisibility of workers—particularly immigrant ones—is only compounded when their food*ways* are the things that become hypervisible. When consumers exoticize and clamor for Latinx food items, ingredients, and culinary customs, they might not really "see" Latinx food laborers at all, or only consider them a means to a delicious end product. And for some eaters, there is no cognitive dissonance in simultaneously holding a desire for ethnic food with a deep xenophobia toward the corresponding ethnic populations. Acknowledging this contradiction, and the binaries of pleasure and politics we erect around food, are two beginning steps we can take.

We also need to hold governments and food industries accountable for their dependence on people's precarity. Even before the nation's founding, colonists relied on enslaving others to labor in plantation and monoculture systems, or recruited other labor through convict leasing and debt peonage, tenant farming, and sharecropping. Later, during the twentieth and twenty-first centuries, US government and agribusiness interests acquired an appetite for foreign guestworkers. Our nation's food labor force began with, and still includes, people who are not privileged in terms of race or citizenship status. Food workers are now overwhelmingly US Latinx, Indigenous and Afro-Latin American, Caribeño, guestworker, and undocumented people. These populations are all more vulnerable to exploitation, retaliation, firing, and deportation. To defend using this vulnerable labor, food industry employers praise them for their stronger work ethic and agreeing to "do work that Americans won't do." They might pay them wages higher than the ones they could earn in their home countries, but these are still not livable wages in the United States. Since the New Deal, the agricultural industry has continued to evade the institution of a minimum wage, overtime pay, and collective bargaining rights for its workers. It sticks to the exceptionalist argument that, because of seasonality and perishable products, labor unions and strikes should not be allowed in its realm. But if we paraphrase sociologist Margaret Gray, agribusiness has long enjoyed a massive subsidy in the form of farmworkers' indigence.[5]

Meanwhile, the US government and its lawmakers praise guestworker programs as economic panaceas and frame them in languages of migrant freedom, consent, and agency. People participate in these programs of their own volition, politicians argue, and can make significant money to bring home. In reality, there is very little consent or agency once someone has been contracted as a guestworker—these people are kept in cycles of debt and confined in multiple ways during their term of work, making their lives similarly precarious to those of undocumented workers. An H-2 program haunted by the ghosts of *bracerismo* keeps wages low, conditions substandard, and workers chronically deportable.[6]

Many of us already have personal philosophies regarding animals and the environment that influence our eating choices. If one is a vegetarian or vegan, one cares about the welfare of animals or the effects that certain animal products have on the body. If one eats meat and eggs, the labels "hormone-free," "humane certified," or "pasture raised" might be important. If one wants to reduce the environmental damage caused by transporting food, the labels "local" or "sustainable" imply a shorter distance between producer and consumer. Many of us are now accustomed to seeing labels like "organic," "fair trade," or "farm to table" on our food items and restaurant menus, but none of these labels necessarily translate to "ethical" in terms of human labor practices. Some farm owners and organizations around the country are walking the walk when it comes to making and selling *fair labor* food. One successful campaign has been the Fair Food Program created by the Florida-based Coalition of Immokalee Workers. The African Americans who made up the majority of Immokalee region farmworkers were succeeded in the 1970s by Haitian, Mexican, and Central American labor. The CIW, founded in 1993, tried to address workers' grievances about wage theft, substandard housing, and labor trafficking and violence by developing a code of conduct for the tomato industry. The agreement—which the CIW convinced various growers, stores, and fast-food chains to sign on to—stipulates that if a participating employer pays workers fairly, meets health and safety requirements, and cooperates with a third-party monitoring agency, they can receive a "Fair Food" label affixed to their tomatoes. After growers signed on, the CIW struck against and boycotted large corporations including Taco Bell, Burger King, McDonald's, Whole Foods, Trader Joe's, Walmart, Aramark, and Sodexo until they agreed to buy their tomatoes from Fair Food farmers, equaling a price difference of a penny more per pound. This small price hike convinced tomato growers not to further cut the wages of their farmworkers.[7] By recognizing that multiple links in the food chain—worker, supplier, and buyer—need to cooperate at once, the CIW has created a model to replicate in other industries. There are other emergent fair food programs and food worker victories. The Comité de Apoyo a los Trabajadores Agrícolas (Agricultural Workers Support Committee), which organizes mostly Latinx and Indigenous immigrant farmworkers in the mid-Atlantic states, leads an Agricultural Justice Project that develops social justice standards for organic and sustainable food businesses. The project has its own "Food Justice Certified" label for growers and business owners. These projects, along with the incremental victories in the Fight for Fifteen minimum wage campaigns that began in 2012, inspire us to imagine a different future in which fair food becomes the norm, rather than the exception, in the United States.

The pleasurable foodscapes of our imagination—whether they are bucolic vegetable fields and dairy farms, pristine supermarkets, or trendy street food carts and restaurants—do not square with the past and present experiences of humans who have been hidden, confined, or marginalized as they work to give us food. If we want to create a truly healthy and sustainable food system for the future, we cannot leave healthy and sustainable labor practices out of the conversation. We may have to become more open to different models of food production and service, such as no-tipping restaurants that raise menu prices to give staff a living wage and benefits. Zazie, a San Francisco restaurant that has been tip-free for many years, explains on its menu, "All of our menu prices include a living wage, revenue share, paid family leave, fully funded health and dental insurance, paid time off, and a 401(K) with employer match for all of our hard working employees." Future restaurateurs drafting their business plans can imagine different models that consider the fair treatment and compensation of their employees. And in thinking of the next generation—the children of current food workers—it is incumbent upon us to recognize if they are inheriting precarity or experiencing new forms of it, such as being DACA recipients in limbo, or the expected caretakers for aging farm and food workers who will never receive pensions or Social Security.

Dreams and romantic notions about how food gets to us—from harvesting to cooking to service and everything in between—are tempered if we acknowledge that there has been long-standing pain and invisibility in the history of every link in the food chain. But just as the problematic elements of the food system have been constructed by people over time, they can be dismantled by people over time. This book could not tell the stories of all the food workers who deserved them, or of all the places in the Northeast United States that deserved them. It has sought, however, to provoke a desire to excavate more of those stories and to show, through the lens of Latinx communities' experiences in one region, how food workers in this nation are still awaiting their feast. They hunger for visibility, respect, and fair treatment that would allow greater security and pleasure in their lives. Historically, the United States has consumed Latinx "others"—in the form of their labor, their cuisine, and the attractive foodscapes they have helped to create and maintain. If we can better satisfy the cravings of those who have been overlooked, we can create a food culture that prioritizes human nourishment instead of depletion.

NOTES

Abbreviations

AGN	Archivo General de la Nación, Mexico City
Centro	El Centro Archive, Center for Puerto Rican Studies, Hunter College, City University of New York, New York
Galarza Papers	Ernesto Galarza Papers, Department of Special Collections, Stanford University Libraries, Stanford, California
Golden Cage	Golden Cage Oral History Project, Vermont Folklife Center, Middlebury, Vermont
Morrisville hearing	Joint Hearing before the New York State Senate Standing Committee on Agriculture and Standing Committee on Labor, Public Hearing to Hear Public Testimony on the Proposed Farmworkers Fair Labor Practices Act, SUNY Morrisville, Morrisville, New York, 25 April 2019, https://legislation.nysenate.gov/pdf /hearings/04-25-19%20NYS%20Senate%20Hearing%20 Farmworkers%20FINAL.txt/
MRWC	Maine Rural Workers Coalition Papers, Maine Historical Society, Portland, Maine
NARA CP	National Archives and Research Administration, College Park, Maryland
NOAA	New Bedford Processing Workers, 2007–10, National Oceanic and Atmospheric Administration Voices Oral History Archives, National Oceanic and Atmospheric Administration, Silver Spring, Maryland
North Country	Dairy Farm Workers in New York's North Country Interview Collection, Library of Congress, Washington, DC
Reuther	Walter P. Reuther Library, Wayne State University, Detroit, Michigan
Ross Papers	Fred Ross Papers, Department of Special Collections, Stanford University Libraries, Stanford, California
Smithtown hearing	Joint Hearing before the New York State Senate Standing Committee on Agriculture and Standing Committee on Labor, Public Hearing to Hear Public Testimony on the Proposed Farmworkers Fair Labor Practices Act, William H. Rogers Building, Smithtown, New York, 26 April 2019, www.nysenate.gov/sites/default /files/04-26-19_nys_joint_farmworkers_hearing_long_island _final_0.pdf

WTW   Working the Waterfront: New Bedford, Massachusetts Occupational Folklife Project, Library of Congress, Washington, DC

ZMP   Zarela Martínez Papers, Arthur and Elizabeth Schlesinger Library, Radcliffe Institute for Advanced Study, Harvard University, Cambridge, Massachusetts

Introduction

1. "Migrants Say Eatery in Maine Forbade Use of Spanish," *Baltimore Sun*, 22 November 2000, http://articles.baltimoresun.com/2000-11-22/news/0011220093_1_migrant -workers-speaking-spanish-file-a-complaint; Lee Burnett, "The Employer's Side: They're Subs until They Get Hurt," *Maine Times*, 30 November–6 December 2000, 7; Cindy Rodriguez, "Mexicans: Auburn Restaurant Biased," *Lewiston Sun Journal*, 22 November 2000, A3; "Spanish Speakers Claim Bias at Eatery," *Bangor Daily News*, 23 November 2000, 1.

2. Faith Karimi and Eric Levenson, "Man to Spanish Speakers at New York Restaurant: 'My Next Call Is to ICE,'" CNN, 17 May 2018, www.cnn.com/2018/05/17/us/new-york -man-restaurant-ice-threat/index.html; Mythili Sampathkumar, "Woman Filmed Harassing Spanish Speakers in Colorado Supermarket," *Independent* (UK), 4 October 2018, www.independent.co.uk/news/world/americas/spanish-woman-supermarket-video -white-woman-colorado-hispanic-a8568971.html; Megan Menchaca, "'Taco Truck Tammy' Incident Leads to Protest with Tacos and Mariachi Band," *Austin American-Statesman*, 15 April 2019, www.statesman.com/story/news/2019/04/15/taco-truck-tammy -incident-leads-to-protest-with-tacos-and-mariachi-band/5433330007/; Gianluca Mezzofiore, "A Burger King Manager Was Told to 'Go Back to Mexico' for Speaking Spanish in a Florida Fast Food Restaurant," CNN, 11 July 2019, www.cnn.com/2019/07/11/us /burger-king-mexico-florida-spanish-trnd/index.html.

3. Rachel Slocum, "Race in the Study of Food," *Progress in Human Geography* 35 (June 2011): 313.

4. Niraj Chokshi, "'Taco Trucks on Every Corner': Trump Supporter's Anti-immigration Warning," *New York Times*, 2 September 2016, www.nytimes.com/2016/09 /03/us/politics/taco-trucks-on-every-corner-trump-supporters-anti-immigration-warning .html?_r=0; Russell Contreras, "99% of Americans Live Near a Mexican Restaurant," *Axios*, 11 January 2024, www.axios.com/2024/01/11/mexican-restaurants-nearby-food -influence-culture; Catherine E. Shoichet, "There Isn't a Taco Truck on Every Corner. But There's a Mexican Restaurant in Nearly Every U.S. County," CNN, 23 January 2024, www.cnn.com/2024/01/23/us/mexican-restaurant-locations-us-county-cec/index.html; L.V. Anderson, "Oral History of Breakfast Tacos Recalls an Era When Tacos Were Shameful," *Slate*, 12 August 2013, https://slate.com/culture/2013/08/oral-history-of -breakfast-tacos-texas-monthlys-interviews-with-austin-tamale-house-owners-recalls -prejudice-against-mexican-food.html.

5. Lucy M. Long, "Culinary Tourism," in *The Oxford Handbook of Food History*, ed. Jeffrey M. Pilcher (New York: Oxford University Press, 2012), 396–400; Mark Padoongpatt, *Flavors of Empire: Food and the Making of Thai America* (Oakland: University of California Press, 2017), 13. For more on culinary tourism, see Jennie Germann-Molz, "Eating Difference: The Cosmopolitan Mobilities of Culinary Tourism," *Space and Culture* 10, no. 1 (2007): 77–93.

6. Vicki Ruiz, "Citizen Restaurant: American Imaginaries, American Communities," *American Quarterly* 60, no. 1 (March 2008): 6.

7. Anthony Bourdain, "Under the Volcano," Tumblr post, 3 May 2014, http://anthony bourdain.tumblr.com/post/84641290831/under-the-volcano.

8. Madison Park, "Protestors Shout 'Shame' at Kirstjen Nielsen as She Dines at Mexican Restaurant," CNN, 20 June 2018, www.cnn.com/2018/06/20/politics/kirstjen -nielsen-mexican-restaurant-protest/index.html; Jessica Sidman, "The Kirstjen Nielsen Protest at a DC Mexican Restaurant Was a Watershed Moment," *Washingtonian*, 21 June 2018, www.washingtonian.com/2018/06/21/the-confrontation-of-kirstjen-nielsen -at-a-dc-mexican-restaurant-was-a-watershed-moment-heres-how-it-really-went-down/.

9. Joann Lo and Ariel Jacobson, "Human Rights from Field to Fork: Improving Labor Conditions for Food-Sector Workers by Organizing across Boundaries," *Race/Ethnicity: Multidisciplinary Global Contexts* 5, no. 1 (Autumn 2011): 61.

10. Liz Robbins, "Owner Was Target, but Restaurant Workers Are Swept Up in Immigration Raids," *New York Times*, 11 November 2016, www.nytimes.com/2016/11/12 /nyregion/immigration-workplace-raids-buffalo.html.

11. Gabriel Haslip-Viera, "The Evolution of the Latina/o Community in New York City: Early Seventeenth Century to the Present," in *Hispanic New York: A Sourcebook*, ed. Claudio Remeseira (New York: Columbia University Press, 2010), 18; Carmen Teresa Whalen, "Latinos/as in the Northeast: A Historic Overview," in "The Future of Latinos in the United States: Law, Opportunity, and Mobility," white paper for the American Bar Foundation, 3–4; Marta V. Martínez, *Latino History in Rhode Island: Nuestras Raíces* (Charleston, SC: History Press, 2014), 17–18; Jesse Hoffnung-Garskof, *Racial Migrations: New York City and the Revolutionary Politics of the Spanish Caribbean* (Princeton, NJ: Princeton University Press, 2019); Carolina González and Seth Kugel, *Nueva York: The Complete Guide to Latino Life in the Five Boroughs* (New York: St. Martin's Griffin, 2006), 1.

12. To date, there are valuable anthologies that address Latinx lives in New England and the East Coast, as well as state- and city-specific monographs. For anthologies, see Gabriel Haslip-Viera and Sherrie L. Baver, eds., *Latinos in New York: Communities in Transition* (Notre Dame: University of Notre Dame Press, 1997); Andrés Torres, *Latinos in New England* (Philadelphia: Temple University Press, 2006); David Carey and Robert Atkinson, eds., *Latino Voices in New England* (Albany: SUNY Press, 2009); Thomas A. Arcury and Sara A. Quandt, *Latino Farmworkers in the Eastern United States: Health, Safety and Justice* (New York: Springer, 2009); and Remeseira, *Hispanic New York*. For labor studies linking the East Coast, Latin America, and the Caribbean, see Cindy Hahamovitch, *The Fruits of Their Labor: Atlantic Coast Farmworkers and the Making of Migrant Poverty, 1870–1945* (Chapel Hill: University of North Carolina Press, 1997); David Griffith, *American Guestworkers: Jamaicans and Mexicans in the U.S. Labor Market* (Philadelphia: University of Pennsylvania Press, 2006); Edwin Meléndez, *Sponsored Migration: The State and Puerto Rican Postwar Migration to the United States* (Columbus: Ohio State University Press, 2017); Ismael García Colón, *Colonial Migrants at the Heart of Empire* (Oakland: University of California Press, 2020). State and city-specific studies include Sarah Mahler, *Salvadorans in Suburbia: Symbiosis and Conflict* (New York: Pearson, 1996); Carmen Whalen, *From Puerto Rico to Philadelphia: Puerto Rican Workers and Postwar Economies* (Philadelphia: Temple University Press, 2001); Robert Smith, *Mexican New York: Transnational Lives of New Immigrants* (Berkeley: University of California

Press, 2005); Jesse Hoffnung-Garskof, *A Tale of Two Cities: Santo Domingo and New York after 1950* (Princeton, NJ: Princeton University Press, 2010); José Itzigsohn, *Encountering American Faultlines: Race, Class, and the Dominican Experience in Providence* (New York: Russell Sage, 2011); Llana Barber, *Latino City: Immigration and Urban Crisis in Lawrence, Massachusetts, 1945–2000* (Chapel Hill: University of North Carolina Press, 2017); and Teresa Mares, *Life on the Other Border: Farmworkers and Food Justice in Vermont* (Oakland: University of California Press, 2019).

13. Jeffrey Pilcher, *Qué Vivan los Tamales! Food and the Making of Mexican Identity* (Albuquerque: University of New Mexico Press, 1998), and *Planet Taco: A Global History of Mexican Food* (New York: Oxford, 2012); Gustavo Arellano, *Taco USA: How Mexican Food Conquered America* (New York: Scribner, 2013); Alyshia Gálvez, *Eating NAFTA: Trade, Food Policies, and the Destruction of Mexico* (Oakland: University of California Press, 2018). For studies of labor and food, see, for example, Sarah Besky and Sandy Brown, "Looking for Work: Placing Labor in Food Studies," *Labor* 12, no. 1–2 (2015): 19–43; Seth Holmes, *Fresh Fruit, Broken Bodies: Migrant Farmworkers in the United States* (Berkeley: University of California Press, 2013); and Lori Flores, *Grounds for Dreaming: Mexican Americans, Mexican Immigrants, and the California Farmworker Movement* (New Haven, CT: Yale University Press, 2016). For studies about xenophobia and the "Latino threat" concept, see Otto Santa Ana, *Brown Tide Rising: Metaphoric Representations of Latinos in Contemporary Public Discourse* (Austin: University of Texas Press, 2002); and Leo Chavez, *The Latino Threat: Constructing Immigrants, Citizens, and the Nation* (Palo Alto, CA: Stanford University Press, 2013).

14. Natalia Molina, *A Place at the Nayarit: How a Mexican Restaurant Nourished a Community* (Oakland: University of California Press, 2022), xiii.

15. The H-2 visa program is the second-oldest guestworker program in world history after South Africa's and the longest running in US history. Cindy Hahamovitch, *No Man's Land: Jamaican Guestworkers in America and the Global History of Deportable Labor* (Princeton, NJ: Princeton University Press, 2011), 6.

16. For more on recovering and translating Black Latinidad, see Lorgia García Peña, *Translating Blackness: Latinx Colonialities in Global Perspective* (Durham, NC: Duke University Press, 2022).

17. Ashanté M. Reese, *Black Food Geographies: Race, Self-Reliance, and Food Access in Washington, D.C.* (Chapel Hill: University of North Carolina Press, 2019).

Chapter One

1. Ernesto Galarza, "Some Problems of the Mexican War Workers at Present Employed in the United States," 30 July 1945, 5; memo to Secretario del Trabajo y Previsión Social from Andrés Iduarte, 7 August 1945, 3, 5. Both from folder 10, box 17, Galarza Papers.

2. David Griffith, *American Guestworkers: Jamaicans and Mexicans in the U.S. Labor Market* (Philadelphia: University of Pennsylvania Press, 2006), 32.

3. Matt Garcia, "Setting the Table: Historians, Popular Writers, and Food History," *Journal of American History* 103, no. 3 (December 2016): 664.

4. Ismael García-Colón, *Colonial Migrants at the Heart of Empire: Puerto Rican Workers on U.S. Farms* (Oakland: University of California Press, 2020), 34–35, 37, 39–40; Meléndez, *Sponsored Migration: The State and Puerto Rican Postwar Migration to the United States* (Columbus: Ohio State University Press, 2017), 37.

5. Karl Jacoby, *The Strange Career of William Ellis: The Texas Slave Who Became a Mexican Millionaire* (New York: W. W. Norton, 2016), 132; David A. Badillo, "An Urban Historical Portrait of Mexican Migration to New York City," *New York History* 90, no. 1/2 (Winter/Spring 2009): 110.

6. "Corrido Pensilvanio," reprinted by the Historical Society of Pennsylvania, https://hsp.org/sites/default/files/corridopennsylvania.pdf. Original found in Paul S. Taylor, *Mexican Labor in the United States, Vol II* (Berkeley: University of California Press, 1931).

7. García-Colón, *Colonial Migrants*, 38.

8. Cindy Hahamovitch, *No Man's Land: Jamaican Guestworkers in America and the Global History of Deportable Labor* (Princeton, NJ: Princeton University Press, 2011), 2; Maria L. Quintana, *Contracting Freedom: Race, Empire, and U.S. Guestworker Programs* (Philadelphia: University of Pennsylvania Press, 2022).

9. On nostalgia, see C. Nadia Seremetakis, "The Breast of Aphrodite," in *The Tasting Culture Reader: Experiencing Food and Drink*, ed. Carolyn Korsmeyer (London: Bloomsbury, 2005); and Fred Davis, "Yearning for Yesterday: A Sociology of Nostalgia," in *The Collective Memory Reader*, ed. Jeffrey K. Olick, Vered Vinitzky-Seroussi, and Daniel Levy (Oxford: Oxford University Press, 2011).

10. García-Colón, *Colonial Migrants*, 151.

11. Ernesto Galarza, "The Mexican Railroad Worker's Camps at Jackson and Ypsilanti, Michigan," 2, 4, RG 59: Department of State, Mexico file, folder 811.504, box 4852, NARA; Ernesto Galarza, "A Study of the Problems of the Mexican Nationals in the Nine Camps of the Cucamonga, Upland, Ontario, and Chino Districts of San Bernardino County, California," Summer 1944, 10, folder 8, box 17, Galarza Papers; Fredy González, "Chinese Braceros? Chinese Mexican Workers in the United States during World War II," *Western Historical Quarterly* 48 (Summer 2017): 137–57.

12. See, for example, letters to Manuel Ávila Camacho from Luis Cárdenas Romero, 6 October 1944, file 26822 (also 29433); Miguel G. Salas, 9 October 1944, file 27666 (also 30644); Blandino Trinidad Martínez, 11 October 11 1944, file 27426 (also 30512); Ubaldo Reyes Guazo, 13 October 1944, file 27546 (also 30413); Gabriel Morales Reyes, 25 October 1944, file 28577 (also 31519); Rosendo Martínez Acosta, Carlos Vergara Zamudio, Felipe Calderón González, Carlos González Calles, and Alejo Ramírez Calderón, 1 November 1944, file 29369 (also 32312), Francisco Rosas, Ramón Serrano, et al., 29 September 1944, file 26028/28556; file 25121; file 23970/26529. All from Ávila Camacho Papers, 546.6/120, AGN.

13. Letters to Manuel Ávila Camacho from Carlos del Río, Luis Álvarez Hernández, et al., 6 March 1944, file 6264/7095 and Delfino Loya, Municipal President of Panindícuaro, Michoacan, 22 February 1944, file 4721/5408. Both from Ávila Camacho Papers, AGN. For more on braceros leaving Mexico, see Alberto García, *Abandoning Their Beloved Land: The Politics of Bracero Migration in Mexico* (Oakland: University of California Press, 2023).

14. Letters to Manuel Ávila Camacho from Simón Nájera, 2 October 1944, file 26348 (also 28774); Francisco Zaragoza G. Martín, Corona Ibarra, et al., 28 February 1944, file 5353 (also 6064); and files 25363, 27294, 24911, and 24976. All from Ávila Camacho Papers, AGN.

15. Letters to Manuel Ávila Camacho from Angela Velarde de Madrigal, 25 October 1944, file 28782 (also 31778) and Elvira Moreno, 21 February 1944, file 4816 (also 5598). Both from Ávila Camacho Papers, AGN.

16. Quintana, *Contracting Freedom*, 1.

17. González, "Chinese Braceros?," 137; Marta V. Martínez, *Latino History in Rhode Island: Nuestras Raíces* (Charleston, SC: History Press, 2014), 19–21, 51; Lilia Fernández, "Of Immigrants and Migrants: Mexican and Puerto Rican Labor Migration in Comparative Perspective, 1942–1964," *Journal of American Ethnic History* 29, no. 3 (Spring 2010): 17.

18. Neil Foley, *Mexicans in the Making of America* (Cambridge, MA: Belknap, 2017), 131; Rita Halle Kleeman, "Hi Amigos!," *New York Herald Tribune*, 21 October 1943.

19. Ernesto Galarza, "Some Problems of the Mexican Braceros Employed in the United States," Personal and confidential memorandum, 28 August 1944, English version, 11, folder 1, box 6, Galarza Papers; Ernesto Galarza, Personal and confidential memorandum on Mexican Contract Workers in the United States, 28 August 1944, 7, RG 59: Department of State, Mexico file, folder 811.504, box 4852, NARA; Ernesto Gamboa, *Bracero Railroaders: The Forgotten World War II Story of Mexican Workers in the U.S. West* (Seattle: University of Washington Press, 2018), 91.

20. Ernesto Galarza, "A Study of the Problems of the Mexican Nationals in the Nine Camps," 9.

21. Letter to Hon. Nelson A. Rockefeller, Assistant Secretary of State, from Threlkeld Commissary Company, 19 March 1945, 1, 3; letter to M. C. Threlkeld Jr. from Wilson R. Buie, Lt. Colonel, Corps of Engineers, Director of Labor, War Food Administration, 4 April 1945, 1. Both from RG 59: Department of State, Mexico file, folder 811.504, box 4852, NARA CP.

22. "Imported Mexican War Emergency Workers and the Community," *American Federation of International Institutes (New York City) Bulletin* in conjunction with American War Community Services Inc, no. 1 (July 1945): 5, folder 8, box 17, Galarza Papers; Chantel Rodríguez, "Health on the Line: The Politics of Citizenship and the Railroad Bracero Program of World War II," PhD diss., University of Minnesota, 2013, 187; Hahamovitch, *No Man's Land*, 64, 80.

23. Galarza, "Some Problems of the Mexican Braceros," 28 August 1944 version, 10–11.

24. Letter to Manuel Ávila Camacho from Eugenio Ramírez Delgado, 19 August 1944, file 23412 (also 25960), box 0793, Ávila Camacho Papers 546.6/120-1, AGN; letter to Sr. Rafael de la Colina from Marian Lantz, 17 September 1974, series III, folder 9, box 5, Galarza Papers; memo to Secretario del Trabajo y Previsión Social from Andrés Iduarte, "Visita a los camps de Kennebunk, Rigby Barracks y Oakland, Maine, de la Boston and Maine Railroad Co.," 7 August 1945, 4–5, folder 10, box 17, Galarza Papers.

25. Gamboa, *Bracero Railroaders*, 144; Galarza, "The Mexican Railroad Worker's Camps at Jackson and Ypsilanti, Michigan," 1.

26. Andrés Iduarte, report to the Señor Secretario del Trabajo y Provisión Social, 6 February 1945, 1–3, folder 9, box 17, Galarza Papers.

27. Letter to Mexican Consul in Detroit from Ernesto Vieyra Avendaño, 21 April 1945, 1–2, translated from the Spanish by the author, RG 59: Department of State, Mexico file, folder 811.504, box 4852, NARA CP.

28. Galarza, "Some Problems of the Mexican War Workers," 30 July 1945, 5; James C. Scott, *Weapons of the Weak: Everyday Forms of Peasant Resistance* (New Haven, CT: Yale University Press, 1985), xvi; James C. Scott, *Decoding Subaltern Politics: Ideology, Disguise, and Resistance in Agrarian Politics* (New York: Routledge, 2013), 65.

29. Telegram to John D. Coates (Chief, Foreign Labor Section, Bureau of Placement, War Manpower Commission) from G. H. Minchin, Santa Fe, 23 March 1945; letter to Leon Bosch, Associate Director, Food Rationing Division, Office of Price Administration

from John D. Coates, 27 March 1945, 2. Both from RG, 59, Department of State, Mexico file, folder 811.504, box 4852, NARA CP.

30. Letter to Mexican Ambassador from E. J. Schremp, 24 May 1945; letter to John Willard Carrigan from Thomas C. Murray Jr., 27 June 1945; letter to R. C. Tanis, Acting Chief, Division of Mexican Affairs, from John D. Coates, 18 August 1945. All from RG 59: Department of State, Mexico file, folder 811.504, box 4852, NARA CP.

31. "Community Minded Young Men, the Church, and the Mercer County Federation of YMCAs at Work with Young Men from Mexico, 1945," folder 4, box 6, Galarza Papers.

32. Letter to Arthur Garfield Hays, ACLU New York Counsel, from lawyer Israel Bernstein, 17 August 1945; memo to Secretario del Trabajo y Previsión Social from Andrés Iduarte, 7 August 1945, 1; letter to Charles E. Gurney from Arthur Garfield Hays, 31 July 1945; letter to Ernesto Galarza form Clifford Forster, ACLU New York Staff Counsel, 11 September 1945; letter to Clifford Forster from Israel Bernstein, 10 September 1945. All from folder 10, box 17, Galarza Papers.

33. Letter to Ávila Camacho from José F. Hernández Serrano and Reynaldo Aguirre Miranda on behalf of the Alianza de Braceros, 2 July 1945, file 17466 (also 20215), box 0793, Ávila Camacho Papers, 546.6/120-1, AGN.

34. "Imported Mexican War Emergency Workers," 6; Ernesto Galarza, Notes on Tapia Montana, 26 August 1945, folder 9, box 5, Ernesto Galarza Papers; "The World from Washington by Senator 97," *Worldover Press*, 26 September 1945, folder 8, box 17, Galarza Papers; Gamboa, *Bracero Railroaders*, 118; S. Goldek, Physician's Report of Personal Injury and Flores-López statement, 14 March 1945, folder 1, box 6, Galarza Papers; Galarza statement on Antonio Feliciano Ramírez case, n.d., 4, folder 9, box 17, Galarza Papers; transcript of interview with Antonio Feliciano Ramírez, folder 9, box 17, Galarza Papers; Galarza, "The Mexican Railroad Worker's Camps at Jackson and Ypsilanti," 2.

35. "Imported Mexican War Emergency Workers," 3.

36. Hahamovitch, *No Man's Land*, 4, 93; Meléndez, *Sponsored Migration*, 75, 191, 200.

37. Letter to John D. Coates from John Willard Carrigan, 3 June 1946. RG 59: Department of State, folder 811.504, box 4854, NARA CP.

38. Hahamovitch, *No Man's Land*, 3, 20, 43–45, 48, 79–80.

39. Carmen Whalen, *From Puerto Rico to Philadelphia: Puerto Rican Workers and Postwar Economies* (Philadelphia: Temple University Press, 2001), 53; Fernández, "Of Immigrants and Migrants," 15–16; Meléndez, *Sponsored Migration*, 42.

40. Meléndez, *Sponsored Migration*, 56–58, 86–87, 201; *New York Daily News*, 12 October 1947, 100–101; García-Colón, *Colonial Migrants*, 132.

41. García-Colón, *Colonial Migrants*, 110.

42. Migration Division, "How to Hire Agricultural Workers from Puerto Rico," 1957, 3, folder 4, box 30, Galarza Papers; Michael Staudenmaier, "'Mostly of Spanish Extraction': Second-Class Citizenship and Racial Formation in Puerto Rican Chicago, 1946–1965," *Journal of American History* 104, no. 3 (December 2017): 682; Meléndez, *Sponsored Migration*, 128, 139, 199–200; García-Colón, *Colonial Migrants*, 88–89.

43. Meléndez, *Sponsored Migration*, 88, 206.

44. Reports for weeks ending 20 January 1956; 1 March 1956; 8 March 1956; 15 March 1956; 22 March 1956; 5 April 1956; 13 April 1956; 19 April 1956; 24 May 1956; 28 June 1956; 23 May 1957; 1 May 1958; 8 May 1958; 21 May 1959; 28 May 1959; 20 April 1961; 4 October 1962. All from folders 1–17, box 2416, Series: Cumulative Weekly Reports of Arrivals, 1956–82, Centro.

45. Meléndez, *Sponsored Migration*, 203.

46. I acknowledge that "wetback" is a derogatory term and place it in quotes because of its actual use in historical sources.

47. "Migratory Labor in American Agriculture," Report of the President's Commission on Migratory Labor, 1951, 78; Fernández, "Of Immigrants and Migrants," 8; Cristina Salinas, *Managed Migrations: Growers, Farmworkers, and Border Enforcement in the Twentieth Century* (Austin: University of Texas Press, 2018), 12; Meléndez, *Sponsored Migration*, 208.

48. García-Colón, *Colonial Migrants*, 151, 155.

49. Eileen J. Suárez Findlay, *We Are Left without a Father Here: Masculinity, Domesticity, and Migration in Postwar Puerto Rico* (Durham, NC: Duke University Press, 2014), 111.

50. Meléndez, *Sponsored Migration*, 208; García-Colón, *Colonial Migrants*, 137.

51. Quintana, *Contracting Freedom*, 181–82.

52. Hanna Garth, "Alimentary Dignity: Defining a Decent Meal in Post-Soviet Cuban Household Cooking," *Journal of Latin American and Caribbean Anthropology* 24, no. 2 (2019): 430, 436.

53. Meléndez, *Sponsored Migration*, 208, 210.

54. Jorge Colón to Anthony Vega, "Progress Report on Projects," 21 July 1967, folder 10, box 507, Farm Labor Program, Growers Association Files, Centro.

55. US Congress, "Migrant and Seasonal Farmworker Powerlessness," Hearings, Ninety-First Congress, First and Second Sessions on Farmworker Legal Problems, Subcommittee on Migratory Labor, Senate Committee on Labor and Public Welfare, 8 August 1969, Washington, DC, 1783–86.

56. "Puerto Rican Migrants Upset Upstate Town," *New York Times*, 17 July 1966, 1; García-Colón, *Colonial Migrants*, 176–77.

57. Birds Eye Food, Inc. contract, ca. 1968–70, 7–8, 10, 14, folder 1, box 506, Farm Labor Program, Growers Association Files, Centro; New York State Department of Labor, Division of Employment, "Clearance Order for Agricultural Labor," Spring 1968, folder 3, box 507, Farm Labor Program, Growers Association Files, Centro.

58. Alan Perl, memo, 25 April 1968, folder 3, box 506, Farm Labor Program, Growers Association Files, Centro; letter to Birds Eye management from Horacio Rodriguez Sanchez, 22 August 1974, 2, folder 9, box 506, Farm Labor Program, Growers Association Files, Centro.

59. My emphasis. García-Colón, *Colonial Migrants*, 113; memo to Ruben Natal from Birds Eye, 28 May 1968, folder 3, box 506, Farm Labor Program, Growers Association Files, Centro.

60. Notices of termination for Juan Serrano Rosario, 16 August 1968; Efran D. Rivera, 1 September 1968; Mario Velásquez, 12 September 1968; Regino Encarnación Vega, 16 September 1968; and Rafael Ayala Laboy, 19 August 1968. All from folder 3, box 506, Farm Labor Program, Growers Association Files, Centro.

61. Termination notices of Santos Márquez Figueroa, 11 September 1968; Juan Báez, 12 September 1968; Luis A. Tartabu, 16 September 1968. All from folder 3, box 506, Farm Labor Program, Growers Association Files, Centro.

62. Termination notices for Efraim Echavarría, 5 August 1968 and Elmo Serrano, 19 August 1968, folder 3, box 507; termination notice of José Hernández, 11 September 1973, folder 8, box 506. Both from Farm Labor Program, Growers Association Files, Centro.

63. Termination notices of Rafael Enrique Rodríguez, 9 September 1968; Félix Rodríguez Dides, 9 September 1968; Rodríguez David Rivera, 13 September 1968; Juan Alberto Báez Nazario, 30 September 1968; José Nazario Báez, 30 September 1968; Juan Hernández, 30 September 1968; Ismael Nazario, 30 September 1968; and Carlos Rivera Boirie, 2 October 1968. All from folder 3, box 506, Farm Labor Program, Growers Association Files, Centro.

64. Termination notices of Juan José Moreu, 18 August 1970; Benjamin Bega, 27 August 1970, Emilio Ayala and Antonio Ayala, 27 August 1970; Claudio Ponce, 3 September 1970; Richard M. González and Rafael Rivera, 4 September 1970; Daniel Vázquez, Juan Martínez, and Julio Daniel Berenguer Rivera, 14 September 1970; Efrain Colón Cruz, 24 September 1970. All from folder 6, box 506, Farm Labor Program, Growers Association Files, Centro.

65. Quitting notice of Ascencio Vázquez, 21 August 1970, folder 6; quitting notice of Efrain Rodríguez, 30 September 1971, folder 7. Both from box 506, Farm Labor Program, Growers Association Files, Centro.

66. Deductions sheet for week ending 8 October 1978, folder 2, box 507, Farm Labor Program, Growers Association Files, Centro; employee agreements of Maximino Rodríguez and Fernando Pratt, 24 October [no year], folder 9, box 506, Farm Labor Program, Growers Association Files, Centro.

67. Migration Division, Fact Sheet on Puerto Ricans in the United States, 2, folder 41, box 33, UFW Administration Department Files Collection, part 2, Reuther; Felipe Hinojosa, *Apostles of Change: Latino Radical Politics, Church Occupations, and the Fight to Save the Barrio* (Austin: University of Texas Press, 2021), 96; Jeffrey R. Backstrand and Stephen Schensul, "Co-Evolution In An Outlying Ethnic Community: The Puerto Ricans of Hartford, Connecticut," *Urban Anthropology* 11 no. 1 (Spring 1982), 10; Lana Dee Povitz, *Stirrings: How Activist New Yorkers Ignited a Movement for Food Justice* (Chapel Hill: University of North Carolina Press, 2019), 33, 35.

68. Gustavo Arellano, *Taco USA: How Mexican Food Conquered America* (New York: Scribner, 2013), 43, 58–59, 126; Jeffrey M. Pilcher, "Eating Mexican in a Global Age: The Politics and Production of Ethnic Food," in *Food Chains: From Farmyard to Shopping Cart*, ed. Warren Belasco and Roger Horowitz (Philadelphia: University of Pennsylvania Press, 2009), 164.

69. Vicki Ruiz, "Citizen Restaurant: American Imaginaries, American Communities," *American Quarterly* 60, no. 1 (March 2008): 7; Arellano, *Taco USA*, 30, 42, 45–46; Camille Begin, *Taste of the Nation: The New Deal Search for America's Food* (Urbana: University of Illinois Press, 2016), 113. For more on the Chili Queens, see Norma L. Cárdenas, "Queering the Chili Queens: Culinary Citizenship through Food Consciousness in the New Borderlands," in *Latin@s' Presence in the Food Industry: Changing How We Think about Food*, ed. Meredith E. Abarca and Consuelo Carr Salas (Fayetteville: University of Arkansas Press, 2016), 121–42; Jeffrey Pilcher and Donna R. Gabaccia, "'Chili Queens' and Checkered Tablecloths: Public Dining Cultures of Italians in New York City and Mexicans in San Antonio, Texas, 1870s–1940s," *Radical History Review* 110 (Spring 2011): 109–26; Monica Perales, "The Food Historian's Dilemma: Reconsidering the Role of Authenticity in Food Scholarship," *Journal of American History* 103, no. 3 (December 2016): 690–93, and Lori Flores, "Latino Labor in the US Food Industry, 1880–1920," *Oxford Encyclopedia of American History*, 17 December 2020, https://doi.org/10/1093/acrefore/9780199329175.013.850.

70. Jeffrey M. Pilcher, "From 'Montezuma's Revenge' to 'Mexican Truffles': Culinary Tourism across the Rio Grande," in *Culinary Tourism*, ed. Lucy M. Long (Lexington: University of Kentucky Press, 2004), 81; Gregory McNamee, *Tortillas, Tiswin, and T-Bones: A Food History of the Southwest* (Albuquerque: University of New Mexico Press, 2017), 187; Donna R. Gabaccia, *We Are What We Eat: Ethnic Food and the Making of Americans* (Cambridge, MA: Harvard University Press, 1998), 160.

71. Arellano, *Taco USA*, 189–90, "Juanita's History," Juanita's Foods website, 27 October 2017, www.juanitas.com/whos-juanita/history/.

72. Jeffrey M. Pilcher, "'Old Stock' Tamales and Migrant Tacos," *Social Research* 81, no. 2 (Summer 2014): 449; Arellano, *Taco USA*, 30; Gabaccia, *We Are What We Eat*, 159–60; McNamee, *Tortillas, Tiswin, and T-Bones*, 186–87; Pilcher, "Eating Mexican in a Global Age," 163.

73. Ruiz, "Citizen Restaurant," 4; George Sanchez, "'Go after the Women': Americanization and the Mexican Immigrant Woman, 1915–1929," Stanford Center for Chicano Research Working Paper Series, no. 6 (1984); Begin, *Taste of the Nation*, 16, 113; "It's Time We Give the Mexican Combo Platter the Credit It Deserves," *Bon Appétit*, 13 February 2020, https://www.bonappetit.com/story/ode-to-combo-platter.

74. Lori A. Flores, "The Career of Zarela Martinez and a Changing Mexican Foodscape in New York City, 1981–2011," *Food, Culture & Society* 26 (2023): 3; Cecilia Márquez, "Becoming Pedro: 'Playing Mexican' at South of the Border," *Latino Studies* 16, no. 4 (December 2018): 461, 468; Pilcher, *Planet Taco*, 131, 167.

75. Jean Grabowski, "Mexico to Avondale in Eight Days, Illegally," *Daily Local News*, 15 December 1975, 1; Cristobal Bonifaz, Pennsylvania ACLU, "The State of Farm Laborers in Chester County," 6 January 1976, 6. Both from folder 41, box 33, UFW Administration Department Files Collection, part 2, Reuther.

76. García-Colón, *Colonial Migrants*, 212.

77. Gloria Bonilla-Santiago, *Organizing Puerto Rican Migrant Farmworkers: The Experience of Puerto Ricans in New Jersey* (New York: Peter Lang, 1988), 59; New York State Department of Labor, "Agriculture and Food Processing Clearance Order," 4 June 1990, folder 5, box 508, Farm Labor Program, Grower Association Files, Centro.

78. Martínez, *Latino History in Rhode Island*, 22, 26, 36–37.

79. Carmen Teresa Whalen, "Latinos/as in the Northeast: A Historic Overview," in "The Future of Latinos in the United States: Law, Opportunity, and Mobility," white paper for the American Bar Foundation, 13, 22; Glenn Hendricks, *The Dominican Diaspora* (New York: Teachers College Press, 1974), 57, 66.

80. Martínez, *Latino History in Rhode Island*, 67, 69–70, 72–74.

81. "Fefa's Market," blog post, accessed 3 March 2024, http://nuestrasraicesri.net//FefasMarket.html.

Chapter Two

1. Edward C. Forst, "Chavez Speaks on Lettuce Workers Strike; Farm Workers Want Chiquita Banana Boycott," *Harvard Crimson*, 6 April 1979, 1, folder 27, box 25 (UFW Office of the President, Cesar Chavez Collection, part 2), Reuther.

2. National Advisory Committee on Farm Labor, "Agribusiness and Its Workers," 1963, 5. Beinecke Library, Yale University; Sarah Stern, "'We Cast Our Lot with the Farm Workers': Organization, Mobilization and Meaning in the United Farm Workers'

Grape Boycott in New York City, 1967–70," honors thesis, NYU Department of History, 30 April 2013, 19.

3. Cindy Hahamovitch, *No Man's Land: Jamaican Guestworkers in America and the Global History of Deportable Labor* (Princeton, NJ: Princeton University Press, 2011), 129–31.

4. See Frank Trentmann, "Consumer Boycotts in Modern History: States, Moral Boundaries, and Political Action," in *Boycotts Past and Present: From the American Revolution to the Campaign to Boycott Israel*, ed. David Feldman (London: Palgrave, 2019).

5. For more on the UFW's boycotts, see Susan Ferriss and Ricardo Sandoval, *The Fight in the Fields: Cesar Chavez and the Farmworkers Movement* (Boston: Mariner, 1998); Miriam Pawel, *The Union of Their Dreams: Power, Hope, and Struggle in Cesar Chavez's Farm Worker Movement* (London: Bloomsbury, 2010); Marshall Ganz, *Why David Sometimes Wins: Leadership, Organization, and Strategy in the California Farm Worker Movement* (New York: Oxford, 2010); Frank Bardacke, *Trampling Out the Vintage: Cesar Chavez and the Two Souls of the United Farm Workers* (New York: Verso, 2012); Matthew J. Garcia, *From the Jaws of Victory: The Triumph and Tragedy of Cesar Chavez and the Farm Worker Movement* (Berkeley: University of California Press, 2014); Heidi Tinsman, *Buying into the Regime: Grapes and Consumption in Cold War Chile and the United States* (Durham, NC: Duke University Press, 2014); Miriam Pawel, *The Crusades of Cesar Chavez: A Biography* (London: Bloomsbury, 2015); and Lori A. Flores, *Grounds for Dreaming: Mexican Americans, Mexican Immigrants, and the California Farmworker Movement* (New Haven, CT: Yale University Press, 2016).

6. Steven V. Roberts, "Grape Strike: Still a Hard Road to Settlement," *New York Times*, 29 June 1969, E5.

7. William Frieburger, "War Prosperity and Hunger: The New York Food Riots of 1917," *Labor History* 25, no. 2 (1984): 217–21, 224–27.

8. Felipe Hinojosa, *Apostles of Change: Latino Radical Politics, Church Occupations, and the Fight to Save the Barrio* (Austin: University of Texas Press, 2021), 17, 98, 100–101; Lana Dee Povitz, *Stirrings: How Activist New Yorkers Ignited a Movement for Food Justice* (Chapel Hill: University of North Carolina Press, 2019), 2; Johanna Fernández, *The Young Lords: A Radical History* (Chapel Hill: University of North Carolina Press, 2020), 10, 123–24.

9. "Farm Union Pins Its Hopes on Victory in Coast Grape Strike," *New York Times*, 2 October 1967, 43; Gladwin Hill, "New Era Ahead in Farm Labor," *New York Times*, 17 April 1966, 208.

10. Peter Bart, "Focus Is Shifted in Grape Strike: Pressure Against Growers Is Exerted in Boycott," *New York Times*, 20 February 1966, 64; Peter Bart, "Schenley to Bargain with a Grape Union," *New York Times*, 7 April 1966, 28; Dick Meister, "'La Huelga' Becomes 'La Causa,'" *New York Times*, 17 November 1968, 84.

11. Lawrence E. Davies, "Grape Strikers Score Gov. Brown as March Ends," *New York Times*, 11 April 1966, 18.

12. "Farm Union Pins Its Hopes on Victory in Coast Grape Strike," *New York Times*, 2 October 1967, 43; Sidney E. Zion, "Union Asks Court for Boycott Help: Says Company Sells Grapes under Different Labels," *New York Times*, 13 February 1968, 24; memo to Frank Murphy from Frank Myers, 22 December 1967, folder 8, box 13 (UFWOC Boston, Office Files, Other Areas #1), Reuther.

13. For a sample of hunger strikes during this period, see "'Strike' to Ease Famine:

Student Assembly Calls for Wheatless Meals in Colleges," *New York Times*, 27 April 1946, 8; "Sean M'Caughey Dies after Hunger Strike," *New York Times*, 11 May 1946, 18; Lindesay Parrott, "Japan's Rail Men End Hunger Strike: Act as Cabinet Seeks Approval of Occupation for Bonus Pay—Regime Seen in Bad Spot," *New York Times*, 14 December 1949, 20; "Striking French Miners to Stop Eating Monday," *New York Times*, 3 February 1962, 3; "Vietnamese Students in Paris Stage Silent Anti-Diem Hunger Strike," *New York Times*, 28 August 1963, 3; "Bolivian Tin Miners Agree to Call Off Hunger Strike," *New York Times*, 23 October 1963, 9.

14. Lawrence K. Altman, "Hunger Strike: What Is Role of Physicians?," *New York Times*, 20 January 1981, 47.

15. Peter Matthiessen profile of Cesar Chavez, *New Yorker*, 21 and 28 June 1969, folder 8, box 3 (UFWOC Boston files), Reuther.

16. Wallace Turner, "Head of Farm Workers Union Ends 25-Day Fast in California," *New York Times*, 11 March 1968, 22.

17. Letter to Ron Jones from Jane C. Brown, 16 April 1968, folder 10, box 16 (UFW Office of the President, series 2—Boycott Offices), Reuther; letter to Ken Sitz from Jane Brown, 22 August 1968, folder 15, box 14 (Boycott Correspondence New York State, 1969–70), Reuther.

18. "Grapes Dumped in Harbor Symbolize Calif. Labor Protest," *Sunday Herald Traveler*, 18 August 1968, 6, folder 10, box 1 (UFWOC Boston Clippings Series), Reuther; "Calif. Pickers Plan 'Boston Grape Party,'" *Boston Globe*, 16 August 1968, 2; Nick Peck, "Grapes Dumped in Harbor to Support Pickers," *Boston Globe*, 18 August 1968, 34; "Hingham Housewives Picket in Support of Grape Strike," *Patriot Ledger*, 28 August 1968, 6.

19. John Herbers, "Kennedy Role as the Candidate of Poor Is Sought by McGovern," *New York Times*, 14 August 1968, 26; "Gifts of Grapes Rouse Legislators," *Philadelphia Inquirer*, 20 September 1968, 3; "Nixon Backs Growers in Labor Fuss," *Bangor Daily News*, 19 September 1968, 23.

20. Hubert Stewart, "A Man Pledged to Stop Grapes," *Philadelphia Inquirer*, 26 August 1968, 25. As Jennifer Robin Terry has shown, children walked picket lines, volunteered in union offices, made signs, attended meetings, translated between Spanish and English for their parents and other members, and sold the union newspaper *El Malcriado*. Jennifer Robin Terry, "Niños por La Causa: Child Activists and the United Farm Workers Movement, 1965–1975," *Pacific Historical Review* 92, no. 2 (Spring 2023): 227–59.

21. Press release, folder 10, box 16 (UFW Office of the President, series 2—Boycott Offices), Reuther; photograph of UFW demonstrators, *Boston Globe*, 23 December 1968, 30; untitled newspaper article, 22 December 1969, folder 12, box 1 (UFWOC: Boston, Clippings Series, series 1), Reuther.

22. "Chavez Sets 3 Speeches in Boston," *Boston Globe*, 10 October 1969, 34; "Grape Boycott Begins in City with Pickets," *Hartford Courant*, 27 November 1968, 22; Stern, "'We Cast Our Lot,'" 39–40.

23. Letter to Cesar Chavez from Elma Gonzalez, 24 March 1969, 1–2, folder 11, box 14 (UFW Office of the President—series 2—Boycott Offices), Reuther.

24. Letter to Cesar Chavez from Everardo Garcia, 23 May 1969, folder 15, box 14 (UFW Office of the President—series 2—Boycott Offices), Reuther.

25. Hendrik Hertzberg, "Cesar Chavez in New York City," *New Yorker*, 15 November 1969, 20–21; letter to John Manila from Jane C. Brown, 5 December 1968, folder 3, box 10

(UFW Office of the President—series 2—Boycott Offices), Reuther; Steven V. Roberts, "Grape Boycott: Struggle Poses a Moral Issue," *New York Times*, 12 November 1969, 48; "A.F.L.-C.I.O. Opening Boycott of G.E. Products," *New York Times*, 28 November 1969, 66; Chris Hall, "Boycott 'Doesn't Represent' Grape Farm Workers," *Providence Journal*, 16 December 1968; Meister, "'La Huelga' Becomes 'La Causa.'"

26. Larry Adelman, "Demonstrators Boycott Grapes at Local Store," *The Dartmouth*, 7 October 1969, and "Co-op Management Halts Sale of Boycott-Provoking Grapes," *Valley News*, n.d., folder 16, box 2 (UFWOC: Boston, Clipping Series, Boycott Activities), Reuther; "Grape Boycott Gains New Support in Maine," *Maine State Labor News*, July 1969, folder 37, box 1 (UFWOC Boston Clippings Series), Reuther; Patricia McGowan "Catholic College Graduate Aids in Organizing Grape Boycott in Fall River, New Bedford," unknown publication, n.d., folder 36, box 1 (UFWOC Boston Clippings Series), Reuther; "Hunger Strike Slated by Grape Boycotter," unknown publication, 23 September 1969, folder 20, box 2 (UFWOC: Boston, Clipping Series, Boycott Activities), Reuther; letter from Katy Dawson to New England boycott office, 13 August 1969, and letter to UFWOC Delano office from John Wabbott, 13 August 1969. Both from folder 10, box 14 (UFW Office of the President—series 2—Boycott Offices), Reuther.

27. Margaret Rose, "'Woman Power Will Stop Those Grapes': Chicana Organizers and Middle-Class Female Supporters in the Farm Workers' Grape Boycott in Philadelphia, 1969–1970," *Journal of Women's History* 7, no. 4 (Winter 1995): 7; US Bureau of Commerce, Census Report FT 410, "Grapes, Fresh: Exports from the United States by Specified Country of Destination, 1968," folder 7, box 16 (UFW Office of the President, series 2), Reuther.

28. US Congress, "Migrant and Seasonal Farmworker Powerlessness," hearings before the Senate Subcommittee on Migratory Labor of the Committee on Labor and Public Welfare, Ninety-First Congress, First and Second Sessions on Farmworker Legal Problems, 8 August 1969 (Washington, DC: US Government Printing Office, 1970), 1731, 1733, 1748, 1753, 1759–60; Donald Janson, "2 South Jersey Poultry Farms Accused of Housing Workers in Chicken Coops," *New York Times*, 20 July 1976, 21.

29. Dolores Huerta, "Statistics on New York Boycott," 2, folder 34, box 24 (UFW Administration Files Collection), Reuther; Ed Chiera, UFW Documentation Project Online Discussion, 169, https://libraries.ucsd.edu/farmworkermovement/disc/December[1]%20 REVISED.pdf; Barbara L. Baer and Glenna Matthews, "You Find a Way: The Women of the Boycott," *Nation*, 23 February 1974, 233–34, 238.

30. "6 Unions Are Sued by Grape Growers," *New York Times*, 13 July 1968, 28; Meister, "La Huelga Becomes La Causa," 90; "Grape Boycott by Minority Groups Most Unfair," *Produce News*, 31 August 1968, folder 1, box 1 (UFWOC: Boston, Clippings Series), Reuther.

31. Lana Dee Povitz, "Nourishing Progressive Ideals in Dark Ages: Boycotts at the Park Slope Food Coop in the 1970s," *Social History* 12, https://muse.jhu.edu/article/763453; Margaret E. Rose, "Women in the United Farm Workers: A Study of Chicana and Mexicana Participation in a Labor Union, 1950-1980," PhD diss., University of California Los Angeles, 1988, 82; Dolores Huerta, UFWOC New York Office Memo, 29 December 1968, 4, folder 34, box 24 (UFW Administration Files Collection), Reuther; letter of instructions from Dolores Huerta to boycotters, 26 September 1968, folder 11, box 5 (UFWOC Boston Correspondence Files), Reuther; letter to William Vaughan from Robert A. Petronella, 10 January 1980, folder 18, box 24 (UFW Office of the President, part 2), Reuther;

letter to the UFCW from UFW New England boycott director David M. Martínez, n.d., 2, folder 18, box 24 (UFW Office of the President, Cesar Chavez Collection, part 2), Reuther.

32. "A&P Boycott Backed by Huntington Hartford," *New York Times*, 14 September 1968, 61; Huerta, "Statistics on New York Boycott," 2; *Brooklyn Boycott News*, 12 August 1969, folder 38, box 121 (UFW Administration Files), Reuther.

33. Letter to Joseph Giumarra from Columbia University Student Council, 14 February 1968, and letter to Joseph Giumarra from Michael Novick, 15 February 1968. Both from folder 27, box 6 (UFWOC Boston Correspondence Files #2), Reuther; letter to Joseph Giumarra from Local 89, 28 February 1968, folder 31, box 6 (UFWOC Boston Correspondence Files #2), Reuther.

34. Letters to Joseph Giumarra from the Club Cívico Cultural Hijos de Camuy, 19 February 1968; Bohio Borincano Social and Athletic Club Inc., 19 February 1968; and the Asociación Nacional de Choferes Puertorriqueños e Hispanos, Inc., 20 February 1968. All from folder 28, box 6 (UFWOC Boston Correspondence Files #2), Reuther; letters to Joseph Giumarra from the Puerto Rican Voters of the Lower East Side, 21 February 1968 and La Sultana de Oeste (Bronx), both from folder 29, box 6 (UFWOC Boston Correspondence Files #2), Reuther; letters to Joseph Giumarra from the Asociación Arroyanos Ausentes Inc., 23 February 1968; Yauco Civic and Social Club, 24 February 1968; the Sociedad Naranjiteños Unidos, 26 February 1968; and Club Cívico Deportivo Bayamones, 26 February 1968. All from folder 30, box 6 (UFWOC Boston Correspondence Files #2), Reuther; letter to Joseph Giumarra from Rev. Domingo I. Rosado, 13 March 1968, folder 34, box 6 (UFWOC Boston Correspondence Files #2), Reuther; letter to Joseph Giumarra from Andrés Echeguren, Círculo Social Cubano, 28 March 1968, folder 37, box 6 (UFWOC Boston Correspondence Files #2), Reuther.

35. Will Lissner, "3 A. & P. Stores Firebombed; Link to Grape Strike Studied," *New York Times*, 24 October 1968, 26. For more on the UFW's alliance with the Black Panther Party, see Lauren Araiza, *To March for Others: The Black Freedom Struggle and the United Farm Workers* (Philadelphia: University of Pennsylvania Press, 2014).

36. Huerta, "Statistics on New York Boycott," 2.

37. Rose, "Women in the United Farm Workers," 78–80; Huerta memo; "Statistics on New York Boycott," 2; *Brooklyn Boycott News*; letter to Cesar Chavez and Larry Itliong from Andy Imutan, 12 June 1969, 1, folder 34, box 24 (UFW Administration Files), Reuther; letter to Cesar Chavez from Marcia B. Goodman, 31 January 1969, folder 14, box 14 (UFW Office of the President—series 2—Boycott Offices), Reuther.

38. Margaret Rose, "Traditional and Nontraditional Patterns of Female Activism in the United Farm Workers of America, 1962 to 1980," *Frontiers: A Journal of Women Studies* 11, no. 1 (1990): 30; Rose, "Woman Power," 6, 10–12.

39. Rose, "Woman Power," 12–14; memo to Cesar Chavez from Hope López, folder 7, box 3 (UFW Philadelphia Boycott Office, part 1), Reuther.

40. Rose, "Woman Power," 8–9.

41. Stern 28; *La Voz de la SIU*, November 1968, folder 7, box 16 (UFW Office of the President, series 2), Reuther.

42. For more on this conference and Mexican American organizing around hunger in the 1960s, see Janett Barragán Miranda's forthcoming book *Hungering for Equality*.

43. East Coast Migrant Health Project report, January 1973, 3, folder 11, box 6, Ross Papers.

44. Rose, "Woman Power," 13, 15–17; Carmen Whalen, *From Puerto Rico to Philadelphia: Puerto Rican Workers and Postwar Economies* (Philadelphia: Temple University Press, 2001), 2, 170.

45. Letter to the editor from Jane K. Dixon, "Says Grapes Are Immoral Buy," *Hartford Courant*, 19 August 1969, 22; "College Girls Picket on Grape Sales," *Newport Daily News*, 19 November 1968, 4; Rose, "Woman Power," 22.

46. Rose, "Woman Power," 16–17.

47. *Philadelphia Evening Bulletin*, 14 July 1969, 1, folder 14, box 1 (UFW Philadelphia Boycott Office), Reuther.

48. Rose, "Woman Power," 18–19; Lori A. Flores, "An Unladylike Strike Fashionably Clothed: Mexicana and Anglo Women Garment Workers against Tex-Son, 1959–1963," *Pacific Historical Review* 78, no. 3 (August 2009): 393–94.

49. Rose, "Woman Power," 18–20.

50. Lynn Litterine, "Supermarket Sit-In Family Affair," *Record* (New Jersey), 17 September 1969, B-13; "Life of Cesar Chavez—A Fight against Injustice," *Record*, 12 October 1969, 17; "Grape Hero Breaks Fast," *Newport Daily News*, 11 October 1969, 14; "Hunger Strike Slated by Grape Boycotter," 23 September 1969, and "2,000 Signers Back Fasting Seminarian," both from folder 20, box 2 (UFWOC: Boston, Clipping Series, Boycott Activities), Reuther; memo to Boycotters from New York Crew, folder 22, box 5 (UFWOC Boston Correspondence Files), Reuther.

51. UFWOC New Jersey organizing committee newsletter, n.d., 2, folder 11, box 14 (UFW Office of the President—series 2—Boycott Offices), Reuther; William F. Buckley Jr., "The Victory of Cesar Chavez," *Boston Globe*, 14 August 1970, 13.

52. Buckley, "Victory of Cesar Chavez"; Steven V. Roberts, "Grape Strike: Still a Hard Road to Settlement," *New York Times*, 29 June 1969, E5; Tom Wolfe, *Radical Chic and Mau-Mauing the Flak Catchers* (London: Picador, 2009), 5, 43–44.

53. Wolfe, *Radical Chic*, 42.

54. Wolfe, *Radical Chic*, 43–46; Charlotte Curtis, "Southampton Meets 'La Causa,'" *New York Times*, 30 June 1969, 44.

55. "Chavez Tells of Pesticides," *Providence Evening Bulletin*, 29 September 1969, 31; "Chavez Scores Grape Growers on Pesticide Use," *New York Times*, 30 September 1969, 19; "McFarland: Too Much Cancer," *Food and Justice: Magazine of the Union Farm Workers of America* 3, no. 4 (May 1986): 7, http://libraries.ucsd.edu/farmworkermovement/ufwarchives/foodjustice/10_May86_001.pdf; Warren J. Belasco, *Appetite for Change: How the Counterculture Took on the Food Industry* (Ithaca, NY: Cornell University Press, 2007), 139; Monica Moore, "Hidden Dimensions of Damage: Pesticides and Health," in *The Fatal Harvest Reader: The Tragedy of Industrial Agriculture*, ed. Andrew Kimbrell, 133–35 (Washington, DC: Island, 2002).

56. Jonathan Maslow, "The Plight of the Puerto Rican Migrant," *Star*, folder 41, box 33 (UFW Administration Department Files Collection, part 2), Reuther; Frances Moore Lappe, *Diet for a Small Planet* (New York: Ballantine, 1991), 135–36; Belasco, *Appetite for Change*, 69.

57. "Fiesta at Church Celebrates Arrival Here of Union Grapes," *Philadelphia Inquirer*, 20 July 1970, 8; Rose, "Woman Power," 22–23.

58. "Grape Pickers Explain," *Record*, 16 April 1970, 2.

59. Thomas McCarthy, "No Grapes and No Gripes," *Long Island Press*, 30 June 1974, folder 14, box 2 (UFW Central Administration Files Collection), Reuther.

60. UFWOC New Jersey organizing committee newsletter, n.d., 1, folder 11, box 14 (UFW Office of the President—series 2—Boycott Offices), Reuther; letter to Cesar Chavez from Andrea O'Malley, 2 October 1970, folder 12, box 10 (UFW Office of the President—series 2—Boycott Offices), Reuther; List of Hueblein Products, folder 5, box 16 (UFW Office of the President—series 2—Boycott Offices), Reuther.

61. Jean Hewitt, "Here to Spur Boycott of Lettuce, Farm Workers Urge: Remember the Grape," *New York Times*, 9 October 1970, 60; Eleanor Blau, "Chavez Asks Lettuce-Boycott Support," *New York Times*, 30 November 1970, 32; Bronx boycott newsletter, 11 November 1970, folder 7, box 130 (UFW Administration Files), Reuther; Bronx press release, folder 14, box 14 (UFW Office of the President—series 2—Boycott Offices), Reuther; "Lettuce Workers Picket Dix," *Newark Evening News*, 12 January 1971, folder 33, box 24 (UFW Administration Files Collection), Reuther.

62. Roberts, "Grape Boycott: Struggle Poses a Moral Issue"; letter to Jim Lollis from Joseph Lutsky, 26 May 1969, folder 3, box 16 (UFW Office of the President—series 2—Boycott Offices), Reuther.

63. Suffolk County Human Rights Commission, "Report of the Suffolk County Migrant Task Force," 9 February 1970, 1, 4–6, 9, 11, addendums 1 and 3, folder 47, box 28 (UFW Administration Department Files Collection, part 2), Reuther; Jane Snider, "Three Deny Labor Camp Health Counts," *Newsday*, 11 November 1975; Ismael García-Colón, *Colonial Migrants at the Heart of Empire: Puerto Rican Workers on U.S. Farms* (Oakland: University of California Press, 2020), 203; "Two Farm Unions Agree on Merger," *New York Times*, 21 June 1976, 60L. For more on Long Island farm labor and camps, see Mark A. Torres, *Long Island Migrant Camps: Dust for Blood* (Charleston, SC: History Press, 2021).

64. Ronald Sullivan, "2 Poverty Aides Seized at Jersey Migrant Camp," *New York Times*, 8 August 1970, 19; UFW Memos, "New Jersey Farm Worker Information" and "Farm Workers in New Jersey," folders 9 and 33, box 34 (UFW Administration Department Files Collection, part 2), Reuther; "UFWOC and the Jersey Farm Workers," *El Malcriado*, 1 November 1970, 14, http://libraries.ucsd.edu/farmworkermovement/ufwarchives/elmalcriado/Dalzell/November%201,%201970.pdf.

65. José Gómez, flyer, n.d. [ca. 1970–73]; letter to New Jersey AFL-CIO Affiliates from President Charles H. Marciante, 24 November 1970; "Five Sit-Ins Arrested in Food Boycott," *Record*, 24 December 1970, B22; "Halt Protest on Lettuce," *Newark Sunday News*, 10 January 1971, C6; New Jersey UFWOC Newsletter. All from folder 33, box 24 (UFW Administration Files Collection), Reuther.

66. Ronald Sullivan, "New Jersey Court Rules Farmers Can't Prohibit Visits to Migrants," *New York Times*, 12 May 1971, 1. For more on *Folgueras v. Hassle*, see Emily Prifogle, "Rural Social Safety Nets for Migrant Farmworkers in Michigan, 1942–1971," *Law & Social Inquiry* 46, no. 4 (April 2021): 1022–61.

67. "Glassboro Center Farm Workers Met to Discuss Problems," *Community Migrant Ministry (Ministerio Migrante de la Comunidad) Newsletter*, 22 June 1972, 2, folder 20, box 33 (UFW Administration Files Collection, part 2), Reuther; UFW Memo, "New Jersey Farm Worker Information," and Elissa Papirno, "Food Triggers Tobacco Camp Work Halt," unknown publication, 13 April 1973. Both from folder 7, box 30 (UFW Administration Files Collection, part 2), Reuther.

68. Flyer, "End America's Harvest of Shame," and memo, "Sopas por La Causa." Both from folder 7, box 28 (UFW Administration Department Files Collection, part 2),

Reuther; Estelle Sammis, "Tears, Cheers for Chavez," *Long Island Press*, 3 July 1974, folder 14, box 2 (UFW Central Administration Files, part 1/2); Ann-Mary Currier, "Non-feast Planned on Common," *Boston Globe*, 27 November 1969; "Growing Pains," *Adelante* (Pittsburgh UFW newsletter), ca. 1971–73, 1, and "Farmworkers' Non-meal," *El Clarin* (UFW Philadelphia newsletter), 1. Both from folder 11, box 26 (Philadelphia Boycott 1971–73 Collection), Reuther.

69. Douglas A. Campbell, "Up, Up, Up Go Nation's Food Costs," *Philadelphia Inquirer*, 26 October 1980, 37; Emily E. LB. Twarog, *Politics of the Pantry: Housewives, Food and Consumer Protest in Twentieth Century America* (New York: Oxford, 2017), 1, 96, 98; "Growing Pains," 2; Allyson P. Brantley, *Brewing a Boycott: How a Grassroots Coalition Fought Coors and Remade American Consumer Activism* (Chapel Hill: University of North Carolina Press, 2021), 52.

70. "New Labor Law Expected to Set Off Arizona Clash," *New York Times*, 11 June 1972, 46; "Telegrams to Cesar" compilation, 5, folder 14, box 3 (UFW Office of the President, series 2 files), Reuther.

71. "Chavez Fasting to Protest Arizona Farm Labor Law," *New York Times*, 15 May 1972, 23; "Chavez Continues a Fast in Arizona: Protests Farm Labor Law—McGovern Backs Him," *New York Times*, 21 May 1972, N50; Anthony Ripley, "Chavez Ends Fast at Kennedy Rites: Says Sacrifices of Workers 'Will Not Be in Vain,'" *New York Times*, 5 June 1972, 65; Athia Hardt, "Chavez Ends 24-Day Fast; Heart May Be Damaged," *Arizona Republic*, 5 June 1972, folder 13, box 3 (UFW Office of the President, part 2 files), Reuther.

72. UFW Press release, 19 July 1974, folder 39, box 29 (UFW Administration Department Files Collection, part 2), Reuther; Sam Washington, "Chavez's Brother Begins LI Fast," *Newsday*, 24 July 1974; "Recent Events on Long Island" document, 2, folder 34, box 32 (UFW Administration Department Files Collection, part 2), Reuther; UFW press release, 23 July 1974, folder 14, box 2 (UFW Central Administration Files Collection), Reuther. The late 1970s continued to be characterized by fasts around the world. See, for example, "Jailed I.R.A. Chief Ends Hunger Strike: New Slaying in Belfast," *New York Times*, 17 January 1973, 4; "Irish Sisters in British Jail End 3 Week Hunger Strike," *New York Times*, 8 June 1974, 10; "Fast Is Begun in India to Press for a State Election," *New York Times*, 8 April 1975, 3; "70 U.S. Prisoners Are Said to End Mexican Jail Fast," *New York Times*, 9 September 1976, 30; "Lima Journalists Begin a Fast," *New York Times*, 20 March 1979, A3; Altman, "Hunger Strike," 47.

73. Letter to UFW headquarters from Ithaca UFW committee, 8 January 1971, folder 36, box 24; "Chicanos Demand Union Lettuce," *Pitt News* (University of Pittsburgh), 24 February 1971, folder 10, box 26; and Letter to UFW Keene headquarters from Tina Nannarone, 19 December 1972, folder 9, box 26, all from UFW Administration Department Files, Reuther; Povitz, *Stirrings*, 102; Povitz, "Nourishing Progressive Ideals," 15, 17; Galleria Loisaida flyer, "United Farmworkers Benefit Night," ca. 1975–80, folder 5, box 27 (UFW Office of the President, Cesar Chavez Files, part 2), Reuther.

74. Winthrop Griffith, "Is Chavez Beaten?," *New York Times*, 15 September 1974, 258; *Church World* (Maine), 5 April 1979, and Marc Grossman, "Chavez Urges Chiquita Banana Boycott," 4. Both from folder 27, box 25 (UFW Office of the President, Cesar Chavez Collection, part 2), Reuther; "Parade Here Backs Efforts by Chavez to Unionize Farms," *New York Times*, 11 May 1975, 55.

75. Felicia Kornbluh, "Food as a Civil Right: Hunger, Work, and Welfare in the South after the Civil Rights Act," *Labor* 12, nos. 1–2 (2015): 140; Mary Potorti, "Feeding

Revolution: The Black Panther Party and the Politics of Food," *Radical Teacher* 98 (2014): 45–46; Bill Collins, "The 'Terrible 10' Cast in Roles of Food Day Villains," *Philadelphia Inquirer*, 17 April 1975, C1.

76. Flyer for benefit dinner, 27 March 1976, and UFW Newsletter, Providence Office, 11 March 1976. Both from folder 12, box 10 (UFWOC Boston Clippings Series), Reuther; Toronto UFW recipe book, folder 38, box 23 (UFW New York Boycott Records, part 2), Reuther.

77. Affidavits from Jeffrey Thornell, Armin Kartagener, and Isadore Abramowitz; court document *Waldbaum v. UFW* and individuals, 31 July 1975, 2. All from folder 24, box 28 (UFW Administration Department Files Collection, part 2), Reuther; testimony from Carmen Blanco, 6 October 1975, and Vigil Statements of Rita Cassel and Marie LeDoux. All from folder 34, box 27 (UFW Administration Department Files Collection, part 2), Reuther.

78. Affidavit of Beatrice C. Sittner, 4 August 1975; Kenneth Urban testimony, undated; Ruth L. Kane testimony, 4 August 1975. All from folder 34, box 27 (UFW Administration Department Files Collection, part 2), Reuther; press release, 22 April 1976, 1, folder 24, box 28 (UFW Administration Department Files Collection, part 2), Reuther.

79. Joyce Starr, "Chavez Leads Pickets in Protest," *Waterbury Republican*, 1 August 1974, folder 8, box 1 (UFW Central Administration Files Collection), Reuther; UFW press release, "Cesar Chavez to Visit Connecticut"; "New England Visit" memo, 1–3, and "Chavez Lauds N.E. Support," *Bridgeport Post*, 7 August 1974, 1–3. All from folder 8, box 1 (UFW Central Administration Files Collection), Reuther; "Cesar Chavez Visits Maine," *Nashua Telegraph*, 7 August 1974, 51; boycott tour schedule, April 9–15, 1979, folder 12, box 19 (UFW Office of the President, Cesar Chavez Collection, part 2), Reuther; Boston boycott report, 16 April 1979, 1, and 1 May 1979, 2. Both from folder 18, box 24 (UFW Office of the President, Cesar Chavez Collection, part 2), Reuther.

80. UFW benefit concert program, 22 December 1976, folder 5, box 27 (UFW Office of the President, Cesar Chavez Collection, part 2), Reuther; UFW benefit concert/rally program, 29 April 1976, and "New York Labor Presents a United Farmworker Benefit," 1976 flyer. Both from folder 13, box 28 (UFW Administration Department Files Collection, part 2), Reuther.

81. Press release, 27 July 1979, 3–4, folder 12, box 19 (UFW Office of the President, Cesar Chavez Collection, part 2), Reuther.

82. Statement of Cesar E. Chavez before the Subcommittee on Labor of the Senate Committee on Labor and Public Welfare, 16 April 1969, 9, folder 5, box 5 (UFWOC Boston Correspondence Files), Reuther; Dolores Huerta, memo, 29 December 1968, 2, folder 34, box 24 (UFW Administration Files Collection), Reuther.

83. Ana R. Minian, *Undocumented Lives: The Untold Story of Mexican Migration* (Cambridge, MA: Harvard University Press, 2018), 161; Mario Sifuentez, *Of Forests and Fields: Mexican Labor in the Pacific Northwest* (New Brunswick, NJ: Rutgers University Press, 2016), 75; Syracuse UFW Support Committee resignation letter, 6 September 1974, and letter to Mary Jo Fink from Linda Maddaus, 10 September 1974. Both from folder 4, box 31 (UFW Administration Department Files Collection Part 2), Reuther; "Brooklyn 1977" transcript, 45, folder 14, box 20, Ross papers.

84. "Emergency—Help the Grape Strikers!," leaflet, ca. 1973, folder 17, box 2 (UFW Central Administration Files Collection), Reuther.

85. "Q&A with Cesar Chavez," *Boston Globe*, 15 April 1979, 2; UFW Boston Newsletters, July 1979, folder 12, box 10 (UFWOC Boston Clippings Series), Reuther.

86. Minian, *Undocumented Lives*, 3, 58.

87. "Horrible Event in New York," *El Malcriado*, 7 October 1966, 4. UFW Documentation Project, UC Santa Barbara, https://libraries.ucsd.edu/farmworkermovement /ufwarchives/elmalcriado/1966/October%207,%201966_PDF.pdf.

88. George Anastasia, "Organizing New Jersey's Puerto Rican Migrants Keeps Angel Dominguez Involved in 'the Struggle,'" *Philadelphia Inquirer*, 8 December 1974, G-1-2; García-Colón, *Colonial Migrants*, 206; Bonilla-Santiago, *Organizing Puerto Rican Migrant Farmworkers*, 66; letter to Jim Drake from Marilu Sánchez, 31 January 1971, 2, folder 5, box 23 (UFW New York Boycott Records, part 2), Reuther.

89. "New York Boycott Project Plan," 15–16 September 1979, folder 12, box 19 (UFW Administration Department Files Collection, part 2), Reuther.

90. Christian O. Paiz, *The Strikers of Coachella: A Rank-and-File History of the UFW Movement* (Chapel Hill: University of North Carolina Press, 2023), 254.

91. See Garcia, *From the Jaws of Victory*; Pawel, *Crusades of Cesar Chavez*; and Flores, *Grounds for Dreaming*, for more on the purges.

92. Paiz, *Strikers of Coachella*, 18–19.

93. "National Fast for Life," *Food and Justice*, October 1988, 6–7, http://libraries.ucsd .edu/farmworkermovement/ufwarchives/foodjustice/34_Oct88_001.pdf; "Fast for Life Still Multiplying," January 1989, 3–7, http://libraries.ucsd.edu/farmworkermovement /ufwarchives/foodjustice/36_Jan89_001.pdf; "Boycott Booming," *Food and Justice*, September 1989, 10–13, http://libraries.ucsd.edu/farmworkermovement/ufwarchives /foodjustice/37_Sep89_001.pdf; "Where to Find Us," *Food and Justice*, May 1988, 10–11, http://libraries.ucsd.edu/farmworkermovement/ufwarchives/foodjustice/31_May88 _001.pdf.

Chapter Three

1. Suzanne Hamlin, "Tex-Mex Fever Hits Manhattan," *New York Daily News*, 2 April 1981, 2–3.

2. "Taco Nation," *Bon Appétit*, www.bonappetit.com/story/taco-nation, 13 February 2020.

3. José R. Ralat, "The Demand for 'Authenticity' Is Threatening Kansas City's Homegrown Tacos," *Eater*, 23 April 2019, www.eater.com/2019/4/23/18294269/kansas-city -tacos-origin-parmesan. For more on South of the Border, see Cecilia Márquez, "Becoming Pedro: 'Playing Mexican' at South of the Border," *Latino Studies* 16, no. 4 (December 2018): 461–81.

4. Jeffrey Pilcher, *Planet Taco: A Global History of Mexican Food* (New York: Oxford, 2012), 145–46, 163, 166; Gregory McNamee, *Tortillas, Tiswin, and T-Bones: A Food History of the Southwest* (Albuquerque: University of New Mexico Press, 2017), 186; Jeffrey M. Pilcher, "Eating Mexican in a Global Age: The Politics and Production of Ethnic Food," in *Food Chains: From Farmyard to Shopping Cart*, ed. Warren Belasco and Roger Horowitz (Philadelphia: University of Pennsylvania Press, 2009), 168–69.

5. Hamlin, "Tex-Mex Fever," 2–3.

6. Melissa Fuster, *Caribeños at the Table: How Migration, Health, and Race Intersect in New York City* (Chapel Hill: University of North Carolina Press, 2021), 25, 29, 38; Donna R. Gabaccia, *We Are What We Eat: Ethnic Food and the Making of Americans* (Cambridge, MA: Harvard University Press, 1998), 166; Simone Cinotto, *The Italian American Table: Food, Family, and Community in New York City* (Champaign: University of Illinois Press,

2013); Pedro A. Regalado, "Storefront Archives: Looking Back with Justo Martí," *Platform* (blog), www
.platformspace.net/home/storefront-archives-looking-back-with-justo-marti, 13 April 2021.

7. Jeffrey M. Pilcher, "'Old Stock' Tamales and Migrant Tacos," *Social Research* 81, no. 2 (Summer 2014): 453; Gabriel Haslip-Viera, "The Evolution of the Latina/o Community in New York City: Early Seventeenth Century to the Present," in *Hispanic New York: A Sourcebook*, ed. Claudio Remeseira (New York: Columbia University Press, 2010), 22.

8. Mid-twentieth-century statistics become complicated because the category of "Mexican" introduced in the 1930 US Census was eliminated by 1940 because of protests by some Mexican Americans who argued for their legal categorization as "white." Mike Davis, *Magical Urbanism: Latinos Reinvent the US City* (New York: Verso, 2001), 21; Gabaccia, *We Are What We Eat*, 166; Inés M. Miyares, "Changing Latinization of New York City," in *Hispanic Spaces, Latino Places: Community and Cultural Diversity in Contemporary America*, ed. Daniel D. Arreola (Austin: University of Texas Press, 2004), 151–52; Fuster, *Caribeños*, 34–35.

9. Samuel Betances, "The Latin Diaspora," *New York Magazine*, 7 August 1972, 28.

10. *Bon Appétit*, 50th Anniversary Issue, November 2006, 58; Natalia Molina, "The Importance of Place and Place-Makers in the Life of a Los Angeles Community: What Gentrification Erases from Echo Park," *Southern California Quarterly* 97, no. 1 (February 2015): 69–111.

11. Laura H. Zarrugh, "From Workers to Owners: Latino Entrepreneurs in Harrisonburg, Virginia," *Human Organization* 66, no. 3 (Fall 2007): 240.

12. In 1946 nearly 245,000 US tourists went to Mexico, and by 1953, Mexico was the most common travel destination for US tourists. Márquez, "Becoming Pedro," 480.

13. Adriana Duran, "Recuerda las enseñanzas maternas," *Reforma*, 21 June 2002, 8G; Lisa Ruffin, "Nueva Mexicana: Uptown Tex-Mex," *Texas Home*, July 1983, 111; "We're Talking Turkey with a Mexican Accent," *New York Daily News*, 24 November 1993, folder 6, box 3, ZMP; Zarela Martínez memoir draft, 2009, 14, folder 15, box 6, ZMP; Gabilondo family recipe book, ca. 1970, folder 6, box 5, ZMP; Zarela family history document, 4, folder 4, box 5, ZMP.

14. Christian Lebanese migrants came to Mexico in significant numbers between 1880 and 1910 to escape religious persecution. They introduced shawarma—meat cooked on a vertical rotisserie—to Mexico in the 1920s, filling thick pita bread–like flour tortillas with the meat. These *tacos árabes* morphed into *tacos al pastor* when second-generation Lebanese Mexicans began marinating the meat in pineapple and serving it inside of corn tortillas in the 1950s and 1960s. Sarah Portnoy, *Food, Health, and Culture in Latino Los Angeles* (Lanham, MD: Rowan and Littlefield, 2016), 76; Pilcher, *Planet Taco*, 146.

15. Zarela Martínez, interview with *El Universal*, 26 September 2013, 3, folder 10, box 3, ZMP; Beatriz Terrazas, "Zarela Talks about Food, Flavor and Family," *Dallas Morning News*, 4 March 2005, folder 10, box 3, ZMP; Adriana Durán, "Lleva la esencia de México," n.d., folder 10, box 3, ZMP; Zarela Martínez biography page, folder 11, box 3, ZMP; Martínez memoir draft, 7, 33–34, 222; "Miss Martinez-Gabilondo, Mr. Sanchez Say Vows," *El Paso Times*, 2 March 1975, 5; Zarela Martínez, WalMart presentation, ca. 2003, folder 3, box 30, ZMP; C. Dickinson Waters, "Zarela Martinez: Bringing Mexico North of the Border," *Nation's Restaurant News*, 21 August 2000, 56; "Mujeres inolvidables de nuestra comunidad," *People en Espanol*, May 2002, folder 8, box 3, ZMP; Ruffin, "Nueva Mexicana," 111.

16. Interview with Zarela Martínez by the author, New York City, 9 January 2020.

17. "Zarela Martinez," *Manhattan, Inc.*, November 1989, 24, folder 11, box 3, ZMP.

18. *Gourmet* magazine, October 1988, 108, folder 11, box 3, ZMP; Nicole Carroll, "World-Renowned Chef to Be Featured at Annual Christmas Extravaganza," *El Paso Times*, 3 November 1992, C1; Ruffin, "Nueva Mexicana," 111; Natalie Haughton, "Make-Your-Own Taco Party: Just One Mexican Cookbook Idea," *New York Daily News*, 19 May 1993, 20; Craig Claiborne, "Memorable Dishes from a Master Mexican Chef," *New York Times*, 21 July 1982, C1; Mary Margaret Davis, "French Chefs Say 'Ole!,'" *El Paso Times*, 2 April 1981, 3C.

19. "Zarela Martinez," *Manhattan, Inc.*, November 1989, 24, folder 11, box 3, ZMP; Claiborne party program, 4 September 1982, folder 2, box 7, ZMP.

20. Pilcher, *Planet Taco*, 145; Gustavo Arellano, *Taco USA: How Mexican Food Conquered America* (New York: Scribner, 2013), 183–84.

21. Meredith Goad, "Tastefully Taking on Tacos," *Portland Press Herald*, 11 July 2021, F6; Tom Long, "A Bit of Mexico in Granite State," *Boston Globe*, 23 December 2007, http://archive.boston.com/ae/food/restaurants/articles/2007/12/23/a_bit_of_mexico_in_granite_state/; Marie Bianco, "Mexico Moves In," *Newsday*, n.d., folder 1, box 8, ZMP.

22. Bianco, "Mexico Moves In"; Bryan Miller, "A Bit of Mexico on the East Side," *New York Times*, 7 March 1986, C22; Barbara Costikyan, "Mexican Revolution," *New York Magazine*, 1 August 1983, 22.

23. Zarela Martínez, WalMart presentation, c. 2003, folder 3, box 30, ZMP; "The Hot New Caterers—and the Old Reliables," *New York/Cue*, 21 March 1983, 50, folder 2, box 7, ZMP; Ruffin, "Nueva Mexicana," 111; Mary Margaret Davis, "Showhouse Features Special Cuisine: Manhattan Caterer to Treat Hometown," *El Paso Times*, 16 February 1984, folder 5, box 3, ZMP; Larae Malooly, "El Paso Native Launches Wal-Mart Home Accessory Line," *El Paso Inc.*, B1, folder 5, box 8, ZMP; Aarón Sánchez and Stef Ferrari, *Where I Come From: Life Lessons from a Latino Chef* (New York: Abrams, 2019).

24. Davis, "Showhouse Features Special Cuisine"; Craig Claiborne, "All-American Menus for the Economic Summit," *New York Times*, 18 June 1983, C1, C7; Ellen Brown, "She Sifts the Tex from the Mex," *USA Today*, 10 August 1983, folder 3, box 7, ZMP; Suzanne Hamlin, "From a Creative New Chef: A Mexican Buffet," *Cuisine*, September 1983, 54, 56, folder 3, box 7, ZMP.

25. "The Great Southwest Comes Sizzling into Town," *Avenue*, April 1985, 132, folder 3, box 7, ZMP; contract for Zarela Martínez, 2–4, folder 10, box 6, ZMP; Jay Jacobs, "Specialités de la Maison: New York," *Gourmet*, September 1985, 32.

26. Costikyan, "Mexican Revolution," 22; Bob Daily, "Chili Daze in Manhattan," *Ultra*, April 1986, 61, 96, folder 3, box 7, ZMP.

27. Molly O'Neill, "Mexican Jumping Scenes," *Harper's Bazaar*, March 1987, 222, 238; Patricia Sharpe, "We Remember Ninfa Laurenzo," *Texas Monthly*, August 2001, www.texasmonthly.com/articles/we-remember-ninfa-laurenzo/; Meredith May, "Ninfa Laurenzo," *Texas Handbook Online*, https://tshaonline.org/handbook/online/articles/dgn01.

28. For more, see Molina, "The Importance of Place and Place-Makers," and Natalia Molina, *A Place at the Nayarit: How a Mexican Restaurant Nourished a Community* (Oakland: University of California Press, 2022).

29. Krishnendu Ray, *The Ethnic Restaurateur* (New York: Bloomsbury, 2016), 140; James Villas, "America's Great New Women Chefs: Artists In the Kitchen," *Town and Country*, October 1985, 212, 214; Carroll, "World-Renowned Chef," C1.

30. Arthur Schwartz, "Mex Master," *New York Daily News*, n.d., folder 3, box 7, ZMP;

Gael Greene, "Home on Two Ranges," *New York Magazine*, 30 November 1987, 90; Martínez bio page, folder 11, box 3, ZMP.

31. Madeline Y. Hsu, "On the Possibilities of Food Writing as a Bridge between the Popular and the Political," *Journal of American History* 103, no. 3 (December 2016): 683.

32. Zarela Martínez, Mexico travel diary, *New York*, 1985–87, 1–4, folder 8, box 8, ZMP; "Great Recipes from Regional and International Cookbooks," *CO Camera* (Boulder), 9 December 1992, folder 5, box 3, ZMP; Zarela Martínez, "The Seafood of Veracruz," *Los Angeles Times*, 21 October 1998, H4; Constance Quan, "The Making of the Menu," *New York Daily News*, 7 June 1989, folder 11, box 3, ZMP; Barbara Hansen, "New York's Favorite Mexican Cook," *Los Angeles Times*, n.d., H17, folder 2, box 4, ZMP; Carrie Helms Tippen, Heidi S. Hakimi-Hood, and Amanda Milian, "Cookery and Copyright: A History of One Cookbook in Three Acts," *Gastronomica* 19, no. 4 (Winter 2019): 6.

33. Anne Goldman, "'I Yam What I Yam': Cooking, Culture, and Colonialism," in *De/Colonizing the Subject*, ed. Sidonie Smith and Julia Watson (Minneapolis: University of Minnesota Press, 1992), 171, 192; Charlotte Druckman, *Skirt Steak: Women Chefs on Standing the Heat and Staying in the Kitchen* (San Francisco: Chronicle Books, 2012), 156; Meredith E. Abarca, *Voices in the Kitchen: Views of Food and the World from Working-Class Mexican and Mexican American Women* (College Station: Texas A&M University Press, 2006), 119.

34. Martínez interview with the author; Zarela Martínez, *Food from My Heart: Cuisines of Mexico Remembered and Reimagined* (New York: Macmillan, 1992); Zarela Martínez, *The Food and Life of Oaxaca: Traditional Recipes from Mexico's Heart* (Hoboken: Wiley, 1997); Zarela Martínez, *Zarela's Veracruz: Cooking and Culture in Mexico's Tropical Melting Pot* (Boston: Houghton Mifflin, 2001).

35. Bryan Miller, "A Bit of Mexico on the East Side," *New York Times*, 7 March 1986, C22; Nancy Harmon Jenkins, "It's Called Mexican, but Is It Genuine?," *New York Times*, 23 April 1986, C1.

36. Email to author from Zarela Martínez, 4 October 2020.

37. O'Neill, "Mexican Jumping Scenes," 222, 238; Gael Greene, "The Whole Enchilada," *New York Magazine*, 23 January 1995, 38; Zarela restaurant menus, folder 2, box 41, ZMP; Bryan Miller, "Hot Mexican and Homey American," *New York Times*, 1 January 1988, 28; Bryan Miller, "Where to Contemplate the Passing of the Year," *New York Times*, 30 December 1990, 35; interview with Edward Bonuso by the author, Queens, NY, 6 May 2021.

38. Druckman, *Skirt Steak*, 240; Ruth Reichl, *Garlic and Sapphires: The Secret Life of a Critic in Disguise* (London: Penguin, 2005), 65.

39. 1988 Zagat New York City restaurant survey, 9, 14.

40. Bonuso interview; Amy Besa and Romy Dorotan comments to the author, Writing History Seminar, Columbia University, 12 April 2019; Martínez interview with the author; Sánchez and Ferrari, *Where I Come From*, 31.

41. Bryan Miller, "Restaurants," *New York Times*, 23 August 1991, C20; "Best Mexican Restaurant: Zarela," *Midtown East Resident*, 30 September 1991, and Barbara Costikyan, "Great New Places to Have a Party," unknown publication, 13 November 1989. Both from folder 11, box 3, ZMP.

42. Samuel Betances, "The Latin Diaspora," *New York Magazine*, 7 August 1972, 28; David A. Badillo, "An Urban Historical Portrait of Mexican Migration to New York City," *New York History* 90, nos. 1–2 (Winter/Spring 2009): 114, 117–18; Seth Kugel, "How Brooklyn Became New York's Tortilla Basket," *New York Times*, 25 February 2001,

www.nytimes.com/2001/02/25/nyregion/new-yorkers-co-how-brooklyn-became-new
-york-s-tortilla-basket.html; Nico Madrigal-Yankowski, "Tortilla Triangle," ArcGIS Stor-
yMaps, 16 December 2019, https://storymaps.arcgis.com/stories/e1375d6134b344
aba3527338b406c22a; Eric Asimov, "$25 and Under," *New York Times*, 29 May 1992, C20.

43. Robert Smith, *Mexican New York: Transnational Lives of New Immigrants* (Berkeley: University of California Press, 2005), 22; Francisco L. Rivera-Batiz, "The State of
Newyorktitlan: A Socioeconomic Profile of Mexican New Yorkers," Russell Sage Foundation, 15 September 2003, 16; Greene, "Whole Enchilada," 38. Again, these census figures
are assuredly undercounts that excluded undocumented immigrants.

44. Milagros Ricourt and Ruby Danta, *Hispanas de Queens: Latino Panethnicity in a
New York City Neighborhood* (Ithaca, NY: Cornell University Press, 2003), 4.

45. Javier Castaño, "La naciente comunidad mexicana en Astoria," *El Diario La Prensa*,
5 May 1994, 6; Ruth Gomberg-Muñoz, *Labor and Legality: An Ethnography of a Mexican
Immigrant Network* (New York: Oxford University Press, 2010), 58.

46. Claudia Torrens, "Familia mexicana seduce con su mole la Costa Este," Associated
Press, 4 August 2018, https://apnews.com/article/e0a91096e65e4573b882e251b56ea077;
Pilcher, "'Old Stock' Tamales," 454–55.

47. Madrigal-Yankowski, "Tortilla Triangle"; Joel Millman, "El Triángulo de las Tortillas," *El Norte* (Monterrey, Mexico), 18 July 1997, 16.

48. Marta V. Martínez, *Latino History in Rhode Island: Nuestras Raíces* (Charleston,
SC: History Press, 2014), 44, 47, 52, 103.

49. Andrew Sandoval-Strausz, *Barrio America: How Latino Immigrants Saved the
American City* (New York: Basic Books, 2019).

50. Krishnendu Ray, "Street Vending, Street Food: Mobility and Diversity Out in the
Open," *Gastronomica* 20, no. 1 (2020): 10.

51. Greene, "Whole Enchilada," 44.

52. Eric Asimov, "$25 and Under," *New York Times*, 17 March 1995, C22; Nina Siegal,
"Four Corners," *New York Times*, 30 July 2000, CY11; Anthony Ramirez, "Where
East Meets Tex-Mex: The Asian Owners of Fresco Tortilla Are Not Flattered by Their
Imitators," *New York Times*, 2 February 1997, CY4; Sylvia Carter, "Me Gusta Mexicana,"
New York Newsday, 3 February 1993, 59; Molly O'Neill, "Kiss Those Burritos Adios! Real
Mexican Food Is Here," *New York Times*, 25 August 1993, C6.

53. Gabaccia, *We Are What We Eat*, 219; *Seinfeld*, season 4, episode 3, 1992; Carter, "Me
Gusta Mexicana," 59; Greene, "Whole Enchilada."

54. Calvin Sims, "Tortillas Gain More and More Aficionados in U.S.," *New York
Times*, 23 September 1992, D1; Cara de Silva, "The Hottest Wrap in Town," *New York
Newsday*, 28 July 1993, 57; Portnoy, *Food, Health, and Culture*, 25; Glenn Collins, "The
Americanization of Salsa," *New York Times*, 9 January 1997, D1, D17.

55. "Restaurants—Go, Consider, Stop," *Forbes*, 8 November 1993, 24; Kari Milchman,
"Classic Cocina," *A&E*, folder 10, box 3, ZMP.

56. Letter to Zarela Martínez from P. Wheeler Gemmer, 4 April 1994, folder 5, box 14,
ZMP.

57. Pilcher, *Planet Taco*, 201; Eric Asimov, "Now in New York: True Mexican," *New
York Times*, Dining Out section, 26 January 2000, 6.

58. Krishnendu Ray, "Ethnic Succession and the New American Restaurant Cuisine,"
in *The Restaurants Book: Ethnographies of Where We Eat*, ed. David Beriss and David
Sutton (Oxford: Berg, 2007), 104–5.

59. Suzanne Hamlin, "Adding Spice to the Big Apple," *HER New York*, October 29–

November 8, 1993, 48; "Day of the Dead Festival Features Oaxacan Foods," *Sun Bulletin*, 20 October 1995, folder 6, box 3, ZMP.

60. Caroline Dipping, "All-Time Favorites: Culinary Stars Share Most Beloved Dishes," *San Diego Union-Tribune*, 29 December 1999, 1.

61. Memo to Natalia Lorenzo of Goya from Zarela Martínez, 29 October 1993, folder 2, box 32, ZMP.

62. "From Mexico with Love," *Christian Science Monitor*, 24 September 1986, 28.

63. Martínez interview with the author.

64. Jesse Hoffnung-Garskof, *A Tale of Two Cities: Santo Domingo and New York after 1950* (Princeton, NJ: Princeton University Press, 2010), 226; Christian Krohn-Hansen, *Making New York Dominican: Small Business, Politics, and Everyday Life* (Philadelphia: University of Pennsylvania Press, 2013).

65. For more on Central Americans and Long Island pre-1995, see Sarah J. Mahler, *American Dreaming: Immigrant Life on the Margins* (Princeton, NJ: Princeton University Press, 1995).

66. Diana R. Gordon, *Village of Immigrants: Latinos in an Emerging America* (New Brunswick, NJ: Rutgers University Press, 2015), viii, 5–6; *Farmingville*, directed by Carlos Sandoval and Catherine Tambini (Long Island, NY: Camino Bluff Productions, 2004), 79 min.; John S. and Nancy Duncan, "Can't Live with Them, Can't Landscape without Them: Racism and the Pastoral Aesthetic in Suburban New York," *Landscape Journal* 22 (2003): 91, 94; Edward S. Casey and Mary Watkins, *Up against the Wall: Re-imagining the U.S.-Mexico Border* (Austin: University of Texas Press), 160.

67. Enrique Soria, "No hay arreglo en México Mágico," *El Diario La Prensa*, 16 May 1994, 6; Ana M. Ledo, "Continuan abusos contra empleados indocumentados: Cinco meses de trabajo sin salario alguno," *El Diario La Prensa*, 20 May 2001, 3.

68. Francisco L. Rivera-Batiz, "Newyorktitlan: A Socioeconomic Profile of Mexican New Yorkers," *Regional Labor Review* 6 (Spring/Summer 2004): 33–34.

69. Rivera-Batiz, "Newyorktitlan," 35–36; Smith, *Mexican New York*, 25.

70. Elaine Louie, "Tamales Are Hot, as in Popular," *New York Times*, Dining section, 22 May 2002, F1; Smith, *Mexican New York*, 20.

71. Manuel E. Avendaño, "Empuje inmigrante," *El Diario La Prensa*, 6 August 2010; Seth Kugel, "Destination: Neza York," *New York Times*, 15 February 2004, CY4; Miyares, "Changing Latinization," 56, 154; Ricourt and Danta, *Hispanas de Queens*, 4.

72. Andy Newman, "First the Mexicans, Then the Food," *New York Times*, 21 June 2001, B1.

73. Florence Fabricant, "Farewell, Danzón," *New York Times*, 1 May 2002, F10; Sánchez and Ferrari, *Where I Come From*.

74. Ruiz, "Citizen Restaurant," 10; Leticia Leizens, "Star Power," *HFN Magazine*, 20 August 2005, folder 10, box 3, ZMP; *Latina Magazine*, March 2006, 138; Zarela Casa—Hispanic Cookware Line, July 2005, folders 13 and 14, box 42, ZMP; Malooly, "El Paso Native Launches Wal-Mart Home Accessory Line," B4; Zarela Martínez, Wal-Mart presentation, c. 2003, folder 3, box 30, ZMP; "Executive Summary, Zarela Casa for Wal-Mart," folder 15, box 41, ZMP; "Inspirados por Zarela," *Siempre Mujer*, 3 February 2005, folder 2, box 8, ZMP; *Latina Magazine*, November 2004, 144; Ann Zimmerman, "Wal-Mart's Hispanic Outreach," *Wall Street Journal*, 31 May 2005, www.wsj.com/articles /SB111749282480946506.

75. "Zarela: Life with Parkinson's," television show proposal, 4, 8, folder 5, box 42, ZMP.

76. Rachel Wharton, "Mexican Revolution: A Favorite City Cuisine Just Keeps Getting

More Authentic," *New York Daily News*, 15 September 2006, 71–72; Dan Saltzstefn, "The Makings for Authentic Tortillas," *New York Times*, 22 July 2009, D3.

77. Seth Kugel, "The Bronx Discovers Its Own Inner Mexico," *New York Times*, 2 April 2004, E30; Ricourt and Danta, *Hispanas de Queens*, 46; Badillo, "Urban Historical Portrait," 107; Zaida Cortés, "La 'Pequeña Oaxaca' crece en el norte de NY," *Diario de México*, 5 December 2016.

78. Carolina González, "Women Chefs Like Sue Torres and Zarela Martinez Shake Up Mexican Dining," *New York Daily News*, 5 May 2010, folder 5, box 41, ZMP; Amy Zimmer, "Mexican Restaurant Closes on East Side after 23 Years," *DNAInfo*, 15 February 2011, www.dnainfo.com/new-york/20110214/manhattan/mexican-restaurant-closes-on-east-side-after-more-than-two-decades/; Florence Fabricant, "Zarela Is Closing," *New York Times*, 1 February 2011, https://dinersjournal.blogs.nytimes.com/2011/02/01/zarela-is-closing/.

79. Ray, *Ethnic Restaurateur*, 95; Marian Burros, "Diner's Journal," *New York Times*, 9 January 2004, E30; "Making a Stand-Up Meal of the Sit-Down Taco," *New York Times*, 2 October 2013, D1; Javier Cabral, "Why Did It Take a White Chef to Pique My Interest in My Own Mexican Culture?," *Bon Appetit*, 13 February 2020, www.bonappetit.com/story/mexican-food-greatest-cuisine.

80. Dylan Gottlieb, "'Dirty, Authentic . . . Delicious': Yelp, Mexican Restaurants, and the Appetites of Philadelphia's New Middle Class," *Gastronomica* 15, no. 2 (Summer 2015): 39–41; Sara Kay, "Yelp Reviewers' Authenticity Fetish Is White Supremacy in Action," *Eater NY*, 18 January 2019, https://ny.eater.com/2019/1/18/18183973/authenticity-yelp-reviews-white-supremacy-trap.

81. Lisa Heldke, "But Is It Authentic? Culinary Travel and the Search for the 'Genuine Article,'" in *The Taste Culture Reader: Flavor, Food, and Meaning*, ed. Carolyn Korsmeyer (Oxford: Berg, 2005), 388; Monica Perales, "The Food Historian's Dilemma: Reconsidering the Role of Authenticity in Food Scholarship," *Journal of American History* 103, no. 3 (December 2016): 691.

82. Perales, "Food Historian's Dilemma," 690–93.

83. Mark Padoongpatt, *Flavors of Empire: Food and the Making of Thai America* (Oakland: University of California Press, 2017), 187.

84. "Making a Stand-Up Meal," D5; Alyshia Gálvez, *Eating NAFTA: Trade, Food Policies, and the Destruction of Mexico* (Oakland: University of California Press, 2018), 32–33; Frank Bruni, "Skipping Dessert for Mexican Food," *New York Times*, 22 February 2012, D1.

85. Alison Hope Alkon and Rafi Grosglik, "Eating (with) the Other: Race in American Food Television," *Gastronomica* 21, no. 2 (Summer 2021): 4. Latinx food entrepreneurs are of course not exempt from being labor rights violators. Seven former employees of Cosme, including a sommelier and four Latino workers, organized to sue chef Enrique Olvera for violating federal and state labor laws regarding minimum wage and overtime pay. Víctor Fuentes, "Demandan ex empleados a chef," *El Norte*, 14 August 2019, 3.

Chapter Four

1. Susan Young, "Maine 97% White, Least Diverse in Nation," *Bangor Daily News*, 16 June 2001, 11; Michael Casey, Associated Press, "Maine Becomes More Diverse but Still Whitest State in the Nation," https://apnews.com/article/maine-census-2020-8d72d29af8c5e528b4197634bbdda8c1.

2. David Carey Jr., "Situating Latino Voices in a New England Community," in *Latino Voices in New England*, ed. David Carey Jr. and Robert Atkinson (Albany: SUNY Press, 2009), 4–5; David Carey, Jr., "Comunidad Escondida: Latin American Influences in Nineteenth-Century Portland" in *Creating Portland: History and Place in Northern New England*, ed. Joseph Conforti (Durham: University of New Hampshire Press, 2005), 91, 94, 108; Maine Center for Economic Policy, "The Growing Latin American Influence: Opportunities for Maine's Economy," 2009, 4, www.mecep.org/wp-content/uploads /2014/09/Latinos-in-the-Maine-Economy-4-23-2009.pdf; "The Spanish Literary Club," *Portland Sunday Times*, 3 April 1881, 1.

3. Edward D. Murphy, "Migrants Indispensable to (Maine) State's Economy," *Portland Press Herald*, 22 September 2002, www.freerepublic.com/focus/f-news/755304/posts.

4. Steven G. Vegh, "The Changing Face of Maine," *Portland Press Herald*, 22 June 1999, 2; "The Growing Latin American Influence," 8.

5. Brinda Sarathy, *Pineros: Latino Labour and the Changing Face of Forestry in the Pacific Northwest* (Vancouver: University of British Columbia Press, 2012), 47; Monica W. Varsanyi, "Immigration Policy Activism in U.S. States and Cities: Interdisciplinary Perspectives," in *Taking Local Control: Immigration Policy Activism in U.S. Cities and States*, ed. Monica W. Varsanyi (Palo Alto, CA: Stanford University Press, 2010), 10; Carmen Teresa Whalen, "Latinos/as in the Northeast: A Historic Overview," in "The Future of Latinos in the United States: Law, Opportunity, and Mobility," white paper for the American Bar Foundation, 18, 20; Andres Torres, *Latinos in New England* (Philadelphia: Temple University Press, 2006), 4.

6. Bill Caldwell, "Turner Farmer Shelling Out a Million Every Day," *Maine Sunday Telegram*, 1 April 1973, 12A; "Success Story: How Jack DeCoster Inherited 100 Hens," *Maine Times*, 18 February 1977, 2–3, 9–15, 18–19; John H. Gormley Jr., "DeCoster Builds Dual Image," *Maine Sunday Telegram*, 8 November 1992, 1A, 10A.

7. "Success Story," 8–10; Peter A. Dammann, "Why Can't Anyone Keep Children from Being Mangled in Machines?," *Maine Times*, 26 January 1979, 12; "DeCoster and OSHA," *Maine Times*, 1 June 1979, 14; Joe Fassler, "Timeline of Shame: Decades of DeCoster Egg Factory Violations," *Atlantic*, 16 September 2010, www.theatlantic.com/health/archive /2010/09/timeline-of-shame-decades-of-decoster-egg-factory-violations/63059/.

8. Edward D. Murphy, "Lawyer for DeCoster Quits," *Kennebec Journal*, 1 November 1996, 3; Fassler, "Timeline of Shame"; Clarke Canfield, "New Cargo Route Opens Egg Exports to Far East Markets," *Portland Press Herald*, 18 October 1993, 1.

9. Phone interview with Donald Hoenig by the author, 6 September 2018; interview with Mike Guare by the author, Bangor, ME, 5 October 2018.

10. Associated Press, "State Sues Egg Farm over Migrants," *Portland Press Herald*, 21 May 1992, 6B; Steven G. Vegh, "Mexico Sues DeCoster for Discrimination," *Portland Press Herald*, 19 May 1998, 11A; Robert A. Rusczek, OSHA, "Abatement Verification Audit Report of DeCoster Egg Farms and Its Successors," 16 June 1998, 6, folder 3, box 5, MRWC; Edward D. Murphy, "Farm Workers Targeting DeCoster," *Kennebec Journal*, 30 September 1997, 12; Murphy, "Lawyer for DeCoster Quits," 3.

11. Steven G. Vegh, "Diocese Charges Egg Farm Blocked Workers' Worship," *Portland Press Herald*, 26 July 1994, 1A; Audrey Marra and Tom Whitney, commentary in *Labor Standard Magazine*, October 1999, folder 1, box 1, MRWC.

12. Aviva Chomsky and Claire Holman, "The Hidden Maine: Serfdom at DeCoster Egg Farm," *Maine Progressive* 6, no. 2 (December 1991): 4–5; "The Alien Underground:

DeCoster Fined for Using Illegal Workers," *Maine Times*, 10 March 1989, 3; Associated Press, "State Sues Egg Farm," 6B; Susann Pelletier, "Fowl Play: DeCoster Still Rules the Roost," *Dissident: Maine's Journal of Politics and Culture* 2, no. 8 (February 1997): 5, folder 1, box 5, MRWC.

13. Associated Press, "Workers Say They Were Treated Like Prisoners," *Portland Press Herald*, 30 September 1992, 4B; Associated Press, "State Sues Egg Farm," 6B; Pelletier, "Fowl Play," 5; Fassler, "Timeline of Shame"; James A. Moore, "State Bar Association Approves Plan for Legal Assistance to Needy," *Portland Press Herald*, 25 August 1966, 22; William H. Williamson, "Pine Tree Legal Assistance: Mouthpiece for the Poor," *Maine Sunday Telegram*, 20 October 1968, 20.

14. Liz Chapman, "Jose Soto, Migrants' Friend: DeCoster Nemesis Is Fighter Who Won't Quit," *Lewiston Sun Journal*, n.d., 1997, B2, folder 1, box 6, MRWC; "Rewarding for Fowl Play," *Dissident* 2, no. 8 (February 1997): 1, folder 1, box 5, MRWC.

15. Robert A. Rusczek, OSHA, "Abatement Verification Audit Report of DeCoster Egg Farms and Its Successors," 16 June 1998, 6, folder 3, box 5, MRWC; Murphy, "Farm Workers Targeting DeCoster" and "Lawyer for DeCoster Quits"; Sara Rimer, "In Maine, Egg Empire Is under Fire," *New York Times*, 29 August 1996, www.nytimes.com/1996/08/29/us/in-maine-egg-empire-is-under-fire.html; Fassler, "Timeline of Shame."

16. Pelletier, "Fowl Play"; Andrew Garber, "Fourth Grocery Chain Joins Egg-Farm Boycott," *Kennebec Journal*, 17 August 1996, 2; Kenneth Z. Chutchian, "Can Maine Businesses Exercise Social Responsibility?," *Maine Times*, 25 July 1996, 8.

17. Andrew K. Weegar, "DeCoster 'Dream Team' Walks, Spurring Much Disappointment," *Maine Times*, 14 November 1996, 9; "Rewarding for Fowl Play," 1; Laura Conaway, "DeCoster Egg Farms of Turner," *Casco Bay Weekly*, 23 January 1997, 5.

18. Pelletier, "Fowl Play," 8; Murphy, "Farm Workers Targeting DeCoster," 12; "Saying It with a Straight Face," *Maine Times*, 3 July 1997, 5.

19. Liz Chapman, "Egg Workers Prepare for Vote," *Lewiston Sun Journal*, 25 March 1998, A1; untitled article, *Lewiston Sun Journal*, 22 March 1998, B4, folder 1, box 6, MRWC.

20. Mirta Ojito, "Suburbs Grapple with Change as New Immigrants Arrive," *New York Times*, September 30, 1996; Nancy West, "INS Boosts Immigration Enforcement," *New Hampshire Sunday News*, 7 April 1996, cited in *Rural Migration News* 2, no. 4 (October 1996): https://migration.ucdavis.edu/rmn/more.php?id=146.

21. Robert A. Rusczek, OSHA, "Abatement Verification Audit Report of DeCoster Egg Farms and Its Successors," 16 June 1998, 6, folder 3, box 5, MRWC, 19, 21; notes from MRWC meeting with National Council of La Raza representatives, 29 June 1998, 1–2, folder 6, box 1, MRWC; MRWC meeting with DeCoster Workers, 4 July 1998, 1, folder 6, box 1, MRWC.

22. MRWC meeting minutes, 17 May 1999, 1, folder 4, box 3, MRWC; MRWC meeting with Congressman John Baldacci, 7 September 1999, 1, folder 6, box 1, MRWC.

23. Liz Chapman, "Union Files Protest with Feds," *Lewiston Sun Journal*, 2 April 1998, A1; Liz Chapman, "Egg Workers Prepare for Vote," *Lewiston Sun Journal*, n.d., A7, folder 1, box 6, MRWC.

24. Susan Rayfield and Alan Clendenning, "DeCoster Workers Fear for Future," *Portland Press Herald*, 17 November 1996, 1B; Robert A. Rusczek, OSHA, "Abatement Verification Audit Report of DeCoster Egg Farms and Its Successors," 16 June 1998, 6, folder 3, box 5, MRWC, 43.

25. Cordova eventually received a $60,000 settlement. Press release, "Jack DeCoster's OSHA Record: The Other Side of the Story," 25 June 1998, 2, folder 4, box 5, MRWC; Donna Gold, "Migrant Advocates Say They're Fighting Uphill Battle," *Maine Times*, 25 November 1999, 10; MRWC meeting minutes, 20 June 2002, 2, folder 6, box 3, MRWC; Associated Press, "Following Tour of Egg Farm, Legislators Call for Changes," *Portland Press Herald*, 25 March 1996, 4B.

26. "Migrant Workers Sue DeCoster over Wages," *Portland Press Herald*, 3 February 1994, 4B; Michael Gordon, "Overtime: DeCoster Settlement Upcoming," *Lewiston Sun Journal*, 20 November 1998, B2; Associated Press, "DeCoster Overtime Suit Settlement in Works," *Bangor Daily News*, 5–6 December 1998, folder 1, box 6, MRWC Papers; Michael Gordon, "1,275 DeCoster Workers File Overtime Pay Claims," *Bangor Daily News*, 27 May 1999, A5; "DeCoster at War over Violations," *Lewiston Sun Journal*, 21 May 2000, B1.

27. "Mexico Joins Suit against Egg Farm," *Bangor Daily News*, 19 May 1998, B3.

28. Steven G. Vegh, "Mexico Sues DeCoster for Discrimination," *Portland Press Herald*, 19 May 1998, A1, A11; "Mexico Joins Suit," B3; Fassler, "Timeline of Shame"; Gregory Kesich, "DeCoster Should Pay Settlement, Judge Rules," *Portland Press Herald*, 23 October 2001, 1B.

29. Letter to lawyer Karen F. Wolf from Mexican Vice-Consul (Boston) Germán Murguia-Mier, 5 April 2004, folder 5, box 4, MRWC; "Fact Sheet for Class Action Settlement for Hispanic Workers of DeCoster Egg Farm," 14 November 2002, folder 4, box 5, MRWC; "DeCoster at War over Violations," B1; Gordon, "1,275 DeCoster Workers."

30. MRWC Board of Directors meeting minutes, 9 November 1998, 1, folder 3, box 1, MRWC.

31. Murray Carpenter, "'Nobody Ever Pays Attention to Them,'" *Maine Times*, 30 September 1999, 3.

32. Meg Haskell, "Bodega Adds Spice to Lewiston Life," *Maine Times*, 26 July 2001, 6.

33. Elsa Nuñez, foreword to *Latino Voices in New England*, x; "The Growing Latin American Influence," 43.

34. Shoshana Hoose, "Spanish Is Spoken Here at Armando Vives' Shoeshine," *Portland Press Herald*, 5 October 1997, 1G; Associated Press, "Latinos Establish Community Council of Maine," *Bangor Daily News*, 19 February 1997, 1.

35. Tom Fritzsche, "Maine's Blueberry Rakers Work Very Hard for Not Much Pay," *Portland Press Herald / Maine Sunday Telegram*, 1 October 2006, http://business.maine today.com/news/061001fritzsche.html; Elizabeth Newman, "From the Field," 17 July 2017, www.elizabethnewman.org/from-the-field.html.

36. Daniel Reichman, "Entrepreneurship in a Pickle: Innovation and Arbitrage in the Sea Cucumber Trade," *Anthropological Quarterly* 86, no. 2 (Spring 2013): 568; Jack Aley, "Once Quiet Blueberry Making Noise in Washington," *Portland Press Herald*, 14 September 1974, 1, 12.

37. Pat Sherlock, "Blueberry Pickers' Quarters Called Intolerable," *Portland Press Herald*, 29 August 1974, 1, 10; Larry Lack, "The Trouble in Blueberry Country," *Maine Sunday Telegram*, 27 August 1978, 21A; A. Dammann, "The Wyman Domain," *Maine Times*, 6 October 1978, 16; "Blueberry Pickers Win Back Pay, Old Boxes," *Portland Press Herald*, 28 November 1978, 16; Jeff Clark, "In the Blueberry Fields: Conditions Have Improved but It's Still No Holiday," *Maine Times*, 2 August 1985, 22; "Blueberries: At Work in the Fields of the Lord," *Maine Times*, 3 September 1976, 12.

38. Carpenter, "'Nobody Ever Pays Attention to Them,'" 3; Wild Blueberry Commission of Maine, Pamphlet 2795, 2. Maine Historical Society; Tux Turkel, "Migrant Blues:

Hispanics Increase Flow of Farm Workers," *Maine Telegram*, 26 August 1990, 1B, 14B; Paul Sylvain and Jeanne Curran, "Migrants Chase an Elusive Dream," *Bangor Daily News*, 21 August 1993; Jeanne Curran, "Migrant Workers Sue Machias Firm," *Bangor Daily News*, 5 August 1993.

39. Associated Press, "Annual Harvest Lucrative: Big Bucks Found in Blueberry Fields," *Bangor Daily News*, 30 August 1997, 1; Letitia Baldwin, "Migrants of Maine: Hispanic Workers Playing Larger Role in Blueberry Harvest," *Bangor Daily News*, 12 August 1995, 1.

40. C. Fairfield Estill and S. Tanaka, "Ergonomic Considerations of Manually Harvesting Maine Wild Blueberries," *Journal of Agricultural Safety and Health* 4 (1998): 43–57; Dora Anne Mills, Maine CDC Blog, "Downeast Trip Day #2: Blueberries!," 14 August 2008, http://mainepublichealth.blogspot.com/2008/08/downeast-trip-day-2.html; interview with Blanca Santiago by the author, Portland, ME, 1 October 2018; Ruby Spicer and Paul Kuehnert, *Health Status and Needs Assessment of Latinos in Maine: Final Report*, Maine Department of Human Services, 1 November 2002, 11–12.

41. Carey and Atkinson, *Latino Voices in New England*, 72–73; Paul Sylvain, "INS Returns Illegal Aliens to Mexico," *Bangor Daily News*, 6 August 1993; Associated Press, "Officials Nab Illegal Workers: U.S. Border Patrol Busts 13 in Penobscot," *Bangor Daily News*, 5 August 1995, 1; Mary Anne Clancy, "Raker's Killer Still Being Sought," *Bangor Daily News*, 19 August 1998, 1; "Border Patrol Arrests 68 Migrant Workers," *Bangor Daily News*, 28 July 1999, 1, and Hoose, "Spanish Is Spoken Here," 5G.

42. Associated Press, "Annual Harvest Lucrative," 1; Karen and Michael Foley, "Migrant Workers," *Bangor Daily News*, 19 August 1995, 1.

43. Mary Anne Clancy, "Blueberry Rakers Walk Off Fields," *Bangor Daily News*, 14 August 1998, A1–A2, and "Blue on Blueberries: August Sun Beats Down Growers' Crop Estimates," *Bangor Daily News*, 31 August 1998, A8.

44. Jonathan Levitt, "Her Home Cooking Keeps Laborers in Pick Condition," *Boston Globe*, 30 August 2006, www.smfws.com/art08302006b.htm.

45. New American Economy, "This Family Came to Down East Maine as Migrant Workers, but Left Their Mark as Entrepreneurs," 10 July 2016, www.newamericaneconomy.org/feature/this-family-came-to-down-east-maine-as-migrant-workers-but-left-their-mark-as-entrepreneurs/; "Soup to Nuts: A Mexican Hot Spot in Blueberry Country," *Portland Press Herald*, 20 August 2014, C3, www.pressherald.com/2014/08/20/a-mexican-hot-spot-in-blueberry-country/.

46. Murphy, "Migrants Indispensable," 1F; Reichman, "Entrepreneurship in a Pickle," 570.

47. Jeanne Marie Laskas, "Hecho en América," *GQ*, September 2011, www.gq.com/news-politics/big-issues/201110/illegal-immigration-issue-blueberry-fruit-farmers-gq-october-2011; John May et al., "Evaluation of a Community-Based Effort to Reduce Blueberry Harvesting Injury," *American Journal of Industrial Medicine* 51 (2008): 307.

48. Matt Byrne, "Eighteen Migrant Workers Who Came to Maine," *Morning Sentinel* (Waterville, Maine), 8 July 2014, 1A; Guare interview; *Antoine v. Paul*, US District Court for the District of Maine, decided 15 January 2015; *Damisse v. Paul*, US District Court for District of Maine, decided 4 April 2016.

49. Interview with Maine Mobile Health Program Director Hannah Miller by the author, Milbridge, ME, 11 August 2021; interview with Ian Yaffe by the author, Winter Harbor, ME, 2 October 2018; Guare interview.

50. Interview with Jorge Acero by the author, Zoom, 10 August 2021.

51. John Hale, "Jamaicans Picking Apples at Cornish," *Portland Press Herald*, 13 September 1975, 1; "Why Won't the Unemployed Pick Apples?," *Maine Times*, 3 October

1975, 2, 4; Cindy Hahamovitch, *No Man's Land: Jamaican Guestworkers in America and the Global History of Deportable Labor* (Princeton, NJ: Princeton University Press, 2011), 206–7, 215; Julian E. Barnes, "Locals Welcome Farm Jobs Usually Held by Migrants," *Portland Press Herald*, 24 July 1991, 1A, 8A.

52. Baldwin, "Migrants of Maine," 1; Turkel, "Migrant Blues," 14B; Tux Turkel, "State Plans First Survey of Immigrants," *Portland Press Herald*, 2 June 1999, 1A; Abby Zimet, "Workers Fight Farmer," *Maine Sunday Telegram*, 19 October 1986, 1, 8.

53. David Griffith, *American Guestworkers: Jamaicans and Mexicans in the U.S. Labor Market* (Philadelphia: University of Pennsylvania Press, 2006), xi; Lori A. Flores, "Wreathed in Worry, Pining for Protection: Latino Forestry Workers and Historical Traumas in Maine," *Journal of American History* 109, no. 4 (March 2023): 833. For more on Mexican labor migration to Canada, see Tanya Basok, *Tortillas and Tomatoes: Transmigrant Mexican Harvesters in Canada* (Montreal: McGill-Queen's University Press, 2002).

54. Acero interview. For more on Latinx pineros in Maine, see Flores, "Wreathed in Worry."

55. "The Growing Latin American Influence," 21.

56. Juana Rodríguez Vásquez interview with the author, Zoom, 29 October 2020.

57. Ann S. Kim, "Growing Roots in Maine," *Portland Press Herald*, 27 January 2006, C1.

58. Reichman, "Entrepreneurship in a Pickle," 566–67; Letitia Baldwin, "Sea Cucumber Plant to Open," *Bangor Daily News*, 27 November 1995, 1; Associated Press, "Sea Cucumber Regulations May be Subjected to Legal Test," *Bangor Daily News*, 21 October 1999, 1.

Chapter Five

1. John R. Gillis, *The Human Shore: Seacoasts in History* (Chicago: University of Chicago Press, 2012), 2.

2. For more on the olfactory history of seafood work, see, for example, Connie Y. Chiang, "Monterey-by-the-Smell," *Pacific Historical Review* 73, no. 2 (May 2004): 183–214.

3. Daniel Reichman, "Entrepreneurship in a Pickle: Innovation and Arbitrage in the Sea Cucumber Trade," *Anthropological Quarterly* 86, no. 2 (Spring 2013): 561, 564; "Sea Cucumbers," Department of Fish and Game, California, 5–2, https://nrm.dfg.ca.gov/FileHandler.ashx?DocumentID=34418&inline; Edward D. Melillo, "Making Sea Cucumbers Out of Whales' Teeth: Nantucket Castaways and Encounters of Value in Nineteenth-Century Fiji," *Environmental History* 20 (2015), 453, 455.

4. Reichman, "Entrepreneurship in a Pickle," 562.

5. Melillo, "Making Sea Cucumbers," 455–57; Nancy Shoemaker, *Pursuing Respect in the Cannibal Isles: Americans in Nineteenth-Century Fiji* (Ithaca, NY: Cornell University Press, 2019), 2, 30.

6. Reichman, "Entrepreneurship in a Pickle," 562–63.

7. Reichman, "Entrepreneurship in a Pickle," 563–65.

8. Jeff Clark, "Invisible Mainers," *Down East Magazine*, August 2008, www.downeast.com/Down-East-Magazine/August-2008/Invisible-Mainers; David A. Fahrenthold, "Filling a Faraway Niche Even in Maine, Latinos' Future Affects Economy," 8 April 2006, www.washingtonpost.com/archive/politics/2006/04/08/filling-a-faraway-niche-span-classbankheadeven-in-maine-latinos-future-affects-economyspan/7baa7ce4-093b-4cd5-a9bf-994f3c5e6946/?utm_term=.cded3461365c; Sanford Phippen, "The People of Winter," in *The Best Maine Stories*, ed. Sanford Phippen (Augusta, ME: Lance Tapley, 1986),

311–12; George H. Lewis, "Shell Games in Vacationland: Homarus Americanus and the State of Maine," in *Usable Pasts: Traditions and Group Expressions in North America*, ed. Tad Tuleja (Logan: Utah State University Press, 1997), 253–54.

9. Reichman, "Entrepreneurship in a Pickle," 568–69; Abby Goodnough, "Maine Town Is Riven by Housing Dispute," *Milbridge Journal*, 14 November 2009, www.theruralcentre .com/doc/Guernsey%20-%20Blueberry%20Report%20ENGLISH.pdf; "The Growing Latin American Influence," 31; Llana Barber, *Latino City: Immigration and Urban Crisis in Lawrence, Massachusetts, 1945–2000* (Chapel Hill: University of North Carolina Press, 2017), 2–3.

10. Lee Burnett, "He Can See Clearly Now: An Undocumented Worker Learns the Hard Way about U.S. Jobs," *Maine Times*, 30 November–6 December 2000, 4, 9.

11. Reichman, "Entrepreneurship in a Pickle," 569–72; Kevin Wack, "Traveling Bodega Brings Migrants Slice of Home," *Los Angeles Times*, 27 July 2003, http://articles.latimes .com/2003/jul/27/news/adna-bodega27; Katherine Cassidy, "Hub for Hispanics Thrives: Down East Harrington's Mexican Store Offers Home Away from Home to Migrants," *Bangor Daily News*, 30 August 2004, 4.

12. "Traveling Bodega"; Judy Harrison, "Mexican Store Proprietor Charged with Visa Misuse," *Bangor Daily News*, 29 June 2007, 1; Judy Harrison, "Escalante Makes First Court Appearance," *Bangor Daily News*, 30 June 2007, 10; Nok-Noi Ricker, "Woman Gets 14 Months for Hiring Illegal Aliens," *Bangor Daily News*, 26 March 2008, 1; "Man Pleads Guilty to Illegal-Alien Charges," *Bangor Daily News*, 4 November 2009, 3; Judy Harrison, "Man Gets Nearly Three Years in Illegal Aliens Case," *Bangor Daily News*, 4 March 2010, 1; Judy Harrison, "Man Gets 1 Year, 1 Day in Identity Theft Case," *Bangor Daily News*, 29 May 2008, 6.

13. Mary Anne Clancy, "INS Arrests 5 Illegal Aliens in Milbridge," *Bangor Daily News*, 22 April 1998, 1; Diana Graettinger, "Border Agents Arrest Illegal Aliens in Beals," *Bangor Daily News*, 2 March 2000, 1.

14. Reichman, "Entrepreneurship in a Pickle," 565, 569.

15. Bill Nemitz, "Search for Illegal Aliens Alienates City," *Portland Press Herald*, 30 January 2004, 1; Blethen Maine News Service, "Restaurant Workers Face Deportation after Arrest," *Portland Press Herald*, 5 May 2004, 8B; David Carey, Jr., and Robert Atkinson, eds., *Latino Voices in New England* (Albany: SUNY Press, 2009), 2; Carey, Jr., "Comunidad Escondida," 113–114; Ann S. Kim, "Mexican Citizen Charged after Raids at Restaurants," *Portland Press Herald*, 19 November 2011, A1 and back page; Kevin Thomas, "Latino Players Taste Maine Life," *Portland Press Herald*, 27 June 2004, D1.

16. Leslie Bridgers and Ann S. Kim, "Mexican Eateries Temporarily Shut Following Arrests," *Portland Press Herald*, 23 September 2011, B1, B3; Amy Calder, "Volunteers Help to Keep Mexican Restaurant Running," *Maine Sunday Telegram*, 2 October 2011, B4.

17. Clark, "Invisible Mainers"; New American Economy, "The Contributions of New Americans in Maine," August 2016, 1, 6, 28, https://research.newamericaneconomy.org /wp-content/uploads/2017/02/nae-me-report.pdf.

18. Carey and Atkinson, *Latino Voices*, 2; US Census Bureau, "Quick Facts on Maine," www.census.gov/quickfacts/me; Maine Center for Economic Policy, "The Growing Latin American Influence: Opportunities for Maine's Economy," 2009, 4, www.mecep.org /wp-content/uploads/2014/09/Latinos-in-the-Maine-Economy-4-23-2009.pdf; 23, 27, 31–32, 46.

19. John Richardson, "Immigrant Labor Fuels Waterfront Economy," *Portland Press Herald*, 9 February 2001, 1A; Hansi Lo Wang, "Maine's Immigrants Boost Workforce of Whitest, Oldest State in US," WYNC broadcast, 20 April 2017, www.wnyc.org/story

/maines-immigrants-boost-workforce-of-whitest-oldest-state-in-us/; Craig Idlebrook, "Latinos Putting Down Roots Downeast," *Working Waterfront*, 1 September 2008, www.workingwaterfront.com/articles/Latinos-putting-down-roots-Downeast/12610/.

20. Lewis Loflin, "Illegal Aliens Get Government Housing in Maine, Whites Need Not Apply," *Bristolblog.com*, n.d., www.sullivan-county.com/racism/maine_housing.htm; Abby Goodnough, "Maine Town Is Riven by Housing Dispute," *Milbride Journal*, 14 November 2009, www.theruralcentre.com/doc/Guernsey%20-%20Blueberry %20Report%20ENGLISH.pdf; Ann S. Kim and Josie Huang, "Maine's Black Population Doubles: Resettled Somali Refugees and Hispanic Workers Are Changing Maine's Makeup," *Portland Press Herald*, 5 August 2006, A1; Sharon Kiley Mack, "Milbridge Housing Plan Needs One More Permit," *Bangor Daily News*, 26 July 2010, www .bangordailynews.com/2010/07/26/news/milbridge-housing-plan-needs-1-more-permit/; Idlebrook, "Housing Blocked"; interview with Ian Yaffe by the author, Winter Harbor, ME, 2 October 2018.

21. Benjamin Fleury-Steiner and Jamie Longazel, "Neoliberalism, Community Development, and Anti-immigrant Backlash in Hazleton, Pennsylvania," in *Taking Local Control: Immigration Policy Activism in U.S. Cities and States*, ed. Monica W. Varsanyi (Palo Alto, CA: Stanford University Press, 2010), 159, 163.

22. Jill Esbenshade et al., "The 'Law-and-Order' Foundation of Local Ordinances: A Four-Locale Study of Hazleton, PA, Escondido, CA, Farmers Branch, TX, and Prince William County, VA," in Varsanyi, *Taking Local Control*, 265; Jamie Longazel, *Undocumented Fears: Immigration and the Politics of Divide and Conquer in Hazleton, Pennsylvania* (Philadelphia: Temple, 2016), 2; Leo Chavez, *The Latino Threat: Constructing Immigrants, Citizens, and the Nation* (Palo Alto, CA: Stanford University Press, 2013), 43.

23. Longazel, *Undocumented Fears*, 258–59.

24. Lewis, "Shell Games," 250–52; David Foster Wallace, "Consider the Lobster," *Gourmet*, August 2004, 55; Daniel Luzer, "How Lobster Got Fancy," *Pacific Standard Magazine*, 7 June 2013, https://psmag.com/economics/how-lobster-got-fancy-59440; Colin Woodard, *The Lobster Coast: Rebels, Rusticators, and the Struggle for a Forgotten Frontier* (New York: Penguin, 2005), 170, 241.

25. For more on Puerto Rican seaside labor see David Griffith and Manuel Valdés Pizzini, *Fishers at Work, Workers at Sea: A Puerto Rican Journey through Labor and Refuge* (Philadelphia: Temple University Press, 2002), 3, 32, 56.

26. Letter to Commissioner of Immigration and Naturalization, Washington, DC, from S. H. Howes, District Director of Immigration and Naturalization, Boston, 26 March 1935; report by Boston immigrant inspector B. L. Boyle, 19 March 1935, 1–2. Both from RG 85: Records of the Immigration and Naturalization Service, Subject and Policy Files, 1893–1957, file unit 55607/457, box 7590, National Archives and Research Administration, Washington, DC.

27. Interview with Debra Kelsey by Madeleine Hall-Arber, New Bedford Fishing Heritage Center, 5 January 2017, WTW, www.loc.gov/resource/afc2016036.afc2016036 _03866_ph01/?r=-0.335,-0.006,1.75,0.889,0.

28. Griffith and Pizzini, *Fishers at Work*, 85; Barber, *Latino City*, 68–69; oral history interview with Anonymous by Corinn Williams, 20 February 2010, NOAA, https://voices .nmfs.noaa.gov/sites/default/files/2018-08/anonymous%2C%2013.pdf.

29. See, for example, oral history interview with Anonymous by Corinn Williams, n.d., NOAA, http://s837454701.onlinehome.us/changing/NI-rights.htm; oral history interview with Anonymous #11 by Corinn Williams, 21 May 2009, NOAA, https://voices

.nmfs.noaa.gov/sites/default/files/2018-08/anonymous_11.pdf; and oral history interview with Anonymous #6 by Corinn Williams, 29 July 2008, NOAA, https://voices.nmfs .noaa.gov/sites/default/files/2018-08/anonymous_6.pdf.

30. Interview with Jaime Rivera by Madeleine Hall-Arber, 23 March 2017, WTW, www.loc.gov/resource/afc2016036.afc2016036_03901_ph01/.

31. Interview with Tomás Calil by Corinn Williams, 21 January 2017, WTW, www.loc .gov/item/2020655287/.

32. Interview with Rosa Herrera by Corinn Williams, 9 June 2017, WTW, www.loc .gov/item/2020655292/; Anonymous #6 interview.

33. Interview with Virginia Martins by Madeleine-Hall Arber, 15 November 2016, WTW, www.loc.gov/item/2020655268/.

34. Interview with Jim Mercer by Madeleine-Hall Arber, 13 April 2017, WTW, www .loc.gov/item/2020655269/; interview with Cindy Pettway by Madeleine-Hall Arber, 10 November 2016, WTW, www.loc.gov/item/2020655271/.

35. Interview with Alexander Chavis by Corinn Williams, 25 March 2017, WTW, www.loc.gov/resource/afc2016036.afc2016036_03925_ph02/; interview with Sebastián Ayala by Madeleine Hall-Arber, 23 March 2017, WTW, www.loc.gov/resource/afc2016036 .afc2016036_03824_ph02/.

36. Interview with Héctor Grave by Corinn Williams, 14 December 2016, WTW, www.loc.gov/item/2020655290/.

37. Interview with Valeriano García by Corinn Williams, 11 June 2017, WTW, www .loc.gov/item/2020655289/.

38. Interview with Guadalupe (no last name provided) by Corinn Williams, 8 June 2017, WTW, www.loc.gov/item/2020655291/.

39. Interview with Anonymous #15 by Corinn Williams, 26 August 2010, NOAA, https://voices.nmfs.noaa.gov/sites/default/files/2018-08/anonymous_15.pdf.

40. Interview with Anonymous by Corinn Williams, http://s837454701.onlinehome .us/changing/NI-adjusting.htm.

41. Ayala interview; interview with Rosa Herrara by Corinn Williams, 9 June 2017, WTW, www.loc.gov/item/2020655292/. For inspiring reading about Latinos' current relationship to the ocean, see Cirse Gonzalez, "Nuestro Océano y la Costa: Latino Connections to the Ocean and Coast," white paper for the Hispanic Access Foundation, posted 11 June 2020, https://hispanicaccess.org/news-resources/research-library/item/893 -nuestro-oceano-y-la-costa-latino-connections-to-the-ocean-and-coast.

42. Comment by "Fisherman" underneath Rachel Wachman, "'This Is My Mission': Helena DaSilva Hughes and the Immigrants' Assistance Center," *New Bedford Light*, 19 September 2023, https://newbedfordlight.org/this-is-my-mission-helena-dasilva -hughes-and-the-immigrants-assistance-center/; interview with Eoin Rochford by Madeleine Hall-Arber, 4 January 2017, WTW, www.loc.gov/item/2020655273/.

43. Interview with Kevin Hart by Madeleine Hall-Arber, 17 January 2017, WTW, www.loc.gov/item/2020655265/.

44. Interview with João Bernardo by Corinn Williams, 11 June 2017, WTW, www.loc .gov/item/2020655286/.

45. Hannah Dreier, "The Kids on the Night Shift," *New York Times Magazine*, 18 September 2023, www.nytimes.com/2023/09/18/magazine/child-labor-dangerous-jobs.html; Will Sennott, "Feds Probe Child Labor Issues in New Bedford Seafood Plants," *New Bedford Light*, 18 December 2023, https://newbedfordlight.org/feds-and-state-probe -child-labor-issues-in-new-bedford-seafood-plants/.

46. Wachman, "'This Is My Mission.'"

47. Interview with Anonymous by Corinn Williams, NOAA, http://s837454701
.onlinehome.us/changing/NI-rights.htm.

48. Will Sennott, "OSHA Signs Up to Protect New Bedford's Immigrant Seafood
Workers," *New Bedford Light*, 5 July 2023, https://newbedfordlight.org/osha-signs-up-to
-protect-new-bedfords-immigrant-seafood-workers/.

49. Sennott, "OSHA Signs Up to Protect New Bedford's Immigrant Seafood Workers."

50. David Griffith, *American Guestworkers: Jamaicans and Mexicans in the U.S. Labor
Market* (Philadelphia: University of Pennsylvania Press, 2006), 52, 56.

51. Christine Knott, "Contentious Mobilities and Cheap(er) Labour: Temporary Foreign Workers in a New Brunswick Seafood Processing Community," *Canadian Journal of
Sociology* 41, no. 3 (2016): 378–79, 381, 386.

Chapter Six

1. Teresa Mares, *Life on the Other Border: Farmworkers and Food Justice in Vermont*
(Oakland: University of California Press, 2019), 12; Teresa Mares et al., "Using Chiles and
Comics to Address the Physical and Emotional Wellbeing of Farmworkers in Vermont's
Borderlands," *Agriculture and Human Values* 37 (2020): 199.

2. Mares et al., "Using Chiles and Comics," 200; Mares, *Life on the Other Border*, 13;
State of Vermont, Agency of Agriculture, Food, and Markets home page, accessed 31
March 2024, https://agriculture.vermont.gov/food-safety/milk-dairy; Kathleen Sexsmith,
"'But We Can't Call 911': Undocumented Immigrant Farmworkers and Access to Social
Protection in New York," *Oxford Development Studies* 45, no. 1 (2017): 97.

3. Teresa M. Mares, Naomi Wolcott-MacCausland, and Jessie Mazar, "Eating Far from
Home: Latino/a Workers and Food Sovereignty in Rural Vermont," in *Food across Borders*,
ed. Matt Garcia, E. Melanie DuPuis, and Don Mitchell (New Brunswick, NJ: Rutgers
University Press, 2017), 182; Mares et al., "Using Chiles and Comics," 197, 200; Mares, *Life
on the Other Border*, 12.

4. Sexsmith, "'But We Can't Call 911,'" 97.

5. Mares et al., "Eating Far from Home," 182; Susannah McCandless, "Mapping the Carceral Countryside: Affect, Mobility and Gender in the Lived Spaces of Vermont Latino Farmworkers," paper presented at the AAG 105th Annual Meeting, Las Vegas, NV, March 2009.

6. Mares, *Life on the Other Border*, 11; Timothy A. Wise, *Eating Tomorrow: Agribusiness, Family Farmers, and the Battle for the Future of Food* (New York: New Press, 2019),
216, 219; Mares et al., "Using Chiles and Comics," 200; Susannah McCandless, "Carceral
Landscapes, Invisible Laborers: Mexican Farmhands in Vermont Dairy Agriculture,"
research talk, Center for Research on Vermont, 2 April 2009, https://archive.org/details
/RETNCRV2009SusannahMcCandlessMexicanFarmhands.

7. Interview with Fabian Martinez, Waltham, VT, 19 December 2007, Golden Cage.

8. Interview with Pedro/Leonel by Chris Urban, New Haven, VT, 13 December 2007,
Golden Cage; interview with Freddie Hernández García by Chris Urban, 11 December
2007, Golden Cage.

9. Steve Tammelleo, "Food Policy, Mexican Migration and Collective Responsibility,"
in *Just Food: Philosophy, Justice, and Food*, ed. Jill M. Dieterle (Lanham, MD: Rowan and
Littlefield, 2015), 105–6. For more on borderland deaths, migrant loss, and transnational
responsibility, see Jason DeLeon, *The Land of Open Graves: Living and Dying on the Migrant Trail* (Oakland: University of California Press, 2015).

10. Interview with Raoul, 8 November 2007, Golden Cage.

11. Interview with Inocente by Chris Urban, New Haven, VT, 13 December 2007, Golden Cage; Wise, *Eating Tomorrow*, 222; Julie C. Keller, *Milking in the Shadows: Migrants and Mobility in America's Dairyland* (New Brunswick, NJ: Rutgers University Press, 2019), 75; interview with Philip Livingston (pseudonym), New Haven, VT, 20 December 2007, Golden Cage; Jeremy Slack, Daniel E. Martinez, and Scott Whiteford, eds., *The Shadow of the Wall: Violence and Migration on the U.S.-Mexico Border* (Tucson: University of Arizona Press, 2018), xvi, 4, 5.

12. Keller, *Milking in the Shadows*, 2, 32, 43–44.

13. Interview with Daniel and Brenda Finney by Hannah Harvester, 5 April 2013, and interview with Mark Akins by Hannah Harvester, 17 January 2013, both from North Country, www.loc.gov/item/2020655445/ and www.loc.gov/item/2020655450/; Wise, *Eating Tomorrow*, 5; interview with John D. Peck by Jill Breit, 15 January 2013, North Country, www.loc.gov/item/2020655468/. The USDA's definition of a small dairy farm is an operation that has fewer than 100 milk cows. A medium farm has between 100 and 499 cows, and a large one has more than 500. Mares, *Life on the Other Border*, 13.

14. Interview with Jason Hatch, Ferrisburg, VT, 12 December 2007, and interview with Kevin Cahart, Waltham, VT, 19 December 2007. Both from Golden Cage. Interview with Kevin and Phyllis Acres by Varick Chittenden and Hannah Harvester, Madrid, NY, 6 February 2013, North Country, www.loc.gov/item/2020655451/; interview with Ben Dykema, North Ferrisburg, VT, 15 November 2007, Golden Cage; interview with Doug Moser and Patty Beyer by Hannah Harvester, 3 April 2013, North Country, www.loc.gov /item/2020655447/.

15. Testimony of Yusuf Abdul-Qadir, Morrisville hearing.

16. Interview with anonymous farmer by Chris Urban, Bristol, VT, 12 December 2007, Golden Cage; Kathleen Sexsmith, "Milking Networks for All They're Worth: Precarious Migrant Life and the Process of Consent on New York Dairies," in Garcia, DuPuis, and Mitchell, *Food across Borders*, 201.

17. Anonymous farmer interview; Sexsmith, "'But We Can't Call 911,'" 96, 101; Rural and Migrant Ministry, "Farmworker Testimonies: Stories from the Field" pamphlet, 2019, 9; Mares, *Life on the Other Border*, 41.

18. Fabian Martínez interview; Pedro/Leonel interview; Livingston interview.

19. "Farmworker Testimonies: Stories from the Field," 9; Morrisville hearing.

20. Dykema interview; Akins interview.

21. Mares, *Life on the Other Border*, 8; interview with Blake Gendebien by Hannah Harvester, Lisbon, NY, 13 March 2013, North Country, www.loc.gov/resource/afc2012033 .afc2012033_00500_ms01/?st=pdf; interview with Nancy "Mama" Sabin, 20 December 2007, Charlotte, VT, Golden Cage.

22. Acres interview; "Same Bed, Different Dreams," *This American Life*, 1 May 2015, www.thisamericanlife.org/556/transcript; Keller 88.

23. Interview with Mary Mendoza by the author, Middlebury, VT, 2 September 2019.

24. Keller, *Milking in the Shadows*, 104; Hernández García interview; Raoul interview; Martínez interview, all from Golden Cage. Translations from Spanish to English, and mixing of the two languages, are done by the author.

25. B. Amore, *Invisible Odysseys: Art by Mexican Farmworkers in Vermont* (Benson: Kokoro, 2012), 6, 33.

26. Hatch interview.

27. Hunt interview.

28. Testimony of Dustin Bliss, Smithtown hearing; Livingston interview; anonymous farmer interview.

29. Gendebien interview; Akins interview; Inocente interview.

30. Hunt interview.

31. Interview with Adrienne and Nick Gilbert by Varick Chittenden, 1 August 2013, Parishville, NY, North Country, www.loc.gov/resource/afc2012033.afc2012033_00544_ph/?st=gallery; Mendoza interview.

32. See Julie Stumpf, "The Crimmigration Crisis: Immigrants, Crime, and Sovereign Power," *American University Law Review* 52, no. 2 (2006): 367–419; and Elliott Young, *Forever Prisoners: How the United States Made the World's Largest Immigration Detention System* (New York: Oxford University Press, 2020).

33. Gendebien interview; Sexsmith, "Milking Networks," 202; Hernández García interview.

34. Dykema interview.

35. Judy Harrison, "3 Arrested at Clinton Dairy Farm Plead Guilty to Fraud," *Bangor Daily News*, 22 August 2008, 6; McCandless, "Carceral Landscapes." Donald Trump reactivated Secure Communities right after his inauguration in January 2017, but President Joe Biden's Department of Homeland Security replaced it with the Priority Enforcement Program, which authorized the detention of aliens convicted of certain enumerated crimes or posing a danger to public safety. Ana R. Minian, *Undocumented Lives: The Untold Story of Mexican Migration* (Cambridge, MA: Harvard University Press, 2018), 234; Mares, *Life on the Other Border*, 154–55; Congressional Research Service, "The Biden Administration's Immigration Enforcement Priorities: Background and Legal Considerations," updated 9 December 2022, https://sgp.fas.org/crs/homesec/LSB10578.pdf.

36. Mares, *Life on the Other Border*, 31.

37. Hunt interview.

38. Mares, *Life on the Other Border*, 67; Mares et al., "Eating Far from Home," 182.

39. Alyshia Gálvez, "*Paqueteros* and *Paqueteras*: Humanizing a Dehumanized Food System," *Gastronomica* 21, no. 1 (2021): 27–37.

40. *Silenced Voices*, documentary film by Sam Mayfield, Brendan O'Neill, and Gustavo Terán for the Vermont Migrant Farmworker Solidarity Project, www.youtube.com/watch?v=Q3DRQVbV6LM.

41. Lorena Muñoz, "Latino/a Immigrant Street Vendors in Los Angeles: Photo-documenting Sidewalks from Back Home," in Sarah Portnoy, *Food, Health, and Culture in Latino Los Angeles* (Lanham, MD: Rowan and Littlefield, 2016), 150; Mares, *Life on the Other Border*, 59–60.

42. *Silenced Voices*.

43. Aurora Almendral, "Immigrant Farm Workers, the Hidden Part of New York's Local Food Movement," WYNC segment, 21 November 2012, www.wnyc.org/story/252235-upstate-new-york-immigrant-farmworkers-are-hidden-part-locally-grown-food-movement/.

44. Alyshia Gálvez, *Eating NAFTA: Trade, Food Policies, and the Destruction of Mexico* (Oakland: University of California Press, 2018), 160, 164.

45. Mares, *Life on the Other Border*, 25–26, 88, 94–95, 104–5, 109; Mares et al., "Using Chiles and Comics," 202.

46. Melissa Pasanen, "Viva el Sabor Reveals Mexican Cooking Traditions in the Farmworker Community," *Seven Days Vermont*, 27 July 2021, www.sevendaysvt.com/vermont/viva-el-sabor-reveals-mexican-cooking-traditions-in-the-farmworker-community

/Content?oid=33479039. I thank the students in Professor Lana Dee Povitz's class at Middlebury College for making me aware of Viva el Sabor.

47. Oscar Lopez and Maria Abi-Habib, "Ending a Decade-Long Decline, More Mexicans Are Migrating to U.S.," *New York Times*, 1 July 2022, www.nytimes.com/2022/07/01/world/americas/migrants-mexico-texas.html.

48. Amore, *Invisible Odysseys*, 68–69.

49. Hunt interview; *Rural Migration News* 12, no. 12 (April 2006), http://migration.ucdavis.edu/rmn/more.php?id=1103_0_2_0.

50. Dykema interview.

51. Hunt interview.

52. Raoul interview; Inocente interview; Hernández García interview.

53. Pedro/Leonel interview.

54. Minian, *Undocumented Lives*; Inocente interview; Marek Bennett, Andy Kolovos, and Teresa Mares, eds., *El viaje más caro: Historias de trabajadores migrantes de agricultura, dibujadas por artistas de New England* (Middlebury: Vermont Folklife Center, 2023).

55. Mendoza interview; Sexsmith, "'But We Can't Call 911,'" 105.

56. Mares et al., "Using Chiles and Comics," 200; Keller, *Milking in the Shadows*, 108; Sexsmith, "Milking Networks," 202; McCandless, "Carceral Landscapes."

57. Mares, *Life on the Other Border*, 151, 153; *Silenced Voices*.

58. Testimony of Nora Catlin, Smithtown hearing; J. D. Allen and María del Mar Piedrabuena, "Farm Workers' Union Protests Pindar Vineyards as Contract Negotiations Stall," WSHU (NPR), 21 November 2022, www.wshu.org/long-island-news/2022-11-21/farm-workers-union-protests-pindar-vineyards-as-contract-negotiations-stall; testimonies of Kim Skellie, Bill Banker, and Judi Whittaker, Morrisville hearing.

59. Testimonies of Jeff Rottkamp and Lisa Zucker, Smithtown hearing.

60. Testimony of Herbert Engman, Morrisville hearing.

61. Testimonies of Brett Bossard and Zaid Kurdieh, Morrisville hearing; testimony of Dustin Bliss, Smithtown hearing.

62. Testimonies of Jon Greenwood, Matthew Critz, Lupareo Pérez-Carbajal, and Leandro Mateo-Gaytán, Morrisville hearing; Margaret Gray and Emma Kreyche, "The Hudson Valley Farmworker Report: Understanding the Needs and Aspirations of a Voiceless Population," Bard College Migrant Worker Project, 2007, 8, www.adelphi.edu/pdfs/farmworker.report.pdf.

63. Margaret Gray and Olivia Heffernan, "What New York Farmworkers Have Earned," *New York Daily News*, 2 October 2020, www.nydailynews.com/opinion/ny-oped-what-new-york-farmworkers-have-earned-20201002-6ahzrzeyrfgmbjeh4di3hquz5q-story.html?

64. David Schildknecht, "Wind, Water, and Long Island's Wealth of Wines," *World of Fine Wine*, no. 16 (2007): 147, 149; Catlin testimony.

65. L. Stephen Velasquez, "Doing It with 'Ganas': Mexicans and Mexican Americans Shaping the California Wine Industry," *Southern California Quarterly* 100, no. 2 (Summer 2018): 227; Kathleen A. Brosnan, "The Lifting Fog: Race, Work, and the Environment," *Environmental History* 24 (2019): 16–17; interview with Rafael Flores by the author, White River Junction, VT, 13 April 2023; interview with Todd Trzaskos by the author, Bethel, VT, 13 April 2023; interview with David Keck by the author, Jeffersonville, VT, 13 August 2022; interview with Deirdre Heekin, Vergennes, VT, 14 April 2023.

66. Marisa Fox, "A Day with the North Fork's Vine Keepers," *North Forker*, October 2021, https://northforker.com/2021/10/the-vine-keepers/.

67. Brianne Ledda and Melissa Azofeifa, "New York's First Farmworker Union Is Formed at Pindar Vineyards," *Suffolk Times*, 14 October 2021, https://suffolktimes .timesreview.com/2021/10/new-yorks-first-farmworker-union-is-formed-at-pindar -vineyards/; Amir Khafagy, "A Year Later, New York's First Farm Workers Union Struggles to Secure Its First Contract," *Documented NY*, 12 December 2022, https:// documentedny.com/2022/12/12/new-york-farmworkers-farm-workers-union/; author conversation with Pindar tasting room employee, 18 October 2021.

68. Allen and Piedrabuena, "Farm Workers' Union Protests Pindar Vineyards"; Sarah Minkewicz, "Agriculture community fights to ensure fairness for farmworkers and rights to unionize," 21 February 2024, www.wivb.com/news/local-news/western-new-york /agriculture-community-fights-to-ensure-fairness-for-farmworkers-and-rights-to -unionize/.

69. Hannah Selinger, "When ICE Detains One of Your Food Community's Own," 13 April 2018, *Edible East End*, www.edibleeastend.com/2018/04/13/when-ice-detains -one-of-your-food-community-own/; Mark Segal, "Green Card Was in Sight," *East Hampton Star*, 19 April 2018, www.easthamptonstar.com/archive/green-card-was-sight; Chelsia Rose Marcius, Elizabeth Elizalde, and Rich Schapiro, "Lawyers Protest as ICE Agents Detain Defendant," *New York Daily News*, 24 April 2018, www.nydailynews.com/new-york /lawyers-protest-ice-agents-detain-defendant-staten-island-article-1.3952546.

70. Selinger, "When ICE Detains"; Segal, "Green Card"; Marcius et al., "Lawyers Protest."

71. Eunice Hyunhye Cho, American Civil Liberties Union National Prison Project, "Unchecked Growth: Private Prison Corporations and Immigration Detention, Three Years into the Biden Administration," 7 August 2023, www.aclu.org/news/immigrants -rights/unchecked-growth-private-prison-corporations-and-immigration-detention-three -years-into-the-biden-administration; Segal, "Green Card"; email to the author from Hannah Selinger, 26 August 2022. Also see Nancy Hiemstra, *Detain and Deport: The Chaotic U.S. Immigration Enforcement Regime* (Athens: University of Georgia Press, 2019).

72. Ginia Bellafante, "The Perilous Existence of a Hamptons Day Laborer," *New York Times*, 7 April 2024, www.nytimes.com/2024/04/07/nyregion/hamptons-workers -long-island.html.

73. Julia Moskin, "Working Class or Upper Crust, Tacos for All in the Hamptons," *New York Times*, 19 August 2008, www.nytimes.com/2008/08/20/dining/20east.html.

74. Roland Barthes, *Mythologies* (New York: Noonday, 1957 [1972]), 60–61.

Chapter Seven

1. Jeffery C. Mays and Andy Newman, "Virus Is Twice as Deadly for Black and Latino People than Whites in N.Y.C.," *New York Times*, 8 April 2020, www.nytimes.com/2020 /04/08/nyregion/coronavirus-race-deaths.html?; Anita Chabria, "Many California Farmworkers Fear a Winter of Hunger and Homelessness amid the Pandemic," 25 October 2020, www.latimes.com/california/story/2020-10-26/central-valley-farmworkers-hunger -evictions-coronavirus-covid19; Adrian Carrasquillo, "Nearly Two-Thirds of Latinos Have Lost Jobs or Face Economic Hardship Due to Coronavirus Outbreak, Poll Finds," *Newsweek*, 17 April 2020, www.newsweek.com/nearly-two-thirds-latinos-have-lost-jobs -face-economic-hardship-due-coronavirus-outbreak-poll-1498417; Perla Trevizo, "El COVID-19 golpea Texas y los hispanos son quienes más mueren," *ProPublica*, 31 July 2020, www.propublica.org/article/it-cost-me-everything-in-texas-COVID-19-takes-a -devastating-toll-on-hispanic-residents.

2. Mya Frazier, "The Poultry Workers on the Coronavirus Front Line: 'If One of Us Gets Sick, We All Get Sick,'" *Guardian*, 17 April 2020, www.theguardian.com/environment /2020/apr/17/chicken-factory-tyson-arkansas-food-workers-coronavirus.

3. David Bacon, "Guest Workers on U.S. Farms Are in the Eye of the Coronavirus Storm," *Equal Times*, 28 May 2020, www.equaltimes.org/guest-workers-on-us-farms -are-in?lang=en; Mike Dorning, "Getting Covid Gets You Fired When You're a Food Worker on a Visa," *Bloomberg*, 31 July 2020, www.bloomberg.com/news/articles/2020 -07-31/u-s-visa-rules-trap-migrant-workers-in-virus-infested-dorms; Brooke Jarvis, "The Scramble to Pluck 24 Billion Cherries in Eight Weeks," *New York Magazine*, 12 August 2020, www.nytimes.com/2020/08/12/magazine/cherry-harvest-workers.html.

4. Scott Hennessee, "COVID-19 Outbreak, Death among Santa Maria Farm Workers," *News Channel 12 3 11*, 14 July 2020, https://keyt.com/health/coronavirus/2020/07/14 /COVID-19-outbreak-death-among-santa-maria-farm-workers/.

5. National Center for Farmworker Health, "COVID-19 in Rural America: Impact on Farms & Agricultural Workers," 1 February 2021, www.ncfh.org/msaws-and-COVID-19 .html; Eric Russell, "COVID-19 Cases among Blueberry Workers Worsen Farm Labor Shortage," *Portland Press Herald*, 3 August 2020, www.pressherald.com/2020/08/03 /COVID-19-cases-among-blueberry-workers-worsen-farm-labor-shortage/; Kate Cough, "Third Cluster of Cases Reported among Blueberry Workers," *Ellsworth American*, 4 August 2020, www.ellsworthamerican.com/maine-news/health-news/third-cluster-of-cases -reported-among-blueberry-workers/; Kate Cough, "More Blueberry Workers Test Positive for Virus," *Ellsworth American*, 6 August 2020, 1; "COVID-19 Shelters for Migrant Workers," 29 October 2020, www.manomaine.org/news/COVID-19-shelters-for-migrant -workers.

6. Tracey Tully, "How You Get Your Berries: Migrant Workers Who Fear Virus, but Toil On," *New York Times*, 5 July 2002, www.nytimes.com/2020/07/05/nyregion/nj -migrant-workers-COVID-19.html; Patricia Mazzei, "Florida's Coronavirus Spike Is Ravaging Migrant Farmworkers," *New York Times*, 18 June 2020, www.nytimes.com/2020 /06/18/us/florida-coronavirus-immokalee-farmworkers.html.

7. Ian Spiegelman, "What's Being Done to Protect California Farmworkers from COVID-19? Not Enough, Experts Say," *Los Angeles Magazine*, 9 September 2020, www .lamag.com/citythinkblog/farmworkers-COVID-19-california/; National Center for Farmworker Health, "COVID-19 in Rural America"; Tony Nuñez, "Farmworkers Worked despite Positive COVID-19 Tests for Fear of Job Loss, Study Shows," *Pajaronian*, 15 December 2020, https://pajaronian.com/farmworkers-worked-despite-positive -COVID-19-tests-for-fear-of-job-loss-study-shows/.

8. Miriam Jordan, "Thousands of Farmworkers Are Prioritized for the Coronavirus Vaccine," *New York Times*, 1 March 2021, www.nytimes.com/2021/03/01/us/coronavirus -vaccine-farmworkers-california.html; National Center for Farmworker Health, "COVID-19 in Rural America"; Alma Patty Tzalain, "I Harvest Your Food. Why Isn't My Health 'Essential'?," *New York Times*, 15 April 2020, www.nytimes.com/2020/04/15 /opinion/covid-farmworkers-paid-leave.html.

9. Magaly Licolli, "As Tyson Claims the Food Supply Is Breaking, Its Workers Continue to Suffer," *Civil Eats*, 30 April 2020, https://civileats.com/2020/04/30/as-tyson -claims-the-food-supply-is-breaking-its-workers-continue-to-suffer/; Angela Steusse and Nathan T. Dollar, "Who Are America's Meat and Poultry Workers?," Economic Policy Institute, 24 September 2020, www.epi.org/blog/meat-and-poultry-worker -demographics/.

10. Patricia Escárcega, "The Not-So-Subtle Racism of American Food Culture," *Playboy*, 8 February 2021, www.playboy.com/read/the-playboy-symposium-the-not-so-subtle-racism-of-american-food-culture; Michael Pollan, "The Sickness in Our Food Supply," *New York Review*, 11 June 2020, www.nybooks.com/articles/2020/06/11/COVID-19-sickness-food-supply/; Gosia Wozniacka, "Poor Conditions at Meatpacking Plants Have Long Put Workers at Risk," *Civil Eats*, 17 April 2020, https://civileats.com/2020/04/17/poor-conditions-at-meatpacking-plants-have-long-put-workers-at-risk-the-pandemic-makes-it-much-worse/.

11. Michael Grabell and Bernice Yeung, "Meatpacking Companies Dismissed Years of Warnings but Now Say Nobody Could Have Prepared for COVID-19," *ProPublica*, 20 August 2020, www.propublica.org/article/meatpacking-companies-dismissed-years-of-warnings-but-now-say-nobody-could-have-prepared-for-COVID-19.

12. Licoli, "As Tyson Claims"; "As COVID Spikes in California, Latinx Workers Who 'Keep the State Going' See Up to 5x the Deaths," *Democracy Now*, 22 July 2020, www.democracynow.org/2020/7/22/california_covid_19_latinx_community; Thomas Yazwinski, "3 Workers Killed, 277 Infected in Coronavirus Outbreak at E. Wash. Beef Plant," KEPR-TV News and KOMO News, 16 May 2020, https://katu.com/news/local/3-workers-killed-277-infected-in-coronavirus-outbreak-at-e-wash-beef-plant; Frazier, "The Poultry Workers"; Vivian Ho, "'Everyone Tested Positive': COVID Devastates Agriculture Workers in California's Heartland," *Guardian*, 8 August 2020, www.theguardian.com/us-news/2020/aug/08/california-COVID-19-central-valley-essential-workers; Leah Douglas, Georgia Gee, and Derek Kravitz, "Documents Show Scope of COVID-19 in North Carolina Meat Industry," *Fern*, 11 December 2020, https://thefern.org/2020/12/documents-show-scope-of-COVID-19-in-north-carolina-meat-industry/; Wozniacka, "Poor Conditions at Meatpacking Plants"; "As COVID Spikes in California"; Julia Lurie, "'Everyone Is Tired of Always Staying Silent': Inside a Worker Rebellion in the Central Valley," *Mother Jones*, January/February 2021, www.motherjones.com/politics/2020/12/farmworkers-labor-rebellion-worker-central-valley/.

13. AFL-CIO, "Death on the Job: The Toll of Neglect," 25 April 2019, 3, https://aflcio.org/reports/death-job-toll-neglect-2019; Lisa Held, "OSHA Faulted for Not Doing More to Protect Workers from COVID-19," *Civil Eats*, 16 June 2020, https://civileats.com/2020/06/16/osha-faulted-for-not-doing-more-to-protect-workers-from-COVID-19/; Rachel Wachman, "'This Is My Mission': Helena DaSilva Hughes and the Immigrants' Assistance Center," *New Bedford Light*, 19 September 2023, https://newbedfordlight.org/this-is-my-mission-helena-dasilva-hughes-and-the-immigrants-assistance-center/.

14. Interviews with Richard Rocha by the author, April 2020, telephone, and 2 January 2024, Alice, TX.

15. "Hunts Point Market Workers in the Bronx Win Wage Increase after Week-Long Strike," *Democracy Now*, 25 January 2021, www.democracynow.org/2021/1/25/headlines/hunts_point_market_workers_in_the_bronx_win_wage_increase_after_week_long_strike.

16. Brendan Seibel, "Grocery Stores Continue to Push Back against Hazard Pay for Workers," *Civil Eats*, 25 February 2021, https://civileats.com/2021/02/25/grocery-stores-continue-to-push-back-against-hazard-pay-for-workers/; Bao Ong, "A New Delivery App Dedicated to New York City Bodegas Just Launched," *Time Out New York*, 24 March 2020, www.timeout.com/newyork/news/a-new-delivery-app-dedicated-to-new-york-city-bodegas-just-launched-032420.

17. As of 2020, there were an estimated 25,476 food truck businesses in the United States. Lori Flores, "Latino Labor in the U.S. Food Industry, 1880–2020," *Oxford Research*

Encyclopedia of American History, published online 17 December 2020, https://doi.org
/10.1093/acrefore/9780199329175.013.850.

18. Annie Correal and Andrew Jacobs, "'A Tragedy Is Unfolding': Inside New York's
Virus Epicenter," *New York Times*, 9 April 2020 (updated 5 August 2020), www.nytimes
.com/2020/04/09/nyregion/coronavirus-queens-corona-jackson-heights-elmhurst.html.

19. Sarah Portnoy, *Food, Health, and Culture in Latino Los Angeles* (Lanham, MD:
Rowan and Littlefield, 2016), 103; Ginette Wessel, "Relaxing Regulatory Controls: Vendor
Advocacy and Rights in Mobile Food Vending," in *Food Trucks, Cultural Identity, and
Social Justice: From Loncheras to Lobsta Love*, ed. Julian Agyeman et al. (Cambridge, MA:
MIT Press, 2017), 28.

20. Chris Crowley, "New York's Street Vendors Just Scored a Major Victory," *Grub
Street*, 28 January 2021, www.grubstreet.com/2021/01/nyc-intro-1116-vendor-permits
-increased.html.

21. Esther Tseng, "Undocumented Restaurant Workers Have Held the Industry Together. Now They Stand to Lose the Most," *Civil Eats*, 28 May 2020, https://civileats
.com/2020/05/28/undocumented-restaurant-workers-have-held-the-industry-together
-now-they-stand-to-lose-the-most/.

22. Saru Jayaraman, *Behind the Kitchen Door* (Ithaca, NY: ILR Press, 2013), 70.

23. Khushbu Shah, "The Customer Is Not Always Right," *Food and Wine*, 29 December
2020, www.foodandwine.com/fwpro/customer-is-not-always-right; Monica Hesse, "'Take
Off Your Mask': Boorish Customers Have Found a Way to Make Sexual Harassment
Even More of a Hazard," *Washington Post*, 10 December 2020, www.washingtonpost
.com/lifestyle/style/masks-restaurant-harassment-pandemic/2020/12/09/d8100674-397b
-11eb-9276-ae0ca72729be_story.html.

24. Josh Dzieza, "Revolt of the Delivery Workers," *New York Magazine* and *Verge*,
13 September 2021, www.curbed.com/article/nyc-delivery-workers.html.

25. Martha Guerrero, "Migrant Gig Workers Organize in New York City: Deliveristas
Unidos & the Fight to Regulate Food Delivery Apps," Immigration and Ethnic History
Society Online, 12 December 2022, https://iehs.org/migrant-gig-workers-organize-in
-new-york-city-deliveristas-unidos-the-fight-to-regulate-food-delivery-apps/.

26. Samantha Melamed, "'We're Essential,'" *Philadelphia Inquirer*, 20 May 2020,
www.inquirer.com/health/coronavirus/a/coronavirus-COVID-19-philadelphia-food
-grocery-delivery-doordash-instacart-grubhub-uber-eats-20200520.html.

27. Claudia Irizarry Aponte and Josefa Velasquez, "NYC Food Delivery Workers Band
to Demand Better Treatment," *City*, 6 December 2020, www.thecity.nyc/work/2020
/12/6/22157730/nyc-food-delivery-workers-demand-better-treatment; "Repartidores
denuncian que algunas apps y restaurantes se embolsan sus propinas," *Puntualizando.net*
(Los Angeles), 9 December 2019, https://puntualizando.net/2019/12/09/repartidores
-denuncian-que-algunas-apps-y-restaurantes-se-embolsan-sus-propinas/; Guerrero, "Migrant Gig Workers."

28. Aponte and Velasquez, "NYC Food Delivery Workers"; Guerrero, "Migrant Gig
Workers"; Dzieza, "The Revolt of the Delivery Workers."

29. Dzieza, "Revolt of the Delivery Workers"; Edgar Sandoval, "'My Turn to Get
Robbed': Delivery Workers Are Targets in the Pandemic," *New York Times*, 9 March 2021,
www.nytimes.com/2021/03/09/nyregion/delivery-workers-robberies-nyc.html; Guerrero,
"Migrant Gig Workers"; María Luisa Paúl and Marisa Iati, "They Fled Venezuela—
and transformed D.C.'s food delivery scene," *Washington Post*, 21 April 2024, www
.washingtonpost.com/dc-md-va/2024/04/22/moped-delivery-drivers-dc/.

30. Jill M. Dieterle, *Just Food: Philosophy, Justice, and Food* (Lanham, MD: Rowan and Littlefield, 2015), 39–40; National Center for Farmworker Health, "COVID-19 in Rural America"; Amy and Stephanie Borkowsky, "The Food and COVID-19 NYC Archive: Mapping the Pandemic's Effect on Food in Real Time," *Gastronomica* 20, no. 4 (Winter 2020): 8–11; Martha Guerrero, "The Excluded Workers Fund: New York's Reckoning with Undocumented Labor during the COVID-19 Pandemic," Immigration and Ethnic History Society (blog), 6 March 2023, https://iehs.org/the-excluded-workers-fund-new -yorks-reckoning-with-undocumented-labor-during-the-COVID-19-pandemic/.

31. Robby Lewis-Nash, "'Food from People to People': Mutual Aid Program Feeds Thousands with Barrier-Free Aid," *Maine Beacon*, 22 February 2021, https://mainebeacon .com/food-from-people-to-people-mutual-aid-program-feeds-thousands-with-barrier -free-aid/; "A Week in the Life of Mano en Mano," 26–30 July 2021, www.manomaine .org/news/a-week-in-the-life-of-mano-en-mano-july-26-30-2021; Gillian Graham, "Pandemic Reveals Race Disparities around Food Security in Maine," *Portland Press Herald*, 28 March 2021, B2.

32. Grace Dickinson, "Bright Yellow 'Community Refrigerators' Pop Up to Feed Those in Need across Philadelphia," *Philadelphia Inquirer*, 8 August 2020, www.inquirer.com /news/community-fridge-project-mama-tee-philadelphia-hungry-coronavirus-20200808 .html.

33. Aimee Bender, *The Particular Sadness of Lemon Cake* (New York: Anchor, 2010).

Conclusion

1. Jill M. Dieterle, *Just Food: Philosophy, Justice, and Food* (Lanham, MD: Rowman and Littlefield, 2015), ix; Gideon Lichfield, "From the Editor," *MIT Technology Review* 124, no. 1 (January/February 2021): 2.

2. David Foster Wallace, "Consider the Lobster," *Gourmet* (August 2004).

3. Lisa M. Heldke, "Food Politics, Political Food," in *Cooking, Eating, Thinking: Transformative Philosophies of Food*, ed. Deane W. Curtin and Lisa M. Heldke (Bloomington: Indiana University Press, 1992), 322.

4. Michael Pollan, *The Omnivore's Dilemma: A Natural History of Four Meals* (New York: Penguin, 2006), 254.

5. Margaret Gray, *Labor and the Locavore: The Making of a Comprehensive Food Ethic* (Berkeley: University of California Press, 2013), 143.

6. Though it is very rare, guestworker unionization is possible. In September 2004, a Farm Labor Organizing Committee boycott of Mt. Olive Pickle Company in North Carolina ended with a collective bargaining agreement for 8,000 farmworkers on more than 1,000 farms. This deal marked the first union representation and contract for guestworkers in the United States. Allison Kidd, "Union Access to Migrant Farmworkers: The Mt. Olive Pickle Company, Cucumber Farmers, and Farmworkers," *Labor Lawyer* 20, no. 3 (Winter/Spring 2005): 342.

7. For more, see Susan L. Marquis, *I Am Not a Tractor! How Florida Farmworkers Took on the Fast Food Giants and Won* (Ithaca, NY: Cornell University Press, 2017); and Barry Estabrook, *Tomatoland: How Modern Industrial Agriculture Destroyed Our Most Alluring Fruit* (Kansas City: Andrews McMeel, 2011).

INDEX

Page numbers in italics refer to illustrations.

agricultural industry: and child labor, 30, 45; in Connecticut, 33; during COVID, 11, 182, 183, 185; and exploitation of foreign labor, 5, 18, 19, 30, 45; and guest-workers, 7, 16, *17*, 18, 19, 21, 31–38, *33*, 40, 41; and lack of oversight, 112, 117, 121; in Maine, 106, 110, 122, 126; in New Hampshire, 22; in New York State, 55, 67, 173, 175; and NAFTA, 92, 155; in Rhode Island, 22; in Vermont, 154. *See also specific agricultural sectors*

agricultural workers: Black American, 106; Caribbean, 113, 122, 124; Central American, 113; and COVID, 182, 183; and H-2 visa program, 10, 124, 125, 174, 182, 199; and labor organizing, 19, 107, 113, 119, 155, 176; in Maine, 106, 110, 122, 126; Mexican-origin, 18, 113; in New York State, 155, 183; and pesticides, 64–65, 72, 111, 118, 175; Puerto Rican, 16, 32, 33, 113; undocumented, 5, 11, 34, 41, 71, 72, 92, 106, 111, 112, 118, 125, 154, 156, 161, 162, 166, 172–74, 178, 183. *See also* Bracero Program; braceros; DeCoster Farms; Farm Placement Program (FPP); farmworkers; UFW; *and specific agricultural sectors*

apple industry, and workers, 1, 16, 41, 53, 106, 123–24, 153–54, 184

Asociación de Trabajadores Agrícolas (ATA), 67, 73

Bahamians, 7, *17*, 23, 31
Biden, Joe, 165, 169, 170, 187, 238n35
Birds Eye (company), 36–38
Black Panther Party, 47, 57, 64, 69, 216n35
Black workers: in crab processing, 152; employers' displacement of, 5, 7, 10; and

Latinidad, 10, 206n16; and labor organizing, 57; as migrants, 106; mistreatment of, 67, 124

blueberry industry: during COVID, 182, 183; health and safety hazards in, 116, 117, 118; litigation against, 117, 120–22; in Maine, 1, 10, 106, 107, 116–23; and mechanization, 122; in New Jersey, 41, 67, 106, 183

blueberry workers: Caribbean, 10, 41, 107, 120–22, 123; Latin American, 1, 107, 117–19; in Maine, 1, 10, 106, 116–23; housing of, 117, 120–21

border. *See* Canada-US border; US-Mexico border

Border Patrol, 11, 72, 155, 156; raids by, 111, 119, 137, 138, 139, 165, 166

Boston: Latinx people in, 6, 32, 42; Mexican restaurants in, 83; UFW in, 47–51, 58, 68, 70, 71, 72, 73

boycotts: of eggs, 111–12; of grapes, 8, 43, 48–53, *54*, *58*, 73, 74; of lettuce, 8, 43, 66–67, 69, 71; of wine, 8, 43. *See also* DeCoster Farms; UFW

Bracero Program, 7, 15–17, 20, 21, 29, 34, 124; decline of, 30, 31, 41, 71. *See also* braceros

braceros, 22, 25, 30; and food protests, 8, 15, 20–31; and Good Neighbor discourse, 8, 20, 21, 27, 28, 29; and health and safety hazards, 29, 30

British West Indies Temporary Alien Labor Program, 16, 20–21

broccoli industry, and labor, 1, 37, 106, 123, 124, 125, 137

Bronx, 57; during COVID, 187, 192; Latinx people in, 79, 99, 101; Mexican food in, 93, 99, 101; UFW in, 66. *See also* New York City

Brooklyn: food protests in, 37; Latinx people in, 37, 38, 99; Mexican food in, 91, 93, 94, 101; UFW in, 55–57, 65, 69. *See also* New York City

Bureau of Employment and Migration (BEM), 31, 32

California, 3; braceros in, 22, 23; and COVID, 181, 183, 184, 185, 193; food protests in, 20; Mexican food in, 39, 77, 91; ties to Northeast of, 46–52, 56–60, 65–66, 74; UFW in, 8, 43

Camacho, Manuel Ávila, 21, 29

Campbell Soup Company, 19, 31, 67, 95, 110

Canada-US border, 6, 11, 108; and surveillance, 118, 132, 155, 161, 163, 165–67, 172, 177

Canadians, 10, *17*, 106, 116, 123, 125, 146. *See also* Indigenous peoples of Canada

Caribbean (place), 5, 105

Caribbean migrants, 6, 16, 18, 21, 31, 104, 113; in agriculture, 10, 107, 113, 122, 123; in Maine, 10, 107, 108, 113, 122, 123, 125; and food protests, 23; in Massachusetts, 132, 152; in New York City, 101; in New York State, 55; in seafood industry, 131, 132, 152; in timber, 125; xenophobia against, 3

Central Americans: in agriculture, 1, 110, 117–19, 125; in dairy industry, 154, 156, 157, 162; fleeing civil war, 74, 92, 144; and immigration discourse, 72, 150; in Maine, 1, 106, 117–19, 125, 132, 137, 138; and migrant journeys, 144, 157; in New Bedford, 143, 144, 150, 151, 152; in New York State, 98, 154, 162; in poultry industry, 112; in seafood industry, 132, 133, 137, 138, 143, 144, 152; and trauma, 4, 151; undocumented, 5, 154; in Vermont, 156, 157; violence against, 3, 9, 98

Chavez, Cesar: East Coast tours of, 52, 53, 73–74; fasting of, 49–50, 68, 69, 74; and labor strikes and boycotts, 8, 46, 48–49, 51, 66; media depictions of, 48, 49, 53; views on undocumented immigration, 9, 71, 72. *See also* UFW

chefs: Anthony Bourdain, 3, 81; with white privilege, 103, 188; women, 102, 103, 104. *See also* Martínez, Zarela

children: in boycotts and protests, 55, 61, 70; in hunger discourse, 48, 70; at work, 30, 45, 109, 150–51

Chinese cuisine, and Mexican cuisine, 81, 96

Chinese Latin Americans, 20, 23, 79

Chinese people, and restaurants, 96, 139

Clinton, Bill, 95, 156, 165

Colombia, 41, 101

Colombians, 6; in agriculture, 113; and food, 179; in Maine, 113, 125; in New England, 41; in New York City, 79, 92, 99; in Rhode Island, 93

community fridges, 12, 193, *194*

Connecticut, 6; agriculture in, 33; braceros in, 22, 30; Dominicans in, 42; food protests in, 68; labor organizing in, 67; Puerto Ricans in, 16, 32, 33, 38, 68; tobacco industry in, 16, 33, 67, 68; UFW in, 52, 53, 70

COVID-19: and border anxieties, 169, 170; and essential food workers, 11–12, 181–95; and food insecurity, 12, 182, 192, 193; mutual food aid during, 12, 182, 192–95; and wage issues, 182, 185, 187, 190, 191, 192

crimmigration, 11, 166, 169, 177

Cuba, 6, 36

Cubans: and grape boycott, 57; in Maine, 6, 29, 105, 106, 115; in New York City, 78, 79, 92; in Rhode Island, 41, 93

culinary tourism, 2, 11, 79, 105, 153, 155, 175

dairy industry: and declining profits, 157; in New York State, 11, 159, 160; in Vermont, 11, 154–74, *159*, 179–80

dairy workers: advocacy for, 172–73; and assertions of personhood, 171; Central American, 154, 156, 157, 162, 164, 172; and crimmigration, 166, 169; and employer relations, 155, 161, 163–67, 171, 174; and food insecurity, 167, 168, 169; and grocery procurement, 155, 165–69, 172; and health and safety of, 160, 169,

171–72; and housing, 155, 156, 160, 162, 172, 173; and deportation fears, 155, 161, 163, 165–67, 170, 171; and labor organizing, 155; in Maine, 166; Mexican-origin, 157, 158, *159*, 162, 163, 164, 166, 167, 171; and migrant journeys, 155–57, 163; in New York State, 159, 160, 162; occupational knowledge of, 160–61; undocumented, 154, 156, 161, 162, 166, 172; in Vermont, 154–74, *159*, 179–80

Deblois, ME, 119; Wyman company in, 116, 117, 118–20, 122, *123*

DeCoster, August, 108–15. *See also* DeCoster Farms

DeCoster Farms: anti-unionism of, 109, 112, 113; and animal mistreatment, 109, 110; consumer boycott against, 111–12; and hazardous conditions, 109–10, 113–14; INS sweeps at, 111; litigation against, 109, 114, 115; OSHA investigation of, 111–14

Delano, CA, 48, 49, 50, 59

Delaware, 32, 33, 62, 67

delivery workers, food, 11, 12, 182; and collective safety structures, 191; and COVID, 190–92; and protests, 192; and wage insecurity, 190, 191, 192

Department of Homeland Security (DHS), 4, 238n35

Department of Labor, US (USDOL): and litigation, 109; and Puerto Rican workers, 16, 31, 36, 37; and seafood industry investigations, 150, 152

Dominican Republic, 10, 16, 79

Dominicans, 6, 90; in Connecticut, 42; as cultural brokers, 115, 116; and food establishments, 42, 79, 90, 93, 97; INS sweeps against, 97; in Maine, 115, 116; in Massachusetts, 42, 132, 143, 144, 146; in New Jersey, 144; in New York City, 41, 42, 79, 92, 97, 99, 101; in Pennsylvania, 142; in Rhode Island, 42, 93; in seafood industry, 143, 146–47

East Harlem, 47, 78, 83; and Mexican food, 93, 94. *See also* New York City

Ecuadoreans, 6, 79, 92, 98, 99, 140, 177, 178

egg industry, 1, 10, 108–15. *See also* DeCoster Farms

egg workers: and labor organizing, 112, 113; Latin American, 1, 10, 111, 112, 113, 114; in Maine, 1, 10, 108–15. *See also* DeCoster Farms

El Salvador. *See* Salvadorans

English language: instruction given to migrants, 22, 28, 32, 162, 165, 182; and xenophobia, 1, 2, 30, 99, 142; spoken by migrants, 1, 146

Europeans, 6, 125, 143, 178

Fair Labor Standards Act, 19, 109

Farm Placement Program (FPP), 15, 16, 21, 31–41, *33*. *See also* Puerto Ricans; Puerto Rico

farmworkers, 3; and COVID, 11, 182–84; and lack of New Deal protections, 5, 18, 19, 31; and Farmworkers Fair Labor Practices Act, 155, 173, 175–76; and food protests, 7–9, 15, 19–23, 25–31, 34, 36, 46, 48, 51, 56, 66, 68, 71, 72–74, 119; and food insecurity, 8, 168; and media exposés, 45–46, 60, 142; and pesticide exposure, 64, 72, 118; and substandard housing, 55, 67, 72; and wages, 30, 41, 42, 45, 48, 67, 72, 160, 172, 199, 200. *See also* Farm Placement Program (FPP); UFW; *and specific agricultural sectors*

Florida: anti-immigrant policies of, 192; migratory labor from, 106, 110, 156, 169, 183

food entrepreneurship, Latinx, 39, 74, 84; as food protest, 42, 112, 198; in the Hamptons, 178; in Maine, 10, 115, 120, 126, 137, 140; and Mexican cuisine, 9, 39, 77–103, 120, 140; in New York City, 9, 77–103; of *paqueteros*, 11, 167, 179, 191; in Rhode Island, 93; of women, 85–86, 102, 103, 104, 169. *See also* Martínez, Zarela

food processing industry, 5, 182, 184–86. *See also* Birds Eye (company); DeCoster Farms; sea cucumber industry; seafood industry

food protests, 68–70; of braceros, 8, 15,
20–31; of farmworkers, 7–9, 15, 19–23,
25–31, 34, 36, 46, 48, 51, 56, 66, 68, 71,
72–74, 119; and Good Neighbor Policy
discourse, 20, 27, 28; of women, 46, 47;
on Long Island, 68, 69; in Maine, 25, 115,
116, 120, 126, 137, 140; in New Jersey, 23;
in New York City, 37, 47, 94, 189, *189*; in
Philadelphia, 68
food truck businesses, 2, 93, 94, 108, 120,
137, 187, 242n17. *See also* street food
vendors
foodways, Latin American, 1, 2, 6, 12, 20,
21, 40, 169, 198
fridges, community, 12, 193, *194*

Galarza, Ernesto, 20, 22, 26, 27, 203
Good Neighbor Policy, 8; and food protests, 20, 27, 28
grape boycotts, 8, 43, 46, 48–53, *54*, 55–74
passim, *58*. *See also* UFW
Guatemala, 41, 138, 144
Guatemalans: in agriculture, 113, 184; in
dairy industry, 156, 162, 164; and entrepreneurship, 147; in Long Island, 175; in
Maine, 110, 111, 112, 113, 138; in Massachusetts, 144, 146, 147, 150, 151; and
migration journeys, 144; and mutual
aid, 169; in New England, 41; in New
Hampshire, 112; in New York State,
175; occupational knowledge of, 175; in
Rhode Island, 93; in seafood industry,
138, 144, 145, 146, 150, 151; in Vermont,
156, 162, 164, 169; in wine industry,
175
guestworker programs, 5, 8, 15, *17*, 18, 19, 31,
125, 152, 199. *See also* Bracero Program;
braceros; British West Indies Temporary
Alien Labor Program; Farm Placement
Program (FPP); H-2 visa program; Migration Division Farm Labor Program

Haitians, 3, 199; in blueberry industry, 10,
120–22; and COVID, 182; in Maine, 10,
105, 120–22, 182; in New York City, 90;
in seafood industry, 143
Hazleton, PA, 141–42

health hazards: and community aid, 47,
116, 118, 120, 122, 125, 141, 171, 172, 193;
in dairy industry, 155, 160, 169, 171–72;
of delivery workers, 190, 191; during
COVID, 181, 182, 183, 184, 185, 186, 187,
190, 191, 192; of farmworkers, 15, 16, 29,
30, 31, 34, 35, 45, 46, 60, 109–11, 116, 117,
118, 142, 183, 184; and migrant trauma,
4, 151, 166, 169, 171, 191; and pesticides,
64–65, 72, 111, 118, 175; in restaurants,
12, 189; in seafood industry, 136, 137,
151, 152; in wine industry, 72, 73, 155. *See
also* Occupational Safety and Health
Administration (OSHA)
housing, substandard, 11, 16, 18, 19, 32, 36,
60; at Birds Eye, 37; in blueberry industry, 116, 117, 118, 120–21, *123*; and braceros, 22, 29, 30; in broccoli industry,
124; and community aid, 172, 182; in
dairy industry, 162; at DeCoster Farms,
111, 112, 114, 117; of farmworkers, 55, 67,
72, 178, 182; litigation against, 141; in
seafood industry, 152; in wine industry,
178
H-2 visa program, 10, 124, 125, 132, 152, 174,
178, 182, 199, 206n15
Hudson Valley, 16, 101, 154, 168, 174
Huerta, Dolores, 8, 46, 47, 55–58
hunger: discourses of, 9, 45, 47, 48, 57, 59,
69, 70, 71, 72; emotional, 12, 169; physiological, 8, 12, 50, 168
hunger strikes, 21, 48, 49, 50, 51, 61, 62, 74.
See also Chavez, Cesar; López, Hope;
UFW

immigrants: backlash to, 107, 141, 142, 162;
and crimmigration, 11, 166, 169, 177;
"hard worker" essentialization of, 150,
158, 159; fear of deportation of, 11, 72, 99,
139, 155, 161, 163, 165–67, 171; and illegal
aliens trope, 3, 72, 111, 118, 170; and
Latino threat trope, 7, 138–39; migrant
journey accounts of, 41, 118, 144, 145,
146, 156, 157, 169, 171, 183; and nostalgias,
19, 20, 34, 149, 167; and occupational
knowledge, 5, 147, 160–61; as precariat,
4, 6, 46, 152; surveillance of, 11, 118, 132,

155, 165–67, 172, 177. *See also* Border Patrol; Department of Homeland Security (DHS); immigrants, undocumented; Immigration and Customs Enforcement (ICE); Immigration and Naturalization Service (INS); Immigration Reform and Control Act (IRCA); racism; xenophobia; *and specific nationalities*

immigrants, undocumented: Cesar Chavez's views on, 9, 71, 72; and COVID, 181, 183, 189, 191, 193, 198, 199; and dairy labor, 154, 156, 161, 162, 166, 172; as precariat, 4, 5, 34, 92, 99, 103, 125, 198, 199. *See also* Border Patrol; Department of Homeland Security (DHS); immigrants; Immigration and Customs Enforcement (ICE); Immigration and Naturalization Service (INS); Immigration Reform and Control Act (IRCA); racism; xenophobia; *and specific nationalities*

Immigration and Customs Enforcement (ICE), 2, 4, 5, 11, 137, 166, 177

Immigration and Naturalization Service (INS), 34, 71, 111, 143; "Operation Bodega," 97; "Operation Wetback," 34; raids by, 4, 138

Immigration Reform and Control Act (IRCA) (1986), 9, 72, 74, 92, 111, 124

Imutan, Andy, 55, 64

Indigenous peoples of Canada: Mi'kmaq, 106, 116; Passamaquoddy, 116; Penobscot, 116

Indigenous peoples of Latin America, 30; Maya, 93, 144, 146, 147, 172; Zapotec, 30, 191

Irizarry, Juan, 67, 73

Italians, 7; and food establishments, 89, 90, 93, 96, 190; in New York City, 78, 94, 99; in seafood industry, 141, 143

Itliong, Larry, 8, 46, 216n37

Jamaicans, 10, 31; in agriculture, 16, 41, 67, 106, 113, 123–25; and IRCA, 124; in Maine, 106, 123, 124, 125; in New Jersey, 7; in New York State, 7, 66; in Pennsylvania, 7

Kennedy, Robert F., 46, 50, 68, 74, 214n19, 219n71

labor recruiters, 16, 111, 117, 120, 138, 182

Latin America: appropriated food from, 2, 3; crises and violence in, 41, 80, 105, 115, 118, 144, 169; and food flows, 1, 7, 74, 80, 91, 93, 125, 137, 167, 179; hunger strikes in, 48; and labor migration, 10, 115, 120, 137, 149, 167. *See also* North American Free Trade Agreement (NAFTA); Puerto Rico; *and names of individual countries in Latin America*

Latin Americans: in agricultural industry, 10, 107, 113; in Maine, 10, 107, 124, 126–27, 133–42; in Massachusetts, 145, 147; in seafood industry, 145; in timber industry, 125. *See also* Latinx people; *and specific nationalities*

Latinx people: and COVID, 19, 30, 165, 181–95; discrimination towards, 4, 27, 29, 32, 52, 68, 97–99, 107, 114, 141; and food protests, 15–43, 45–74; and hard workers trope, 150, 158, 159; impact on New York City, 77–104; and invisibility, 3–7, 104–7, 118, 126, 140, 155, 167, 170, 178, 198–201; and loneliness and isolation, 34, 155, 161, 162, 163, 165–67, 171; in New England seafood, 131–52; and occupational knowledge, 5, 147, 160–61; as sustaining pastoral New England, 153–80; undervaluation of foodways of, 2, 9, 89, 95, 96, 102–4

lettuce, 23, 40, 171; and boycotts against, 8, 43, 46, 48, 65–71

lobster, 131; in Maine, 10, 125, 126, 134, 142, 143. *See also* seafood industry; seafood workers

Long Island, 11; agriculture, 67, 175; Central Americans in, 98, 175; food protests in, 68, 69; Hamptons, 154, 155, 177, 178; hate crimes against day laborers in, 98; Jamaicans in, 66; Mexican-origin people in, 98; Puerto Ricans in, 33, 67; South Americans in, 79, 98, 177; UFW in, 52, 57, 70; wine industry in, 154, 155, 175–80

López, Hope, 47, 58–61, 65, 216n39

Los Angeles, 18, 39, 52; during COVID, 187, 189; and Mexican food, 77, 78, 85; UFW in, 58, 68

Maine, *135*; Africans in, 106; agriculture in, 106, 122, 126; anti-Latinx racism in, 107, 141; apple industry in, 1, 106, 123–24; attitudes toward immigrants in, 126, 139–41; blueberry industry in, 1, 10, 106, 107, 116–23; Border Patrol in, 119, 139; braceros in, 10, 25, 28; broccoli industry in, 106, 124; Caribbean peoples in, 10, 33, 105, 106, 107, 108, 111, 113, 115, 118, 120–22, 123, 124, 125, 140, 143; Central Americans in, 1, 105, 106, 110, 111, 112, 113, 117–19, 125, 132, 136, 137, 138, 143; demographics of, 105, 106, 107, 139, 140; during COVID, 182, 193; egg industry in, 1, 108–15; INS in, 138; lobster industry in, 10, 125, 126, 134, 142, 143; Mexican-origin people in, 10, 25, 105, 106, 110, 111, 114, 117–20, 132, 138, 141, 143, 166; Nova Scotians in, 105, 116, 118, 125; potato industry in, 106, 125; sea cucumber industry in, 106, 107, 126–27, 132–42; South Americans in, 113, 125, 140; timber industry in, 107, 116, 123, 125; UFW in, 53
Maine Mobile Health Program (MMHP), 122, 182
Maine Rural Workers Coalition (MRWC), 113, 115, 116, 136, 137
Manhattan, 2, 9, 39, 80; Cubans in, 78; Dominicans in, 97; during COVID, 192; and grape boycott, 52, 57, 64, 66; INS sweeps in, 97; Mexican food establishments in, 78, 79, 80, 84, 88, 89, 90, 91, 92, 93, 94, 95, 98, 101; Mexican-origin people in, 79, 98, 99; Salvadorans in, 91. *See also* New York City
Martínez, Zarela, 9, 10, 79, *85*, *87*; early career of, 81–82; and entry in New York City food scene, 83–84; and views on sexism in restaurant industry, 85, 86; and trip to Mexico, 87–88; and Zarela restaurant, 89–91; and discourses about Mexican food, 95, 96; and views on

Chicano and Mexican identities, 97; legacy of, 102–4
Massachusetts, 67, 83, 143; braceros in, 22; Cape Verdeans in, 64, 132, 143; Dominicans in, 42, 144; and grape boycott, 53; Mayans in, 144, 146, 147; Portuguese in, 132, 143, 145, 146, 150; Puerto Ricans in, 32, 33, 64; Salvadorans in, 146, 149. *See also* Boston; New Bedford, MA; seafood industry; seafood workers
Maya K'iche'. *See* Indigenous peoples of Latin America
meat-processing industry, and workers, 11, 142, 183, 184, 185
Mexican Americans, 2, 8, 10, 67, 97, 106, 110, 117, 216n42; and changing US demographics, 16; and immigration sweeps, 34; as food entrepreneurs, 39, 103; student activism of, 52; and US Census categories, 222n8. *See also* UFW
Mexican consulates and consuls, 1, 8, 15, 19, 21, 22, 114
Mexican food, 2–4, 8, 9; in California, 39, 77, 91; and culinary nostalgia, 26; discourses about, 3, 40, 81, 89, 90, 95, 96; mainstream acceptance of, 20, 38, 40, 77–78, 94–95; in New York City, 9, 77–103, 191, 193; and the Northeast, 83; in TV dinners and dinner kits, 39, 40, 77; undervaluation of, 95, 96, 102–4. *See also* Martínez, Zarela
Mexican-origin people, 1, 7, 8; in agriculture, 1, 18, 41, 110–14, 116–20, 125; and COVID, 185, 191; in dairy industry, 157, 158, *159*, 162, 163, 164, 166, 167, 171; as delivery workers, 191; and food boycotts, 45–74; and food entrepreneurship, 9, 77–103; as guestworkers, 7, 8, 10, *17*, 125, 152; and immigration sweeps, 4, 40, 111, 138, 139, 140; in Maine, 1, 10, 105, 106, 110, 111, 114, 117–20, 132, 138, 141, 143, 166; in Massachusetts, 6, 143, 146, 147; in New England, 41; in New York City, 6, 18, 77–103, *100*; in New York State, 98, 154, 162; in Pennsylvania, 41; as railroad workers, 15, 20, 21, 22, 25–30; in Rhode Island, 6, 93; in seafood industry, 132,

138, 141, 143, 146, 152; and US Census, 222n8; and US demographics, 16, 18, 101; in Vermont, 156–158, *159*, 163, 164, 166, 167, 169, 171; violence and xenophobia against, 3, 98, 141. *See also* braceros; UFW

Mexican restaurants, 20, 40, 95; immigration raids on, 140; internationally, 78; in Maine, 83, 121, 139, 140; in Massachusetts, 83; and nativism, 1–4; in New Hampshire, 83; in New York City, 78–104; in Philadelphia, 103; and social media, 102; in Southwest, 39; undervaluation of, 2, 9, 89, 96, 102, 103; and wage theft, 98. *See also* Martínez, Zarela

Mexico, 25, 26, 29, 92, 101, 156, 170; and labor litigation, 114; revolution in, 6, 18

Michigan, 20, 26, 32, 33, 49

Migrant and Seasonal Agricultural Worker Protection Act (AWPA), 112, 121, 122

Migration Division Farm Labor Program, 7

Milbridge, ME, 139; Central Americans in, 136, 138; Mexican-origin people in, 120, 138; Mexican restaurant in, 121, *121*; community tensions in, 10, 141, 146; seafood industry in, 126, 132, 134, 136, 137

multiracial coalitions, 60, 113, 119, 182

mutual food aid, 182, 192–95

NAFTA. *See* North American Free Trade Agreement (NAFTA)

Native Americans, 10, 116, 119, 120, 125

New Bedford, MA, 127; attitudes toward migrants, 11, 149–50; Cape Verdeans in, 132, 143; Caribbean people in, 132, 143, 144, 146, 152; Latin Americans in, 143, 144, 145, 146, 147, 150, 151, 152; child labor in, 150–51; Mayans in, 144, 146, 147; Portuguese in, 132, 143, 145, 146, 150; seafood industry in, 10, 132, 143–52; UFW in, 49; as whaling hub, 143, 152

New Deal, 5, 18, 19, 40

New England, 205n12; culinary tourism, 11; image of, as a "white" place, 6; Latinx people in, 41, 107, 143; seafood industry, 126, 131–52

New Hampshire: agriculture, 22; grape boycott, 53; INS sweeps in, 112; Latin Americans in, 22, 33, 107, 112; Mexican restaurant in, 83

New Jersey, 7, 16; blueberry industry in, 106, 183; braceros in, 28, 30; Caribbean people in, 7, 16, 23, 31–36, 41, 144; labor organizing in, 19, 67; Mexican Americans in, 67; and *State v. Shack*, 67; UFW in, 53, 56, 57, 62, 65, 66. *See also* Seabrook Farms

New York City, 6, 9; Caribbean people in, 31, 37, 41, 42, 60, 79, 90, 99, 101; during COVID, 181, 188, 192, 193; food entrepreneurs in, 9, 77–103, 167; food protests in, 47, 189; Mexican-origin people in, 6, 18, 77–103, *100*; Mexican restaurants in, 78–104; South Americans in, 79, 99, 192; street food in, 93, 94; UFW in, 50, 53, 55–58, 70, 73, 74. *See also* Bronx; Brooklyn; East Harlem; Manhattan; Queens; Staten Island

New York State, 6, 7, 11, 22; agriculture in, 55, 106, 173; Caribbean laborers in, 55; Central Americans in, 154, 162, 175; and COVID, 183; dairy industry in, 11, 153, 157, 159, 160, 162; and Farmworkers Fair Labor Practices Act, 155, 173, 175–76; and grape boycott, 52, 53, 56, 57, 70; Mexican-origin people in, 154, 162; migrant labor in, 55; wine industry in, 11

North American Free Trade Agreement (NAFTA), 9, 74, 92, 144, 155

Northeast: diverse Latinx demographic of, 10, 16, 18, 21, 41, 64, 106, 112, 131, 141; image of, as "white" place, 6, 108; as "other" border zone, 6; significance of, to UFW, 46, 48, 66–70, 74; as tied to Pacific world, 133. *See also* Canada-US border: and surveillance

Obama, Barack, 165, 166

Occupational Safety and Health Administration (OSHA), 111–14, 122, 152, 160, 185, 186

Old El Paso (company), 40, 83, 95

oral history, 7, 148, 155, 156–57, 163

paqueteros, 11, 167, *168*, 179
Pennsylvania: and Asociación de Trabaja-
dores Agrícolas (ATA), 67; and
COVID, 183; and grape boycott, 62; and
guestworker programs, 7, 16, 33; Jamai-
cans in, 7; Mexican-origin people in, 7,
18, 41; Puerto Ricans in, 7, 16, 33, 41, 60.
See also Hazleton, PA
Peruvians, 6, 79, 92, 140
pesticides, 64–65, 72, 111, 118, 175
Philadelphia: braceros in, 15, 25; and
COVID, 193; food protests in, 47, 68;
Mexican food entrepreneurship in, 103;
mutual food aid in, 193; and women
UFW leaders, 49, 51, 58–62, 65, 73
Pine Tree Legal Assistance, 109–11, 117,
120, 122, 124
Pittsburgh, PA, 50, 53, 58, 68, 73, 117
Portland, ME, 29, 114, 126; Africans in, 115,
139; Border Patrol raids in, 139; Cesar
Chavez in, 70; and COVID, 193; egg
industry in, 109, 114; fish processing in,
141; mutual aid in, 193; immigrant advocacy in, 116, 139; Latin Americans in, 6,
29, 114, 115, 116, 139; Mexican restaurants
in, 83. *See also* Maine
potato industry, and workers, 67, 106, 125
poultry industry, and workers, 5, 112, 156,
184, 185
Providence, RI, 6, 22; grape boycott, 49, 58,
70; Latinx and Indigenous populations
in, 6, 42, 93. *See also* Rhode Island
Puerto Ricans: in agricultural labor,
10, 16, *17*, 32, 33, *33*, 36–38, 41, 67, 113;
in Connecticut, 16, 32, 33, 38, 68; in
Delaware, 32, 33, 67; in egg industry,
111, 113; and food protests, 19, 31–40, 68;
and guestworker statistics, 16, 32, 33;
and health and safety hazards, 34, 35,
64; on Long Island, 33, 67; in Maine, 33,
106, 111, 118, 140, 143; in Maryland, 31;
in Massachusetts, 16, 32, 33, 64, 144; in
Michigan, 32, 33; in New England, 41; in
New Hampshire, 22, 33; in New Jersey,
16, 31–36, 41; in New York City, 31, 37,
38, 60, 78, 99; in Pennsylvania, 7, 16, 33,
41, 60; in railroad labor, 31; in seafood

labor, 144; and substandard wages, 38; in
tobacco labor, 16, 33; and xenophobia, 2,
32, 36. *See also* Farm Placement Program
(FPP)
Puerto Rico, 22, 32, 35, 36, 37; and labor
litigation, 41; and Migration Division
Farm Labor Program, 7. *See also* Farm
Placement Program (FPP)

Queens, NY, 65, 99, 101; during COVID,
188; Latin Americans in, 79, 92, 94, 99;
food entrepreneurs in, 93, 94, 101. *See
also* New York City

racism: in food labor, 2–3, 8, 28, 29, 107;
lawsuits concerning, 114, 141; after 9/11,
142; and violence, 2, 98, 118, 141
railroad labor, 5; and Mexican-origin
people, 15, 20, 21, 22, 25–30; and Puerto
Ricans, 31. *See also* Bracero Program;
braceros
restaurants: Chinese, 96, 139; during
COVID, 12, 177, 189–90; and devaluation of Latinx labor, 81; and health
hazards, 12, 189; immigration raids in,
4, 139; and labor invisibility, 5, 200;
and racism, 2, 23, 25. *See also* Mexican
restaurants
Rhode Island: agriculture in, 22; Latin
Americans in, 22, 33, 41, 42, 93. *See also*
Providence, RI

Salvadorans: in agriculture, 113; in dairy
industry, 156, 172; and food insecurity,
144; in Maine, 113, 136; in Massachusetts, 145, 146, 149; and migration journeys, 144, 145, 146; in New York City,
91, 92; in seafood labor, 136, 145, 146; in
Vermont, 156, 172
Seabrook Farms, 19, 23, 25, 35, 67
sea cucumber industry, 126–27, 133–43; and
Latinx labor, 132, 136, 138, 141; in Maine,
106, 107, 126–27, 133–42; as link between
Northeast and Pacific, 133
seafood industry, 6, 10, 105, 106, 108, 116;
and child labor, 150–51; of New England
coast, 131–52

seafood workers: as boon to local economies, 140; Cape Verdean, 132, 143; Caribbean, 131, 132, 143, 144, 146, 147, 152; Central American, 132, 133, 137, 138, 143, 144, 145, 146, 150, 151, 152; and emotive power of the coast, 131–32, 149; and gender discrimination, 147; and H-2 visa program, 124, 152; invisibility of, 6, 106; Italian, 141, 143; and labor organizing, 151–52; Latin American, 143, 145, 146, 147, 152; and migration journeys, 144; in New Bedford, 143–51; occupational knowledge of, 145; Portuguese, 132, 143, 145, 146, 150; as precariat, 186; upward mobility of, 146–47. *See also* sea cucumber industry

slavery, 4, 6, 18

South Americans, 3, 21, 79, 105

Spanish language, 27; and marginalization of Indigenous peoples, 30; and xenophobia, 1, 2, 179

Staten Island, 93, 99

State v. Shack (1971), 67, 110

street food vendors, 12, 39, 74, 80, 81, 93, 94, 96; and COVID, 182, 187–89

strikes, hunger, 21, 48, 49, 50, 51, 61, 62, 74

strikes, labor, 12, 19, 25, 27, 43, 68; against grape growers, 48, 51, 52, 56, 59, 62, 72; against lettuce growers, 66; in Maine blueberry industry, 119

sugar, 16, 27, 51, 105, 124, 144

Taco Bell, 77, 95, 200

tacos: and anti-immigrant rhetoric, 2; as commodity, 7, 40; as cultural craze, 102; and generalizations about Latinx people, 5, 7

tamales, 3, 7, 39, 77, 81, 169; in New York City, 82, 84, 89, 91, 93, 94, 101; and street vending, 120, 167, 179

taquerías, 4, 5, 74, 93, 94, 96, 99, 101

Teamsters, 66, 72, 73

Tejanos, 16, 117, 124

Texas, 1, 112, 125; anti-immigrant policies in, 192; braceros in, 22; and COVID, 181, 186; food workers in, 186, 187; and Mexican food, 39, 40, 77, 83, 84, 91; Northeast migrant labor from, 18, 22,

52, 78, 110, 113, 117, 157; UFW in, 49, 73; Venezuelans in, 192

Tex-Mex cuisine, 8, 20, 77–79, 83, 84

tortillas, 7, 40, 62, 64, 77, 83, 222n14; and culinary nostalgia, 23, 26; and entrepreneurship, 137, 167, 168, 179; and food protests, 20, 22, 23; and Mexican food craze, 9, 80, 91, 93, 95, 99; in workers' diet, 23, 144, 168

Trump, Donald, 2, 3, 4, 165, 182, 184, 185, 238n35

UFW, 8, 9, 46; in California, 49, 58; litigation by, 49; in the Northeast, 48–53, *54, 63*; tensions within, 71–73; women leadership in, 46–48, 55–65. *See also* Chavez, Cesar; Huerta, Dolores; López, Hope

United Farm Workers. *See* UFW

United Farm Workers Organizing Committee (UFWOC). *See* UFW

US-Canada border. *See* Canada-US border

US-Mexico border, 3, 6, 71, 91, 107, 142, 170, 171

Venezuelans, 6, 192

Vermont, 53, 182, 183; and agriculture, 154; and bucolic veneer of, 153, 170; Central Americans in, 156, 157, 162, 164, 169, 172; dairy industry in, 11, 152, 154–74, 179–80; Latinx people in, 107, 156–71 passim

violence: in food labor, 2, 10; in labor activism, 19, 20, 52, 67, 73; toward Latina workers, 98; in migrant journeys, 41, 118, 144, 169, 171. *See also* racism; xenophobia

wages, low-level, 4, 5, 7, 8; in dairy and wine, 160, 172, 173; during COVID, 182, 185, 187, 190, 191, 192; and guestworkers, 16, 18, 19, 25, 26, 30, 34, 36, 38, 41, 42; in Maine, 107, 109, 114, 115, 116, 117, 119, 124; in Mexican foodscapes, 92, 98, 99; in New England seafood, 150, 152; perpetuated by ethnic succession, 5, 152; reinforced by consumers, 81, 96; and UFW boycotts, 45, 48, 49, 65, 72

Walmart, 101, 156, 164, 166
War Manpower Commission (WMC),
    27, 31
Washington, DC, 39, 48, 55, 73, 192
white demographic, 1, 2, 6; and privilege
    as chefs, 103, 188; and responses to im-
    migrants, 107, 119, 141, 142, 162, 179;
    and taste for Mexican food, 39–40; and
    UFW support, 59
wine industry: and crimmigration, 177–79;
    and Fair Farmworkers Practices Act, 155,
    175–76; in Long Island, 11, 152, 154, 174,
    175–80
wine workers, 155, 175, 176, 177
Wisconsin, 32, 33, 49, 52, 107, 183
women: in food protests, 47; in seafood
    labor, 145; sexism against, 99, 147, 148,

190; in UFW, 46, 55, 57, 60, 65; in
    wreath labor, 125
World War II, 5, 6, 40, 98; guestworker
    programs in, 7, 8, 15–40. See also Bracero
    Program; braceros; Farm Placement
    Program (FPP)

xenophobia, 2, 3, 5, 9, 11, 141, 142, 149, 162,
    198, 206n13; and "go back to Mexico!"
    slogan, 2, 141. See also racism

YMCA, 22, 28, 209n31
Young Lords Organization, 47–48

Zapotec, 30, 191. See also Indigenous
    peoples of Latin America